AA004404

ICDS 2020

The Fourteenth International Conference on Digital Society

November 21 – 25, 2020

Valencia, Spain

ICDS 2020 Editors

Jaime Lloret Mauri, Polytechnic University of Valencia, Spain
Samantha Papavasiliou, University of Adelaide, South Australia, Australia
Sunil Choenni, Rotterdam University of Applied Sciences | Ministry of Justice and Security, The Hague, The Netherlands
Mortaza S. Bargh, Rotterdam University of Applied Sciences | Ministry of Justice and Security, The Hague, The Netherlands

Printed from e-media with permission by:

Curran Associates, Inc.
57 Morehouse Lane
Red Hook, NY 12571

Some format issues inherent in the e-media version may also appear in this print version.

International Academy, Research, and Industry Association (IARIA)
412 Derby Way
Wilmington, DE 19810

Phone: (408) 893-6407
Fax: (408) 527-6351

petre@iaria.org

Additional copies of this publication are available from:

Curran Associates, Inc.
57 Morehouse Lane
Red Hook, NY 12571 USA
Phone: 845-758-0400
Fax: 845-758-2633
Email: curran@proceedings.com
Web: www.proceedings.com

Table of Contents

ICDS 2020

Forward

The Fourteenth International Conference on Digital Society (ICDS 2020) covered a large spectrum of topics related to advanced networking, applications, social networking, security and protection, and systems technologies in a digital society.

Nowadays, most of the economic activities and business models are driven by the unprecedented evolution of theories and technologies. The impregnation of these achievements into our society is present everywhere, and it is only question of user education and business models optimization towards a digital society.

Progress in cognitive science, knowledge acquisition, representation, and processing helped to deal with imprecise, uncertain or incomplete information. Management of geographical and temporal information becomes a challenge, in terms of volume, speed, semantic, decision, and delivery.

Information technologies allow optimization in searching an interpreting data, yet special constraints imposed by the digital society require on-demand, ethics, and legal aspects, as well as user privacy and safety.

The event was very competitive in its selection process and very well perceived by the international scientific and industrial communities. As such, it is attracting excellent contributions and active participation from all over the world. We were very pleased to receive a large amount of top quality contributions.

We believe that the ICDS 2020 contributions offered a panel of solutions to key problems in all areas of digital needs of today's society.

We take here the opportunity to warmly thank all the members of the ICDS 2020 technical program committee as well as the numerous reviewers. The creation of such a broad and high quality conference program would not have been possible without their involvement. We also kindly thank all the authors that dedicated much of their time and efforts to contribute to the ICDS 2020. We truly believe that thanks to all these efforts, the final conference program consists of top quality contributions.

This event could also not have been a reality without the support of many individuals, organizations and sponsors. In addition, we also gratefully thank the members of the ICDS 2020 organizing committee for their help in handling the logistics and for their work that is making this professional meeting a success.

We hope the ICDS 2020 was a successful international forum for the exchange of ideas and results between academia and industry and to promote further progress on the topics of digital society.

ICDS 2020 Chairs

ACHI 2020 General Chair
Jaime Lloret Mauri, Polytechnic University of Valencia, Spain

ICDS 2020 Steering Committee
Lasse Berntzen, University College of Southeast, Norway
Claus-Peter Rückemann, Westfälische Wilhelms-Universität Münster (WWU) / DIMF / Leibniz Universität Hannover, Germany

ICDS 2020 Advisory Committee
Åsa Smedberg, Stockholm University, Sweden
Jaroslaw Kozlak, AGH University of Science and Technology, Krakow, Poland

ICDS 2020
Committee

ICDS 2020 General Chair
Jaime Lloret Mauri, Polytechnic University of Valencia, Spain

ICDS 2020 Steering Committee
Lasse Berntzen, University of South-Eastern Norway, Norway
Claus-Peter Rückemann, Westfälische Wilhelms-Universität Münster (WWU) / DIMF / Leibniz Universität Hannover, Germany

ICDS 2020 Advisory Committee
Åsa Smedberg, Stockholm University, Sweden
Jaroslaw Kozlak, AGH University of Science and Technology, Krakow, Poland

ICDS 2020 Technical Program Committee
Chiniah Aatish, University of Mauritius, Mauritius
Mohamad Ibrahim Al Ladan, Rafik Hariri University, Lebanon
Laura Alcaide Muñoz, University of Granada, Spain
Ludivine Allienne, Université Picardie Jules Verne - laboratoire CURAPP-ESS, France
Kambiz Badie, ICT Research Institute, Iran
Ilija Basicevic, University of Novi Sad, Serbia
Najib Belkhayat, Cadi Ayyad University of Marrakech, Morocco
Lasse Berntzen, University of South-Eastern Norway, Norway
Aljosa Jerman Blazic, SETCCE Ltd. / IT association at Chamber of commerce, Slovenia
Mahmoud Brahimi, University of Msila, Algeria
Martim Brandao, University of Oxford, UK
Justin F. Brunelle, The MITRE Corporation, USA
Maria Chiara Caschera, CNR-IRPPS, Italy
Sunil Choenni, Dutch Ministry of Justice and Security / Rotterdam University of Applied Sciences, Netherlands
Yul Chu, University of Texas Rio Grande Valley (UTRGV), USA
Soon Ae Chun, City University of New York, USA
Kathy Clawson, University of Sunderland, UK
María E. Cortés-Cediel, Universidad Complutense de Madrid, Spain
Arthur Csetenyi, Budapest Corvinus University, Hungary
Fisnik Dalipi, Linnaeus University, Sweden
Monica De Martino, CNR-IMATI (National research Council, Institute of applied Mathematics and Information technology), Italy
Joakim Dillner, Karolinska University Laboratory | Karolinska University Hospital - Center for Cervical Cancer Prevention, Sweden
Higor dos Santos Pinto, Universidade Federal Fluminense, Brazil
Ilie Cristian Dorobat, "Politehnica" University of Bucharest, Romania

Copyright Information

The Privacy Funnel from the Viewpoint of Local Differential Privacy

Milan Lopuhaä-Zwakenberg
Department of Mathematics and Computer Science
Eindhoven University of Technology
Eindhoven, the Netherlands
email: m.a.lopuhaa@tue.nl

Abstract—**In the Open Data approach, governments want to share their datasets with the public, for accountability and to support participation. Data must be opened in such a way that individual privacy is safeguarded. The Privacy Funnel is a mathematical approach that produces a sanitised database that does not leak private data beyond a chosen threshold. The downsides to this approach are that it does not give worst-case privacy guarantees, and that finding optimal sanitisation protocols can be computationally prohibitive. We tackle these problems by using differential privacy metrics, and by considering local protocols which operate on one entry at a time. We show that under both the Local Differential Privacy and Local Information Privacy leakage metrics, one can efficiently obtain optimal protocols; however, Local Information Privacy is both more closely aligned to the privacy requirements of the Privacy Funnel scenario, and more efficiently computable. We also consider the scenario where each user has multiple attributes, for which we define *Side-channel Resistant Local Information Privacy*, and we give efficient methods to find protocols satisfying this criterion while still offering good utility. Exploratory experiments confirm the validity of these methods.**

Keywords—Privacy funnel; local differential privacy; information privacy; database sanitisation; complexity.

I. INTRODUCTION

Under the Open Data paradigm, governments and other public organisations want to share their collected data with the general public. This increases a governments transparency, and it also gives citizens and businesses the means to participate in decision-making, as well as using the data for their own purposes. However, while the released data should be as faithful to the raw data as possible, individual citizen's private data should not be compromised by such data publication.

To state this problem mathematically, let $\mathcal{X}$ be a finite set. Consider a database $\vec{X} = (X_1, \cdots, X_n) \in \mathcal{X}^n$ owned by a data aggregator, containing a data item $X_i \in \mathcal{X}$ for each user i (For typical database settings, each user's data is a vector of attributes $X_i = (X_i^1, \cdots, X_i^m)$; we will consider this in more detail in Section V). This data may not be considered sensitive by itself, however, it might be correlated to a secret S_i. The aggregator wants to release the database to the general public while preventing adversaries from retrieving the secret values S_i. For instance, X_i might contain the age, sex, weight, skin colour, and average blood pressure of person i, while S_i is the presence of some medical condition. To publicise the data without leaking the S_i, the aggregator releases a privatised database $\vec{Y} = (Y_1, \cdots, Y_n)$, obtained from applying a sanitisation mechanism $\mathcal{R}$ to $\vec{X}$. One way to formulate this is by considering the *Privacy Funnel*:

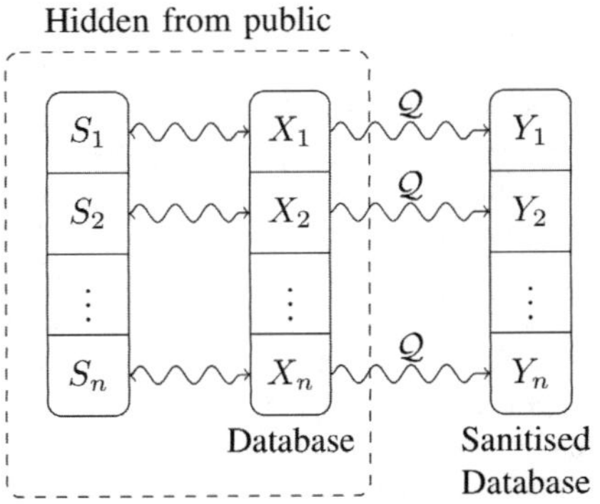

Figure 1. Model of the Privacy Funnel with local protocols.

Problem 1. (Privacy Funnel, [4]) *Suppose the joint probability distribution of $\vec{S}$ and $\vec{X}$ is known to the aggregator, and let $M \in \mathbb{R}_{\geq 0}$. Then, find the privatization mechanism $\mathcal{R}$ such that $\mathrm{I}(\vec{X};\vec{Y})$ is maximised while $\mathrm{I}(\vec{S};\vec{Y}) \leq M$.*

There are two difficulties with this approach:

1) Finding and implementing good privatization mechanisms that operate on all of $\vec{X}$ can be computationally prohibitive for large n, as the complexity is exponential in n [6] [14].
2) Taking mutual information as a leakage measure has as a disadvantage that it gives guarantees about the leakage in the average case. If n is large, this still leaves room for the sanitisation protocol to leak undesirably much information about a few unlucky users.

To deal with these two difficulties, we make two changes to the general approach. First, we look at *local* data sanitisation, i.e., we consider optimization protocols $\mathcal{Q}\colon \mathcal{X} \rightarrow \mathcal{Y}$, for some finite set $\mathcal{Y}$, and we apply $\mathcal{Q}$ to each X_i individually; this situation is depicted in Figure 1. These can be efficiently implemented. Second, to ensure strong privacy guarantees even in worst-case scenarios, we take stricter notions of privacy, based on Local Differential Privacy (LDP) [11].

The structure of this paper is as follows. In Section II, we define the mathematical setting of our problem. We discuss two privacy notions, LDP and Local Information Privacy (LIP), and discuss their relation to the Privacy Funnel. In Sections III and IV, we show that for a given level of LDP or LIP, respectively, one can efficiently find the optimal sanitisation protocol. In Section V, we consider the setting where every X_i is a vector of attributes, and we show how to make protocols that protect against side-channel attacks. In Section VI, we numerically assess the methods presented in this paper.

II. Mathematical Setting

The database $\vec{X} = (X_1, \cdots, X_n)$ consists out of a data item X_i for each user i, each an element of a given finite set $\mathcal{X}$. Furthermore, each user has sensitive data $S_i \in \mathcal{S}$, which is correlated with X_i; again we assume $\mathcal{S}$ to be finite (see Figure 1). We assume each (S_i, X_i) is drawn independently from the same distribution $p_{S,X}$ on $\mathcal{S} \times \mathcal{X}$ which is known to the aggregator through observing $(\vec{S}, \vec{X})$ (if one allows for non-independent X_i, then differential privacy is no longer an adequate privacy metric [5] [16]). The aggregator, who has access to $\vec{X}$, sanitises the database by applying a sanitisation protocol (i.e., a random function) $\mathcal{Q}\colon \mathcal{X} \to \mathcal{Y}$ to each X_i, outputting $\vec{Y} = (Y_1, \cdots, Y_n) = (\mathcal{Q}(X_1), \cdots, \mathcal{Q}(X_n))$. The aggregator's goal is to find a $\mathcal{Q}$ that maximises the information about X_i preserved in Y_i (measured as $\mathrm{I}(X_i; Y_i)$) while leaking only minimal information about S_i.

Without loss of generality we write $\mathcal{X} = \{1, \cdots, a\}$ and $\mathcal{Y} = \{1, \cdots, b\}$ for integers a, b. We omit the subscript i from X_i, Y_i, S_i as no probabilities depend on it, and we write such probabilities as p_x, p_s, $p_{x|s}$, etc., which form vectors p_X, $p_{S|x}$, etc., and matrices $p_{X|S}$, etc.

As noted before, instead of looking at the mutual information $\mathrm{I}(S;Y)$, we consider two different, related measures of sensitive information leakage known from the literature. The first one is an adaptation of LDP, the *de facto* standard in information privacy [11]:

Definition 1. (ε-LDP) *Let $\varepsilon \in \mathbb{R}_{\geq 0}$. We say that $\mathcal{Q}$ satisfies ε-LDP w.r.t. S if for all $y \in \mathcal{Y}$ and all $s, s' \in \mathcal{S}$ one has*

$$\frac{\mathbb{P}(Y = y|S = s)}{\mathbb{P}(Y = y|S = s')} \leq \mathrm{e}^{\varepsilon}. \tag{1}$$

This is less strict than the 'standard' notion of ε-LDP, which measures the information about X leaked in Y. This reflects the fact that we are only interested in hiding sensitive data, rather than all data; it is a specific case of what has been named 'pufferfish privacy' [12]. The advantage of LDP compared to mutual information is that it gives privacy guarantees for the worst case, not just the average case. This is desirable in the database setting, as a worst-case metric guarantees the security of the private data of all users, while average-case metrics are only concerned with the average user. Another useful privacy metric is *Local Information Privacy* (LIP) [9] [16], also called Removal Local Differential Privacy [8]:

Definition 2. (ε-LIP) *Let $\varepsilon \in \mathbb{R}_{\geq 0}$. We say that $\mathcal{Q}$ satisfies ε-LIP w.r.t. S if for all $s \in \mathcal{S}$ and $y \in \mathcal{Y}$ we have*

$$\mathrm{e}^{-\varepsilon} \leq \frac{\mathbb{P}(Y = y|S = s)}{\mathbb{P}(Y = y)} \leq \mathrm{e}^{\varepsilon}. \tag{2}$$

Compared to LDP, the disadvantage of LIP is that it depends on the distribution of S; this is less relevant in our scenario, as the aggregator, who chooses $\mathcal{Q}$, has access to the distribution

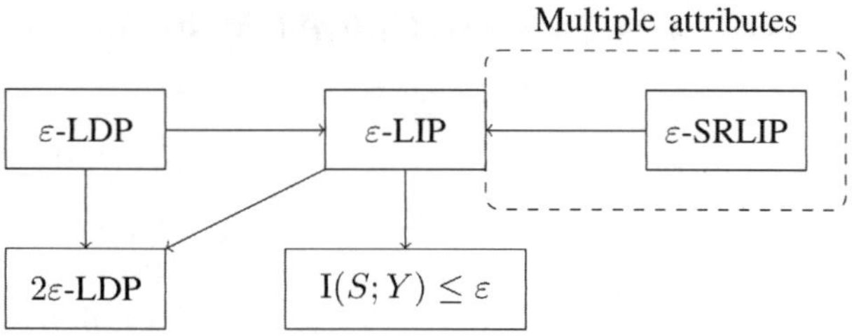

Figure 2. Relations between privacy notions. The multiple attributes setting is discussed in Section V.

of S. The advantage of LIP is that is more closely related to an attacker's capabilities: since $\frac{\mathbb{P}(Y=y|S=s)}{\mathbb{P}(Y=y)} = \frac{\mathbb{P}(S=s|Y=y)}{\mathbb{P}(S=s)}$, satisfying ε-LIP means that an attacker's posterior distribution of S given $Y = y$ does not deviate from their prior distribution by more than a factor e^{ε}. The following Lemma outlines the relations between LDP, LIP and mutual information (see Figure 2).

Lemma 1. (See [16]) *Let $\mathcal{Q}$ be a sanitisation protocol, and let $\varepsilon \in \mathbb{R}_{\geq 0}$.*

1) *If $\mathcal{Q}$ satisfies ε-LDP, then it satisfies ε-LIP.*
2) *If $\mathcal{Q}$ satisfies ε-LIP, then it satisfies 2ε-LDP, and $\mathrm{I}(S;Y) \leq \varepsilon$.*

Remark 1. *One can choose to employ more stringent privacy metrics for LDP and LIP by demanding that $\mathcal{Q}$ satisfy ε-LIP (ε-LDP) for a set of $p_{S,X}$, instead of only one [12]. Letting $p_{S,X}$ range over all possible distributions on $\mathcal{S} \times \mathcal{X}$ yields standard LIP (LDP) (i.e., w.r.t. X).*

In this notation, instead of Problem 1 we consider the following problem:

Problem 2. *Suppose $p_{S,X}$ is known to the aggregator, and let $\varepsilon \in \mathbb{R}_{\geq 0}$. Then, find the sanitisation protocol $\mathcal{Q}$ such that $\mathrm{I}(X;Y)$ is maximised while $\mathcal{Q}$ satisfies ε-LDP (ε-LIP, respectively) with respect to S.*

Note that this problem does not depend on the number of users n, and as such this approach will find solutions that are scalable w.r.t. n.

III. Optimizing $\mathcal{Q}$ for ε-LDP

Our goal is now to find the optimal $\mathcal{Q}$, i.e., the protocol that maximises $\mathrm{I}(X;Y)$ while satisfying ε-LDP, for a given ε. We can represent any sanitisation protocol as a matrix $Q \in \mathbb{R}^{b \times a}$, where $Q_{y|x} = \mathbb{P}(Y = y|X = x)$. Then, Q defines a sanitisation protocol $\mathcal{Q}$ satisfying ε-LDP if and only if

$$\forall x\colon \ \sum_y Q_{y|x} = 1, \tag{3}$$

$$\forall x, y\colon \ 0 \leq Q_{y|x}, \tag{4}$$

$$\forall s, s', y\colon \ (Q\, p_{X|s})_y \leq \mathrm{e}^{\varepsilon} (Q\, p_{X|s'})_y. \tag{5}$$

As such, for a given $\mathcal{Y}$, the set of ε-LDP-satisfying sanitisation protocols can be considered a closed, bounded, convex polytope Γ in $\mathbb{R}^{b \times a}$. This fact allows us to efficiently find optimal protocols.

Theorem 1. *Let $\varepsilon \in \mathbb{R}_{\geq 0}$. Let $\mathcal{Q}\colon \mathcal{X} \to \mathcal{Y}$ be the ε-LDP protocol that maximises $\mathrm{I}(X;Y)$, i.e., the protocol that solves Problem 2 w.r.t. LDP.*

1) *One has $b \leq a$.*
2) *Let Γ be the polytope described above. Then one can find $\mathcal{Q}$ by maximising a convex function on Γ.*

This result is obtained by generalising the results of [10]: there this is proven for regular ε-LDP (i.e., w.r.t. X), but the arguments given in that proof hold just as well in our situation; the only difference is that their polytope is defined by the ε-LDP conditions w.r.t. X, but this has no impact on the proof. Together, these results reduce our problem to a finite optimisation problem: By point 1, we only need to consider $\mathcal{Y} = \mathcal{X}$, and, by point 2, we only need to find the set of vertices of Γ, a $a(a-1)$-dimensional convex polytope.

One might argue that, since the optimal $\mathcal{Q}$ depends on $\mathrm{p}_{S,X}$, the publication of $\mathcal{Q}$ might provide an aggregator with information about the distribution of S. However, information on the distribution (as opposed to information of individual users' data) is not considered sensitive [13]. In fact, the reason why the aggregator sanitises the data is because an attacker is assumed to have knowledge about this correlation, and revealing too much information about X would cause the aggregator to use this information to infer information about S.

IV. Optimizing $\mathcal{Q}$ for ε-LIP

If one uses ε-LIP as a privacy metric, one can find the optimal sanitisation protocol in a similar fashion. To do this, we again describe $\mathcal{Q}$ as a matrix, but this time a different one. Let $q \in \mathbb{R}^b$ be the probability mass function of Y, and let $R \in \mathbb{R}^{a \times b}$ be given by $R_{x|y} = \mathbb{P}(X = x | Y = y)$; we denote its y-th row by $R_{X|y} \in \mathbb{R}^a$. Then, a pair (R, q) defines a sanitisation protocol $\mathcal{Q}$ satisfying ε-LIP if and only if

$$\forall y\colon\ 0 \leq q_y, \tag{6}$$

$$Rq = \mathrm{p}_X, \tag{7}$$

$$\forall y\colon\ \sum_x R_{x|y} = 1, \tag{8}$$

$$\forall x, y\colon\ 0 \leq R_{x|y}, \tag{9}$$

$$\forall y, s\colon\ \mathrm{e}^{-\varepsilon}\,\mathrm{p}_s \leq \mathrm{p}_{s|X}\, R_{X|y} \leq \mathrm{e}^{\varepsilon}\,\mathrm{p}_s\,. \tag{10}$$

Note that (10) defines the ε-LIP condition, since for a given s, y we have $\frac{\mathrm{p}_{s|X} R_{X|y}}{\mathrm{p}_S} = \frac{\mathbb{P}(S=s|Y=y)}{\mathbb{P}(S=s)} = \frac{\mathbb{P}(Y=y|S=s)}{\mathbb{P}(Y=y)}$. (In)equalities (8–10) can be expressed as saying that for every $y \in \mathcal{Y}$ one has that $R_{X|y} \in \Delta$, where Δ is the convex closed bounded polytope in $\mathbb{R}^{\mathcal{X}}$ given by

$$\Delta = \left\{ v \in \mathbb{R}^{\mathcal{X}} :\ \begin{array}{c} \sum_x v_x = 1, \\ \forall x: 0 \leq v_x, \\ \forall s: \mathrm{e}^{-\varepsilon}\,\mathrm{p}_s \leq \mathrm{p}_{s|X}\, v \leq \mathrm{e}^{\varepsilon}\,\mathrm{p}_s \end{array} \right\}. \tag{11}$$

As in Theorem 1, we can use this polytope to find optimal protocols:

Theorem 2. *Let $\varepsilon \in \mathbb{R}_{\geq 0}$. Let $\mathcal{Q}\colon \mathcal{X} \to \mathcal{Y}$ be the ε-LIP protocol that maximises $\mathrm{I}(X;Y)$, i.e., the protocol that solves Problem 2 w.r.t. LIP.*

1) *One has $b \leq a$.*
2) *Let Δ be the polytope described above, and let $\mathcal{V}$ be its set of vertices. Then one can find $\mathcal{Q}$ by solving a $\#\mathcal{V}$-dimensional linear optimization problem.*

This is proven for $\varepsilon = 0$ (i.e., when S and Y are independent) in [15], but the proof works similarly for $\varepsilon > 0$; the main difference is that the equality constraints of their (10) will be replaced by the inequality constraints of our (10), but this has no impact on the proof presented there. Since linear optimization problems can be solved fast, again the optimization problem reduces to finding the vertices of a polytope. The advantage of this approach, however, is that Δ is a $(a-1)$-dimensional polytope, while Γ is $a(a-1)$-dimensional. The time complexity of vertex enumeration is linear in the number of vertices [1], while the number of vertices can grow exponentially in the dimension of the polyhedron [2]. Together, this means that the dimension plays a huge role in the time complexity, hence we expect finding the optimum under LIP to be significantly faster than under LDP.

V. Multiple Attributes

An often-occuring scenario is that a user's data consists out of multiple attributes, i.e., $X_i = (X_i^1, \cdots, X_i^m) \in \mathcal{X} = \prod_{j=1}^m \mathcal{X}^j$. This can be problematic for our approach for two reasons:

1) Such a large $\mathcal{X}$ can be problematic, since the computing time for optimisation both under LDP and LIP will depend heavily on a.
2) In practice, an attacker might sometimes utilise side channels to access to some subsets of attributes X_i^j for some users. For these users, a sanitisation protocol can leak more information (w.r.t. to the attacker's updated prior information) than its LDP/LIP parameter would suggest.

To see how the second problem might arise in practice, suppose that X_i^1 is the height of individual i, X_i^2 is their weight, and S_i is whether i is obese or not. Since height is only lightly correlated with obesity, taking $Y_i = X_i^1$ would satisfy ε-LIP for some reasonably small ε. However, suppose that an attacker has access to X_i^2 via a side channel. While knowing i's weight gives the attacker some, but not perfect knowledge about i's obesity, the combination of the weight from the side channel, and the height from the Y_i, allows the attacker to calculate i's BMI, giving much more information about i's obesity. Therefore, the given protocol gives much less privacy in the presence of this side channel.

To solve the second problem, we introduce a more stringent privacy notion called *Side-channel Resistant LIP* (SRLIP), which ensures that no matter which attributes an attacker has access to, the protocol still satisfies ε-LIP with respect to the attacker's new prior distribution. One could similarly introduce

SRLDP, and many results will still hold for this privacy measure; nevertheless, since we concluded that LIP is preferable over LDP, we focus on SRLIP. For $J \subset \{1, \cdots, m\}$, we write $\mathcal{X}^J = \prod_{j \in J} \mathcal{X}^j$ and its elements as x^J.

Definition 3. (ε-SRLIP). *Let $\varepsilon > 0$, and let $\mathcal{X} = \prod_{j=1}^m \mathcal{X}^j$. We say that $\mathcal{Q}$ satisfies ε-SRLIP if for every $y \in \mathcal{Y}$, for every $s \in \mathcal{S}$, for every $J \subset \{1, \cdots, m\}$, and for every $x^J \in \mathcal{X}^J$ one has*

$$\mathrm{e}^{-\varepsilon} \leq \frac{\mathbb{P}(Y = y | S = s, X^J = x^J)}{\mathbb{P}(Y = y | X^J = x^J)} \leq \mathrm{e}^{\varepsilon}. \tag{12}$$

In terms of Remark 1, $\mathcal{Q}$ satisfies ε-SRLIP if and only if it satisfies ε-LIP w.r.t. $\mathrm{p}_{S,X|x^J}$ for all J and x^J. Taking $J = \varnothing$ gives us the regular definition of ε-LIP, proving the following Lemma:

Lemma 2. *Let $\varepsilon > 0$. If $\mathcal{Q}$ satisfies ε-SRLIP, then $\mathcal{Q}$ satisfies ε-LIP.*

While SRLIP is stricter than LIP itself, it has the advantage that even when an attacker has access to some data of a user, the sanitisation protocol still does not leak an unwanted amount of information beyond the knowledge the attacker has gained via the side channel. Another advantage is that, contrary to LIP itself, SRLIP satisfies an analogon of the concept of *privacy budget* [7]:

Theorem 3. *Let $\mathcal{X} = \prod_{j=1}^m \mathcal{X}^j$, and for every j, let $\mathcal{Q}^j \colon \mathcal{X}^j \to \mathcal{Y}^j$ be a sanitisation protocol. Let $\varepsilon^j \in \mathbb{R}_{\geq 0}$ for every j. Suppose that for every $j \leq m$, for every $J \subset \{1, \cdots, j-1, j+1, \cdots, m\}$, and every $x^J \in \mathcal{X}^J$, $\mathcal{Q}^j$ satisfies ε^j-LIP w.r.t. $\mathrm{p}_{S,X|x^J}$. Then $\prod_j \mathcal{Q}^j \colon \mathcal{X} \to \prod_j \mathcal{Y}^j$ satisfies $\sum_j \varepsilon^j$-SRLIP.*

The proof is presented in Appendix A. This theorem tells us that to find a ε-SRLIP protocol for $\mathcal{X}$, it suffices to find a sanitisation protocol for each $\mathcal{X}^j$ that is $\frac{\varepsilon}{m}$-LIP w.r.t. a number of prior distributions. Unfortunately, the method of finding an optimal ε-LIP protocol w.r.t. one prior $\mathrm{p}_{S,X}$ of Theorem 2 does not transfer to the multiple prior setting. This is because this method only finds one (R, q), while by (7) we need a different (R, q) for each prior distribution. Therefore, we are forced to adopt an approach similar to the one in Theorem 1. The matrix Q^j (given by $Q^j_{y^j|x^j} = \mathbb{P}(\mathcal{Q}^j(x^j) = y^j)$) corresponding to $\mathcal{Q}^j \colon \mathcal{X}^j \to \mathcal{Y}^j$ satisfies the criteria of Theorem 3 if and only if the following criteria are satisfied:

$$\forall x^j : \sum_{y^j} Q^j_{y^j|x^j} = 1, \tag{13}$$

$$\forall x^j, y^j : 0 \leq Q^j_{y^j|x^j}, \tag{14}$$

$$\forall J, x^J, s, y^j : \mathrm{e}^{-\varepsilon/m} (Q^j \, \mathrm{p}_{X^j|x^J})_{y^j} \leq (Q^j \, \mathrm{p}_{X^j|s,x^J})_{y^j}, \tag{15}$$

$$\forall J, x^J, s, y^j : (Q^j \, \mathrm{p}_{X^j|s,x^J})_{y^j} \leq \mathrm{e}^{\varepsilon/m} (Q^j \, \mathrm{p}_{X^j|x^J})_{y^j}. \tag{16}$$

Similar to Theorem 1, we can find the optimal Q^j satisfying these conditions by finding the vertices of the polytope defined by these equations. In terms of time complexity, the comparison to finding the optimal ε-LIP protocol via Theorem 2 versus finding a ε-SRLIP protocol via Theorem 3 is not straightforward. The complexity of enumerating the vertices of a polytope is $\mathcal{O}(ndv)$, where n is the number of inequalities, d is the dimension, and v is the number of vertices [1]. For Δ of Theorem 2 we have $d = a - 1$ and $n = a + 2c$. By contrast, for the polytope defined by (13–16) satisfies $d = a^j(a^j - 1)$ and $n = (a^j)^2 + 2c \prod_{j' \neq j} (a^{j'} + 1)$. Finding v for both these polytopes is difficult, but in general $v \leq \binom{n}{d}$. Since this grows exponentially in d, we expect Theorem 3 to be faster when the a^j are small compared to a, i.e., when m is large. We will investigate this experimentally in the next section.

VI. Experiments

We test the feasibility of the different methods and privacy definitions by performing small-scale experiments on synthetic data. All experiments are implemented in Matlab and conducted on a PC with Intel Core i7-7700HQ 2.8GHz and 32GB memory. We compare the computing time for finding optimal ε-LDP and ε-LIP protocols for $c = 2$ and $a = 5$ for 10 random $\mathrm{p}_{S,X}$, obtained by generating each $\mathrm{p}_{s,x}$ uniformly from $[0, 1]$ and then rescaling. We take $\varepsilon \in \{0.5, 1, 1.5, 2\}$; the results are in Figure 3. As one can see, Theorem 2 gives significantly faster results than Theorem 1; the average computing time for Theorem 1 for $\varepsilon = 0.5$ is 133s, while for Theorem 2 this is 0.0206s. With regards to the utility $\mathrm{I}(X; Y)$, since ε-LDP implies ε-LIP, the optimal ε-LIP protocol will have better utility than the optimal ε-LDP protocol. However, as can be seen from the figure, the difference in utility is relatively low.

Note that for bigger ε, both the difference in computing time and the difference in $\mathrm{I}(X; Y)$ between LDP and LIP become less. This is because of the probabilistic relation between S and X, for ε large enough, any sanitisation protocol satisfies ε-LIP and ε-LDP. This means that as ε grows, the resulting polytopes will have less defining inequalities, hence they will have less vertices. This results in lower computation times, which affects LDP more than LIP. At the same time, the fact that every protocol is both ε-LIP and ε-LDP will result in the same optimal utility.

In Figure 4, we compare optimal $\frac{\varepsilon}{2}$-LDP protocols to optimal ε-LIP protocols. Again, LIP is significantly faster than LDP. Since ε-LIP implies $\frac{\varepsilon}{2}$-LDP, the optimal $\frac{\varepsilon}{2}$-LDP has higher utility; again the difference is low.

We also perform similar comparisons for multiple attributes, for $c = 2$, $a_1 = a_2 = 3$ and $a_3 = 4$, comparing the methods of Theorems 2 and 3. The results are presented in Figure 5. As one can see, Theorem 3 is significantly slower, with Theorem 2 being on average 476 times as fast. There is a sizable difference in utility, caused on one hand by the fact that ε-SRLIP is a stricter privacy requirement than ε-LIP, and on the other hand by the fact that Theorem 3 does not give us the optimal ε-SRLIP protocol.

VII. Conclusions and Future Work

Local data sanitisation protocols have the advantage of being scalable for large numbers of users. Furthermore, the

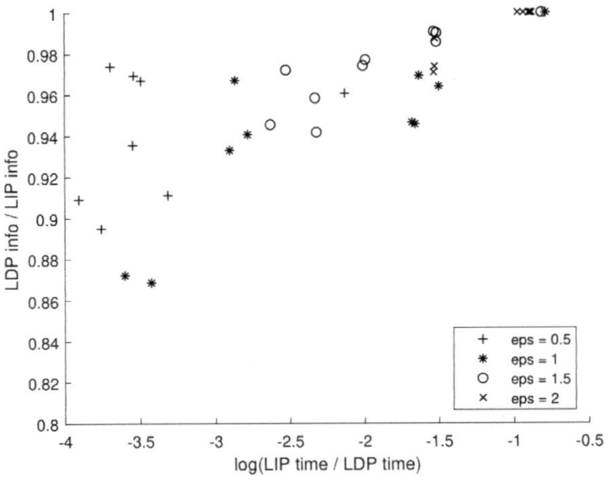

Figure 3. Comparision of computation time and $\mathrm{I}(X;Y)$ for ε-LDP protocols found via Theorem 1 and ε-LIP protocols found via Theorem 2, for random $\mathrm{p}_{S,X}$ with $c = 2$, $a = 5$, and $\varepsilon \in \{0.5, 1, 1.5, 2\}$.

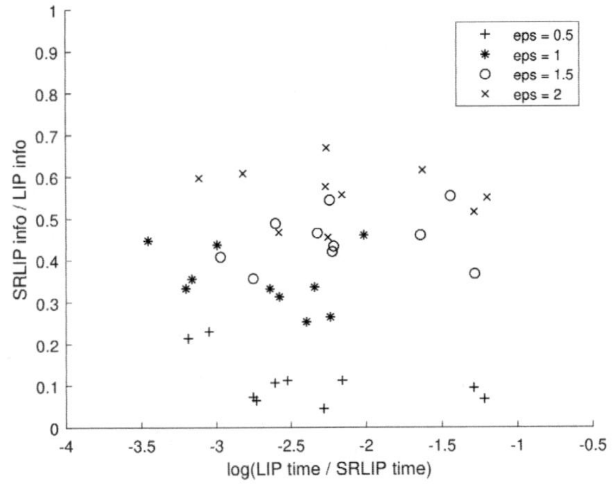

Figure 5. Comparison of computation time and $\mathrm{I}(X;Y)$ for ε-(SR)LIP-protocols found via Theorems 2 and 3, for random $\mathrm{p}_{S,X}$ with $c = 2$, $a_1 = a_2 = 3$, $a_3 = 4$, and $\varepsilon \in \{0.5, 1, 1.5, 2\}$.

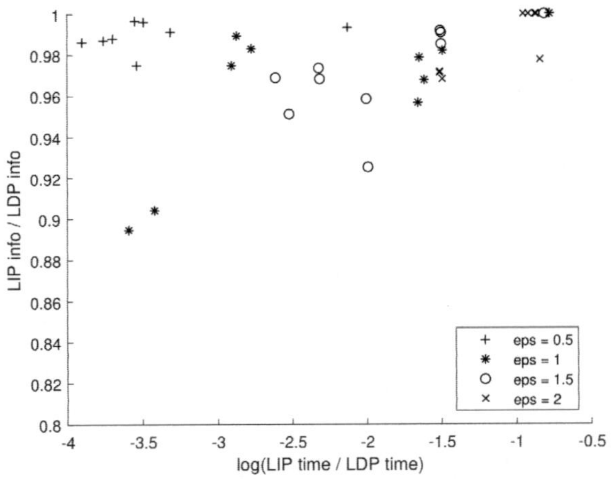

Figure 4. Comparision of computation time and $\mathrm{I}(X;Y)$ for ε-LDP protocols found via Theorem 1 and $\frac{\varepsilon}{2}$-LIP protocols found via Theorem 2, for random $\mathrm{p}_{S,X}$ with $c = 2$, $a = 5$, and $\varepsilon \in \{0.5, 1, 1.5, 2\}$.

advantage of using differential privacy-like privacy metrics is that they provide worst-case guarantees, ensuring that the privacy of every user is sufficiently protected. For both ε-LDP and ε-LIP we have found methods to find optimal sanitisation protocols. Within this setting, we have found that ε-LIP has two main advantages over ε-LDP. First, it fits better within the privacy funnel setting, where the distribution $\mathrm{p}_{S,X}$ is (at least approximately) known to the estimator. Second, finding the optimal protocol is significantly faster than under LDP, especially for small ε. If one nevertheless prefers ε-LDP as a privacy metric, then it is still worthwile to find the optimal $\frac{\varepsilon}{2}$-LIP protocol, as this can be found significantly faster, at a low utility cost.

In the multiple attributes setting, we have shown that ε-SRLIP is a more sensible privacy metric than ε-LIP, since without this requirement a protocol can lose all its privacy protection in the presence of side channels. Unfortunately, however, experiments show that we pay for this both in computation time and in utility. Nevertheless, because of the robustness of ε-SRLIP, it remains the preferred privacy notion in this setting.

For further research, two important avenues remain to be explored. First, the aggregator's knowledge about $\mathrm{p}_{S,X}$ may not be perfect, because they may learn about $\mathrm{p}_{S,X}$ through observing $(\vec{S}, \vec{X})$. Incorporating this uncertainty leads to robust optimisation [3] , which would give stronger privacy guarantees. Second, it might be possible to improve the method of obtaining ε-SRLIP protocols via Theorem 3. Examining its proof shows that lower values of ε^j may suffice to still ensure ε-SRLIP. Furthermore, the optimal choice of $(\varepsilon^j)_{j \leq m}$ such that $\sum_j \varepsilon^j = \varepsilon$ might not be $\varepsilon^j = \frac{\varepsilon}{m}$. However, it is computationally prohibitive to perform the vertex enumeration for many different choices of $(\varepsilon^j)_{j \leq m}$, and as such a new theoretical approach is needed to determine the optimal $(\varepsilon^j)_{j \leq m}$ from ε and $\mathrm{p}_{S,X}$.

ACKNOWLEDGEMENTS

This work was supported by NWO grant 628.001.026 (Dutch Research Council, the Hague, the Netherlands). The author thanks Jasper Goseling and Boris Škorić for helpful discussions.

REFERENCES

[1] D. Avis and K. Fukuda, "A pivoting algorithm for convex hulls and vertex enumeration of arrangements and polyhedra," *Discrete and Computational Geometry*, vol. 8, no. 1, pp. 174–190, 1992.
[2] I. Bárány and A. Pór, "On 0-1 Polytopes with Many Facets," *Advances in Mathematics*, vol. 161, no. 2, pp. 209–228, 2001.
[3] D. Bertsimas, V. Gupta, and N. Kallus, "Data-driven robust optimization," *Mathematical Programming*, vol. 167, no. 2, pp. 235–292, 2017.
[4] F.P. Calmon et al., "Principal Inertia Components and Applications," *IEEE Transactions on Information Theory*, vol. 63 no. 8, pp. 5011–5038, 2017.

[5] P. Cuff and L. Yu, "Differential Privacy as a Mutual Information Constraint," *ACM SIGSAC Conference on Computer and Communications Security 2016*, pp. 43–54, 2016.

[6] N. Ding and P. Sadeghi, "A Submodularity-based Agglomerative Clustering Algorithm for the Privacy Funnel," Unpublished preprint, *arXiv:1901.06629*, 2019 (retrieved: February, 2020).

[7] C. Dwork, F. McSherry, K. Nissim, and A. Smith, "Calibrating noise to sensitivity in private data analysis," *Theory of Cryptography Conference*, pp. 265–284, 2006.

[8] Ú. Erlingsson et al., "Encode, Shuffle, Analyze Privacy Revisited: Formalizations and Empirical Evaluation," Unpublished preprint, *arXiv:2001.03618*, 2020 (retrieved: February, 2020).

[9] B. Jiang, M. Li, and R. Tandon, "Local Information Privacy with Bounded Prior," *IEEE International Conference on Communications*, pp. 1–7, 2019.

[10] P. Kairouz, S. Oh, and P. Viswanath, "Extremal Mechanisms for Local Differential Privacy," *Advances in Neural Information Processing Systems*, vol. 27, pp. 2879–2887, 2014.

[11] S. P. Kasiviswanathan, H. K. Lee, K. Nissim, S. Raskhodnikova, and A. Smith, "What can we learn privately?," *SIAM Journal of Computing*, vol. 40, no. 3, pp. 793–826,2011.

[12] D. Kifer and A. Machanavajjhala, "Pufferfish: A Framework for Mathematical Privacy Definitions," *ACM Transactions on Database Systems*, vol. 39, no 1., pp. 1–36, 2014.

[13] M. Lopuhaä-Zwakenberg, B. Škorić, and N. Li, "Information-theoretic metrics for Local Differential Privacy protocols," Unpublished preprint, *arXiv:1910.07826*, 2019 (retrieved: February, 2020).

[14] F. Prasser, F. Kohlmayer, R. Lautenschläger, and K. A. Kuhn, "ARX - A Comprehensive Tool for Anonymizing Biomedical Data," *AMIA Annual Symposium Proceedings*, pp. 984–993, 2014.

[15] B. Rassouli and D. Gündüz, "On Perfect Privacy and Maximal Correlation," Unpublished preprint, *arXiv:1712.08500*, 2017 (retrieved: February, 2020).

[16] S. Salamatian, F.P. Calmon, N. Fawaz, A. Makhdoumi, and M. Médard, "Privacy-Utility Tradeoff and Privacy Funnel," Unpublished preprint, http://www.mit.edu/~salmansa/files/privacy_TIFS.pdf, 2020 (retrieved: February, 2020).

APPENDIX A
PROOF OF THEOREM 3

For $J \subset \{1, \cdots, m\}$ and $j \in \{1, \cdots, m\}$, we write $J[j] := J \cup \{1, \cdots, j-1\}$. Furthermore, we write $\mathcal{X}^{\setminus J} = \prod_{j \notin J} \mathcal{X}^j$, and its elements as $x^{\setminus J}$. We write $\varepsilon := \sum_j \varepsilon^j$. We then have

$$
\begin{aligned}
\mathrm{p}_{y|s,x^J} &= \sum_{x^{\setminus J}} \mathrm{p}_{y|x}\, \mathrm{p}_{x^{\setminus J}|s,x^J} && (17)\\
&= \mathrm{p}_{y^J|x^J} \sum_{x^{\setminus j}} \left(\prod_{j \notin J} \mathrm{p}_{y^j|x^j} \right) \mathrm{p}_{x^{\setminus J}|s,x^J} && (18)\\
&= \mathrm{p}_{y^J|x^J} \sum_{x^{\setminus j}} \prod_{j \notin J} \mathrm{p}_{y^j|x^j}\, \mathrm{p}_{x^j|s,x^{J[j]}} && (19)\\
&= \mathrm{p}_{y^J|x^J} \prod_{j \notin J} \sum_{x^j} \mathrm{p}_{y^j|x^j}\, \mathrm{p}_{x^j|s,x^{J[j]}} && (20)\\
&= \mathrm{p}_{y^J|x^J} \prod_{j \notin J} \mathrm{p}_{y^j|s,x^{J[j]}} && (21)\\
&\leq \mathrm{p}_{y^J|x^J} \prod_{j \notin J} \mathrm{e}^{\varepsilon^j}\, \mathrm{p}_{y^j|x^{J[j]}} && (22)\\
&\leq \mathrm{e}^{\varepsilon}\, \mathrm{p}_{y^J|x^J} \prod_{j \notin J} \mathrm{p}_{y^j|x^{J[j]}} && (23)\\
&= \mathrm{e}^{\varepsilon}\, \mathrm{p}_{y|x^J}\,. && (24)
\end{aligned}
$$

The fact that $\mathrm{e}^{-\varepsilon}\, \mathrm{p}_{y|x^J} \leq \mathrm{p}_{y|s,x^J}$ is proven analogously.

Framework for a User-friendly Statistical Disclosure Control Tool

Anshika Rawat[1], Mortaza S. Bargh[2], Afshin Amighi[3] and Marijn Janssen[4]
[1,4] Delft University of Technology, Delft, The Netherlands
[2] Research and Documentation Centre, Ministry of Justice and Security, The Hague, The Netherlands
[3] Rotterdam University of Applied Sciences, Rotterdam, The Netherlands
Email: [1] a.rawat-1@student.tudelft.nl [2] m.shoae.bargh@wodc.nl [3] a.amighi@hr.nl [4] m.f.w.h.a.janssen@tudelft.nl

Abstract—**Public organisations are opening more and more data to increase their transparency. But more often than not, data cannot be opened without modification due to data protection issues. There are Statistical Disclosure Control (SDC) tools that can help to accomplish this. However, these tools are not intuitive for end-users, especially for those who are not deeply familiar with data science. The end-users are mostly public servants who want to open data. Therefore, the main objective of this paper is to develop a framework for a user-friendly tool based on data disclosure methods and usability guidelines for protecting microdata. The developed framework can be used to design and evaluate a tool that can be used by data controllers within the Dutch governmental institutions for anonymising data. This contributes to the sharing of more data with the public or between organisations with a minimised risk of disclosing the identity of the individuals the data is about.**

Keywords–Statistical Disclosure Control; Data Protection.

I. Introduction

Each year, colossal amounts of data is collected and generated through court proceedings and administrative procedures of the Dutch justice department. This data is generally gathered by many independent organisations that are involved in the Dutch justice system, like the Public Prosecution Service, courts, the Central Fine Collection Agency and the Dutch Police. However, this data is not shared amongst intuitions or made accessible to the public. This is because sharing of such data sets carries an inherent privacy risk. Disclosure of personal data is considered as one of the main threats for data opening. Therefore, only a small proportion of this data is made available to the public to protect the identity of the people the data is about. This impacts the transparency of these organisations because the full potential of these data sets cannot be achieved, as it is paramount to protect the privacy of the respondents of the data because of laws like General Data Protection Regulation (GDPR) [1].

For this reason, the Dutch Ministry of Justice and Security has taken upon itself to enhance its transparency, accountability and efficiency by setting up an open data programme that aims at stimulating the sharing of its data sets with the public or with other organisations [1]. The data sets pertain to information that is gathered by the justice branch of the Dutch government.

It is for this reason that the Research and Documentation Centre (abbreviated as WODC in Dutch) of the Dutch Ministry of Justice and Security is conducting a research on a tool that can be used to anonymize data so that personal data can be protected while maintaining the usefulness of the data. This tool is based on SDC methodologies. SDC refers to methods that try to prevent statistical data from disclosing confidential information about specific respondents, who may be individuals or enterprises [2].

A. Problem Definition

Sizable research has been conducted on appropriate SDC techniques and has been implemented in the form of software tools. Despite the elegance and extensiveness of these solutions, these tools are not widely used by data controllers in public organisations in the Netherlands. The simple reason is that they are complicated, time-consuming to learn and use, and their usage requires a deep understanding of data science. Another reason is that people who implement these techniques, especially statistical agencies, do not widely share, in substantial detail, their knowledge and experience using SDC and about the process of creating safe data with other agencies [3]. This makes it difficult for those organisations who are motivated to implement this solution but are new to the process to get all the relevant information they need to apply these techniques in practice.

B. Research Objective

This project is concerned with the analysis, design and evaluation of a framework for a set of SDC usage guidelines that can be translated into a standardised tool which is user-friendly, time-efficient and intuitive for its intended target user groups. The target user groups of this tool are data controllers within the Dutch public organisations like the Dutch Ministry of Justice and Security.

C. Research Questions

To achieve this, the main objective of this project can be realised by the following five research questions:

1) What is the present state of the SDC tools in use?
2) What are the conceptual SDC methods in practice?
3) How can these conceptual guidelines be transformed into an intuitive tool for the target group?
4) What is the preferred design option, given the needs and skills of the target group and given the organizational setting?
5) How is the preferred design perceived by the target group?

The rest of the paper is structured as follows. In Section 2, we provide a literature overview to introduce key concepts.

Section 3 explains the research methodology to be undertaken. Finally, we conclude the work in Section 4.

II. Literature Overview

In this section, the concept of SDC on data sets relevant for this paper is introduced. In addition to this, the current state of SDC tools is also outlined to show that there is a need for a more user-friendly SDC tool.

A. *Conceptual guidelines of SDC*

According to the literature, the key guideline of SDC is to protect structured data so that it can be released without giving away the identity of specific individuals or entities [4]. Structured data refers to data that is stored in a structured way, such as a database or spreadsheets. Thus, this technique of anonymising data can be applied to a wide range of data sets, most commonly to microdata and tabular data sets. Microdata refers to data at the individual respondent level. On the other hand, tabular data is aggregate data structured as rows and columns containing information or contributions of a group of respondents. The common output that is offered by national statistical agencies is tabular data [5]. Hutchison & Mitchell distinguish the different data protection methods that can be applied to microdata and tabular data respectively [6]. However, this paper is only concerned with microdata sets and its protections methods. Microdata records include personal data such as direct identifiers which reveal the identity of the person right away. Examples include the name of the person or their address. This is a direct risk to privacy and such identifiers are usually removed or redacted. However, the inherent risk that the data faces is assumed in terms of 'linkage' of sensitive data with identified data [4]. The attributes in the data set that are used in this linkage are termed quasi-identifiers or indirect identifiers. These identifiers do not explicitly reveal the identity of the individual, but are used in combination with other indirect identifiers to re-identify an individual. It is assumed that direct identifiers in the data sets that reveal the identity of the individual such as name, citizenship number, etc, are removed from the data set. However, the literature also indicates that quasi-identifiers cannot simply be removed from the data set. Hundepool provides two reasons for this, first, the data may be required for analysis and, second, the data may already be available to an attacker [4]. Therefore, when designing an SDC tool, the common risks to privacy that can be realised through 'linkage' can be classified into three types [7]. They are:

1) Identity disclosure: It is the foremost risk of re-identification in which the individual can be pinpointed by a specific data entry.
2) Attribute disclosure: This is a primary risk that arises when additional information can be inferred about an individual from the data shared through different data sets or other users.
3) Membership disclosure: A risk in which the attacker is able to determine whether some particular data about an individual may or may not be contained in the data set through data linkage.

Hence, an SDC tool should address the above mentioned risks. On further investigating the literature, it was found that SDC techniques also differ in the way the anonymised data is released. The data release methods can be classified into three types, namely, Public Use Files (PUFs), Scientific Use Files (SUFs) and data made available in a controlled research centre [3]. PUFs are relevant for this topic as this is the data which is made openly accessible to anyone. Because of the public nature of these files, they require protection much larger in the extent to other release types. Therefore, it can be inferred that the design of the tool must have the proper data disclosure capabilities to minimise the risk to user privacy.

However, SDC techniques cannot guarantee the elimination of risk, but they help in reducing the risk to an acceptable level. This is illustrated as a risk-utility trade-off in the SDC process [3]. This trade-off is characterised by the risk of disclosure and the utility of the data for the end-user. The trade-off between the two signifies that, to maximise utility from the data, the risk has to be maximised as well. Figure 1 shows the plot between risk and utility. Zero risk of disclosure is accompanied by the release of no data, whereas data released without disclosure is accompanied by maximum risk. Therefore, SDC techniques have to achieve an optimal point on the risk-utility plot where the maximum utility can be achieved at an acceptable disclosure risk. This is an important concept to remember when comparing and selecting appropriate SDC techniques/methods and choosing the right parameters to mask the data. This understanding should also be reflected in the implementation of the proposed tool. Additionally, the protection methods for microdata should try to reduce the three common risks to privacy by finding the optimal trade-off between risk and quality of data in terms of information loss.

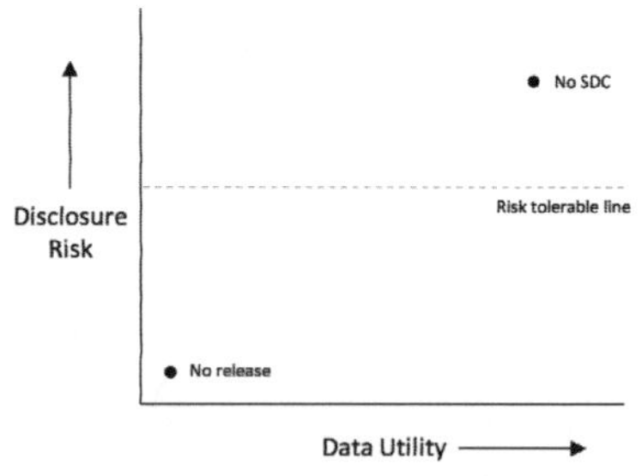

Figure 1. Plot of Risk-Utility Trade-off

The issue of data anonymization is still a complex subject which requires expertise to translate the necessary guidelines for achieving a simplified tool to the point that it can be used by a target group with minimal knowledge of statistics and data science. In the Netherlands, there is no current infrastructure to sanitise confidential data to make it available for external use. Often, data is not released at all and stored away only for authorised personnel to see. This implies that the full potential of this data is never realised, as it cannot be shared for use for conducting research or for other scientific purposes due to GDPR violation. Thus, there is a need to develop a simple-to-use tool or at least a software environment that can harness some basic data anonymisation technique so that data controllers can adopt some minimal practices of sanitizing data and release them to the public.

This brings us to the question of how can the complexity of SDC techniques be reduced or hidden by an agreeable user-interface? One way to reduce the complexity of the issues is to explore already existing tools that can be simplified so as to present the data controllers with a less than perfect solution, but still something that can tentatively be adopted by them. A simple-to-use interface can guide users through complex data protection methods. Prasser & Kohlmayer suggest that data controllers follow the onion layer principle in which data is protected in a series of multiple layers as there is no single method to protect data sets [7]. These steps including legal agreements, as well as collecting and storing that data, which is absolutely necessary. These measures are already being followed because of regulations like GDPR and by executing a Data Protection Impact Assessment (DPIA).

B. SDC Tools

There are quite a few SDC tools that are available, notably μ-Argus [4], sdcMicro [8] and ARX [9]. Multiple comparative studies have highlighted the capabilities of these tools when compared to each other. The literature shows that tools like μ-Argus implement a broad range of SDC methodologies. On the downside, this tool is a closed-source application which is no longer in active development. SdcMicro is an additional package for existing statistical software. It provides elementary anonymization techniques and has limited support to other specific data transformations. Prasser et al. analyse that the limitation of these tools relate to scalability issues when handling large data sets, incomplete support of privacy criteria and methods of data transformation and, most significantly, these tools require complex configuration by Information Technology (IT) experts [9].

In contrast, ARX is an open-source software which addresses the issues that other tools lack. It provides a broad range of efficient data anonymization methods along with a cross-platform user-interface. This graphical front-end provides multiple perspectives for configuring, exploring and analysing the data. But the main reason ARX stands out is that the framework is designed to prevent tight coupling of subsystems and ensure extensibility. This has helped the developers of ARX provide a stand-alone software library with a public Application Programming Interface (API), which can be used for integrating with other systems.

Even though ARX is the preferred tool of choice, it is not widely used for the simple reason that its many functionalities make this tool quite complex. The extensive features provided by ARX can be quite overwhelming to a user with basic knowledge of this field. The many terminologies used in the graphical front-end of ARX might be unknown to a common user, making this tool not intuitive. ARX also provides a user manual guide and an in-built setup assistant (wizard), but it does not help in reducing its complexity. Gould & Lewis suggest that the different components of a software – operating environment, user platform and reference manuals or materials usually fail to interact cohesively to create a conception that the user eventually deals with, as these components are designed separately [10].

As a result, there is a need to design and implement a tool which would be easier to learn and adopt. The findings suggest that sdcMicro and μ-Argus do not provide the flexibility or the scalability that can be used as a potential development environment for a new user-friendly implementation of an SDC tool. Instead, the availability of the extensive APIs of ARX coupled with its continuous development, testing and documentation due to active development makes this tool ideal for developing a tool that harvests the potential of the ARX tool itself, but in an environment that may be more suited to data controllers and their levels of SDC related knowledge.

C. User Interface Design

Designing a user interface for a software often involves a considerable investment of time and effort which can be reduced by adhering to previously established design guidelines [11]. These guidelines can serve as a starting point for establishing software requirements and development of the framework. Most of these guidelines explore aspects of the user interface design on data entry, data display and Human-Computer Interaction (HCI). However, not all guidelines can be applied to the design and have to be filtered for tailoring the framework design to fit the needs of the target group.

Another technique that can be used for capturing and describing the functional requirements of a software tool is use-case modelling [12]. Use-cases describe all those scenarios in which a user can interact with a system [13]. Writing effective use-cases can help in realising the goals of the different stakeholders. It can also lead to stakeholder driven requirement analysis taking into account the possibility of conflicting requirements [14].

Moreover, Morris & Dillon argue in their paper that developers can gather inputs on user perception of the usefulness or ease of use of the system based on preliminary designs of software tools [15]. The paper suggests that these early formulations of user perception of a system have an influence on whether users will actually use that system [15]. The literature also suggests that capturing predictive measures of user acceptance, even before the user has an opportunity to interact with the software, can lead to correlations between perceived usefulness and eventual user adoption of the software [16].

In conclusion, guidelines and requirement analysis can help in formulating a preliminary design of the framework. This can result in detecting user perceptions early in the design cycle, leading to reduced cost and effective time management.

III. RESEARCH METHODOLOGY

The nature of this project requires an understanding of SDC methodologies and their architecture so that they can be translated into design guidelines for the proposed framework. Additionally, the ARX tool has to be evaluated for the comprehension of its capabilities and how those capabilities can be exploited so that the framework can be built upon features that can eventually result in the implementation of a new tool. Design guidelines for a user interface software have to be formalised in conjunction with the goals of the stakeholders to realise the requirements of the framework. Furthermore, use-case modelling and qualitative data analyses can lead to a final design. Lastly, the design has to be evaluated to map it against the goals of all the stakeholders. The five research questions mentioned previously can help in achieving a generalised framework for an SDC tool.

Research questions 1 and 2 can be answered by conducting a literature study that can help in understanding the present state of the current SDC technologies, methods and their required guidelines. By doing this, shortcomings of the current state of the art can be understood and the most relevant ones can be handled in the framework. The literature study can also help in making an informed decision on the models and methods of data anonymization that should be part of the proposed framework. Thus, the first two research questions can help in formulating generalised SDC guidelines. The research also calls upon investigating into HCI, which happens through the user interface design. This can help in further shaping the design guidelines and features of a primary tool and translating it into an intuitive software design. Literature study can further help in answering research question 3. The literature can also reveal insights into user perception and behaviour for the early adoption of the tool. Thus, the first three questions can help in defining a set of guidelines and characteristics of the framework.

Next, to further understand the target group, a qualitative analysis research method approach will be undertaken to understand the requirements of the tool in an organisational setting. This involves conducting semi-structured interviews consisting of open-ended questions with the target group. Such type of interviews can be successful in delving deeper into the content matter which would have otherwise been difficult in structured or focus interviews [17]. The interviews will be conducted with individuals from target organisations within the Dutch public institutions like WODC, Dutch Police, etc.

The guidelines can then be finalised using the literature study and insights gained during the qualitative analysis. Once the guidelines have been agreed upon, requirement engineering can be done via use-case modelling. Next, a framework can be designed for the SDC tool, thereby answering research question 4.

Lastly, the design of the framework has to be validated by the target user-group. A mock-up of the new tool can be made using the framework to see how it is perceived by the target users. The research can explore the design and evaluation of the tool by applying different techniques such as heuristic evaluation, usability testing, use of guidelines and the cognitive walk-through method [18]. Heuristic evaluation and usability testing require the involvement of User Interface (UI) specialists. This is not feasible for this project. Therefore, the use of guidelines and cognitive walk-through techniques can help in finding serious as well as general problems with the usability of the tool without the need for a UI specialist. Thus, the final research question can be answered by conducting a survey and by applying the previously mentioned usability techniques. The result of the survey should be analysed to accommodate the recommendations to make improvements in the framework.

IV. CONCLUSION

In this position paper, we have identified a problem in practice regarding data disclosure tools and how they are not used by data controllers in public organisations in the Netherlands. We proposed a solution direction to address this problem by designing a framework for a simpler and more user-friendly implementation of an SDC tool.

REFERENCES

[1] M. S. Bargh, R. Meijer, and M. Vink, "On statistical disclosure control technologies: For enabling personal data protection in open dara settings," Research and Documentation Center WODC, The Hague, The Netherlands, Tech. Rep., Cahier 2018-20.

[2] J. Domingo-Ferrer and V. Torra, "Disclosure risk assessment in statistical data protection," Journal of Computational and Applied Mathematics, vol. 164, 2004, pp. 285–293.

[3] T. Benschop, C. Machingauta, and M. Welch, "Statistical Disclosure Control: A Practice Guide," 2019.

[4] A. Hundepool, J. Domingo-Ferrer, L. Franconi, S. Giessing, R. Lenz, J. Naylor, and P. De Wolf, "Handbook on Statistical Disclosure Control," ESSnet on Statistical Disclosure Control, 2010.

[5] J. Domingo-Feffer, A. Oganian, and V. Torra, "Information-theoretic disclosure risk measures in statistical disclosure control of tabular data," in Proceedings of the International Conference on Scientific and Statistical Database Management (SSDBM), Jan. 2002, pp. 227–231.

[6] D. Hutchison and J. C. Mitchell, "Privacy in Statistical Databases," in Proceedings of the CENEX-SDC Project International Conference, 2006.

[7] F. Prasser and F. Kohlmayer, Putting Statistical Disclosure Control into Practice: The ARX Data Anonymization Tool, 2015, chapter 6, pp. 111–148, in book, Gkoulalas-Divanis, A. and Loukides, G. (Eds.), Medical Data Privacy Handbook, ISBN: 978-3-319-23633-9.

[8] M. Templ, "Statistical disclosure control for microdata using the r-package sdcmicro," Transactions on Data Privacy, vol. 1, no. 2, Aug. 2008, pp. 67–85.

[9] F. Prasser, F. Kohlmayer, R. LautenschlÃger, and K. A. Kuhn, "ARX–A Comprehensive Tool for Anonymizing Biomedical Data," in Proceedings of the Annual Symposium / AMIA Symposium, 2014, pp. 984–993.

[10] J. D. Gould and C. Lewis, "Designing for usability-key principles and what designers think," in Proceedings of the Conference on Human Factors in Computing Systems, vol. 28, 1983, pp. 50–53.

[11] S. L. Smith and J. N. Mosier, "Guidelines for designing user interface software," 1986.

[12] B. Anda, H. Dreiem, D. I. K. Sjøberg, and M. Jørgensen, "Estimating Software Development Effort Based on Use Cases — Experiences from Industry," in The Unified Modeling Language. Modeling Languages, Concepts, and Tools, M. Gogolla and C. Kobryn, Eds. Springer Berlin Heidelberg, 2001, pp. 487–502.

[13] D. Rosenberg and K. Scott, Use case driven object modeling with UML. Springer, 1999.

[14] B. G. Cameron, E. F. Crawley, G. Loureiro, and E. S. Rebentisch, "Value flow mapping: Using networks to inform stakeholder analysis," Acta Astronautica, vol. 62, 2008, pp. 324–333.

[15] M. G. Morris and A. Dillon, "How user perceptions influence software use," IEEE Software, vol. 14, no. 4, July 1997, pp. 58–65.

[16] F. D. Davis and V. Venkatesh, "Toward preprototype user acceptance testing of new information systems: implications for software project management," IEEE Transactions on Engineering Management, vol. 51, no. 1, Feb 2004, pp. 31–46.

[17] B. DiCicco-Bloom and B. F. Crabtree, "The qualitative research interview," Medical Education, vol. 40, no. 4, 2006, pp. 314–321.

[18] R. Jeffries, J. R. Miller, C. Wharton, and K. Uyeda, "User interface evaluation in the real world: a comparison of four techniques," in Proceedings of the SIGCHI conference on Human factors in computing systems, 1991, pp. 119–124.

A Review of Frequency Table Disclosure Control from a Microdata Perspective

Alexander Latenko[1], Mortaza S. Bargh[2], Susan van den Braak[3], Marco Vink[4]
[1-4] Research and Documentation Centre, Ministry of Justice and Security, The Hague, The Netherlands
[2] Rotterdam University of Applied science, Research Center Creating 010, Rotterdam, The Netherlands
Email: [1] a.latenko@wodc.nl [2] m.shoae.bargh@wodc.nl [3] s.w.van.den.braak@wodc.nl [4] m.e.vink@wodc.nl

Abstract—**Protecting personal data is a key requirement for properly sharing and opening data. With growing concerns regarding privacy, it is important to ensure that the personal data of individuals is not compromised or made public in Open Data initiatives. For the most part, the personal data protection fields for microdata and tabular data have been researched separately. This separation has caused both fields to have much overlapping research, particularly concerning the privacy and utility of the respective data types. This overlapping research, however, has not been well integrated between the fields. Recently, there have been developments and improvements for protecting microdata that are not being applied to the field of tabular data protection. In this work, the association between microdata and tabular data is formalized and used to link the personal data disclosure risks and the personal data protection models that can be applied to both microdata and tabular data.**

Keywords–Data Protection; Disclosure Scenarios; Frequency Tables; Statistical Disclosure Control.

I. Introduction

Within the process of opening and sharing data, Statistical Disclosure Control (SDC) is applied to reduce the risk of privacy disclosures for individuals while preserving the quality and utility of the data. Minimizing the risk of privacy disclosures is an essential step that needs to be performed in order to adhere to privacy regulations, such as the EU's General Data Protection Regulation (GDPR). As essential as it is for a data controller, i.e., the entity that opens the data, to provide sufficient guarantees of privacy, it is perhaps just as essential for a data user to be provided with similar guarantees of the quality of data. There are different reasons for opening or disseminating data, including, among others, improving transparency and enabling (scientific) research. Census tables are an example of opening data for transparency, where the information in those tables influences public perception and therefore should be as informative as possible. Opening data does not only facilitate research, but has become increasingly necessary for academic work to be acceptable for publication in certain journals [1].

SDC solutions are non-trivial in practical settings as the identification of potential sources of disclosure is a difficult task. This becomes clear from the recent cases where data subjects, the individuals present in the data, were first de-identified (anonymized), but were later re-identified by researchers [2]. Even when SDC methods have been applied on data, re-identification is still sometimes possible. Numerous cases have been discovered, including the infamous cases of disclosure in the microdata of taxi rides from NYC [3] and tabular data containing sensitive health information [4].

To prevent re-identification, an initial identification of the sources and causes of personal data disclosures is required. As such, this work contributes by providing a taxonomy for data disclosures when opening tabular data. Models such as t-closeness [5] and differential privacy [6] have been introduced to provide certain levels of privacy. Such models have mainly been introduced for protecting microdata. However, tabular data and microdata are closely related. We fundamentally formalize the relation between the two data types. This formalization makes it possible to evaluate the relation between SDC models developed for protecting microdata sets and those developed for protecting tabular data sets. Thus, this work improves the unification of the SDC methods and models developed for microdata and tabular data sets. The contribution on this work is focused on frequency tables, which is the most general type of tabular data. The disclosure risks and privacy models for frequency tables mainly hold for other types of tabular data, such as magnitude tables [7]. However, the disclosure risks that affect other specific types of tabular data are not considered in this work.

To the best of our knowledge, this is the first work that aims at unifying the privacy models for microdata and those for tabular data, allowing for comparisons between the privacy models. The rest of this work consists of the formalization of microdata and tabular data, specifically frequency tables, in Section II. The concept of disclosure is introduced in Section III, followed by the attacks that cause personal data disclosures in Section IV. An overview of privacy models is presented in Section V. Lastly, Section VI concludes this work and discusses possible future work.

II. Data Association

In order to unambiguously describe the scenarios where personal data disclosures may take place for tabular data sets, the concept of microdata and tabular data are formalized in this section.

A. Microdata

A microdata set $\mathcal{DS}_M$ comprises N rows, or records, denoted by x^n, where $n = 1, \ldots, N$ and every record x^n corresponds to one individual. Further, every record x^n comprises D attributes. An attribute is denoted by a_i, where $i : 1, \ldots, D$. An attribute a_i has an associated domain of nominal or ordinal values A_i. Domain $A = A_1 \times A_2 \times \ldots \times A_D$ denotes the super domain, which contains all attribute values in $\mathcal{DS}_M$. Every record x^n is defined over A, consisting of attribute values $x_1^n, x_2^n, \ldots, x_D^n$, where $x_i^n \in A_i$, $i : 1, \ldots, D$. Table I is an example of a microdata table.

In the SDC literature for microdata, the set of attributes $\{a_1, a_2, \ldots, a_D\}$ are generally divided into four disjoint sets called: explicit identifiers, quasi identifiers, sensitive attributes, and non-sensitive attributes. *Explicit Identifiers* (EIDs) refer

TABLE I. EXAMPLE OF MICRODATA

	EID	QIDs		SAT	Misc.	
Record	a_1: Name	a_2: Zip	a_3: Age	a_4: Illness	...	a_D
x^1	x_1^1=Jane Doe	x_2^1=2230	x_3^1=15	x_4^1=Cancer	...	x_D^1
$\vdots$	$\vdots$	$\vdots$	$\vdots$	$\vdots$	...	$\vdots$
x^N	x_1^N=...	x_2^N=...	x_3^N=...	x_4^N=...	...	x_D^N

to the set of attributes in the original microdata set $\mathcal{DS}_M$ that structurally and on their own could uniquely identify an individual. Examples of explicit identifiers are an individual's name, home address and unique personal numbers like a 'social security number', 'national health service number', 'voter card identification number', or 'permanent account number'.

Quasi Identifiers (QIDs) refer to the set of attributes in the original microdata set $\mathcal{DS}_M$ that could 'potentially' identify individuals. Identification through QIDs is achieved by using a combination of values, which belong to QID attributes, of a record from the microdata set $\mathcal{DS}_M$. For these values of QID attributes, an intruder, a person or entity that seeks to learn personal information about data subjects, can identify individuals from other known knowledge bases. Knowledge bases can be very specific and personal, such as being acquainted with the data subjects, or general, such as the information from other public data releases. For example, assume that weight, length, hair color, and location are QIDs. Knowing the values of these attributes, an acquaintance may recognize the person uniquely. The QIDs in microdata set $\mathcal{DS}_M$, therefore, capture the so-called background knowledge that intruders have with respect to microdata set $\mathcal{DS}_M$.

Sensitive Attributes (SATs) refer to those attributes that capture privacy-sensitive information about individuals. In the justice domain, for example, this could be the specifics of a crime committed or the remaining duration of a prison sentence, and in the health domain this could be the condition an individual is suffering from. These sensitive attributes are sometimes important for data users for data analytics purposes. Unlike QIDs, SATs are assumed to be unknown outside of the original microdata set $\mathcal{DS}_M$ and, therefore, they are not characterized as background knowledge of intruders.

Non-sensitive Attributes (NATs) refer to all the miscellaneous attributes that are not directly-identifying, quasi-identifying or sensitive in a specific context. For example, someone's favorite color may be considered as a NAT in a microdata set for medical research. We shall use the concepts of EID, QID, SAT and NAT to explain statistical disclosures and the SDC methods for frequency tabular data sets.

B. Frequency Tables

A frequency table, also known as a contingency table, is constructed from a subset of attributes generally referred to as *grouping attributes*. The set of grouping attributes γ, which consists of d attributes, is generally only a small subset of the attributes of the original microdata. As such, the dimension of a frequency table, denoted by d, tends to be (much) smaller than that of the microdata, denoted by D.

A table consists of a number of cells. Every cell C_y, in a tabular data set $\mathcal{DS}_T$, contains an attribute value pattern y, which consists of a combination of grouping attribute values, i.e., $y = \{y_i | y_i \subset A_i, a_i \in \gamma\}$. The set notation has been used here because y_i can represent a single attribute value, for instance, a single age y_i=15 if a_i=Age, or y_i can also be used to represent a set of ages y_i=$\{15, 16\}$. In frequency tables a cell C_y expresses the number of records x^n in the source microdata set $\mathcal{DS}_M$ whose relevant attribute values $x_1^n, x_2^n, \ldots, x_d^n$ fit the attribute value pattern y. Since the records in $\mathcal{DS}_M$ generally have a larger dimension, only a subset of attribute values are counted. For example, in Table I attributes (x_3^n, x_4^n) are counted for all n records when they fit the pattern of (y_3, y_4). Table II is an example of a frequency table with attributes (y_3, y_4) that could have been sourced from the microdata of Table I.

TABLE II. EXAMPLE OF A 2-DIMENSIONAL TABLE CONSTRUCTED FROM TWO ATTRIBUTES IN TABLE I

		a_4(SAT)		m_3=Total
		y_4=Cancer	y_4=HIV	
a_3(QID)	y_3=15	1	2	3
	y_3=16	4	5	9
m_4=Total		5	7	12

In a frequency table, the cell value can be defined as:

$$C_y = |\{x^n | x^n \in \mathcal{DS}_M, \forall y_i \in y : x_i^n \in y_i\}|. \quad (1)$$

In addition to the cells defined in (1), frequency tables also contain total cells, denoted by m_i, that are only comprised of a single attribute value. We refer such cells are *marginals*. Table marginals in tabular data sets are obtained from the projection of the j-ary cube $a_1, a_2, \ldots, a_j$ onto a subset of j attributes, also called j-way marginals [8], where $j < d$. For example, one-way marginal with respect to grouping attribute a_i with value y_i is:

$$m_i(y_i) = \sum_{C_y \in \mathcal{DS}_T,\ \text{given } y_i \text{of } y} C_y.$$

The summation above is over all cells with value y_i. The two-way marginal with respect to attributes a_i and a_j with value y_i and y_j is:

$$m_{i,j}(y_i, y_j) = \sum_{C_y \in \mathcal{DS}_T,\ \text{given } y_i, y_j \text{of } y} C_y. \quad (2)$$

These summations can be used to define marginals for up to d-way marginals.

C. Release

Frequency tables are derived from microdata. Similar to a microdata set, a frequency table provides information about a number of records. A frequency table provides this information about d grouping attributes, while the microdata set $\mathcal{DS}_M$ provides this information for all attributes. When frequency tables have the same dimension as their microdata sources, the data sources contain the same information, albeit being differently structured, which is due to the difference between the definitions of y_i and x_i^n. Compared to frequency tables, microdata generally provides more detailed information, which introduces a higher risk of personal data disclosures.

Tabular data has been used to provide information on a subset of attributes, i.e., the grouping attributes, with those attribute values that are assumed to be interesting for data users. These attributes are selected to be in the y of the table cells. A common example is census data, where the objective is to provide information about the population that is as accurate as possible and is processed minimally. When the objective is to release information for the sake of transparency, tabular data is a common choice.

III. DISCLOSURE CONCEPTS

In this section, we formalize several concepts that are relevant for characterizing personal data disclosures within tabular data sets.

A. Disclosure Elements in Tabular Data Sets

The elements of a tabular data set, or a table in short, that can be used for disclosing someone's personal information are:

1) Grouping attributes $a_1, a_2, \ldots, a_d$, which represent the dimensions of the table.
2) The table description attribute(s) t_{des}, which results from the table caption or the textual explanations embedded in the paragraphs preceding or succeeding the table.

For example, in Table III, there are two attributes a_1 (gender, being male or female) and a_2 (age, being minor or adult). The table also includes a table description in the table caption, saying that the table is about those arrested (acting as $t_{\text{des},1}$) in January 2019 (acting as $t_{\text{des},2}$). Note that, although we denote it as t_{des} for emphasis, a table description attribute is also an attribute from the microdata source.

TABLE III. NUMBER OF ARRESTS IN JANUARY 2019 (ACTING AS $t_{\text{des},1}$ and $t_{\text{des},2}$, RESPECTIVELY).

a_1 : Gender		male	female	Total
a_2 : Age	minor	11	1	12
	adult	62	37	99
Total		73	38	111

B. Re-identification

In SDC methods for protecting microdata sets, the background knowledge of intruders (so-called intruder's prior), which can be used to re-identify data subjects, is mainly modelled in QIDs. In this section, we outline how this approach can be extended to tabular data sets. To explain the attribute mapping for tabular data sets, we use Table III as an example of a frequency table. The cell with value 1 in the table corresponds to one data record in the microdata set from which the table is constructed. This cell can be specified by grouping attribute values a_1 = female and a_2 = minor, and the table description attribute values $t_{\text{des},1}$ = those arrested and $t_{\text{des},2}$ = in January 2019.

The re-identification of the record, corresponding to a cell with value 1, may take place based on any combination of attributes $a_1, a_2, t_{\text{des},1}$ and $t_{\text{des},2}$, which may potentially act as QIDs. For example, in our data set we have a single female minor who has been arrested in January 2019. That means that any intruder who knows someone that fits those QID values uniquely, can identify the person that is counted in Table III. This will be referred to as the *re-identification* of a cell with value 1. Once an individual has been identified to be uniquely part of a cell, any new information or data related to that cell will thus also be attributed to that individual, as described in the following subsection.

Note that for exact re-identification of an individual, corresponding to a cell with value 1 in a frequency table, it is important that just one person fits in the group specified by the values of the grouping, and description attributes, that act as QIDs. This category is also called the *Equivalence Class* (EC) of those QIDs. This uniqueness of the individual corresponding to the cell with value 1, and within the EC of the corresponding QIDs, can be described based on the concepts of sample uniqueness and population uniqueness [9].

Both sample uniqueness and population uniqueness should be defined based on the values of those attributes that act as QIDs. The underlying assumption is that every cell with value 1 (and corresponding microdata record) in the frequency table can potentially be identified based on the QIDs. The QIDs being the background information available to an intruder to link a cell to an actual individual.

Let $|S_{EC}|$ denote the cell value in a frequency table, i.e., the number of data records of the corresponding microdata set. The EC being determined over the values of QIDs of the frequency table. The value of $|S_{EC}|$ determines the degree of uniqueness of the cell (or of the corresponding records/individuals in the microdata set). If $|S_{EC}| = 1$, then the corresponding cell is unique in the published frequency table. A larger value of $|S_{EC}|$ makes the corresponding cells (or records) less unique.

Sample uniqueness is necessary, but it is not enough for re-identification. With respect to the set of the QIDs, we assume that the frequency table (or the corresponding microdata set) is a sample of a larger population microdata set. In other words, all data records in the sample data set (i.e., the frequency table of the corresponding microdata set) are also in the population microdata set denoted by P, where these sample and population microdata sets have been defined over the same attribute value domains. Therefore, both have the same ECs (i.e., the same patterns of the values for the QIDs). Let $|P_{EC}|$ denote the size of the EC, which is determined over the values of the QIDs of the frequency table. The uniqueness of an individual/record in both microdata sets can be defined by $|S_{EC}| = 1$ and $|P_{EC}| = 1$, which are the sizes of the EC in those microdata sets. We note that:

- Population uniqueness results in sample uniqueness (i.e., if $|P_{EC}| = 1$, then $|S_{EC}| = 1$); and
- Sample uniqueness does not necessarily result in population uniqueness (i.e., if $|S_{EC}| = 1$, then $|P_{EC}| \geq 1$).

In practice, given a sufficient number of QIDs, an intruder can fairly accurately estimate the probability that $|S_{EC}| = 1$ results in $|P_{EC}| = 1$. A recent work has shown that the estimations were possible with more than 95% accuracy when there are 15 QIDs [10].

One should also note that while a data controller can easily validate sample uniqueness by investigating the released frequency table (or the corresponding microdata set), this is not always possible for the population uniqueness. The data controller does not necessarily possess the entire population data.

Note that *population uniqueness is necessary, but it is not enough for exact re-identification.* In addition to population uniqueness, whereby the size of an EC in the population data set is 1 (i.e., $|P_{EC}| = 1$), there should be a unique identifier (e.g., an EID) associated with the corresponding EC from the population microdata set, so that the identities can be linked to the cell with a value 1 in the frequency table.

C. Attribution

Some grouping attributes can act as QIDs, as mentioned in the previous subsections, and other attributes can act as SATs. An attribute is a SAT when it contains information that could potentially be harmful for the associated individual or groups when released [11]. The value of a SAT does not contribute to the identification of an individual the way that a QID does, as the SAT is specific to (i.e., known within) the data set to be released. In combination with external data sets, the grouping and table description attributes acting as QIDs could be used to identify individuals and, consequently, reveal the values of the other grouping attributes for those records/individuals.

Table IV provides 4 example cases of the grouping and table description attributes that could act as QIDs and SATs, based on the example given in Table III. Note that in Table IV, attributes $t_{\text{des},1}$ and $t_{\text{des},2}$ are merged into attribute t_{des} for simplifying the presentation. For each case in Table IV, we assume that the corresponding QIDs result in identification for the cell with value 1 in Table III. This is because there is only a single person described by the QIDs, in those cases, in the sample data sets (i.e., sample uniqueness), it is assumed that the population uniqueness holds as well. Note that this is an illustrative example, in practice, often more QIDs are needed to result in population uniqueness and someone's identification with a high certainty. Furthermore, for the sake of simplicity, we assume that all other attributes per case in Table III are SATs.

TABLE IV. FOUR CASES ILLUSTRATING ATTRIBUTION TO SATs, THROUGH IDENTIFICATION BY QIDs IN TABLE III)

	QIDs (already known facts about the cell contributor in the world)	SATs (new facts known about the cell contributor via Table III)
Case 1	a_1, a_2	t_{des}
Case 2	a_1, t_{des}	a_2
Case 3	a_2, t_{des}	a_1
Case 4	a_1, a_2, t_{des}	...?

Disclosure through re-identification on its own may not be an issue, if one guarantees that no more information about the identified individual can been learned. If we examine the SATs column in Table IV, we find that for cases 1-3 we do learn a new attribute value from the released table that describes something extra about the person in the data. Thus, the combination of unique identification and learning a new attribute value about the identified individual can lead to so-called *individual attribution*. Note that the intruder in case 4 may not learn anything new about the data subject, but the case could still be perceived as privacy intrusive because this table aggregates, presents and reaffirms the associations of all grouping attributes and the table description attribute (i.e., a_1, a_2, t_{des}) to the individual.

TABLE V. AN ILLUSTRATION OF GROUP ATTRIBUTION.

Number of arrests ($t_{\text{des},1}$) of minors (a_2) in 2019 ($t_{\text{des},2}$)				
a_1: Gender		Male	female	total
a_3: Crime	hacking	5	5	10
	DUI	15	0	15
Total		20	5	25

Attribution can also occur without identification, for example, intruders can learn something new about a whole group without identifying the individual groups members. This is called *group attribution*. Consider the example in Table V, which is a representation with a more specific set of attributes from Table III. In Table V the grouping attribute a_2 assumes only the 'minor' value, furthermore, the grouping attribute a_3 is included, which only specifies the crime types: hacking and Driving Under Influence (DUI). In Table V, we cannot uniquely identify the records corresponding to the cell with value 5 by knowing the values of just the QIDs a_1 and a_2 because they correspond to 5 records/individuals in this table. Nevertheless, the intruder can learn that the crime type is hacking (i.e., $a_3 =$ hacking), for someone whose QIDs match $(a_1, a_2) =$ (female, minor), without being able to re-identify the exact person from the released table.

IV. SOURCES OF DISCLOSURE

Intruders seek to learn private information about the contributors present in a released table. There are many aspects that matter when trying to assess the risk of disclosure, such as the motivation, means and consequences of a disclosure attempt, which are part of what is called a disclosure scenario [12]. These aspects vary between releases as much as the information within the releases does. Most intruders that are interested in medical data might have little reason to actively seek disclosure risks in tax data, and vice versa. Both groups, however, will use similar attacks to learn about contributors.

Let us assume that the intruder, as background knowledge, has data set D_B, where every record z^n is defined over d'' attributes, some of which are defined from the same attribute domains of the original microdata $\mathcal{DS}_M$. In other words, microdata sets D_B and $\mathcal{DS}_M$ have some attributes in common (only QIDs).

A. Few contributors

When there are few contributors in a cell of a frequency table, the risk of disclosure is fairly high. When there is a single contributor to a cell such that $C_y = 1$, then there is a risk of re-identification. If the intruder has knowledge of the identity of an individual n, whose characteristics fit the pattern y (i.e., the intruders has knowledge of a record $z^{(n)}$ that fits y), and $|P_{EC}| = 1$, then re-identification takes place. Furthermore, if the length of the pattern y is longer than the number of identifying attributes in z^n (i.e., the attributes in z^n acting as QIDs), then we have attribution because the intruder can now learn some attributes that the intruder had not known previously.

A single contributor to a cell is not the only issue. It is possible that the intruder knows some of the individuals that contribute to a cell with a value of more than one, i.e., $C_y > 1$. For example, when the intruder is in the table himself, or when the intruder colludes with some other contributors from the cell to gain information. This information is used to recognize a single individual with certainty, i.e., to subtract the known individuals from a cell with $C_y > 1$ to create a new cell that has $C_y = 1$.

B. Zero Cells

One major source of attribution is the presence of zero cells in the table. Take Table VI as an example, where there are several zero values. When an intruder has in his background knowledge a record $z^n = (Arrest = yes, Gender = Female, \ldots)$, then the intruder immediately learns that the age of the arrested individual is not greater than 21. This is referred to as negative attribution [13], whereby we learn which values cannot be attributed to an individual.

TABLE VI. EXAMPLE OF SKEWED TABLE OF ARRESTS IN 2019 (a_3)

		a_1:Age				marginal
		< 18	$18-21$	$21-29$	$29+$	m_{gender}
a_2:Gender	female	1	37	0	0	38
	male	3	0	21	10	32
marginal	m_{age}	4	37	21	10	70

Negative attribution is a form of disclosure that occurs commonly, as any zero cell in a table could lead to negative attribution. The impact of negative attribution is generally smaller than exact attribution. Learning that someone is not exactly 15 years old, is less impactful than learning that someone is exactly 16 years old. However, as negative attributions are common, multiple negative attributions can be combined to have close to exact attribution. An intruder may learn that everyone in Table VI had been trialed as an adult, which can only happen for 15-year olds or older, resulting in a negative attribution that no one is younger than 16. Now, an intruder can learn from Table VI that any female in the table is between the ages of 16 and 22.

In some cases, zero cells can cause exact attribution. In the case of Table VI, if the intruders know of an individual between the age of 21 and 30 that had been arrested, the intruders will immediately learn that the gender of the individual is male.

C. Differencing

Unfortunately, disclosure risk does not originate only from having cells with few or no contributors. If it had been so, it would have been possible to adjust only the specific cells with low numbers of contributors. The values that cells represent in a table are dependent on each other. For example, the value in one cell could be the summed total of several other cell values (like marginals). When the value of a cell is adjusted for its protection, it is sometimes possible to use the cells that are related to that cell to find the original value of the cell.

Suppression is a common method for tabular protection that hides the number in the cell with a "*", "NULL", or any other string or symbol. Such a symbol clearly indicates that the value of the cell is suppressed [11]. Let us reconsider Table VI, only this time we suppress the values of the first column by publishing a new cell $C'_{female,<18} = *$, instead of the correct value $C_{female,<18} = 1$. An intruder does not directly know the number of contributors belonging to the cell with pattern $(female, < 18)$. Further, assume that the intruder does know the number of contributors that belong to the gender marginal, i.e, the right most column in Table VI. We can subtract all other cell values from the marginal to retrieve the original value:

$$\begin{aligned} C_{female,<18} &= m_{gender}(female) - C_{female,18\text{-}21} \\ &\quad - C_{female,21\text{-}29} - C_{female,29+} \\ &= 1. \end{aligned}$$

This common linear relation between the cells makes it much harder to determine which cell to adjust. In the case of suppression, for example, the problem becomes NP-complete [14]. Aside from marginals, other cells may also have a linear relation with each other. When a table describes some flows, for instance, the number of patients following a certain treatment, then one common relation is that the number of outputs of the flow equals the number of inputs of the flow subtracted by the number of cases still being in the flow (e.g., receiving a treatment). These types of relations are inherent to the domain and the processes that the data tracks. Generally, some domain knowledge is necessary to identify such relations.

D. Linking

When assessing the disclosure risk of a table, it is not enough to only examine the table itself, as the cells in a table can be linked to the background knowledge of the intruder and other tables that may have been released in the past. Generally, different table releases use different source (micro)data, which makes information linking unlikely. However, several specific types of data releases have been identified that have a high risk of disclosure through linking [16]. Linking increases the number of methods, which includes the ones previously discussed, for personal data disclosure.

One situation where data linkage likely leads to disclosure is when the same data is released multiple times with slight alterations, for example, when changing the values of an attribute. This has been identified for microdata as the *republication problem* [15]. The same problem persists in tabular data releases. When a table is published with, for example, a cell value $C_{age=16\text{-}19}$, it is possible to adjust the value of the grouping attribute age and release a cell value of $C_{age=15\text{-}19}$. This adjustment may be done for a variety of reasons, such as a new legislation making the new age group of interest or when a new method for generating tables is implemented. Even when both cells are safe given the disclosure risk mentioned above, the difference between these releases generates a new cell $C_{age=15}$ which may not be safe. We refer to [16] for more extensive examples of disclosure through linking.

When searching for disclosures in data, intruders can use linking and differencing to create more cells with zero or unique contributors. Subsequently, intruders can try to re-identify individuals contributing to those cells and carry out attribution attacks against those individuals. This search process is visualized in Figure 1.

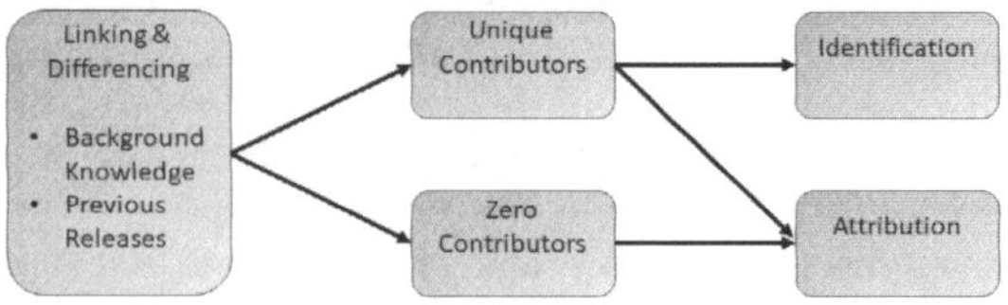

Figure 1. Diagram representing the relation between disclosure sources.

E. Approximate Disclosure

Disclosures do not always happen with complete certainty. If data is appropriately protected, it is possible that none of the disclosure scenarios above occur. When an intruder has some uncertainty in the attribution or re-identification, the intruder could either direct more resources towards confirming the re-identification or attribution (e.g., via linking the newly discovered information with other data sources). It is possible to have approximate disclosures in re-identification and attribution cases.

Re-identification with sampled data almost never happens with complete certainty. An intruder with access to a sampled table, might potentially discover cells representing only one individual, i.e., $C_y = 1$. The intruder might even know a person that fits pattern y. The risk of disclosure may still be fairly small if the intruder has no knowledge of how large the number of similar individuals in the population is. In other words, the value of the corresponding $|P_{EC}|$ could be one, but can also be let us say 100 (i.e, the individual could be unique or 100 individuals could fit that pattern in the population). In the former, the re-identification with certainty can occur. In certain cases, given uniqueness in the sampled data, it is possible to be fairly certain how many individuals fit that pattern in the population. For example, [17] has shown that 86% of the U.S. population is unique given only a few attributes.

Zero cells commonly cause (negative) group attribution, since intruders can learn that no individual in surrounding groups belongs to the pattern represented by the zero cell. It is also common that, instead of zero, there are only very few individuals belonging to one cell and an overwhelming majority belonging to another cell. Consider the distribution of female arrestees in Table VI, where the majority (i.e., 37) are adults, compared to the single arrestee that was a minor. If an intruder seeks to learn information about a female arrestee, the intruder may conclude with fairly high certainty that she is an adult. In many nations it is common for minors' privacy to be additionally protected by law. Thus, an intruder who learns that his target is likely an adult, might become more motivated to spend more resources in tracking his target, as their information may be more easily accessible (relative to a minor).

Differencing and linking can be applied to find cells with few or zero contributors. This can lead to identification and attribution as depicted in Figure 1. When finding these cells, an intruder may approximate the likelihood that an individual, whom the intruder may know, is associated with some sensitive information. This approximate learning is unavoidable to an extent. However, it is important that intruders do not learn too much sensitive information about individuals either exactly or approximately. For this purpose, various privacy models have been devised for protecting frequency tables.

V. Privacy Models

There are various techniques to protect tabular data from attacks. These techniques adjust the table and the cells by suppressing or rounding cells, restructuring table attributes [11] or adding noise [18]. These techniques aim at having a certain level of privacy. The level of privacy is determined by so-called privacy models, which identify the cells or records that could be at risk of disclosure. The privacy models, although researched independently, are fairly similar for tabular data and microdata. In this section, we aim at clarifying these similarities. Furthermore, note that these privacy models cannot guarantee full protection against all disclosures. But, if they are appropriately applied, they can minimize the likelihood that intruders with reasonable resources are able to disclose sensitive information.

A. Exact Risks

One early and fairly common privacy model in microdata is k-anonymity [19]. This model requires that for any pattern of QIDs, $y = (a_1 = i, \ldots, a_d = j)$, there are at least k individuals that belong to that pattern. Similarly, if we use pattern y to define a cell in the table, then when the privacy model is applied on the microdata it also holds for tabular data: $C_y \geq k$.

One major issue with the k-anonymity privacy model is that it does not protect SATs, even though these are commonly released. k-anonymity ensures for every possible QID pattern to have sufficient individuals. This makes it difficult to identify a single individual and, generally, any SAT published will have values distributed across many QID patterns. However, one common source of disclosure risk arises when a SAT value is skewed towards one group. Take pattern y and extend it with a SAT s, let us take gender as s. In this case, it is possible that $C_{y,s=female} = 0$, whereas $C_{y,s=male} = 15$ (we used this example in Table V). We may not be able to identify an individual based on pattern y from the data, but we learn that any individual that falls under pattern y is a male. This is known as a homogeneity attack and can be reduced with the ℓ-diversity model [20]. ℓ-diversity requires that for all QID patterns there are at least ℓ SAT values (note that this requirement holds for every SAT attribute). In the case of gender, requiring 2-diversity means that $C_{y,s=male} \geq 1$ and $C_{y,s=female} \geq 1$, which would prevent zeroes in the case of two genders. If another sensitive value $j =$ bigender would be possible, then with 2-diversity only two cells have to be nonzero and, in this case, one zero would be allowed in $\{C_{y,male}, C_{y,female}, C_{y,bigender}\}$, thus negative attribution can still occur, but at least ℓ possible values prevent exact attribution without extensive background knowledge.

Both k-anonymity and ℓ-diversity have been developed for microdata protection. Similarly, the minimum frequency rule was developed for protecting frequency tables [21]. The minimum frequency rule restricts all cells to contain at least n individuals, i.e., $C_y \geq n$. This is required for a complete pattern y, this includes all the QIDs and SATs. The minimum frequency rule is a more strict model than ℓ-diversity as it prevents any negative attribution. This provides additional protection but may remove too much information in certain cases. ℓ-diversity can already suffer from too much information loss with multiple SATs due to the curse of dimensionality [22]. In protecting frequency tables, the minimum frequency rule requires removing zero cells, which may reduce the number of grouping attributes in order for a table to uphold the rule.

Whether zeroes are acceptable varies by case, as the impact of negative attribution is severely less than of exact attribution. The minimum frequency rule is the strongest in prevention of zero cells, ℓ-diversity prevents exact attribution through zero cells, and k-anonymity leaves the most information for data users, but also provides the least protection against negative or exact attribution through those cells.

B. Approximate Risks

A data controller may prevent exact identification and attribution of individuals, given that intruders have a limited set of resources for re-identification or attribution. However, approximate attribution in some cases might be sufficient for an intruder with enough background knowledge, or resources, to learn sensitive information.

A risk of approximate attribution exists when there is a skew between subgroups, e.g., when almost everyone that fits a certain pattern y belongs to a specific age group. This concern has been identified for microdata, which resulted in Entropy ℓ-diversity being introduced [20]. The entropy restriction requires that individuals that fit pattern y are well distributed across the values of their SATs. For example, for a SAT s in the set of sensitive attributes S, entropy can be defined as:

$$Entropy(y) = -\sum_{s \in S} p(C_{y,s}) \log p(C_{y,s}),$$

where $p(C_{y,s})$ is the fraction of contributors that belong to pattern y and sensitive value s. If $Entropy(y) \geq \log \ell$ holds for all patterns y, then the data is considered safe.

Even with entropy ℓ-diversity, it is still possible to learn something about pattern y. For example, if we take a SAT with value s_1 representing some rare disease and value s_2 some common disease, we can take $p(C_{y,s_1}) \approx p(C_{y,s_2}) \approx 0.5$, which will have very high entropy and be considered to have a low risk of disclosure. Assume the fraction of $p(s_2)$ in the data as a whole is very small ≤ 0.001, then intruders can learn that individuals that fit pattern y have an abnormally large chance of having the rare disease. This is known as the skewness attack and can be prevented with the t-closeness model [5]. The t-closeness model requires the distribution of the attribute values $s \in S$, for every pattern y, to be similar to the distribution of s in the data as a whole.

ℓ-diversity and t-closeness have been developed for microdata. For tabular data, a work recently introduced privacy models that includes an entropy constraint for tabular data [23][24]. The entropy constraint in the model is a generalization of ℓ-diversity and t-closeness. Instead of using the entropy of S over a pattern y, this model restricts the entropy of the distribution over C (all cells). Computing the entropy over C, ignoring the grouping of cells by their SATs, and instead, restricting the entropy for all cells regardless of their SATs or QIDs, allows for more protection on the table as a whole. As ℓ-diversity and t-closeness solely restrict the distributions with respect to SATs, they reduce only the most impactful disclosure risks (on SATs) while maintaining more useful information. However, determining which attributes should be considered as QIDs or SATs is not always a trivial task [25].

C. Differential Privacy

A data controller may not always be able to determine the QIDs and SATs accurately, as it is difficult to know what kind of information is out there. A data controller may be aware of intruders with a lot of resources and background knowledge, but may be unable to specify the means these intruders possess exactly. For such cases, differential privacy models have been developed, originally for microdata [6], and later also introduced for tabular data [26]. ϵ-differential privacy requires that the effect that individuals have on the data is limited. Take data sets DS and DS^*, where the difference between the two is a single individual, the result r (the result of an analysis or a query), for both data sets, has to be similar enough such that:

$$\frac{P(r|DS)}{P(r|DS^*)} \leq e^{\epsilon}. \tag{3}$$

The advantage of applying such a model is that data controllers have a theoretical guarantee for containing personal data disclosures with a tuneable parameter ϵ. This guarantees holds regardless of the information an intruder may possess [6]. This property makes ϵ-differential privacy useful for cases where data controllers do not know much about the intruders' background knowledge. Note that this guarantee applies to the definition of ϵ-differential privacy, according to which the presence or absence of the (personal) data of an individual in a data set must not have an observable impact on the output of an analysis/computation over that data set [6]. Whether this definition of privacy is comprehensive and adequate has not been established yet.

Recently, there has been a significant demand for on-line table generation, which allows the user to query data numerous times, instead of receiving a pre-processed data set. This has advantages for both data user and data controller, but it also comes with the issue that if the data users are also potential intruders, then, they now possess resources for differencing and linking [27][28]. In such environments, especially when data users' queries are minimally controlled, the differential privacy model is indispensable. More syntactic privacy models [29], such as k-anonymity and t-closeness, cannot protect the data against such intruders, unless the queries are restricted or tracked to prevent the intruder's background knowledge from increasing too much.

One issue with differential privacy is that, in order to provide the guarantee (3), a stochastic mechanism is required to transform the data. This transformation is generally achieved by using some distribution of noise [30]. Applying noise or some other stochastic mechanism to transform the data has a probability that the transformed data differs significantly from the original data. This issue in the so-called the range of correctness [29], i.e., the possible original values that the transformed data represents, makes it more difficult to apply the differential privacy model. In cases where it is expected that the published statistics about crime, income, etc., are close to their actual numbers (e.g., when releasing census tables), large potential variations are unacceptable. This issue has been identified in US census data, where due to smaller samples with some outliers, the added variance from the noise could vary between 1000% and 7000% for moderate levels of privacy [31]. There are more variations of differential privacy that vary slightly in the privacy and utility levels but provide similar theoretical guarantees as (3) and require some stochastic mechanism to work as well. For a more extensive view focused on differential privacy, we refer to [30].

VI. Conclusion and Future Work

This study examined privacy models from microdata and tabular literature through a unified formalization. It was found that the personal privacy models in the tabular data literature are more privacy-preserving, and thus require less information to be released than their microdata counterparts. The dimension, i.e., the number of attributes of the data that is published, is generally much larger for microdata than for tabular data. When there are more attributes, intruders may learn more from attribution, additionally, intruders have more attributes at their disposal for re-identification. As such, having stricter privacy models for tabular data may seem counterintuitive.

From the comparison of the privacy models, it becomes clear that the background knowledge is differently assessed between the two data types. The privacy models for tabular data require the same protection for all cells, regardless of the classes, such as QIDs or SATs. If done correctly, using microdata privacy models allows for releasing more data with minimal increase of privacy risks. However, the process of classifying the attributes into QIDs, SAT, etc., is difficult. Due to tabular data being more aggregated by nature, it generally needs to be less transformed/processed (than its microdata counterpart) to provide similar privacy guarantees. For the same reason, the information in tabular data is more robust against stronger privacy models, which means that adhering to stronger privacy models causes less information loss for tabular data. However, as the dimension of tables increases, we suspect that using attribute classes, such as QIDs and SATs, in data privacy models may become unavoidable. Additional research is required into the loss of information from privacy models for various release purposes and dimensions of tables. A different manner to avoid the process of having to assign attribute classes is by applying differential privacy. One issue of differential privacy for tabular data is that the range of correctness for values can become very large. This can increase the variance tremendously, as shown in previous works, which may be unacceptable for common tabular data releases, such as census tables.

Microdata and tabular data are very similar, however, there are differences in practical release purposes that cause tabular data to generally require more accuracy for data users in their privacy models. A possible future work is to assess how protection methods, i.e., the transformation done on the data, differ between microdata and tabular data. Of interest would be to investigate whether similar differences can be found in protection methods, for tabular data and microdata, and whether they depend on the slight differences in the purposes of release for the respective data types.

REFERENCES

[1] I. Hrynaszkiewicz, M. L. Norton, A. J. Vickers, and D. G. Altman, "Preparing raw clinical data for publication: guidance for journal editors, authors, and peer reviewers," Bmj, vol. 340, 2010, p. c181.

[2] C. Culnane, B. I. P. Rubinstein, and V. Teague, "Health Data in an Open World," arxiv preprint, 2017. [Online]. Available: http://arxiv.org/abs/1712.05627

[3] M. Douriez, H. Doraiswamy, J. Freire, and C. T. Silva, "Anonymizing NYC taxi data: Does it matter?" Proceedings - 3rd IEEE International Conference on Data Science and Advanced Analytics, 2016, pp. 140–148.

[4] G. J. Matthews, O. Harel, and R. H. Aseltine, "Privacy protection and aggregate health data: a review of tabular cell suppression methods (not) employed in public health data systems," Health Services and Outcomes Research Methodology, vol. 16, no. 4, 2016, pp. 258–270.

[5] N. Li, T. Li, and S. Venkatasubramanian, "t-closeness: Privacy beyond k-anonymity and l-diversity," 2007 IEEE 23rd International Conference on Data Engineering, no. 2, 2007, pp. 106—-115.

[6] C. Dwork, F. McSherry, K. Nissim, and A. Smith, "Calibrating noise to sensitivity in private data analysis," Lecture Notes in Computer Science (including subseries Lecture Notes in Artificial Intelligence and Lecture Notes in Bioinformatics), vol. 3876 LNCS, 2006, pp. 265–284.

[7] J. Castro, "Statistical disclosure control in tabular data," Advanced Information and Knowledge Processing, vol. 51, no. November, 2010, pp. 113–131.

[8] B. Barak et al., "Privacy, accuracy, and consistency too," Proceedings of the twenty-sixth ACM SIGMOD-SIGACT-SIGART symposium on Principles of database systems, 2007, p. 273.

[9] M. S. Bargh, R. Meijer, and M. Vink, "On statistical disclosure control technologies," Tech. Rep., 2018.

[10] L. Rocher, J. M. Hendrickx, and Y.-A. de Montjoye, "Estimating the success of re-identifications in incomplete datasets using generative models," Nature Communications, vol. 10, no. 1, 2019, p. 3069. [Online]. Available: http://www.nature.com/articles/s41467-019-10933-3

[11] A. Hundepool et al., Statistical Disclosure Control. John Wiley & Sons, 2012.

[12] M. Elliot and A. Dale, "Scenarios of attack: the data intruder's perspective on statistical disclosure risk," Netherlands Official Statistics, vol. 14, no. Spring, 1999, pp. 6–10.

[13] M. Elliot, E. Mackey, K. O'Hara, and C. Tudor, The Anonymisation Decision-Making Framework. UKAN, 2016, vol. 1, no. 2006. [Online]. Available: https://fpf.org/brussels-privacy-symposium-final-papers/

[14] J. P. Kelly, B. L. Golden, and A. A. Assad, "Cell suppression: Disclosure protection for sensitive tabular data," Networks, vol. 22, no. 4, 1992, pp. 397–417.

[15] X. Xiao and Y. Tao, "M-invariance: towards privacy preserving re-publication of dynamic datasets," SIGMOD Conference, 2007, pp. 689–700. [Online]. Available: http://portal.acm.org/citation.cfm?id=1247556

[16] B. C. M. Fung et al., "Privacy-preserving data publishing," ACM Computing Surveys (Csur), vol. 42, no. 4, 2010, pp. 1–53. [Online]. Available: http://portal.acm.org/citation.cfm?doid=1749603.1749605

[17] P. Golle, "Revisiting the uniqueness of simple demographics in the US population," Proceedings of the ACM Conference on Computer and Communications Security, 2006, pp. 77–80.

[18] V. Leaver, "Implementing a method for automatically protecting user-defined Census tables," Joint ECE/Eurostat Worksession on Statistical Confidentiality in Bilbao (December 2009), http://www. unece. org/stats/documents/2009.12. confidentiality. htm, 2009.

[19] P. Samarati and L. Sweeney, "Protecting privacy when disclosing information: k-anonymity and its enforcement through generalization and suppression," 1998.

[20] A. Machanavajjhala, J. Gehrke, D. Kifer, and M. Venkitasubramaniam, "l-Diversity: Privacy beyond k-anonymity," ACM Transactions on Knowledge Discovery from Data, vol. 1, 2007, p. 3.

[21] A. Hundepool et al., "Handbook on Statistical Disclosure Control," Statistical Disclosure Control, 2010, pp. 1–288.

[22] C. C. Aggarwal and P. S. Yu, "A General Survey of Privacy-Preserving Data Mining Models and Algorithms," 2008, pp. 11–52.

[23] L. Antal, N. Shlomo, and M. Elliot, "Measuring Disclosure Risk with Entropy in Population Based Frequency Tables," 2014, pp. 62–78.

[24] ——, "Disclosure Risk Measurement with Entropy in Two-Dimensional Sample Based Frequency Tables," pp. 1–10.

[25] G. T. Duncan and M. Elliot, Statistical confidentiality, 2010.

[26] Y. Rinott, C. M. O'Keefe, N. Shlomo, and C. Skinner, "Confidentiality and differential privacy in the dissemination of frequency tables," Statistical Science, vol. 33, no. 3, 2018, pp. 358–385.

[27] G. Thompson, S. Broadfoot, and D. Elazar, "Methodology for the Automatic Confidentialisation of Statistical Outputs from Remote Servers at the Australian Bureau of Statistics Methodology for the Automatic Confidentialisation of Statistical Outputs from Remote Servers at the Australian Bureau of St," no. October, 2013, pp. 28–30.

[28] N. Shlomo, L. Antal, and M. Elliot, "Measuring disclosure risk and data utility for flexible table generators," Journal of Official Statistics, vol. 31, no. 2, 2015, pp. 305–324.

[29] C. Clifton and T. Tassa, "On syntactic anonymity and differential privacy," Transactions on Data Privacy, vol. 6, no. 2, 2013, pp. 161–183.

[30] C. Dwork, "Differential privacy: A survey of results," Lecture Notes in Computer Science (including subseries Lecture Notes in Artificial Intelligence and Lecture Notes in Bioinformatics), vol. 4978 LNCS, 2008, pp. 1–19.

[31] R. Sarathy and K. Muralidhar, "Evaluating laplace noise addition to satisfy differential privacy for numeric data," Transactions on Data Privacy, vol. 4, no. 1, 2011, pp. 1–17.

On Protecting Microdata in Open Data Settings from a Data Utility Perspective

Afshin Amighi[1], Mortaza S. Bargh[2], Sunil Choenni[3], Alexander Latenko[4], Ronald Meijer[5]
[1,2,3] Rotterdam University of Applied science, Research Center Creating 010, Rotterdam, The Netherlands
[2,3,4,5] Research and Documentation Centre Ministry of Justice and Security, The Hague, The Netherlands
Email: [1] a.amighi@hr.nl [2] m.shoae.bargh@wodc.nl [3] r.choenni@wodc.nl [4] a.latenko@wodc.nl [5] r.f.meijer@wodc.nl

***Abstract*—In modern societies, opening data is playing a crucial role in innovations and economic growth. Public organizations and private enterprises constantly are collecting data. To support the growth of societies, these organizations and enterprises intend to be more active in data opening. However, disclosure of personal data is one of the main threats for data opening. Data transformation techniques for Statistical Disclosure Control (SDC) aim at removing personal data while maintaining the utility of the data at an acceptable level. Applying SDC methods always faces the struggle of maintaining a balance between data utility and personal disclosure risk. In this research, we investigate different options for a common set of transformations for protecting microdata. We study a set of common scenarios which target (or specify) two types of data environments (i.e., those with and without the original microdata sets) and two approaches for privacy protection (i.e., those based on normative heuristics and a formal approach). Employing ARX, we run a series of experiments to observe the behaviours of various measurement factors. At the end, we discuss the consequences of choosing each of the options that can be used by policymakers for opening privacy-sensitive microdata sets.**

Keywords–Data Protection; Disclosure Scenarios; Microdata; Statistical Disclosure Control.

I. Introduction

Often, public organizations and private enterprises collect data about citizens and their clients or employees. These parties collect such personal data directly as the input necessary for provisioning their services (like the contact and demographic information about crime-victims or patients). They may collect personal data also indirectly as the byproduct of their service provisioning (when, for example, a judicial or healthcare process proceeds through a chain of actions and interventions). Consequently, personal data are collected and processed in various forms such as microdata, tabular data, semi-structured data as well as unstructured data.

Governments try to improve their transparency, accountability and efficiency through proactively opening their public funded data sets to the public. Hereby, they intend to support participatory governance by citizens, to foster innovations and economic growth for enterprises, and to enable citizens and organizations to make informed decisions. An important precondition for any data opening is to Open Data responsibly, without violating the fundamental human rights such as privacy, liberty, autonomy and dignity [1]–[3]. Considering the scope of this contribution, we focus on the privacy risks or harms associated with such Open Data initiatives. For example, processing personal data may lead to wrong classification of individuals, adversely impacting their liberty, autonomy and income. Even correctly classifying individuals may be harmful and illegal when, for example, individuals become subject to unjustifiable and/or unjust discrimination [4]. Further, linking such personal data to other data sets can reveal even more privacy-sensitive information about individuals than was initially shared [1][5].

Protecting the privacy of individuals in the open data settings, where the shared data is observable for everybody, including the adversaries, boils down to removing personal data from the shared data while maintaining the utility of the data as much as possible. This operation is called data anonymization in a technical sense, which relates to the data minimization, purpose limitation, and accuracy principles of General Data Protection Regulation (GDPR) i.e., Articles 5-1b/1c/1d. Data anonymization is not an easy task as there have been many supposedly anonymized data sets that were re-identified in practice [6].

A common way for data anonymization is by using SDC methods. These SDC methods are applicable to microdata as well as tabular data (i.e., frequency and magnitude tables). Our scope in this contribution is limited to microdata sets which are structured as a table of records/tuples corresponding to individuals, and attributes corresponding to some (privacy-sensitive) properties of those individuals. Generally, applying SDC methods affects data privacy (or personal data disclosure risks) and data utility inversely, i.e., when one increases the other decreases. In practice, therefore, one should make a trade-off among personal data disclosure risks and the utility of opened data.

In Open Data setting, the purpose of data usage is not predetermined. The data consumers (i.e., the public) should be able to apply any (legitimate) analysis they are interested in. This implies that the objective is to transform microdata such that the risk/threat of personal disclosure becomes negligible (i.e., practically eliminated), while the data utility remains high as much as possible. Inspired by [7], we call such a data publishing as *privacy preserving microdata opening*.

In order to apply SDC methods for protecting personal data in Open Data settings, there is a need for gaining an insight in the utility of data when different SDC protection methods (of varying data protection level) are applied. The objective of this study is to empirically investigate the impact of applying the SDC methods on data utility when opening sensitive microdata sets. Specifically, our research questions can be formalized as: *For a common set of data transformation options, what are data utility and data disclosure implications? What are the implications of these options, which policymakers should consider when opening privacy sensitive microdata sets?*

For this study, we have carried out desk research, expert interviews, and extensive experiments with an SDC software tool called ARX [8]. We identify a number of cases that are relevant for data opening. The results of this study can clarify the difference between the identified cases and demonstrate some of the implications of opting for each of these cases. Legal consultants, legislators and policymakers can use the study results when choosing their strategy for opening privacy-sensitive microdata sets.

The remainder of this paper is organized as follows. In Sections II and III, we provide some related work and the background of and the motivations for data opening. In Section IV, we present two generic approaches for applying SDC methods and in Section V, we define the data quality and data privacy measures used for our experiments. Subsequently, we provide the experiment cases in Section VI. Then, in Section VII, we present the experiments results obtained for a publicly available data set, we reflect on the study results and lay down the limitations of the study. Finally, we draw our conclusions and mention some future research directions in Section VIII.

II. Related Work

One criterion for defining our cases is whether or not the intruder has access to the original microdata set. The issue of whether the original microdata can be used for re-identification of some individuals from a technically anonymized microdata set is elaborated upon in [9] and [10]. Elliot et al. [9] discuss the UK privacy regulations, which recognize two environments: one with the original microdata (as it is often the case for the environment of the data controller) and the other without it. In the first environment, the technically anonymized microdata set is considered as personal data while in the other it is considered as an anonymized data. This is because the entity in possession of the original data (e.g., the data controller) can use the original data set to re-identify some individuals in the technically anonymized microdata set. They also mention that an anonymized data set that is re-identifiable for some party (like data controllers) is personal in the EU jurisdiction. Similarly, El Emam and Malin [10] emphasize that when data controllers are able to re-identify some individuals with the original data set, the data set is not anonymous.

In [11], we build on this argument and further argue that, based on an investigation of the relevant legal regimes, criminal justice data cannot be opened when they are personal. Further, we note that, unlike the claim in [9], the condition of not being personal for everybody (i.e., being anonymous in a GDPR sense) is not unanimously accepted (yet) as a precondition for opening privacy sensitive data sets (like criminal justice system data sets). In this contribution, we extend our previous work [11] by defining a number of possible options for protecting microdata sets against re-identification by parties with and without original microdata sets. Subsequently, we investigate the utility of the resulting microdata sets.

Further, we investigate the utility of an anonymization method that yields a sound (i.e., formally provable) data protection mechanism according to a new definition of privacy (ϵ-differential privacy). The need for formal approaches to define privacy and realize personal data protection rigorously is at the centre of focus in recent studies [12]–[14]. The authors argue that past technologies for protection against personal data disclosure rely on intuitive, heuristic understandings of privacy, and the privacy regulations have often endorsed such heuristic techniques implicitly or explicitly. For example, by making an implicit assumption that re-identification may primarily (or even solely) occur via record linkage, where a record is de-identified by those in a publicly available data set, "many privacy regulations require protecting personal information that can be linked to an individual in order to safeguard against record linkage" [12]. Such regulations, which capture some aspects of normative privacy, do not satisfy all expectations of privacy protection. Therefore, these studies ask for more understanding of the gaps between technical/formal approaches to privacy and the normative approaches to privacy so that future privacy regulations can be improved. Inspired by these works, we investigate the impact of applying a formal privacy protection method (specifically, ϵ-differential privacy) on data utility and compare it with a heuristic normative approach (i.e., k-anonymity) as often applied against record linkage attacks.

Based on the impacts of such solution directions on data utility and on privacy risks, as presented in this contribution, policymakers can make an informed strategy for opening their privacy sensitive microdata sets.

III. Opening Microdata

A. *Motivation(s)*

Governments seek to improve their transparency, accountability and efficiency through proactively opening their publicly funded data sets to the public. Via Open Data, governments intend to support participatory governance by citizens, to foster innovation and economic growth, and to empower citizens and businesses for making informed decisions.

Often, public organizations and privacy enterprises possess personal data about citizens as well as clients, employees or partners in the form of microdata sets. Microdata records may include (privacy-sensitive) properties of individuals (like demographic, behavioral, health and/or business information).

In order to achieve the objectives of Open Data, namely transparency, accountability and efficiency, public organizations strive to open their microdata sets as raw as possible. But, microdata sets pertaining to natural persons (very often) contain (sensitive) personal data (like demographic, behavioral, health and/or business information). Opening such microdata as raw as possible, therefore, can inflict (severe) privacy breaches (i.e., personal data disclosures) with adverse impacts on the fundamental human rights as well as on individuals' dignity, liberty, autonomy and income [1]–[3]. Therefore, protecting the privacy of citizens and individuals is an important precondition for (governmental) organizations in order to open their data responsibly [11].

Further, for validation and reproduction of their results, scientists and scholars are supposed to make their research data available for their peers and the scientific community. These research data are often in the form of microdata. In these cases, the protection of personal data is also one of the preconditions for conducting these researches and, even more importantly, for sharing the research data with the scientific community.

B. *Opening Personal (Sensitive) Data*

Personal data refer to any information that relates to an identified or identifiable natural person (so-called a *data subject*). One can distinguish several types of personal data in legal domains. For example, GDPR discerns three personal data types: Directly identifiable data, indirectly identifiable data, and sensitive data. Directly identifiable data relate to a person straightforwardly, for instance, someone's name or address. Indirectly identifiable data do not relate to a person straightforwardly but may influence the way a person is perceived or treated in the society (for instance, the type of someone's house or car), or may contribute to someone's identification when combined with other data sets. Sensitive data are related to the fundamental rights and freedom of individuals. According to GDPR, sensitive personal data are of two types: (a) Special categories of personal data such as someone's racial or ethnical origins, political opinions, religious or philosophical beliefs, trade union memberships, genetic data, biometric data for the purpose of uniquely identifying a natural person, health data, or sex-life or sexual orientation data; and (b) the personal data related to criminal convictions and offences. If sensitive data are (or can be) related to an identified or identifiable natural person, they may be processed only if the data processing complies with strict data protection measures. Bargh et al. [11] argue that such sensitive data sets can be opened to the public if they are without personal information, i.e., they cannot be related to identified or identifiable natural persons.

A data set can be regarded as without personal information in a given, so-called, *data environment*. When a data controller transforms a microdata set to a protected one, and shares the result with a partner organization, the boundary of the partner organization defines a data environment. Within the scope of this study (i.e., opening data to the public), two types of data environments are interesting to investigate, namely: those with the original microdata set and those without it. Making this distinction is based on the fact that the original microdata set is one of the richest knowledge bases that can be used for linking, via re-identification or attribution [15], the records or attributes in a protected microdata set to natural persons. This richness can be associated with the facts that the protected microdata set is the result of applying SDC methods to the original microdata set and that the original microdata set itself contains one or more identifying attributes (like names and social security numbers). These identifying attributes together with the other attributes in the original microdata set can facilitate linking the records in the protected microdata set to the corresponding identities (thus, to re-identify the records in the protected microdata set). A typical data environment with the original microdata set is that of the data controller.

In [11], it is shown that protecting a microdata set for a data environment without the original microdata set delivers a transformed microdata set that is anonymous in a GDPR sense (i.e., being anonymous for everybody in that data environment), while protecting a microdata set for a data environment with the original microdata set delivers a transformed microdata set that is pseudonymized in a GDPR sense (i.e., being potentially identifiable for a party, for example, the data controller, who is possession of the original microdata set). Note that these two types of data environments exists in Open Data settings in cases where the data controller does not maintain or maintains, respectively, a copy of the original microdata set. In Section III-D, we elaborate further on these two data environments types (i.e., those with the original microdata set and those without it).

C. Protecting Microdata in Open Data Setting

In the context of Open Data, the data spread over and reach all areas, some of which fall out of GDPR jurisdiction. As mentioned above, GDPR requires that sensitive personal data are processed (i.e., shared in case of Open Data) with strict data protection measures. The data protection mechanisms that can be applied to this setting are those that minimize data by stripping off, ideally, all the personal data from the data to be opened. To this end, the data minimization mechanisms can be applied via the following processes:

- Data anonymization: This process ensures "that the risk of somebody being identified in the data is negligible" [9]. Data anonymization aims at hiding the identity and/or the sensitive data of data subjects, while retaining sensitive data for the purpose of data analysis [16]. To achieve this, the so-called SDC methods and tools are used.
- Data de-identification: This process aims at protecting a microdata set against the intrinsic threats by transforming direct identifiers (like names, social security numbers and digitized unique biometrics). This transformation is carried out via replacing direct identifiers with pseudo identifiers, masking/suppressing them or removing them.

Note that the term anonymization above is used in a technological sense (and not in a GDPR sense). Further, note that the term de-identification in North America means anonymization in a technological sense. As part of strict data protection measures, cybersecurity controls such as access control and cryptography are not suitable for protecting data in Open Data settings. In other words, data disclosure threats due to cybersecurity attacks of Information System (IS) hacking and due to decrypting encrypted personal data, while data being in transit, storage and processing, are out of the scope in Open Data settings.

D. Attribute Mapping

The process of applying SDC methods for data anonymization and de-identification starts with the subprocess of dividing the set of the attributes of a microdata set into various categories. This subprocess is called *attribute mapping*. To describe attribute mapping, we start with formalizing the concept of microdata sets. Microdata sets are structured in the form of a table of records/tuples and attributes. Within the context of this study, we assume that every record corresponds to an individual and every attribute corresponds to a (privacy-sensitive) property of the corresponding individual.

More specifically, a microdata set DS_N comprises N rows or records denoted by x^n, where $n : 1, \ldots, N$. We assume that every record x^n corresponds to one individual. Further, every record x^n comprises D attributes, denoted by a_d, where $d : 1, \ldots, D$. Each attribute a_d assumes a nominal or ordinal value from domain A_d (or, in other words, attribute a_d assume a value that is an element of set A_d). Domain $A = A_1 \times A_2 \times \ldots \times A_D$ denotes the super domain, over which all attributes are defined. Every record x^n is defined over A, consisting of attribute values $x_d^n \in A_d$, $d : 1, \ldots, D$.

In attribute mapping, the set of attributes $\{a_1, a_2, \ldots, a_D\}$ are normally divided into four disjoint sets called: Explicit identifiers, quasi identifiers, sensitive attributes, and non-sensitive attributes. *Explicit Identifiers* (EIDs) refer to those attributes in DS_N that structurally and on their own could uniquely identify individuals, i.e., data subjects. Examples of EIDs are a data subject's name and social security number. *Quasi Identifiers* (QIDs) refer to the set of attributes in DS_N that could be used to identify (some of) the data subjects in DS_N. To this end, the QIDs should also be present in some other data sets or information sources together with the corresponding EIDs. The QIDs in microdata set DS_N, therefore, capture the background knowledge that intruders have with respect to data set DS_N. *Sensitive ATtributes* (SATs) refer to those attributes that capture privacy-sensitive information, while conveying useful information for a data analysis purpose (e.g., someone's disease type and salary). Unlike QIDs, SATs are known only within DS_N and, therefore, they cannot be characterized as background knowledge for intruders. *Non-sensitive ATtributes* (NATs) refer to all the other attributes that are not EIDs, QIDs or SATs.

Through attribute mapping, attributes $a_1, a_2, \ldots, a_D$ of microdata set DS_N are divided into 4 disjoint subsets EID, QID, SAT and NAT. Defining the EIDs is straightforward and is based on the intrinsic aspects of microdata set DS_N. Defining NATs becomes trivial once the other three subsets are determined. Defining QIDs and SATs is not straightforward as it depends on subjective and contextual aspects related to the data environment. QIDs capture the background information already known in the so-called *auxiliary information* sources (i.e., in the other data sets than DS_N) about the identities of (some of) the data subjects in DS_N. In other words, in the other data sets one can find a combination of attributes QIDs and one or more EIDs for (some of) the data subjects in DS_N. For illustration, the example in Figure 1 shows an attribute mapping for original microdata set DS_N, assuming the background information available to intruders as shown by the attributes of auxiliary data set A_{aux}. The last row in the figure indicates the attributes of the transformed microdata set DS'_N due to applying SDC methods to microdata set DS_N.

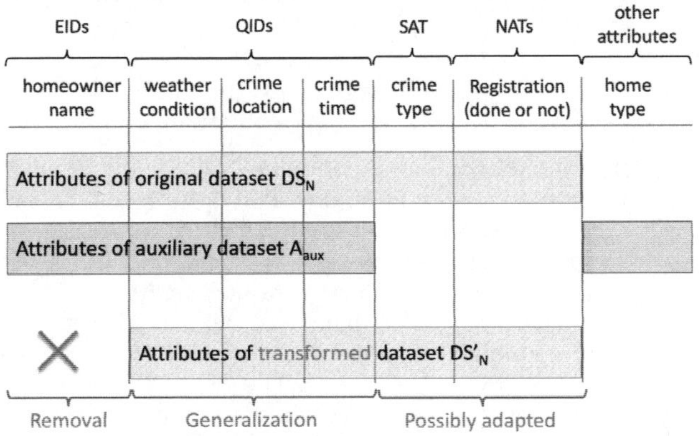

Figure 1. An illustration of attribute mapping for a data environment without the original microdata set.

Some legal frameworks specify specific attributes as SATs. For example, the UK's Data Protection Act (DPA) considers racial or ethnic origin, political opinions, religious beliefs, trade union membership, physical or mental health or condition, sexual life, and some aspects of criminal proceedings as *sensitive personal data* [9]. Further, the situational context and personal preferences (of data subjects) influence an attribute in being considered as a SAT. In some situations, the attributes related to one's income, wealth, credit record and financial deals can be considered as SATs. Attribute religion might be considered as a SAT in some countries and NAT in others.

In environments where the original microdata set DS_N acts as an auxiliary information source (like that of the data controller, as also mentioned in Section III-B), all the other attributes in DS_N with exception of the EIDs act as QIDs. In other words, QIDs, SATs and NATs shown in Figure 1 can act as the extended set of QIDs, given the original and the protected microdata sets, as shown in Figure 2. This extended set of QIDs can facilitate linking the records in the protected microdata set DS'_N to the EIDs in the original microdata set DS_N.

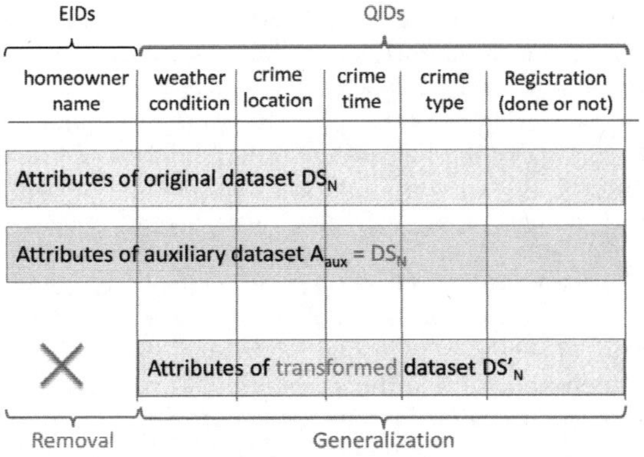

Figure 2. An illustration of attribute mapping for a data environment with the original microdata set.

IV. Guiding Principles for Personal Data Protection

A. Normative Approaches

Often, legal regimes and definitions of privacy are based on the normative and intuitive assumptions "about how pieces of information interact" [12]. According to the normative notions of privacy with respect to data minimization (i.e., data protection via the de-identification and anonymization processes), a given microdata set DS_N is considered as personal data if it can reveal personal information when it is combined with any other auxiliary data set A_{aux} that is available to (legitimate and illegitimate) data recipients (i.e., the intruders). Data set A_{aux} encompasses the background information available to intruders. We note that such auxiliary data sets are growing rapidly in the current Big Data era.

B. Towards Formal Approaches

Dwork et al. [17] showed that it is impossible to enforce the stringent definition of privacy protection as proposed by the current normative definitions, when the intruder has an arbitrary amount of background knowledge. To protect privacy in those microdata sets that are used for statistical computation (and also for Open Data purposes), one should deal with the shortcomings of the heuristic data protection approaches that partially capture the normative notions of privacy. There is currently a trend to move from the current normative heuristics of privacy to the formal privacy protection approaches. For example, some legal scholars advocate to base legal privacy regimes, which are mostly based on the normative and intuitive assumptions about how pieces of information interact, on formal privacy models [12]. Formal privacy models, which are based on mathematically and rigorously proven techniques such as differential privacy [17], are inherently not subject to interpretation in different contexts, particularly in regard to other data sets. In other words, formal concepts do not rely on intuitive assumptions about how pieces of information interact, but rather on the properties of a data set itself which can be examined by scientific and mathematical principles.

A pioneering work that provides a formal definition of privacy is [17] that introduces the ϵ–differential privacy technique. According to this definition, the presence or absence of the (personal) data of an individual in a data set must not have an observable impact on the output of an analysis/computation over that data set. In other words, it requires "the output distribution of a privacy preserving analysis to remain stable under any possible change to a single individual's information" [12]. The technique of ϵ–differential privacy is already deployed in some Information Systems (ISs) currently by, for example, Google, Apple, Uber, and the U.S. Census Bureau. Apple uses the technique in iOS10 for increasing its security and privacy, Google uses it for protecting urban mobility data to ensure that individual users and journeys cannot be identified, and the U.S. Census Bureau wants to apply it to 2020 US census data for safeguarding the information it gathers from the US citizens [12].

One should note that the ϵ–differential privacy technique guarantees privacy protection in the sense defined in the beginning of the previous paragraph. Whether this definition of privacy is comprehensive and adequate is not established. Although the formal approaches and definitions of privacy and privacy protection have not been introduced to legislation and regulations yet, there is a growing trend to do so in academia due to being independent of environmental conditions that are highly dynamic in the era of big and Open Data. Therefore, we shall examine the impact of such approaches and compare it with those of traditional normative approaches in Section VII for a specific formal technique (i.e., an ϵ–differential method implemented in SDC tool ARX, see Subsection VI-E).

V. Data Utility and Risk Measures

In our study, we define five data protection cases as possible scenarios applicable to Open Data settings and observe the data utility per each case. In this section, first, we describe the data utility and data disclosure measures used in the study. In Section VI, we present details of these cases.

To illustrate the notation adopted from this point on, Figure 3 summarizes these notations per each data transformation stage when applying SDC methods. From the original microdata set DS_N, the EIDs are removed or suppressed to obtain microdata set DS'_N. The QIDs of the result are generalized to get microdata set DS''_N. Finally, in order to achieve k-anonymity, some records of DS''_N are suppressed to yield microdata set $DS''_{N'}$. Note that N and N' denote the number of the records in the corresponding data sets, where $N' \leq N$, i.e., the the number of records may decrease in last step in Figure 3.

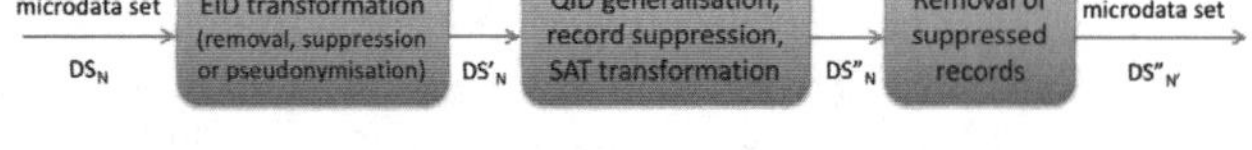

Figure 3. The notation convention used from this point on.

A. General-Purpose Data Utility Measures

Data utility measures are indicators for assessing the usefulness of the data transformations that are applied to the microdata by using SDC methods. There are two categories of data utility measures, the so-called special-purpose measures and general-purpose measures, which depend on whether or not the usage of data is already known, respectively [16]. In this paper, we consider the latter one, as the purpose of data usage is not determined beforehand in Open Data settings (see also the research objective part in Section I). In the following, we explain three general purpose data utility measures of Average Equivalence Class Size, Non-Uniform Entropy, and Granularity from literature in a way that they are provided/realized within ARX tool.

1) Average Equivalence Class Size: The Average Equivalence Class Size (AECS) measure [18] is given by:

$$\text{AECS} = \frac{|DS''_{N'}|}{k \times N_{EC}} = \frac{N'}{k \times N_{EC}},$$

where N_{EC} is the number of the ECs of $DS''_{N'}$. The AECS ≥ 1 and it is a measure of information loss. The higher the value of AECS, the higher is the amount of information loss. If the size of all ECs of microdata set $DS''_{N'}$ is k, then the AECS measure value is one, i.e., its minimum and best value for a given k. The optimization objective of data anonymization here is to reduce the AECS value to 1 (i.e., to find a partitioning that approaches the best case). Apparently, the AECS does not consider the impact of record suppression.

ARX provides the AECS as an information loss measure, which is a bit differently than the definition given above (namely, normalizing without the value of k and with the value of N), as:

$$\text{AECS}_{\text{ARX}} = \frac{1}{N} \times \frac{N'}{N_{EC}}.$$

2) Non-Uniform Entropy Measure: Gionis and Tassa [19] define three measures of information loss, based on information theory entropy rate. They call these measures as the entropy measure, the monotone entropy measure, and the non-uniform entropy measure. These measures are calculated based on the distribution of values in the original microdata set DS_N, given the distribution of values in the transformed microdata set $DS''_{N'}$. For example, let attribute a be a QID, which takes values from set $\{v_1, v_2, \ldots, v_I\}$ in the original microdata set DS_N. In the transformed microdata set $DS''_{N'}$, the values of attribute a are generalized to values $\{v_{1,2}, v_{3,4}, \ldots, v_{I-1,I}\}$, i.e., values v_1 and v_2 in DS_N are generalized to value $v_{1,2}$ in microdata set $D''_{N'}$, and so on. Let a'' denote the attribute in $DS''_{N'}$ that corresponds to attribute a in DS_N, noting that the values of a'' are from $\{v_{1,2}, v_{3,4}, \ldots, v_{I-1,I}\}$. Then, for example, given that $a = v_1$ and $a'' = v_{1,2}$, the information loss due to generalization for this outcome is proportional to

$$-\log_2 \frac{\#\text{ of } v_1}{\#\text{ of } v_{1,2}} = -\log_2 \frac{\#\text{ of } v_1}{\#\text{ of } v_1 + \#\text{ of } v_2}.$$

Let a_m, where $m : 1, \ldots, M$, denote a QID in microdata set DS_N and a''_m denote the corresponding QID in microdata set $DS''_{N'}$. We use $A_m = \{v_m\}$ and $A''_m = \{v''_m\}$ to denote the sets of values of QID a_m and a''_m, respectively. The non-uniform entropy measure is defined in Relation (6) in [19] as (with slight adaptation, using our own notation defined above):

$$E = \sum_{m=1}^{M} \sum_{\substack{v_m \in A_m, \\ v''_m \in A''_m}} - \log_2 Pr(a_m = v_m | a''_m = v''_m)$$

This non-uniform entropy measure is monotonic with respect to generalization. Monotonicity of a measure here means that the measure increases monotonically with increasing degrees of generalization. In other words, if the value v_1 is generalized to value $v_{1,2}$ at level 1 and then to value $v_{1,4}$ at level 2, then the corresponding values of the measure increase when moving from level 1 to level 2. ARX provides a non-uniform entropy-based utility model, which is simply $1 - E$.

3) Granularity: Granularity is an information loss measure defined in [20], which is realized in ARX tool [21][8]. The measure expresses the degree to which the values of an attribute in the transformed microdata set cover the original domain of the attribute.

The information loss for every QID attribute a_m, which is generalized (or suppressed) from domain A_m in original microdata set DS_N to the domain A''_m in the transformed microdata set $DS''_{N'}$, is computed as the average loss for every (i.e., per record) value of that attribute, denoted by $x^n_m \in A_m, n : 1, \ldots, N$. The loss for every value of the QID attribute is calculated based on the generalization taxonomy tree T of that attribute.

For a categorical QID a_m, let M_m denote the total number of leaf nodes in the taxonomy tree T_m of QID attribute a_m. Assume that the value of the QID attribute a_m is generalized to node P_m, at which the sub-tree possesses $M_{p,m}$ leaf nodes. The loss of information when the value of the QID a_m for the n-th record (i.e., value x^n_m) is generalized from a leaf node of tree T_m in the original microdata set to the sub-tree node P_m is calculated by:

$$\text{Information loss for attribute value } x^n_m = \frac{M_{p,m} - 1}{M_m - 1}.$$

When the value of the QID attribute a_m is suppressed, the worst-case information loss occurs, i.e., the generalized node is the root of the taxonomy tree. This worst case leads to information loss $\frac{M_m - 1}{M_m - 1} = 1$ for that suppressed value of the QID attribute.

For numerical QIDs, the information loss can be defined similarly. Consider the value of such a numerical QID attribute a_m for the n-th record (i.e., value x^n_m) is generalized to an interval i defined by the lower and upper end points $L_{m,i}$ and $U_{m,i}$, respectively. Further, assume that the lower and upper bounds of that QID attribute a_m in original data set are L_m and U_m, respectively. Then, the information loss for this value of the QID attribute a_m is given by:

$$\text{Information loss for } x^n_m = (U_{m,i} - L_{m,i})/(U_m - L_m).$$

Indeed, the granularity measure for every value of a QID attribute quantifies the loss when a leaf node value cannot be disambiguated from another leaf node value due to the generalization (i.e., when both belong to the same sub-tree of the generalization node P).

The information loss for the QID attribute a_m is computed by averaging the loss for every (i..e., per record) value of that attribute.

$$\text{Information loss for } a_m = \frac{1}{N} \sum_{n=1}^{N} \text{Information loss for } x^n_m.$$

The granularity measure is the total information loss due to generalizations and suppressions for all QID attributes. It is computed by summing up the information loss of each QID as defined above (assuming that the QID attributes are equally important for identification potentially) and normalizing the outcome. Similar to non-uniform entropy, ARX supports an utility model based on granularity calculated as $1 - \frac{1}{M}\sum_1^M l(a_m)$, where $l(a_m) \in [0, 1]$ is the information loss for a_m.

B. Data Disclosure Risk Measures

In the following, we explain three general purpose data disclosure risk measures of Prosecutor Record at Risk, Journalist Average Risk and Marketeer Success Rate. Note that these risk measures capture those risks associated with the external risks factors, as the background knowledge of intruders is modelled by the QIDs. Therefore, these data disclosure risk measures are applicable to Cases III, IV and V (to be mentioned in the following section). The risks associated with EIDs (i.e., the internal risks factors) and SATs (i.e., the risks associated with attribute linkage and table linkage attacks [16] are not captured by the risks measures studied in the following.

Typical measures for quantifying disclosure risks turn around the concepts of sample uniqueness and population uniqueness. With respect to the set of QIDs, let us assume that microdata set DS_N is a sample of a larger population microdata set denoted by P_L (i.e., $N \leq L$). Alternatively said, all data records in sample microdata set DS_N are also in population microdata set P_L, where microdata sets DS_N and P_L have QIDs in common. Note that for re-identification of (some of) the records, it is necessary that data set P_L includes the combination of attributes EIDs and QIDs. To this end, the EIDs can actually be present in P_L or can potentially be present in P_L in the sense that the intruder can somehow deduce the corresponding EIDs in the future via, for example, interrogation (e.g., asking neighbours), testing (e.g., testing someone's DNA), searching digital media (via search engines like Google and Bing), and so on. Population microdata set P_L can be seen as background information, which does not contain attributes SATs and NATs of DS_N (as, otherwise, these SATs and NATs should have been considered as QIDs).

Let us further assume that the QIDs in microdata sets DS_N and P_L are generalized in the same way, resulting in microdata sets $DS''_{N'}$ and $P''_{L'}$ with the same ECs (i.e., the same patterns of the values for the generalized QIDs). For a given EC, the EC size in $DS''_{N'}$ is smaller than or equal to the EC size in $P''_{L'}$. The uniqueness of a data record (i.e., an individual) in microdata sets $DS''_{N'}$ and $P''_{L'}$ with respect to QIDs can be defined as follows. Assume that the data record belongs to an EC, which has $|EC_S|$ and $|EC_P|$ records in microdata sets $DS''_{N'}$ and $P''_{L'}$, respectively. The sample uniqueness and population uniqueness of the record are defined by $|EC_S| = 1$ and $|EC_P| = 1$, respectively.

We note that population uniqueness results in sample uniqueness (i.e., if $|EC_P| = 1$, then $|EC_S| = 1$); and sample uniqueness does not necessarily result in population uniqueness (i.e., if $|EC_S| = 1$, then $|EC_P| \geq 1$). One should also note that while a data controller can easily validate sample uniqueness by investigating the (to be) released microdata set, the data controller cannot easily validate population uniqueness because population microdata sets are generally inaccessible to data controllers.

It is important to determine/know which of population uniqueness and sample uniqueness is more relevant for estimating data disclosure risks.

- If the intruder knows that an individual's record is in the sample microdata set, as in the case of prosecutor attacker (e.g., the background knowledge that a nosy neighbor has [22][23]), then it is important to investigate sample uniqueness.
- If the intruder is uncertain whether an individual's record is in the sample microdata set, as in the cases of journalist and marketer attackers [22][23], then it is important to investigate population uniqueness. The rationale here is that the (likelihood of a) risk might be not high if a record, which appears alone in an EC in the sample microdata set, shares the same EC with multiple records in the population microdata set.

To further explain these points, let us reconsider a probability model from [24]. Assume a data record belongs to an EC, which has $|EC_S|$ and $|EC_P|$ records in microdata sets $DS''_{N'}$ and $P''_{L'}$, respectively. For a prosecutor attacker, the probability of correctly linking the individual with a record from the sample microdata set is

$$Pr(\text{correct linkage}|\text{being in } DS''_{N'}) = 1/|EC_S|.$$

In this case, sample uniqueness, captured by EC_S above, is important. This measure corresponds to the measure of Prosecutor Record at Risk in ARX, where the maximum prosecutor risk is $\frac{1}{\text{the smallest } |EC_S|}$.

For a journalist attacker with moderate motivation (i.e., the one who stops after looking at the population microdata set without posing further questions or doing further field investigation), the probability of correctly linking the individual with a record from the sample microdata set is

$$\begin{aligned} Pr(\text{correct linkage, being in } DS''_{N'}|\text{ being in } P''_{L'}) &= \\ Pr(\text{correct linkage } | \text{ being in } DS''_{N'}, \text{being in } P''_{L'}) &\times \\ Pr(\text{being in } DS''_{N'}|\text{ being in } P''_{L'}) &= \\ Pr(\text{correct linkage } | \text{ being in } DS''_{N'}) &\times \\ Pr(\text{being in } DS''_{N'}|\text{ being in } P''_{L'}) &= \\ \frac{1}{|EC_S|} \times \frac{|EC_S|}{|EC_P|} = \frac{1}{|EC_P|}. \end{aligned}$$

This measure corresponds to the measure of Journalist Average Risk in ARX, which is the average of this vale for all ECs.

In both journalist and marketeer attacker cases, the population uniqueness, captured by $|EC_P|$ above, is important. Assuming that $|EC_S| \leq |EC_P|$, the worst-case scenario is the prosecutor attacker, i.e., the sample uniqueness. If we are sure that the attacker is unsure about the victim being in the sample data set, then population uniqueness is important.

VI. EXPERIMENTS

In this section, we describe 5 data protection cases that are applicable to Open Data settings. (Note that here we do not claim that these cases represent all possible cases.) From Case I to Case V, we tighten our assumptions on the background information that is available to intruders step-wise and observe the data utility and data disclosure behaviors, based on a number of measures defined in literature. Cases I-IV are based on the normative heuristics, while Case V is based on the formal ϵ–differential privacy model as implemented in ARX.

A. Case I

As the baseline, we consider a microdata with personal information, including identifying attributes. For our experiment, we choose the publicly available Adult data set. It is an excerpt of 32,561 records from the 1994 US census database. The data set is often used in similar studies, like [22][24][25]. As part of data preparation, we consider attribute "hhid" of the Adult data set as an EID, discard attribute "fnlwgt" as it does not convey much information for our purpose, and discard education level in numbers because it is another form of attribute education in categories. This baseline case is subject to personal data disclosures due to intrinsic aspects.

B. Case II: Basic Protection Against Intrinsic Risks

In this case, the EID of the microdata set (e.g., the "hhid" in the case of the Adult data set) is removed, but the other attributes are unchanged. In the past, many practitioners used to characterize this case as anonymized data. Often, the set of explicit identifiers is removed (i.e., filtered), replaced with an unrecognizable value (i.e., masked/suppressed), or replaced with a unique and unrecognizable value (i.e., pseudonymized in a technical sense). Removal, suppression or pseudonymization of EIDs is considered as the first step of applying SDC methods. This first step eliminates the intrinsic risks of personal data disclosures in a microdata set, but is still vulnerable to personal data disclosures due to extrinsic factors [6].

C. Case III: Protection Against Data Linkage by Externs

In this case, a microdata set is without EIDs, but with generalized QIDs (and/or suppressed records), and with untransformed SATs and NATs. The set of the QIDs chosen for Case III is {age, workclass, occupation, race, sex, native-country}, for which the k-anonymity is applied. In our experiments we do not modify SATs (by applying, for example, l-diversity or t-closeness) to contain the complexity of this presentation. Normally, the values of QIDs are transformed by, for example, generalization (e.g., exact ages are changed to age intervals), suppression (e.g., the gender attribute values are replaced with a specific character), or perturbation (e.g., random values are added to the body weight attribute values). Still, this case is subject to extrinsic risks, like record linkage by those who have access to the original microdata set (like data controllers).

A disadvantage of operating according to Case III is that, as the background information increases due to Big Data, the set of QIDs available to intruders expands. Bargh et al. [11] argue that data anonymity in the GDPR sense can be achieved if the data disclosure risks are contained within an acceptably negligible level, considering, among others, available technologies, other data sources, and the costs of re-identification at the time of data anonymization. Data disclosure risks may increase over time due to availability of other data sets and changing environment conditions. Thus, the currently anonymous data may become personal data in the future. This implies that an applied privacy protection mechanism, which results in an anonymous data set currently, may not do so in the future.

D. Case IV: Protection Against All Parties

In this case, a microdata set, which is without EIDs, is protected by considering all other attributes as QIDs. Thus, aligning with the previous case, the microdata set is protected by applying k-anonymity to all attributes that are considered as QIDs. To this end, the QIDs are generalized and some records are suppressed. There are no guarantees that data disclosure risks will not take place, as this case is still subject to some extrinsic risks [7][26].

E. Formal Protection with ϵ-Differential Privacy

In this case, the original microdata set DS_N is stripped off from EIDs, and the result is protected by applying a method that conforms to ϵ-differential privacy definition. For this method, there is a formal guarantee that data disclosure risks will not take place, provided that the definition of ϵ-differential privacy is adopted. Note that this definition of privacy is other than that considered for Cases III and IV. Further, this Case V is subject to some extrinsic risks [7][26].

The tool ARX offers a method for applying ϵ-differential privacy to microdata sets as proposed in [26]. According to this method, first the records of DS_N are presampled and subsequently k-anonymity is applied to all remaining records, while considering all attributes as QIDs, to result in ϵ-differential privacy, as described in [27]. The k-anonymity is applied to the sampled records by generalizing the values of QIDs and suppressing those records that belong to the ECs with less than k records. To this end, the overall privacy budget ϵ is split up into two parts: (a) ϵ_{anon} (denoted by ϵ_a here), used by the anonymization operator, and (b) ϵ_{search} (denoted by ϵ_s here), used by the search strategy. The method proposed in [27], i.e., the SafePub method, satisfies $(\epsilon = \epsilon_a + \epsilon_s, \delta)$–differential privacy, where we should specify:

- δ, which is recommended to be $\frac{1}{N} < \delta < 10^{-4}$ (where N is the size of the input data set). We chose $\delta = \frac{1}{N}$ (based on the recommendation in Section 7.2 in [27]);
- Parameter Steps, which is the number of iterations performed by the search strategy. We chose Steps = 300 (based on the recommendation in Section 8.4 in [27]).
- In order to choose $\epsilon = \epsilon_a + \epsilon_s$ and, consequently ϵ_a and ϵ_s, we chose $\epsilon_s = 0.1$ according to the recommendation in Sections 8.4, 8.5 and 8.6 in [27]. Note that the values of Steps and ϵ_s are related. Consequently, the value of ϵ_a can be varied between 0.1 and 2, as done in Fig 15 in [27]. In turn, $\epsilon = \epsilon_a + 0.1$ varies accordingly.

The relation of SafePub to k-anonymity is described in [26].

VII. RESULTS AND DISCUSSIONS

In order to run our experiments, we have used ARX's API and implemented a layer to specify and execute a series of experiments. We have used this layer to collect all the statistical measurement results for Cases I-V, see Section VI, over a range of parameters. In this section, the results of our experiments from Cases III-V are presented. The main privacy model in our experiments is k-anonymity. To derive the results based on the formal approach (i.e., Case V), our program explores a set of values for ϵ and δ and extracts the corresponding k's. The set of extracted k's is used to perform the experiments using k-anonymity model for the cases III-IV.

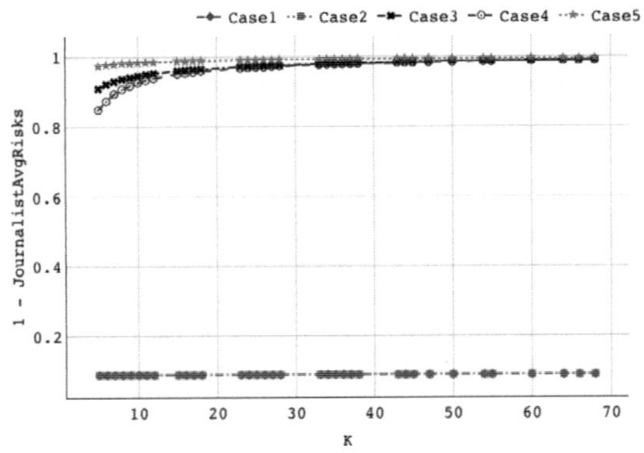

Figure 4. All cases Privacy derived from Journalist Average Risks

The results are visualized in two categories: (1) The behaviour of the risk measures and the utility measures per different values of k (see Figure 5), and (2) The behaviour of data utility versus privacy (see Figure 6). For each category there is a set of graphs that represent the results of our anonymization experiments. All our experiments are performed with the maximum suppression limit and minimum generalization factor as provided in ARX [8]. To present the results in Figure 5 and Figure 6, Cases I and II are omitted as these two cases either had the maximum or the minimum values. Having visualized these two cases would have suppressed the behaviors of Cases III-V. As an example, see Figure 4 where cases I and II show the minimum privacy.

In Figure 5a, the privacy measure of output data is presented. Increasing the value of k yields higher privacy (in this case, lower journalist average risks) which is validated also in Figure 5b and Figure 5c; i.e., the number of records at risk and the highest risk are decreasing. As expected, comparing case III with the other cases, both Figure 5a and Figure 5b justify that even with lower k's, ϵ-differential privacy (Case V) outperforms by a big margin. However, the higher privacy performance in Case V has a drawback of losing quality as depicted in Figure 5d and reaffirmed by Figures 5e and 5f.

The second category of the results, as shown in Figure 6, presents the combined behaviour of a data utility/quality measure versus a data privacy measure in three graphs. As we see from these graphs and as expected, when privacy increases the utility of the data decreases. Interestingly, we can see that Case V operates near the best privacy area, with the lowest data quality. This has to do with the presampling inherent to the ϵ-differential privacy method used, which results in lower disclosure risks and lower data utility values. Comparing the performances of Cases III and IV, we observe that the former behaves closer to the higher values of the data risk and data utility measures. This has to do with having a fewer number of attributes acting as QIDs and being generalized.

For Open Data purposes and from the perspective of protecting privacy, Case V operates better than Case IV, and Case IV operates better than Case III. This performance comes with the cost of having lower data utility, respectively. One should also note that the privacy property that is realized in Cases III and IV differ from that realized in Case V. While the former is based on a normative property (i.e., to prevent record linkage when the transformed microdata is linked with

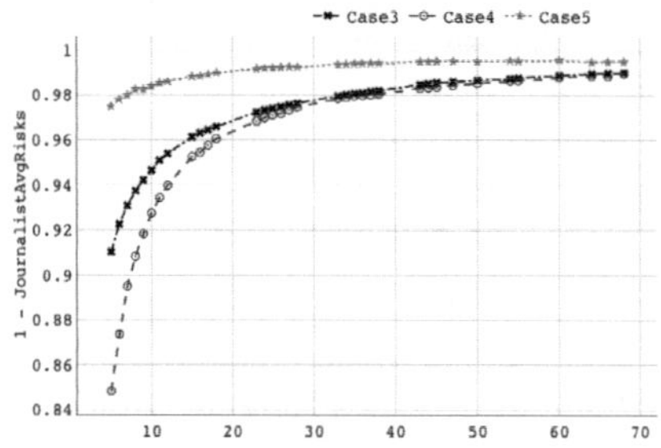

(a) Privacy derived from Journalist Average Risk

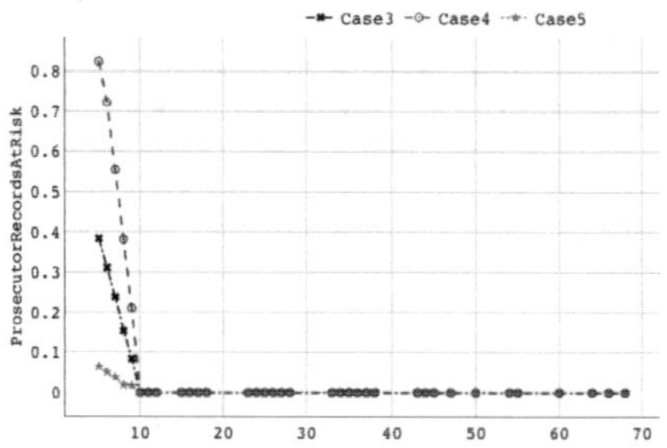

(b) Prosecutor Records At Risk

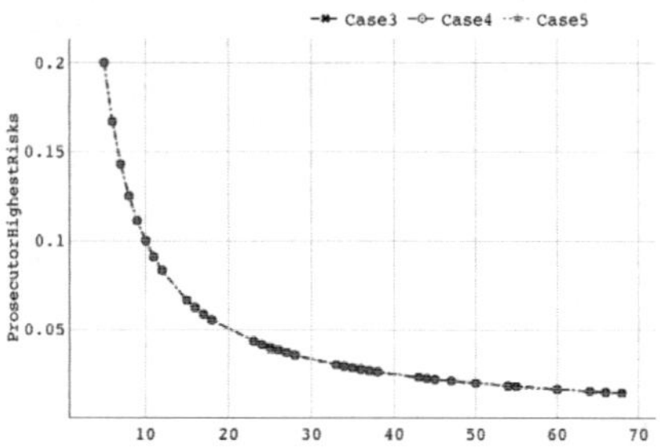

(c) Prosecutor Highest Risk

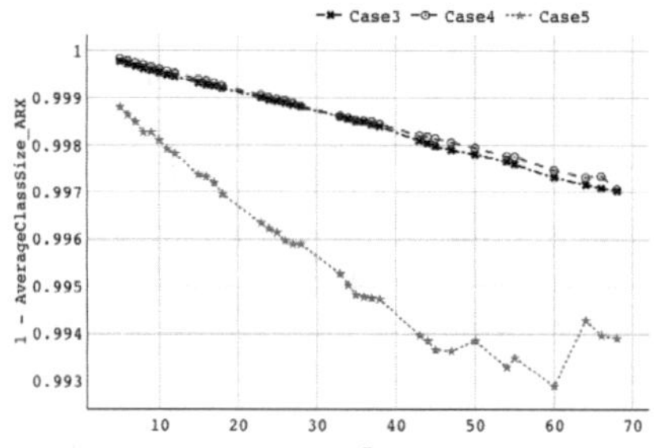

(d) Quality derived from Average Class Size

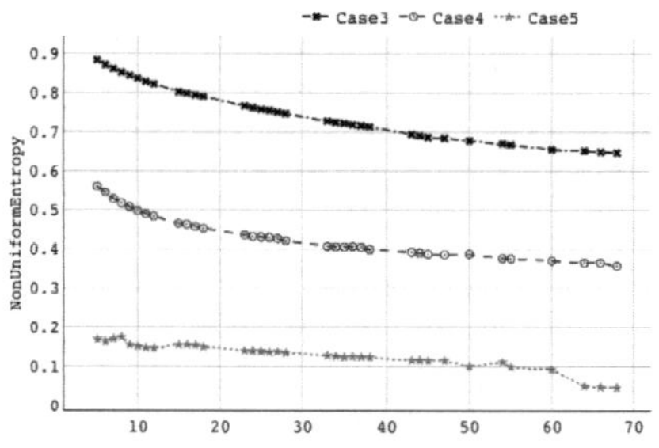

(e) Non Uniform Entropy

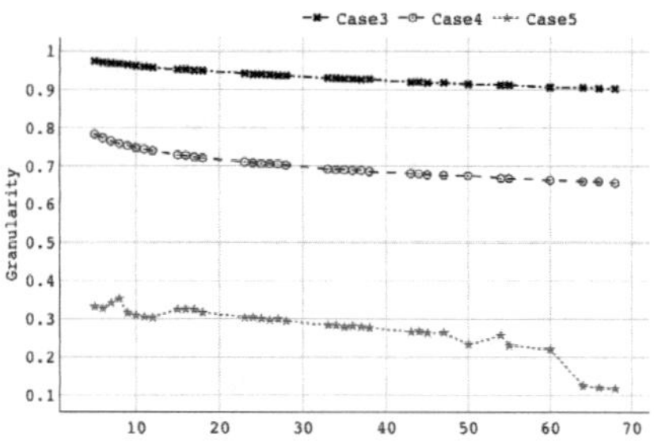

(f) Granularity

Figure 5. Risks and Utility Measurements for $K \in [5, 68]$

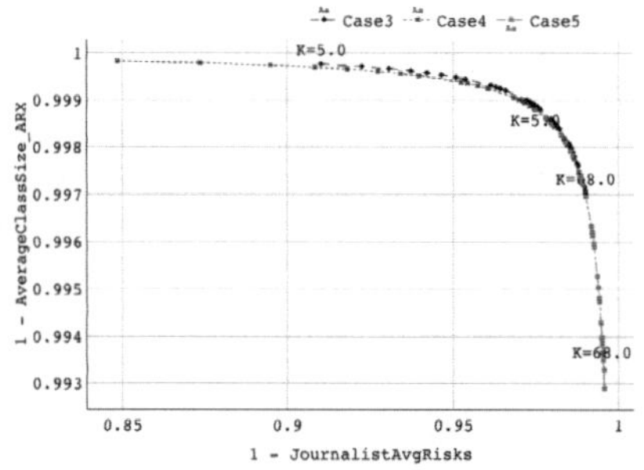

(a) Quality: derived from AverageClassSize per Privacy: derived from JournalistAvgRisks

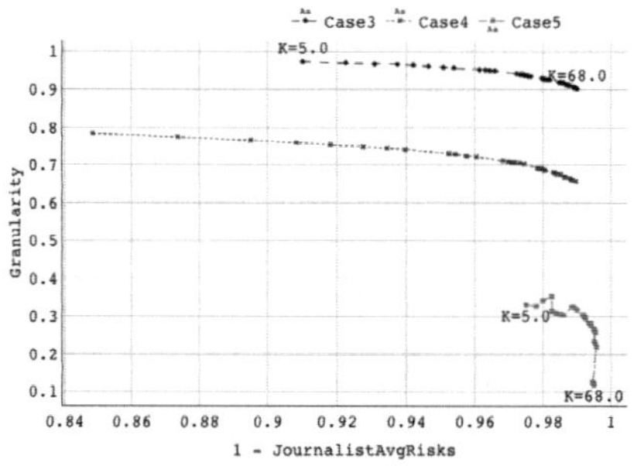

(b) Quality: Granularity per Privacy: derived from JournalistAvgRisks

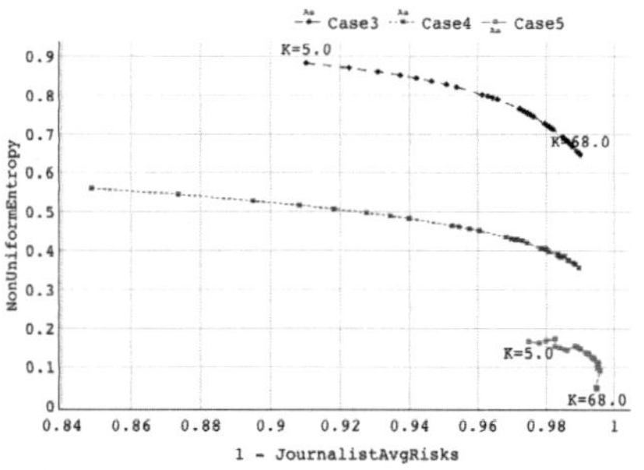

(c) NonUniformEntroy per Privacy: derived from JournalistAvgRisk

Figure 6. Quality per Privacy Measurements

other microdata sets), the latter is based on a formal definition of privacy (i.e., the definition of ϵ-differential privacy that guarantees the presence or absence of the (personal) data of an individual in a data set does not have an observable impact on the output of an analysis/computation over that data set). Whether this definition of privacy is comprehensive and adequate, specially in Open Data settings, is not established scientifically and/or adopted within privacy regimes and data protection regulations.

SDC-based anonymization does not provide a full guarantee against personal data disclosures, nevertheless, applying it is necessary for realizing compliance to the principle that personal data should be processed fairly (see Article 5(1-a) of GDPR). This fairness asks for putting sufficient efforts to protect personal data in a given context. Therefore, we argue that choosing all attributes as QIDs in Case IV or some attributes as QIDs in Case III is the least amount of data anonymization efforts needed to protect personal data according to the normative property of privacy discussed above. But the question remains if this will be sufficient, and will be seen as such, for instance, in the light of the GDPR fairness principle. In the environments where the formal definition of ϵ-differential privacy prevails, then applying the formal model as in Case V can (or even must) be considered. Note that in this work we kept our presentation simple and did not apply complementary data protection methods like l-diversity and t-closeness. In a practical setting, one should consider applying these techniques to contain disclosure risks at an acceptable level based on, among others, the principle of fair processing of data.

VIII. CONCLUSION

In this contribution, we analyzed the consequences of two cases in Open Data settings, namely having access to and having no access to original microdata sets, in terms of data utility. To this end, we applied SDC technologies in a number of steps to minimize privacy risks while maintaining data utility. Opting for Case III, where the opened data might potentially be re-identifiable for parties with the original microdata sets (like the data controller), can yield higher data quality than that in Case IV where the microdata is protected against such parties. On the other hand, opting for Case IV is an attempt to make the transformed microdata anonymous for everybody (e.g., the data controller). For Open Data purposes and from the perspective of protecting privacy, Case V operates better than the other cases. This performance of Case V comes with the cost of having lower data utility relatively to the other cases. We noted that the formal definition of privacy behind Case V is not established widely within privacy regimes and data protection regulations.

In this study, we clarified the difference among a number of solution directions for protecting personal data when publishing microdata sets to the public according to their implications on disclosure risks and utility of data. Based on the results of this contribution, we believe, legal experts, legislators and policymakers can make an informed choice among these options or foresee new solution directions based the here adopted approach.

In the future, we intend to apply the experiments to more real-world data sets. Also, we will explore how to embed the desires of data consumers and data publishers who would like to publish data effectively, while preserving the privacy of data subjects as much as possible. Further, we aim at extending the tool in the direction of having improved data utility and being user friendly for data controllers.

REFERENCES

[1] M. Bargh and S. Choenni, "On preserving privacy whilst integrating data in connected information systems." Academic Conferences and Publishing International, Proc. of the 1st Int. Conf. on Cloud Security Management (ICCSM), October 17-18, Seattle, USA, 2013.

[2] S. Kalidien, S. Choenni, and R. Meijer, "Crime statistics online: potentials and challenges," in *Proceedings of the 11th Annual International Conference on Digital Government Research, Public Administration Online: Challenges and Opportunities, Puebla, Mexico*, May 17-20, 2010, pp. 131–137.

[3] J. Prins, D. Broeders, and H. Griffioen, "iGovernment: A new perspective on the future of government digitisation," *Computer Law Security Review*, vol. 28, no. 3, pp. 273 – 282, 2012.

[4] S. Choenni, M. S. Bargh, C. Roepan, and R. F. Meijer, *Privacy and Security in Smart Data Collection by Citizens*. Cham: Springer International Publishing, 2016, pp. 349–366.

[5] S. W. van den Braak, S. Choenni, R. Meijer, and A. Zuiderwijk, "Trusted third parties for secure and privacy-preserving data integration and sharing in the public sector," in *13th Annual International Conference on Digital Government Research, DG.O, College Park, MD, USA*, June 4-7, 2012, pp. 135–144.

[6] L. Sweeney, "Maintaining patient confidentiality when sharing medical data requires a symbiotic relationship between technology and policy." Artificial Intelligence Laboratory, Massachusetts Institute of Technology, AIWP-WP344, 1997.

[7] N. Li, W. Qardaji, and D. Su, "Provably private data anonymization: Or, k-anonymity meets differential privacy," *CoRR*, vol. abs/1101.2604, 01 2011.

[8] Arx data anonymization tool. https://arx.deidentifier.org/, Date visited: Feb. 2020.

[9] K. O. M. Elliot, F. Mackey and C. Tudor. The anonymisation decision-making framework, technical report by uk anonymisation network (ukan). https://ukanon.net/wp-content/uploads/2015/05/The-Anonymisation-Decision-making-Framework.pdf, Date visited: Feb. 2020.

[10] K. E. Emam and B. Malin. Concepts and methods for de-identifying clinical trial data. https://www.ncbi.nlm.nih.gov/books/NBK285994/, Date visited: Feb. 2020.

[11] M. S. Bargh *et al.*, "Opening privacy sensitive microdata sets in light of GDPR," in *20th Annual International Conference on Digital Government Research, DG.O, Dubai, United Arab Emirates*, June 18-20, 2019, pp. 314–323.

[12] K. Nissim and A. Wood, "Is privacy privacy?" *Philosophical Transactions of the Royal Society A: Mathematical, Physical and Engineering Sciences*, vol. 376, no. 2128, p. 20170358, 2018.

[13] A. Wood *et al.*, "Differential privacy: A primer for a non-technical audience," vol. 21, no. 17. Vanderbilt Journal of Entertainment and Technology Law, 2018, p. 209.

[14] K. Nissim *et al.*, "Bridging the gap between computer science and legal approaches to privacy," vol. 31, no. 2. Harvard Journal of Law Technology, 2018, pp. 687–780.

[15] M. S. Bargh, R. Meijer, and M. Vink, "On statistical disclosure control technologies: For enabling personal data protection in open data settings," Research and Documentation Center WODC, The Hague, The Netherlands, Tech. Rep., 2018.

[16] B. C. M. Fung, K. Wang, R. Chen, and P. S. Yu, "Privacy-preserving data publishing: A survey of recent developments," vol. 42, no. 4, p. 14, 2010.

[17] C. Dwork, F. McSherry, K. Nissim, and A. D. Smith, "Calibrating noise to sensitivity in private data analysis," in *Theory of Cryptography, Third Theory of Cryptography Conference, TCC, New York, NY, USA*, March 4-7, 2006, pp. 265–284.

[18] K. LeFevre, D. J. DeWitt, and R. Ramakrishnan, "Mondrian multidimensional k-anonymity," in *Proceedings of the 22nd International Conference on Data Engineering, ICDE, Atlanta, GA, USA*, April 3-8, 2006, p. 25.

[19] A. Gionis and T. Tassa, "k-anonymization with minimal loss of information," *IEEE Trans. Knowl. Data Eng.*, vol. 21, no. 2, pp. 206–219, 2009.

[20] V. S. Iyengar, "Transforming data to satisfy privacy constraints," in *Proceedings of the Eighth ACM SIGKDD International Conference on Knowledge Discovery and Data Mining, Edmonton, Alberta, Canada*, July 23-26, 2002, pp. 279–288.

[21] F. Prasser, J. Eicher, R. Bild, H. Spengler, and K. A. Kuhn, "A tool for optimizing de-identified health data for use in statistical classification," in *IEEE 30th International Symposium on Computer-Based Medical Systems (CBMS)*, June 2017, pp. 169–174.

[22] F. Prasser, F. Kohlmayer, and K. A. Kuhn, "A benchmark of globally-optimal anonymization methods for biomedical data," in *IEEE 27th International Symposium on Computer-Based Medical Systems, New York, NY, USA*, May 27-29, 2014, pp. 66–71.

[23] K. El Emam, F. K. Dankar, A. Neisa, and E. Jonker, "Evaluating the risk of patient re-identification from adverse drug event reports," *BMC medical informatics and decision making*, vol. 13, no. 1, p. 114, 2013.

[24] F. Prasser, F. Kohlmayer, and K. A. Kuhn, "The importance of context: Risk-based de-identification of biomedical data," *Methods of Information in Medicines*, vol. 55, no. 4, pp. 347–355, 2016.

[25] F. K. Dankar, K. El Emam, A. Neisa, and T. Roffey, "Estimating the re-identification risk of clinical data sets," *BMC medical informatics and decision making*, vol. 12, no. 1, p. 66, 2012.

[26] N. Li, W. H. Qardaji, and D. Su, "On sampling, anonymization, and differential privacy or, *k*-anonymization meets differential privacy," in *7th ACM Symposium on Information, Computer and Communications Security, ASIACCS, Seoul, Korea,*, May 2-4, 2012, pp. 32–33.

[27] R. Bild, K. A. Kuhn, and F. Prasser, "Safepub: A truthful data anonymization algorithm with strong privacy guarantees," *PoPETs*, no. 1, pp. 67–87, 2018.

Customizing eGovernment Support Services: A Value Co-Creation Perspective

Maryanne Scutella
Adelaide Business School
University of Adelaide
Adelaide, Australia
e-mail: maryanne.scutella@adelaide.edu.au

Carolin Plewa and Carmen Reaiche
Adelaide Business School
University of Adelaide
Adelaide, Australia
e-mail: carolin.plewa@adelaide.edu.au,
carmen.reaiche@adelaide.edu.au

Abstract— **Small businesses are an important part of the Australian economic landscape. Therefore, it is important that small businesses be supported to encourage sustainability and growth. One of the complexities in designing and delivering relevant e-Government support services in this context is the diversity of small businesses, in particular when considering their existing resource base (such as experience, knowledge and skills), the resources they are seeking and the way they integrate their own resources with those of others. Customization is proposed to address the diverse nature of resources and resource integration, as it presents resources that are specific and relevant to the business. Indeed, the lack of perceived relevance is understood to act as a barrier to small businesses accessing support services that may be overcome by customization. However, research is yet to consider the role of customization of support services as a way to maximizing resource integration and value co-creation for small businesses. This research aims to address this limitation by developing a framework for increasing value-in-use from support services in the context of e-Government digital support systems. The suggested framework can then build the foundation for future empirical research in this area.**

Keywords- customization; e-Government; value co-creation; resource integration; information overload.

I. INTRODUCTION

Small businesses are complex and diverse in nature, and thus differ greatly in how they derive value from support services. Indeed, some research focuses on small business as a homogenous group [1], treating customers as a broad and rather undefined mass [2]. Even where the research has attempted to look at the clients more closely, there is a tendency to only use socio-demographic and digital divide factors. This is despite general recognition of the heterogeneous nature of small businesses, considering variations not only in the business' size, age, industry also in regards to the capabilities and motivations of their owners and managers [3].

Not only are small businesses more than 'scaled-down' versions of larger firms and need to be treated differently [1], they also differ more broadly in the resources that form part of each firm's make-up. Hence, understanding the complexity and diversity of small business and their resources will be a key focus of this research.

Notably, while limited, existing research suggests a positive impact of public agency support services on small business success and growth [3] as well as employment creation and labor productivity [4], thus indicating the importance of understanding the use of such services and the value small businesses generate as part of that usage process. This importance of small business support is recognized by governments around the world, who offer different types of support services, such as Business Link in the UK [5], many of which are offered online through websites or online portals. Many of such portals seek to cover as many possible facets and questions as possible, so as to account for the diversity of small businesses and their requirements for resources and support.

However, barriers to small businesses exist, limiting their ability fully realize value from such services. In particular, the impact of support services on the effectiveness of small business support programs depend both on the actual content and, importantly, the delivery method [6]. For example, a Canadian study found that more than half the respondents thought the support services offered to small business by public agencies was not suited to their needs, questioning the relevance of the service and related information provided [7]. Furthermore, the number of support services available to small business, together with an accompanying plethora of information, may limit their ability to generate value from these services. Whilst giving small businesses the opportunity to access the information they require; the sheer volume can also be a barrier to finding and utilizing these resources. This concept is commonly referred to as "information overload' and occurs as there are limits to how much information humans can process and use in a certain timeframe [8].

To overcome these issues, research has suggested tailoring content to the user, so that the information provided conforms to businesses better, especially for those experiencing information overload [9]. Indeed, it is the personalization techniques that "can reduce information overload and, hence, increase user satisfaction" [9]. For example, customizing the content to the user may make the service not only more relevant, it may also make it quicker and easier to find the right material [10]. Customization can be defined as "some level of adaptation or tailoring of the process to meet the individual consumer's needs" [11]. Research has shown that support services may experience greater usage if "support becomes more customized and suitable to problems and needs of SME" (Small Business) [3]. Indeed, research in digital services has demonstrated that the impact of human factors in the value co-creation process is greater at the front-end phase of the production of digital products and services [12].

However, although previous research notes the potential importance of customization for small business utilization of support services, research is yet to consider how it enables small businesses to generate value from these services. This is important, however, given that the advancement of small business – may it be in sustainability, growth or other goal – depends on their ability to gain value from the services they draw upon. Furthermore, customization research to date has focused mostly on the offering organization's perspective and not on the user/customer [13][14].

To advance our knowledge, this research draws on the theoretical grounding of value co-creation and resource integration to conceptualize the role of customization in the value co-creation process, providing a user centric approach that has been an identified gap in the existing customization literature. It will also contribute to small business, e-Government and support services research by advancing our conceptual understanding and related managerial recommendations aimed at maximizing the benefits small businesses derive from support services. Building on the conceptual development outlined here, future research can offer empirical support for the appetite of customized small business support and the relationship with factors central to the value co-creation process; a key focus and contribution of this research, which will be introduced in this working paper and expanded in future research.

Indeed, much of the research on customization and value co-creation has occurred in the commerce or retail perspective. However, there are significant differences between e-Government and e-commerce [15]. For example, a pivotal goal of commerce is gaining of profit, which is not a consideration for government. There is also not competition between government departments as each has their own specialty and often actively promote other government departments and services, thus warranting research specifically investigating this context.

Finally, this research will answer calls for research in the value co-creation literature. In particular, [16] call for the role of the customer and their resources that are integrated, with [17] pointing to the need to further investigate the contribution of the customer, which is still underrepresented in the literature. Furthermore, researchers have called for studies into the role of customer participation in the value co-creation process, particularly this from a "business customers has been largely unexplored" [18]. They highlight that more research is needed into business to business offerings, and in particular from the consumer business perspective as much of the previous research at that point was from the seller's perspective. This has also been cited as a limitation in e-Government research with limited research examining e-Government success from a citizen-based perspective [19].

This paper is divided into four sections. Section I contains the introduction, Section II presents the literature review and proposed framework, Section III discusses future research, and Section IV conclusions.

II. LITERATURE REVIEW AND PROPOSED FRAMEWORK

Significant research has examined value co-creation - "the process by which actors (firms and customers) integrate their resources to generate value" [20] - in recent years, emphasizing the role of actors (such as customers) as part of this process. Founded in Service Dominant logic (S-D), value co-creation reflects on the notion that customers are not just passive receivers of value, but that they instead they have a crucial active role in creating value for themselves [21]; both through direct and indirect inputs across multiple stages of utilizing or creating services [22]. Therefore, it is not the service itself that has value but it is a function of how the user utilizes it [23]. Within the S-D logic framework, value-in-use is seen as the outcome of resource integration [17] and the resource integration is a fundamental aspect of the value co-creation process [24]. Hibbert, Winklhofer and Temerak [25] posit that "resource integration is the process by which customers deploy resources as they undertake bundles of activities that create value directly or that will facilitate subsequent consumption/use from which they derive value". Hence, the organizations' role is to ensure that the service is designed, delivered and marketed in such a way as to facilitate the customer integrating resources and thus creating value from the service [26].

The way actors integrate resources and co-create value is by means of value co-creation behavior, and thus the "concrete representation of resource integration that assists in building knowledge about specific behaviors that customers engage in for co-creation of value" [27]. Value co-creation behavior can be defined as customers' participation in the value co-creation process, and as consisting of two higher order dimensions, participation behavior and citizenship behavior [28]. This research will focus on the subdimensions of participation behavior as this is more likely to appear when the client interacts with online support systems. This approach has been taken in previous studies with relation to e-shops [29]. There are four key elements to customer participation behavior. The first is information seeking, the effort to obtain or improve resources. The second is information sharing, third responsible behavior and fourth personal interaction, and thus the relationship between the customer and service provider [28]. While building an important foundation for understanding value co-creation behavior, it is recognized that it may not fully reflect the case of business to business customers [27][28]. This research will therefore examine this concept from a business client perspective.

This research will draw on a recent framework proposed by [30], as it provides a view of the different stages of resource integration and it is proposed that customizations fits naturally into this framework. The first phase relates to an actor matching their resources and what they require with that of the offering organization [30]. This logically requires the actors to be aware of what the potential resources are that may be of relevance. Matching primarily concerns interaction between the actor and the organization's resources. One of the key aspects of resource integration therefore is for the client to be able to find the right resources for them from the offering organization that they can match and then integrate with their existing resources and thus create value.

It is proposed here that customization mainly occurs during the matching phase and will assist in this process by making it easier for actors to match the available resources with their existing resources and specific requirements. This would then have a flow-on effect to the other two phases.

Resourcing is the second phase in the [30] framework and focuses specifically on the integration of resources process. This phase importantly includes the removal of the barriers to resource integration [30]. In the context of this research, customization is proposed to assist in this phase by removing the barrier that may be created by customers perceiving a lack of relevance of services or relevant support material. The assessment of value by the actor themselves forms the main component of the third and final phase.

The framework is highlighted in Figure 1 and conceptualizes the role of customization for value co-creation. In brief, the user brings their existing resources, along with an understanding of the resources they require, to the offering system or organization. The customized offering of the organization then allows the user to utilize their value co-creation behaviors (information seeking, sharing and responsible behavior) to match the resources of they require and have to that being offered, utilize this resource (resourcing), perform a value assessment and thereby derive value from the service and use this to achieve their initial goals (value-in-use). This may then lead to greater satisfaction with the offering organization and other consequences.

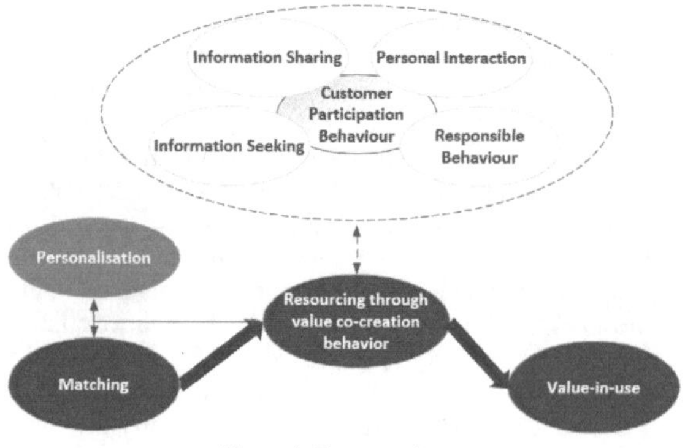

Figure 1. Framework

III. FUTURE RESEARCH

Value co-creation behavior, resource integration and customization literature and current approaches were reviewed to develop a possible framework that could be tested empirically in future research - to determine the validity of the framework generally, and specifically with relation to e-Government small business support.

Future research will look at the case study of an Australian government department and specifically at small business. The data that will be used are from two surveys that have previously been conducted by the organization. The first is on general small business engagement and the second with relation to their specific small business support digital offerings. The two surveys contain discrete populations and will be analyzed separately to address different components of the research questions. Both surveys, however, do contain a variable pertaining to the customers appetite for customization. Whilst the two surveys were conducted for a different purpose, several questions from both surveys have been identified as variables of interest that can be used to investigate the research framework.

IV. CONCLUSION

This research seeks to understand e-Government small business support from the user perspective and how customization can be used to increase the value small businesses drive from these services. A value co-creation framework is used, with a specific focus on resource integration, as a way to frame a customized support service. This research forms basis for proposed future quantitative research.

REFERENCES

[1] S. Holmes and D. Gupta, "Opening Aladdin's cave: Unpacking the factors impacting on small businesses," in Small Business Conditions and Finance A. M. a. J. Simon, Ed., ed Sydney: Reserve Bank of Australia, 2015, pp. 37–56.

[2] B. Distel and J. Becker, "All citizens are the same, aren't they? – Developing an e-government user typology," vol. 10428, ed. 2017, pp. 336-347.

[3] Z. Rakićević, J. Omerbegović-Bijelović, and D. Lečić-Cvetković, "A model for effective planning of SME support services," Evaluation and Program Planning, vol. 54, pp. 30-40, 2016.

[4] T. Cravo and C. Piza, "The impact of business-support services on firm performance: a meta-analysis," Small Business Economics, pp. 1-18, 2018.

[5] K. F. Mole, M. Hart, S. Roper, and D. S. Saal, "Broader or Deeper? Exploring the Most Effective Intervention Profile for Public Small Business Support," Environment and Planning A, vol. 43, pp. 87-105, 2011.

[6] S. Sawang, R. Parker, and D. Hine, "How Small Business Advisory Program Delivery Methods (Collective Learning, Tailored, and Practice - Based Approaches) Affect Learning and Innovation," Journal of Small Business Management, vol. 54, pp. 244-261, 2016.

[7] J. Audet and E. St-Jean, "Factors affecting the use of public support services by sme owners: Evidence from a periphery region of Canada," Journal of Developmental Entrepreneurship, vol. 12, pp. 165-180, 2007.

[8] N. K. Malhotra, "Information Load and Consumer Decision Making," Journal of Consumer Research, vol. 8, pp. 419-430, 1982.

[9] T.-P. Liang, H.-J. Lai, and Y.-C. Ku, "Personalized Content Recommendation and User Satisfaction: Theoretical Synthesis and Empirical Findings," Journal of Management Information Systems, vol. 23, pp. 45-70, 2006.

[10] V. Krishnaraju, S. Mathew, and V. Sugumaran, "Web personalization for user acceptance of technology: An empirical investigation of E-government services," A Journal of Research and Innovation, vol. 18, pp. 579-595, 2016.

[11] Y. Ding and H. T. Keh, "A re-examination of service standardization versus customization from the consumer's perspective," Journal of Services Marketing, vol. 30, pp. 16-28, 2016.

[12] M. Saunila, J. Ukko, and T. Rantala, "Value co-creation through digital service capabilities: the role of human factors," Information Technology & People, vol. 32, pp. 627-645, 2019.

[13] P. Kristensson, J. Matthing, and N. Johansson, "Key strategies for the successful involvement of customers in the co-creation of new technology-based services," International Journal of Service Industry Management, vol. 19, pp. 474-491, 2008.

[14] E. N. Torres, P. Lugosi, M. Orlowski, and G. Ronzoni, "Consumer-led experience customization: a socio-spatial approach," Journal of Service Management, vol. 29, pp. 206-229, 2018.

[15] H. Alshibly and R. Chiong, "Customer empowerment: Does it influence electronic government success? A citizen-centric perspective," Electronic Commerce Research and Applications, vol. 14, pp. 393-404, 2015.

[16] N. Löfberg and M. Åkesson, "Creating a service platform – how to co-create value in a remote service context," Journal of Business & Industrial Marketing, vol. 33, pp. 768-780, 2018.

[17] J. Petri and F. Jacob, "The customer as enabler of value (co)-creation in the solution business," Industrial Marketing Management, vol. 56, pp. 63-72, 2016.

[18] M. Mustak, E. Jaakkola, and A. Halinen, "Customer participation and value creation: a systematic review and research implications," Managing Service Quality: An International Journal, vol. 23, pp. 341-359, 2013.

[19] M. Scott, W. Delone, and W. Golden, "Measuring eGovernment success: a public value approach," European Journal of Information Systems, vol. 25, pp. 187-208, 2016.

[20] M. Paredes, J. Barrutia, and C. Echebarria, "Resources for value co-creation in e-commerce: a review," Electronic Commerce Research, vol. 14, pp. 111-136, 2014.

[21] C. Park, H. Lee, J. Jun, and T. Lee, "Two-sided effects of customer participation: roles of relationships and social-interaction values in social services," Service Business, vol. 12, pp. 621-640, 2018.

[22] K. Ranjan and S. Read, "Value co-creation: concept and measurement," Official Publication of the Academy of Marketing Science, vol. 44, pp. 290-315, 2016.

[23] D. T. de Oliveira and M. N. Cortimiglia, "Value co-creation in web-based multisided platforms: A conceptual framework and implications for business model design," Business Horizons, vol. 60, pp. 747-758, 2017.

[24] M. Kleinaltenkamp, R. J. Brodie, P. Frow, T. Hughes, L. D. Peters, and H. Woratschek, "Resource integration," Marketing Theory, vol. 12, pp. 201-205, 2012.

[25] S. Hibbert, H. Winklhofer, and M. S. Temerak, "Customers as Resource Integrators: Toward a Model of Customer Learning," Journal of Service Research, vol. 15, pp. 247-261, 2012.

[26] S. Iyanna, "Insights Into Consumer Resource Integration And Value Co-Creation Process," Journal of Applied Business Research, vol. 32, pp. 717-728, 2016.

[27] G. Laud and I. O. Karpen, "Value co-creation behaviour – role of embeddedness and outcome considerations," Journal of Service Theory and Practice, vol. 27, pp. 778-807, 2017.

[28] Y. Yi and T. Gong, "Customer value co-creation behavior: Scale development and validation," Journal of Business Research, vol. 66, pp. 1279-1284, 2013.

[29] T. Fotiadis, "Customer Participation, e-Service Quality, Satisfaction: (e)Service Dominant Logic Trinity," Journal of Promotion Management, vol. 25, pp. 394-418, 2019.

[30] A. Caridà, B. Edvardsson, and M. Colurcio, "Conceptualizing resource integration as an embedded process: Matching, resourcing and valuing," Marketing Theory, vol. 19, pp. 65-84, 2019.

A Digital Systems Approach Across eGovernment Services: The Australian Taxation Office and The Health Environment

Samantha Papavasiliou and Carmen Reaiche
Adelaide Business School
University of Adelaide,
Adelaide, Australia
e-mail: samantha.papavasiliou@adelaide.edu.au,
carmen.reaiche@adelaide.edu.au

Abstract— **The public sectors shift to digital first service provision has had a considerable impact on how individuals interact with public sector entities. This research highlights the similar assistance requirements and concerns with different public sector digital services. Evidence for this research is presented through a case study on the Australian Taxation Office and two digital health platforms, MyAgedCare and My Health Record. By understanding the different issues and assistance seeking requirements across the public sector digital services, digital service designers and policy makers can better create services that meet the needs and expectations of users. A primary finding of this research highlights the expectations of users that human interfaces for assistance-seeking are maintained, in order to maximise an individual's capacity to interact with the system successfully.**

Keywords- Digital Health; Assistance Seeking; Digital Inclusiveness; Digital Ecosystem; Public Sector.

I. INTRODUCTION

As public sector services adopt new technologies and start to identify the considerable benefits associated with utilising digital services, the availability and use of legacy systems will decrease [1]. Public sector services are fundamental in a modern society and service availability is crucial. However, with the use of digital services in lieu of legacy systems, especially in the mandatory service space, users are becoming more and more limited in their choices [1]. Therefore, this paper argues that for governments to be truly inclusive, legacy systems must remain in place, to enable and provide access to all who require them.

This paper explores the application of findings from an Australian Taxation Office (ATO) case study, used to understand the barriers and opportunities affecting digital service provision in the public sector. The findings are used to start the discussion on the digital health environment, including the most common Australian digital health platforms known as My Health Record and MyAgedCare [2], both services which are displayed with similar digital formats. This paper does not argue against the use of digital approaches for service provision, however it questions the inclusiveness of providing digital first services in mandatory service space (e.g., tax lodgement or aged care referrals).

The purpose of transitioning public sector services to digital platforms is clear, to provide easy access to government services, and to promote the transformation and delivery of modern and future proof digital services to those who need them [1] [3]. There are millions of Australians who utilise online government services through the central platform "myGov", as well as numerous state government online services [1]. The large numbers utilising the services demonstrate how Australian public sector digital services are well adopted within the community. However, there are still pockets of the community who are struggling to access necessary services [1].

All Australian Public Sector Organisations were impacted by the introduction of the Australian Digital Continuity Policy 2020, mandating the use of digital first channels for every public sector service provided [4]. This policy put considerable pressure on both public sector organisations and service users. Through exploration of previous literature, a considerable gap was identified between what is known about digital service users and non-users, and those individuals who are required to use them. Therefore, the impact of shifting mandatory public sector services to a digital first platform is still largely unknown. As digital first service provision is the way forward for all public sector organisations (especially in Australia), a holistic view of users is needed. Research needs to support and assist users, improve services and inform policy to increase long-term voluntary compliance obligations in a mandatory service space. To support this view, this research is exploring the relevance of previous research based on a case study on the ATO, and comparing them to different services provided by the Australian Department of Health.

This paper will explore the barriers to digital adoption in the public sector space, specifically comparing mandatory and voluntary spaces. These comparisons will be based on understanding that ATO and MyAgedCare services are mandatory and My Health Record being voluntary. This research explores the common reported themes among digital barriers and proposes additional research to be undertaken to address the gaps. The themes will be derived from an ATO case study (conducted previously) and comparing to a pilot study undertaken on MyAgedCare. Additional research has explored the identified barriers to the use of My Health Record (a voluntary service), to understand the similarities across digital health and digital taxation, as well as mandatory and voluntary. Through the use of thematic analysis outlining the barriers to digital adoption, links between the ATO case study and the digital health platforms are introduced to demonstrate the similar issues across the different eGovernment services. By exploring the various barriers and their links to the User Centred Model (Figure 1) the analysis provides lessons learned applicable to both policy makers and digital services designers.

The structure of this paper is divided into six sections. Section one contains the introduction, section two outlines the literature reviewed, section three discusses the ATO, My Health Record and MyAgedCare, the fourth section outlines the methods, the fifth section highlights the results of the study and the final section is the conclusion.

II. Literature Review

A. Digital inclusion

Inclusion is complex as it incorporates numerous concepts including; awareness, acceptance, respect and understanding, to provide equal participation opportunities [5][6]. An inclusive environment encourages people with different characteristics, backgrounds and ways of thinking, to work together to fulfil their potentials [5][6]. These environments require considering both internal and external stakeholder perspectives, and placing equal value on all perspectives regardless of where they originated [7]. Digital inclusiveness is also increasingly complex, as it involves multiple components within the specific digital ecosystem of an individual. Therefore, digital inclusion identifies the importance of access to information and communications technology and the resulting social and economic benefits for users [8]. An individual's level of digital inclusion is impacted by digital skills, connectivity and accessibility. Digital skills include the capacity to use technology to connect with the services (internet and computer), connectivity involves having internet access (the infrastructure) and accessibility is the user friendly digital services that assist in accessing the service [9]. Thus raising the question, does digital health have potential negative implications on levels of digital inclusiveness?

B. Digital divide

One of the most significant issues towards the use of digital public sector services is the digital divide, whereby in Australia more than 2.5 million individuals are still not online [9] and the digital divide is largest in those older than 65 [9]. The digital divide is defined as the gap between individuals or groups with limited access to digital information and services, compared to those who have effective access [9]. With the shift of government services to online delivery methods, there is considerable potential for older Australian's to be disadvantaged from the greater use of emergent and dominant communication technologies [13], as digital services tend to leave older Australian's out [10]. An aging population is vulnerable and in some cases reluctant to use digital technology, raising concerns about ability to use technology, scams, privacy, self-diagnosis resulting from misunderstanding of information and the desire for face-to-face explanations [11]. Thus raising the question, how do digital health platforms affect service use?

The digital divide is an issue that effects lower income earners, individuals with poor access to the internet and/or those individuals who lack the skills to use technology, making it harder to access. Furthermore, lower levels of digital inclusion are associated with individuals who only access internet through mobile devices. Digital exclusion often exacerbates other forms of social exclusion; this includes unemployment, low education and poverty [12]. Therefore, the importance of digital inclusion is undeniable; all Australians require access to both technology and skills to ensure they can take part in every aspect of social and economic life. There are practical concerns for achieving equitable levels of access between different social groups and public services, as society is not homogenous, providing basic accesses to the community is not sufficient. Services provided to citizens by government need to align their design and application to the needs of the community, to encourage digital inclusiveness and begin to breakdown the digital divide.

C. Barriers to eGovernment

Previous research has explored the specific barriers to digital adoption within the eGovernment space. The European Commission, defines a barrier to eGovernment as the, characteristics within the contexts of legal, social, technological, or institutional which negatively impact the development of eGovernment [11, P.3]. This can be caused by users' lack of demand and the obstacles preventing engagement with services, or disincentives for the government to supply the eGovernment services or prevalence of obstacles preventing its supply [12]. This research identified barriers and compiled them into seven key categories; leadership failures, financial inhibitors, digital divide and choice, poor coordination, workplace and organisational inflexibility, lack of trust and poor technical design [12]. However, research suggests that regardless of the platform, the impact of stakeholders (internal and external) can negatively influence its use [13]. Therefore, successful eGovernment platforms depend on understanding the environments in which they operate [14]. These elements including stakeholder inclusiveness should be considered more in-depth, with their relationship to the multiple barriers preventing eGovernment/digital service adoption and their applicability across disciplines.

III. eGovernment Services: ATO and Health

For this research, mandatory environments are classified as "Public Sector Organisations who must by legislation provide Digital Platforms for their services" [15][16]. Whereas mandatory interactions are defined as "Users who meet certain characteristics and must by legislation interact with the public sector service provider to meet these obligations" [15][16]. Therefore, users must engage with providers, but under the digital first mandate expectations around how they do so has changed. In contrast voluntary public sector services are similar to those provided by the private sector, in that an individual can decide whether they want to utilise the service or not.

A. ATO

The ATO was the first service provider to adopt digital first service provision, with the introduction of myTax for individuals, business portals, and tax agent portals. The ATO requires all individuals to interact annually with them to submit their tax return, all individuals who derive income within Australia. Since the digital first transition, the majority of services are digital and require an understanding of both taxation and computer systems. Taxpaying population is in Australia is over 16 million; of these 84% are individuals [16]. The ATO has high digital adoption rates of the MyTax platform, with 95% of individuals eligible to utilise the service [16], however there are still gaps within the population that need to be explored and understood.

Progressively the myTax platform became more inclusive, through annual and ongoing adaptions, and the progressive changes in the manner in which digital adoption and service provision has occurred [17] [18]. Each iteration incorporates the feedback from users to ensure ongoing viability of the platform, while also ensuring ongoing success [24]. The iterative approach of ongoing improvements has been a key component outlining the success of the myTax platform, which makes the platform a good case study on the creation of inclusive government services. This is not to say that the platform is 100% inclusive, there are still issues with accessibility, understanding and willingness to change that impact its use [19].

B. Digital Health

Healthcare systems are becoming significantly more complex, with more professionals becoming involved in each individual patients care, and ever-changing healthcare needs of the population [20]. Healthcare is the product of a complex adaptive system, comprised of people, equipment, processes and institutions which all work together [21]. Healthcare systems operate at their best, by undertaking ongoing improvements. However, when the system fails to improve it negatively impacts the system [22]. Therefore, the research argues that through the application of a systems thinking lens, the complexity of the different interacting internal and external environments within organisations, health systems and society for example, can be better identified and understood. The systems complexity highlights both problems and opportunities and requires responsive organisations and systems capable of adjusting to changes. The ability of the system or components of the system to respond to changes, all depends on one's ability to understand influences [23]. Systems thinking can provide a holistic view and assist in identifying areas requiring revisiting [24].

C. My Health Record

My Health Record is an online platform containing a summary of an individual key medical and health information (including histories). The site provides information for individuals and health practitioners who opted into the service to view medical histories, previous tests, medication (history and current) and diagnosis. The My Health Record platform was piloted in 2016 [25]. The aim of the platform was to provide a single location for all medical details of a patient that is readily available for health practitioners and users. The service is voluntary, there was an opt-out process between 2018 and 2019, where eligible Australians indicated whether or not they wanted the service [25]. To be eligible an individual must be registered with Medicare. Although there are a number of benefits from the provision of the online health record, more than 2.5 million Australians opted out of the platform [26]. The primary reason was privacy concerns, specifically because not only doctors can view the records (any registered health provider can); data can be used for research; once created the record cannot be deleted and there is fear of hacking data [27].

D. MyAgedCare

MyAgedCare is an online platform for individuals aged 65 or older which is the starting point on an individual's aged care journey [28]. The site provides information for government-funded services available at home to enable individuals to continue living independently. The MyAgedCare platform has undergone numerous changes since its launch in 2013, aiming to provide a consistent, streamlined and holistic assessment of clients. However a study published in 2018 demonstrates service demand significantly outweighs supply. With 127,748 on waitlists or not receiving adequate levels of assistance based on their needs [29], and the waitlist growing by 20,000 every six months [30]. Furthermore, 96,000 people waiting since 2013 have found nursing home placements faster than their preferred option of home care, and more than 16,000 people died waiting for services [30]. Numbers are impacted by geographical location, types of services, financial outlay and availability of qualified staff. Although this backlog in services is important to note, it is not the key issue raised in this paper, this study focuses on the implications of MyAgedCare as a digital platform and how this, in turn, affects patient centred care.

Both digital health eGovernment platforms under analysis are relatively new, having not undergone as many iterations as the ATO myTax platform. However, these platforms have a considerable impact on end users and the Australian population, as they are both critical for providing information and links to information that outline individuals health profiles, where and how to access services and has the capacity to act as a facilitator of medical services in Australia. This research intends to highlight the key lessons learned from the ATO digital experience, to help inform digital health service designers, to provide avenues for designers and policy makers to obtain guidance on how to develop more inclusive digital services in this space. Simultaneously, other eGovernment platforms can take advantage of the key learnings from the ATO digital experience, as this is transferable to eGovernment.

IV. METHODS

A qualitative approach was applied to this research. An integration of both interpretative and exploratory approach to obtain an in-depth understanding of the key barriers to digital adoption and how they were overcome was considered appropriate to the ATO, MyAgedCare and My Health Record cases. This approach provides evidence to describe the eGovernment environment and provide insights to promote ongoing service adoption.

This research has two components, the first component was the analysis of the ATO digital experience. The ATO study component for this research used primary data collected during a 4-week period over July 2018. A survey form was provided to 11 call centre operatives who populated numerous fields outlining reasons for call and demographics of callers; to understand why people were seeking assistance. Once collected the data (N = 3,990) was anonymised through aggregation techniques to group like individuals into similar groups to understand the population. As this research was designed to be exploratory in nature, the focus was to understand the different issues facing users, a thematic analysis was completed on the qualitative data obtained.

The second component incorporates the Digital Health sector platforms, My Health Record and MyAgedCare. For the MyAgedCare component of this research, data has been collected from concerns, interpretations and perceptions of various stakeholders engaged with the MyAgedCare platform. Data analysed underpinned the actor's perception on "What do they think of the MyAgedCare platform?". The same method was utilised to explore the My Health Record platform which works on similar digital integration system approach. The main focus of the discussions was to understand what different actor's perceptions are on "What do they think of the My Health Record Platform?". The data was consolidated and anonymised when analysed to identify common themes and trends within the responses. The data collected for this component has been treated as a pilot and comparative form to the ATO digital environment and therefore was only based on answering a singular question. The additional analysis conducted was on existing data provided outlining environmental components.

V. UNDERPINNING FINDINGS: USER CENTRED MODEL

The research adopted an interpretive lens to guide analysis with a systems view. Through the analysis of the 11 call centre operatives' surveys, a conceptual model is proposed for the complete integration of key stakeholders influencing end user digital adoption: User Centred Model (see Figure 1). The key factors and element of this model emerged by observation and interpretation of all the stakeholders and interactive elements within the system and all the parts of the broader environment. The purpose of adopting a systems lens to build this model was to provide a user-centred research approach which can guide policy making as well as provide better support and understanding of the various needs of the different users. This conceptual model contributes to knowledge by initially identifying a number of factors within a user's environment and their degree of impact on willingness or capacity to adopt mandatory digital services.

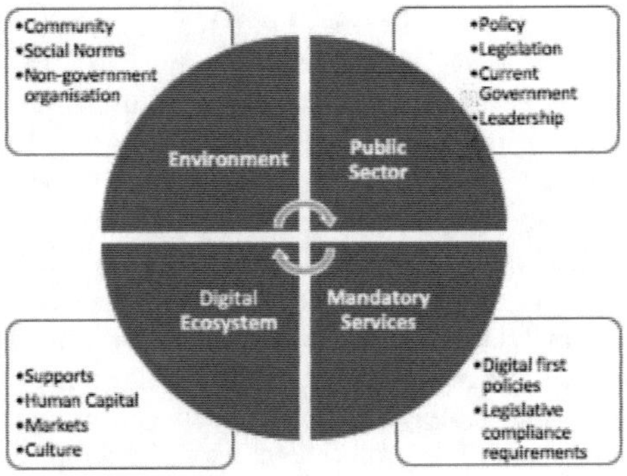

Figure 1. User Centred Model

TABLE I. ATO BARRIERS TO DIGITAL ADOPTION

Theme	Users comments
Platform support and technical support	- Do not know how to access the page - What are the security measures in place? - How do I link between the MyGov and MyTax platforms? - I have not used this before - where is my prefilled data ? - How do I change my details/or name? - The identification questions were incorrect - I am having technical difficulties
Lacks computer skills, preference to use non digital	- I want to use myTax by I don't know how to use a computer - I have no email address or digital presence - Do not own a computer - How do I do this digitally? - I always do my taxes this way - Language barriers prevents the use of digital - Only completes old non digitalised forms
Requires education in the system, platform awareness	- How do I lodge? - Why do I need to? - How does tax work? - Why do I have to pay money? - How does income work? - Where do I put information on the form? - What are tax offsets? - How long does this take? - What is a deduction?

Table 1 outlines the thematic analysis conducted within the ATO, this table demonstrates the different barriers individuals face when interacting with the myTax platform and creates a basis for the analysis of the digital health platforms. The thematic analysis demonstrates that individuals seek assistance and advice on both tax technical components and general platform and technical support. Both of these scenarios are relevant for the digital health space, as language used in services and information provided can have a considerable impact on end users.

When comparing the themes outlined within Table 1, all themes influence an individual capability and willingness to utilise digital services. There are links within each section to legislation, mandatory services and the environmental impacts. From this, the research can infer that there is a lack of understanding of mandatory services, specifically what the legislation is requiring the shift to digital. Therefore, to address this, users need to be informed of the changes and the provision of transparent policies are required, these policies need to be easily interpreted by all users. Furthermore, by understanding how different policies interact with the mandatory services users can be more informed as to the security and safety of their data, without this understanding it is unclear how end users will feel confident and comfortable using the services.

When comparing the findings within Table 1 to the preliminary findings within Tables 2-4, lessons can be learned in relation to the potential inclusiveness of digital services, especially when looking beyond mandatory systems and simply exploring the various policies and involvement of stakeholders. For example, in both mandatory and voluntary systems, an important issue for end users is the security concerns related to their private data, how they access the digital services and their level of digital literacy. The users for these services also differ considerably, which demonstrates interesting findings when it comes to across the board generalisability of barriers to digital inclusiveness.

TABLE II. RESPONSES TO "WHY ARE YOU NOT USING DIGITAL SERVICES?"

Theme	Users comments
Scams/Fraud /Security	- Fear of scams - Not sure which is the real website and which is fraudulent - Computer/cyber security concerns
No computer/ Internet access	- Have no experience utilising a computer or accessing the internet - Unclear on what a digital health service is - Have no access to the internet of computer

The results within Tables 1, 3 and 4, highlight how regardless of platform, the assistance required relates to end-user concerns about terminology, accuracy of information and representation. Furthermore, there is a clear and direct relationship between digital awareness of the operations of online platforms (eGovernment) and the types of questions asked within the digital space (e.g., digital literacy questions, obtaining the correct information).

TABLE III. RESPONSES TO "WHAT DO YOU THINK OF MYAGEDCARE?"

Theme	Users comments
Phoneline	- Rude staff - Staff demanding to speak to client directly despite acknowledgement of advocate availability - Hearing impairment impacting communication - Language barriers
Confusing	- Terminology used by staff - Questions deemed by clients as intrusive and unnecessary - Inaccurate information provided on website - Clients unable to understand the different services and costs involved – written information only with a lack of visual representation - Sometimes inaccurate representation of available services - Availability of services for under 65 years
Difficultly accessing	- Vision impairment - A lack of comprehension - Unreliable or no internet in the home (particularly rural and remote) - Mobility impairment - unable to leave home to use public access computer - Inability to express urgency

TABLE IV. RESPONSES TO "WHAT DO YOU THINK OF MY HEALTH RECORD?"

Theme	Users comments
Privacy	- Confidentially and privacy concerns - Concerns for the ongoing privacy for their data stored online - Unhappy that it cannot be deleted once created - Unclear who can access my records and why? - Allied health services can access my records - What if my medical history is shared an
Confusing	- Terminology used online - Accuracy of information provided on online - Not every doctors client and hospital is represented
Difficultly accessing	- Vision impairment - Do not understand how to use the portal - Low levels of digital literacy - Unreliable or no internet in the home - Mobility impairment - unable to leave home to use public access computer

VI. CONCLUSION

The preliminary findings from the digital health space in comparison to the ATO case study demonstrates significant similarities between the digital/online platforms and the issues associated with digital awareness, acceptance, assistance seeking, accessibility and support. As demonstrated within the results of the ATO case study, the value of face-to-face or human interaction based assistance is still a necessary component of the success of eGovernment service inclusiveness. Digital health too quickly removed the face-to-face component of assistance in regard to both My Health Record and My Aged care, decreasing the inclusiveness and making it difficult for individuals who preferred face-to-face support. Human interaction support is available in this space, however does not provide the same emotional support often expected within the delicate situations evident in healthcare.

My Health Record and MyAgedCare have a considerable amount to learn from the ATO, who have maintained high adoption and satisfaction ratings within their digital service. Furthermore, through multiple iterations, ongoing improvements were made possible, while ensuring that different avenues for obtaining support and assistance were available to suit the user's needs (e.g., in person, over the phone and through intermediaries). What this research has indicated is that the digital health services have moved too quickly in their transition from legacy to digital services. The ATO learned within their transition to digital first services, specifically what legacy systems they could do without and which ones they need to maintain and improve.

REFERENCES

[1] Digital Transformation Agency, Digital Delivery of Government Services: Digital Transformation Agency Submission to the Finance and Public Administration Committee. 2017. Available from: https://www.aph.gov.au/DocumentStore.ashx?id=9d695f6a-2354-4cc5-be0d-913de41b25de&subId=516630. [Retrieved: 10 January, 2020]

[2] Department of Health, Evaluation of my Health Record Participation Trial Report, 2016. Available from: https://www.health.gov.au/internet/main/publishing.nsf/Content/publications-Evaluation-of-the-my-health-record-participation-trials/. [Retrieved: 10 January, 2020]

[3] C. Dilmegani, B. Korkmaz and M. Lundqvist. 'Public Sector Digitalisation – The Trillion Dollar Challenge', McKinsey Business Transition Office, 2014.

[4] National Archives of Australia. Digital Continuity 2020, 2015. Available from: www.naa.gov.au/Information.management /Digital.Continuity.2020. [Retrieved: 10 January, 2020]

[5] S. Thompson. "Defining and Measuring 'Inclusion' Within an Organisation K4D; Helpdesk Report. Brighton", UK: Institute of Development Studies, 2017.

[6] W. Wallace and G, Pillans. Creating an Inclusive Culture: UK Corporate Research Forum, 2016. Available from: http://www.crforum.co.uk/wpcontent/uploads/2016/11/11-Creating-an-Inclusive-Culture-1.pdf. [Retrieved: 10 January, 2020]

[7] OECD. "Inclusive Government for a More Inclusive Society. In Government at a Glance 2015", Paris: OECD Publishing, 2015.

[8] J. Thomas et al. "Measuring Australia's Digital Divide: The Australian Digital Inclusion Index 2018", Melbourne: RMIT University: For Telstra, 2018.

[9] UK Government. Policy Paper: Government Digital Inclusion Strategy, 2014. Available from: https://www.gov.uk/government/publications/government-digital-inclusion-strategy/governmentdigital-inclusion-strategy. [Retrieved: 10 January, 2020]

[10] Aged Care Guide. Digital Inclusion Leaves Older Australian's Out, 2017. Available From: http://www.adedcareguide.com.au/talking-aged-care/digital=inclusion-leaves-older-Australias-out/. [Retrieved: 10 January, 2020]

[11] European Commission. Breaking Barriers to eGovernment; Overcoming Obstacles to Improving European Public Services, 2007. Available from: https:/www.oii.ox.ac.uk/archive/downloads/research/egovbarriers/deliverables/solutions_report/Solutions_for_eGovernment.pdf. [Retrieved: 10 January, 2020]

[12] S. Angelopoulos, F. Kitsios, P. Kofakis and T. Papadopoulos. "Emerging Barriers in eGovernment Implementation", *Proceedings of International Conference on Electronic Government (EGOV 2010)*, pp. 216-225, Lausanne Switzerland (29 August – 2 September). 2010.

[13] M. Yildiz. 2007. eGovernment Research: Reviewing the Literature, Limitations, and Ways Forward, Government Information Quarterly, Vol. 24 No. 3.

[14] S. Papavasiliou, C. Reaiche and P. Ricci. "Digital Adoption: The Need for Truly Inclusive eGovernment Services", Proceeding of the 2019 International Conference on E-Learning, EBusiness, Enterprise Information Systems & eGovernment. pp. 43-49. 2019. ISBN: 1-60132-495-2

[15] S. Papavasiliou, C. Reaiche and P. Ricci. "Digital Interactions Strategy: A Public Sector Case", The Thirteenth International Conference on Digital Society and eGovernments. pp. 19-23. 2019. ISBN: 978-1-61208-685-9

[16] Australian Taxation Office. Individuals, 2019. Available from: https://www.ato.gov.au/About-ATO/Research-and-statistics/In-detail/Taxation-statistics/Taxation-statistics-2016-17/?page=7. [Retrieved: 10 January, 2020]

[17] B. Carmody. ATO Rolls Out myTax to Sole Traders and Contractors for the First Time, 2017. Available from: https://www.smartcompany.com.au/finance/ato-rolls-out-mytax-to-sole-traders-and-contractors-for-the-first-time/. [Retrieved: 10 January, 2020]

[18] A. Coyne. ATO to Kill Off e-Tax, 2015. Available from: https://www.itnews.com.au/news/ato-to-kill-off-e-tax-401902. [Retrieved: 10 January, 2020]

[19] N. Olsen. Tax Administration in a Digital Age: The Australian Experience, 2018. Available from: https://www.ato.gov.au/Media-centre/Speeches/Other/Tax-Administration-in-a-Digital-Age-The-Australian-experience/. [Retrieved: 10 January, 2020]

[20] S. Leyshon and S. McAdam. "Scene Setter: The Importance of Taking A Systems Approach to Persons Centred Care", BMJ. vol. 350. 2015.

[21] J. Clarkson, J. Dean, J. Ward, A. Komashie and T. Bashford,. "A Systems Approach to Healthcare: From Thinking to Practice", *Future Healthcare Journal*. Vol. 5(3). Pp. 151-155. 2018.

[22] J. Braithwaite. "Changing How We Think About Healthcare Improvement", BMJ. vol. 361. 2018.

[23] R.M. Lebeir. Health Care Management: The Contribution of Systems Thinking, University of Hertfordshire, 2006.

[24] A. Gorod, L. Hallo and T. Nguyen. "A Systematic Approach to Complex Project Management: Integration of Command-and-Control and Network Governance", *Systems Research and Behavioural Science*. Vol. 35, pp. 811-837. 2019. doi: 10.1002/sres.2520.

[25] Department of Health. What is My Health Record?, 2019. Available from: https://www.myhealthrecord.gov.au/for-you-your-family/what-is-my-health-record. [Retrieved: 10 January, 2020]

[26] C. Knaus. More than 2.5 million people have opted out of My Health Record, 2019. Available from: https://www.theguardian.com/australia-news/2019/feb/20/more-than-25-million-people-have-opted-out-of-my-health-record. [Retrieved: 10 January, 2020]

[27] A. Bogle. My Health Record: Your Questions Answered on Cybersecurity, Police and Privacy, 2019. Available from: https://www.abc.net.au/news/science/2018-07-15/my-health-record-questions-answers-security-privacy-police/9959622/. [Retrieved: 10 January, 2020]

[28] MyAgedCare. About Us, 2019. Available from: https://www.myagedcare.gov.au/about-us. [Retrieved 10 August, 2019]

[29] National Aged Care Alliance. 2019 Federal Election Position Statement - Getting Aged Care Right for Everyone, 2019. Available from:https://agewellcampaign.com.au/wpcontent/uploads/2019/05/2019-Federal-Election-Position-Statement.pdf. [Retrieved: 10 January, 2020]

[30] S. Lauder and V. Milton. My Aged Care Home Care Wait of Only 12 Months has the Allens Considering Themselves Lucky, 2019. Available from: https://www.abc.net.au/news/2019-05-10/eunice-and-john-allen-wait-for-home-care-package/11098848. [Retrieved: 10 January, 2020]

Soft Skills: A Key Driver for Digital Transformation

Richa Gulati
Business School
University of Adelaide
Adelaide, Australia
e-mail: richa.gulati@adelaide.edu.au

Carmen Haule Reaiche
Business School
University of Adelaide
Adelaide, Australia
e-mail: carmen.reaiche@adelaide.edu.au

***Abstract* - This paper focuses on exploring the value of intangible (soft skills) investments to aid successful digital transformation in organisations. The human capital of a business or an organisation is the key catalyst for implementing change. It is, therefore, important to have a skilled workforce which is capable of adopting and coping with changes such as digital transformation. This research focuses on the importance of soft aspects of digital transformation. Gioia method was adopted to guide the analysis of the data (interviews) for this research. The results are indicative of the important soft skills required to embrace digital transformation and its potential impact on successful implementation.**

Keywords-intangible investment; soft skills; digital transformation; project managers.

I. Introduction

Technology and society are evolving faster than business can naturally adapt and digital transformation is one aspect of this evolution. Technology has changed relationships between customers and organisations, deeply affecting organisational models and management systems [1] [6]. It is an exponential change, which is not just the job of a person or a team, but a collective effort of the whole organisation. It is about the overall improvement of ways of working and efficiency of an organisation [2]. Due to the scale of change and ease of its management, it is often divided into smaller projects, which are then managed to adopt the change [3]. It is worth considering that given the awareness and planning of change, if organisations are ready to face it. And more importantly: What drives it? A single thread that weaves in everything to ultimately produce the outcome is the soft aspect of the organisation. Digital transformation is probably less about digital and more about transformation, which is led by people. Technology is a tool but its actual strength is soft skills [4][5]. This research seeks to address the gap pertaining to soft aspects of digital transformation, which hinders successful implementations and changes management in organisations. It aims to instill the value of investing in intangible aspects of an organisation, which in turn play a key role in their success.

This paper is further divided into four sections, namely, Background, Significance and Research Contribution, Research Approach and, Preliminary Findings and Future Research. Firstly, the background section provides an insight into current situation and context of this research leading to the significance and research contribution section. This section then establishes the importance and possible contributions of this project. The next section of research approach elaborates on the process of data collection and method used by researchers. Lastly, the preliminary findings and future research section summarizes the primary findings of this research and provides insight into the future steps for this project.

II. Background

Digital transformation has become an integral part of organisations in pursuit of growth, expansion, quality and sustainability [1]. One on hand, it allows organisations to enhance organisational efficiency and customer experience, but, on the other hand, it brings tremendous pressure as it demands changes in organisational models and management systems [6][7]. Many organisations adopt a project management approach wherein change management is the key focus [8][9]. However, the key element is the people who drive, accept, adopt and implement this transformation, i.e., the human capital of the organisation [7]. In line with adoption strategies and careful planning, human capital strategies play an important role as well. The project manager needs to plan how to manage, organize, develop, and align people at work to deliver successful customer and employee experiences [10]. It is probably not the strongest of the species that survives, not the most intelligent that survives. It appears to be the one that is the most adaptable to change [11].

Some of the skills required by a manager in order to successfully manage digital transformation are: critical thinking, complex communication, creativity collaboration, flexibility and adaptability, productivity and accountability, building a team that thrives, cultivating a growth mindset, influence, ability to navigate innovation and change, effective collaboration with leaders and across teams. In addition to these, adaptability, creativity, action-oriented, passion, curiosity and management skills also play an important role while managing the team and projects [6] [11]-[15]. From the customer's orientation, it is important to create memorable and meaningful experiences. The most valuable assets for service and experience creation are people, ideas and collaboration [16]. There has been some emphasis on people's aspect in vivid literature, however, the importance of soft skills has not gained much focus as a key driver or backbone of digital transformation, although, it has been a recommendation in those research studies. Thus, this research aims to establish the importance of soft skills in managers.

III. SIGNIFICANCE AND RESEARCH CONTRIBUTION

This research contributes to knowledge by identifying the moderating role of soft skills in digital transformation. The research aims to establish the importance of "people" and their "soft skills" in an organisation by investigating the value of investing in intangible assets, i.e., soft skills of their employees. Prior research has identified key drivers that support digital transformation, however, there has not been enough attention on developing and acquiring the skills needed to maneuver this change. Having an adaptable workforce has become a necessity for business and organisations in order to cope with the changes in their respective domains [12].

IV. RESEARCH APPROACH

This is an exploratory research, which has been conducted in two phases. In the first phase, we explored secondary data comprising of literature and various case studies. This was followed by a second phase of qualitative data collection concentrating on interviews. Prior to running the interviews, a pilot study was conducted to validate the interviews questions.

A. Data

Firstly, a pilot was conducted in which a qualitative data set of nine interviews was collected. The narratives of these interviews were then analysed to verify if the findings were indicative of the information being sought by researchers. Secondly, a total of ten interviews were conducted particularly focusing on project managers in a variety of fields, and this forms the actual data set for this research.

B. Method

Gioia method was used to analyse the data for this research. Gioia is a systematic approach to new concept development and grounded theory articulation [17]. During the analysis, we sieved 1st order concepts, followed by 2nd order themes and finally derived aggregate dimensions. This three step process was adopted to bring in transparency and rigor to the process of inductive research (see Figure 1 for the steps of this process) [18].

In the 1st order concept analysis, researchers adhered to informants terms, with little attempt to distil categories. After data collection, the interviews were transcribed to obtain the first order concepts. As a result, a large number of categories were derived in this step. These were then analysed to identify the themes emerging from data. Once we had 2nd order themes, the finding were then checked against literature to verify that these were "new", i.e., a contribution. As the research progressed to the 2nd order theme, it sought similarities and differences among the 1st order concepts. Upon confirmation that the findings are new, further literature review, and identifying similarities and differences, the aggregate dimensions were finalized. This eventually reduced the number of categories, which were then given labels or phrasal descriptors. Once this data structure of themes and concepts was created, we investigated to distil them further into aggregate dimensions.

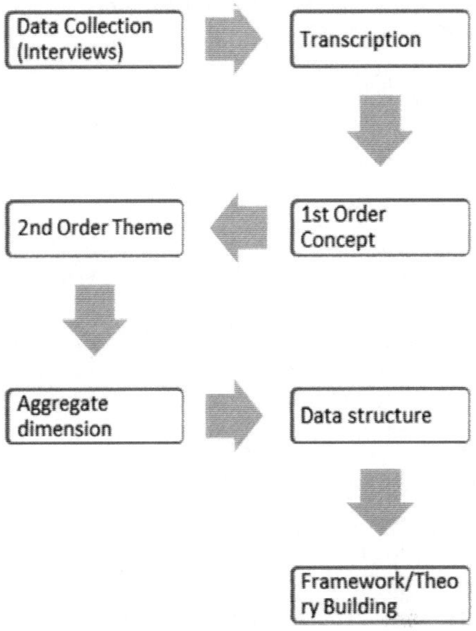

Figure 1. Method.

V. PRELIMINARY FINDINGS AND FUTURE RESEARCH

A successful digital transformation initiative needs to holistically look into customer experience, organisational culture, business model, processes, technologies, leadership and capabilities, and size of the company [7][12][14][19]. In order to have an edge over such rapid changes, companies need to ensure that they are ready to embrace disruptions and fill skills gaps in their organisations. Skills are the most valuable and essential resource in knowledge economy [5]. With markets becoming increasingly complex, complex problem solving, coordinating with others and people management become crucial aspects [20].

From the dataset collected and analysed, project managers have emphasized the importance of soft skills at various avenues. Additionally, they have also shed light on factors, which can impact skills development culture in an organization, for example, the size of the company. "Environment plays an important role in skills development; we might pick up skills according to the need of the environment", indicates the importance of organisations being conducive of developing their workforce. Project managers have highlighted other factors such as size of projects, mentoring, guidance, etc., during the interviews. It was well supported across various domains, such as defense, construction, information technology, etc. Some soft skills considered important by project managers (derived from interviews) are listed in Table I.

TABLE I. ESSENTIAL SOFT SKILLS:PM PERSPECTIVE

Essential Soft Skills: PM Perspective
Communication
Emotional Intelligence
Empathy
Leadership
Motivation
Resistance
Conflict Resolution
Professionalism
Negotiation

In absence of organisational efforts to develop a workforce, project managers mentioned that self-performance, reflection, individual personality, lessons learnt from past projects, type of people they work with, zeal to learn more aid as the factors that motivated them to develop soft skills. One of the key findings also indicated that the majority of the project managers realized the importance of soft skills during their experience and had little or no knowledge prior to work experience. This certainly had some exception for people who were natural leaders or in cases where their upbringing included elements like leadership opportunities, were taught to stand up, parental guidance to manage, sports etc. Some of the motivators mentioned by project managers during the interviews have been summarized in Table II below.

TABLE II. SOFT SKILLS MOTIVATORS

Soft Skills Motivators
Conducive Environment
Reflection : Past Projects
Self – Assessment
Need of Environment
Communication is the Key
Team Management
New Industry/Environment
Collaboration
Mentoring
Team Members
Individual Personalities in Team
Employee Engagement

Though some factors helped practicing project managers to identify the importance of soft skills, in absence of proper training, they struggled with certain issues like the level of comfort colleagues have when getting to the people's side of things, judgmental point of view, underestimating soft skills, being mistaken as trying to micromanage and most importantly finding the right balance of expression. These are some of the preliminary findings from the interviews conducted thus far. A detailed and comprehensive analysis will be conducted once the data collection is complete.

VI. CONCLUSION AND FUTURE RESEARCH

In this research, we have been able to identify some emerging themes from the data collected thus far, which are indicative of the importance of soft skills in digital transformation projects. Essential soft skills such as communication, emotional intelligence, leadership, etc., have been derived from the data set as well. Additionally, the data set is also reflective of soft skills motivators and suggestions for training project managers to groom their soft skills. Even though the data set looks promising at this stage, this research is an ongoing research and future steps have been planned, wherein the researchers aims to conduct a total of 30 interviews (inclusive of 10 already conducted) with project managers across various domains. These interviews will also be analysed using the Gioia method to obtain the findings of the project. The results of this research will not only contribute to the overall development of organisations by identifying key soft skills required by project manager, but also provide a competitive edge over their competitors. This would also aid organisations by encouraging them to reinvest the cost of recruiting new managers into their own assets and developing them further.

REFERENCES

[1] S. Shinde, S. Kimbahune, D. Singh, V. Deshpande, D. Piplani, and K. Srinivasan, mKRISHI BAIF: Digital transformation in livestock services. In Proceedings of the India HCI 2014 Conference on Human Computer Interaction, pp. 148-153, December 2014.

[2] S. Sandeep, IYC World Soft Infrastructure Pvt Ltd. Learning System for Digitalisation of An Educational Institution. U.S. Patent Application 13/122,620, 2011.

[3] P. Parviainen, M. Tihinen, J. Kääriäinen, and S. Teppola. Tackling the digitalization challenge: how to benefit from digitalization in practice. International journal of information systems and project management, 5(1), pp.63-77, 2017.

[4] T. Berger, and B. Frey. Digitalisation, jobs and convergence in Europe: Strategies for closing the skills gap (Vol. 50). Oxford: Oxford Martin School, 2016.

[5] F. KOHLBACHER. Skills 4.0: How CEOs shape the future of work in Asia, 2017.

[6] E. Piccinini, R.W. Gregory, and L.M. Kolbe, Changes in the producer-consumer relationship-towards digital transformation. Changes, 3(4), pp.1634-1648, 2015.

[7] A. Ustundag and E. Cevikcan, Industry 4.0: managing the digital transformation. Springer, 2017.

[8] H. Shaughnessy, Creating digital transformation: strategies and steps. Strategy & Leadership, 2018.

[9] A. Bounfour, Digital futures, digital transformation. Progress in IS. Cham. Springer International Publishing, 10, pp. 978-3, 2016.

[10] G. Westerman, D. Bonnet and A. McAfee, The nine elements of digital transformation. MIT Sloan Management Review, 55(3), pp. 1-6, 2014.

[11] R.S. Schuler, Repositioning the human resource function: transformation or demise? Academy of Management Perspectives, 4(3), pp. 49-60, 1990.

[12] G. C. Kane, D. Palmer, A. N. Phillips, D. Kiron, and N. Buckley, Strategy, not technology, drives digital transformation. MIT Sloan Management Review and Deloitte University Press, 14(1-25), 2015.

[13] P.R. Harris and K.G. Harris. Managing effectively through teams. Team Performance Management: An International Journal, 1996.

[14] A. M. Townsend, S. M. DeMarie, and A. Hendrickson, Virtual teams: Technology and the workplace of the future. IEEE Engineering Management Review, 28(2), pp.69-80, 2000.

[15] I. L. Panel, Digital transformation: A framework for ICT literacy. Educational Testing Service, pp.1-53, 2002.

[16] A. Singh and T. Hess, How Chief Digital Officers promote the digital transformation of their companies. MIS Quarterly Executive, 16(1), 2017.

[17] D. A. Gioia, K. G. Corley and A. L. Hamilton, Seeking qualitative rigor in inductive research: Notes on the Gioia methodology. Organizational research methods, 16(1), pp.15-31, 2013.

[18] K. G. Corley and D. A. Gioia, Identity ambiguity and change in the wake of a corporate spin-off. Administrative science quarterly, 49(2), pp.173-208, 2004.

[19] J. Loonam, S. Eaves, V. Kumar and G. Parry, Towards digital transformation: Lessons learned from traditional organizations. Strategic Change, 27(2), pp.101-109, 2018.

[20] P. Lagadec, Learning processes for crisis management in complex organizations. Journal of Contingencies and Crisis management, 5(1), pp.24-31, 1997.

Research on Criteria for Personal Information Collection Consent Based on Trust

Goo Yeon Lee
Dept. of Computer and Communication Eng.
Kangwon National University
Chuncheon-si, Gangwon-do, Korea
email: leegyeon@kangwon.ac.kr

Hwa Jong Kim
Dept. of Computer and Communication Eng.
Kangwon National University
Chuncheon-si, Gangwon-do, Korea
email: hjkim@kangwon.ac.kr

***Abstract*—In this paper, we study the criteria for determining whether to provide personal information to a service provider based on its trust. The study analyzes the relation between the service provider's trust, the profit gained from subscribing to the service, the expected loss of the potential personal information leakage or misuse, and the activation cost. The analyzed results will be useful for the development of an automated personal information consent algorithm in the future.**

Keywords-trust; personal information; consent; collection.

I. Introduction and Related Work

Generally, when a user wants to use a specific service related to the individual, a personal information collection procedure is performed by the service provider. In case of offline, the consent process for collecting personal information is signed face-to-face. In the online case, the user understands the terms of processing personal information through a screen of a computer or a smart phone, and the consent or rejection indication thereof is performed. However, when we actually agree to the collection of personal information, we worry about whether our personal information may be misused later and some loss occurs.

In many cases, the confidence in a service provider is determined based on its reputation or the past experience of using other services from the provider. However, some users may consent without any prior knowledge of a service provider, which is recommended to avoid because there is a risk of personal information abuse such as voice phishing.

Recently, a lot of researches have been made to measure and utilize mutual or objective trust in the exchange of information between various entities on the Internet. If trusts from different entities on the Internet can be developed and quantified, these trusts can be used when providing personal information to service providers for using specific services.

There are many research and standardization efforts on trust. International Standardization of Trust Technology in ITU-T SG13 and ITU-T Y.3052 document [1] classify trust into direct trust such as belief, faith, confidence and dependence, and indirect trust, such as reputation, recommendation, expectation and experience. In addition, trust value evaluation methods based on knowledge, experience and reputation have been proposed [2][3] and several studies related to trust have been conducted [4]. However, it is considered that there has not been any research on the trust combined with the consent for providing personal information when joining services.

When a trust is applied to the service provider that collects personal information, the user can make a decision on whether to provide personal information based on the trust. However, trust cannot be 100% certain, so no matter how high the trust is, there is a possibility of personal information leakage and misuse. Therefore, there is a tradeoff between the benefit of using the service and the potential loss from personal information leakage and misuse. Accordingly, it is necessary to make an optimal decision to ensure that the benefit can be greater than the potential loss. In this study, we analyze the criteria for judging whether to provide personal information by quantifying the benefit obtained from the service and the risk of personal information exposure and abuse based on the trust of the service provider.

In this paper, we perform an analysis in Section 2 and discuss results in Section 3. Finally, we draw a conclusion in Section 4.

II. Analysis Model

In this section, we analyze the relation between the benefit from using the service and the potential loss due to the exposure or misuse of personal information based on the trust. The followings are definitions of parameters used in this section.

T : It indicates the trust of a provider. It has a value between 0 and 1. A trust of 1 represents the case where the trust is 100%, and 0 represents the case where there is no trust at all. This value is estimated by a trust model. We expect that some trust rating companies like the existing credit rating companies will be formed and users may obtain the trust information of providers from the companies.

R : It presents the risk to be taken by providing personal information. This can be expressed as a function of provider's trust. It has a value from 0 to 1, and has a value of 0 when there is no risk at all and a value of 1 when the risk is 100%.

P : It represents the service profit that a user obtains from using the service. This value may be specified by a user, but a normal value can be recommended as the service is settled.

L : It shows the expected loss if the user's personal information is exposed or misused. This value may be specified by a user, or may use the amount of the court's reimbursement decision for recent personal information leakage.

C : It represents the activation cost. The user does not use the service immediately just because the service profit is greater than the expected loss. Basically, the net profit must be above the activation cost. This value is different depending on the user's disposition and situation.

We consider the risk R for the service provider according to the trust(T). If T is 1, it has 100% confidence and R=0. And if T is 0, it is 100% dangerous and R=1. In general, risk decreases sharply as trust increases from zero, and gradually decreases after some confidence. In other words, risk is convex down when trust changes from 0 to 1. There are many relations that satisfy these conditions, but we choose the following approach. The exponential function is suitable as a function that satisfies these characteristics. If the boundary condition of $R = 1$ when $T = 0$ and $R = 0$ when T=1 is applied, we suggest the following relation.

$$R = \frac{e^{-AT} - e^{-A}}{1 - e^{-A}}, \quad (1)$$

where A is a characteristic constant representing the confidence sensitivity. When A is larger, the risk has smaller value even at the same trust value. On the contrary, when A becomes small, it represents a situation of judicious judgment. In Figure 1, we give a graph of the relationship between T and R when A is 1, 3 and 5. The measurement of A value is outside the scope of this study, so it may be determined sociologically or economically. We expect that trust rating companies will assess the characteristics of a country or society to determine its confidence sensitivity and provide it to users.

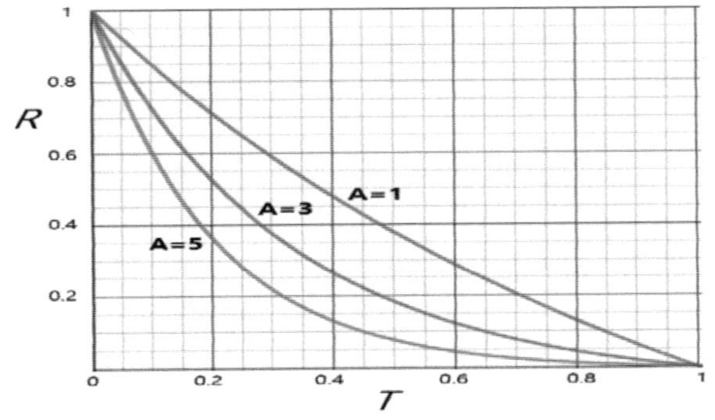

Figure 1. Relation between T and R when A=1, 3 and 5

The user subscribes to the service only when the net profit after subtracting the expected loss from the profit is greater than the activation cost. Here, we use the value of risk R as the probability that personal information will be exposed or misused. Therefore, when the following formula is established, the user provides consent in the agreement procedure to the service provider.

$$P - L \cdot R \geq C \quad (2)$$

Substituting (1) into (2) gives the following equation:

$$P - L \cdot \frac{e^{-AT} - e^{-A}}{1 - e^{-A}} \geq C \quad (3)$$

Solving (3) with respect to T, we get

$$T \geq -\frac{1}{A} \ln \frac{(P-C)(1-e^{-A}) + Le^{-A}}{L} \quad (4)$$

III. RESULTS AND DISCUSSION

From (3) and (4), we have $P_{\min} = C + L$ when T=0 and $P_{\min} = C$ when T=1. That is, the value of P is meaningful when it exists in the interval between C and $C + L$. In Figure 2, we give the graph of minimum trust as P varies when C = 5000KRW(Korean won) and L = 10000KRW. Parameter A was assigned a value of 3.

When P=5000, the profit P from signing up for the service is just equal to C = 5000. In the case, there is no reason to join the service if there is any risk. That means the user can join only if there is no risk of personal information leakage or misuse. When P = 15000, there remains 5000KRW even if 100% loss (L=10000) is assumed. In this case, even if there is a 100% loss of personal information leakage or abuse, motivation for signing up is sufficient. In addition, we can see that when P = 6000, the minimum trust should be about 0.649. However, when P = 11000, the customer will sign up for the service even if the trust is lowered to 0.161.

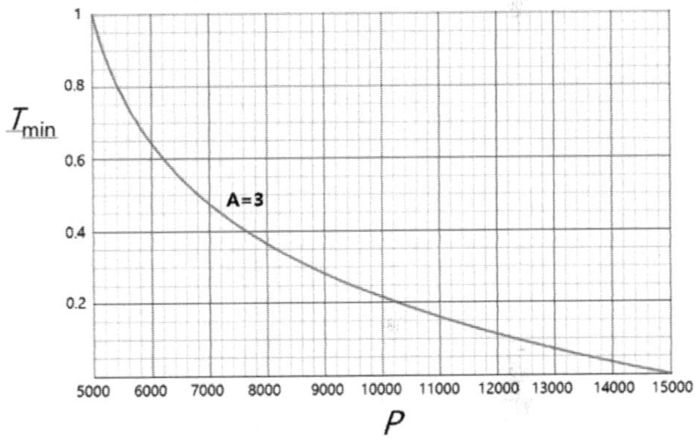

Figure 2. Minimum trust as P varies when C = 5000KRW, L = 10000 KRW and A =3

IV. CONCLUSION

In this paper, we study the case where a user provides personal information to a service provider. In the study, we define the provider's risk based on its trust, and then derive the decision equation for the personal information collection consent by analyzing the profit gained when subscribing the service and the expected loss of the provider's personal information leakage or misuse. The analyzed results will be useful for the consent decision to provide personal information at the time of subscription.

ACKNOWLEDGMENT

This work was supported by Institute for Information & communications Technology Promotion (IITP) grant funded by the Korea government (Ministry of Science and ICT) (No.2018-0-00261, GDPR Compliant Personally Identifiable Information Management Technology for IoT Environment).

REFERENCES

[1] Telecommunication Standardization Sector of ITU, ITU-T Y.3052: Overview of trust provisioning in information and communication technology infrastructures and services, Mar. 2017. Online: https://www.itu.int/rec/T-REC-Y.3052/en [accessed Jan. 2020]

[2] N. B. Truong, T. Um, B. Zhou, and G. M. Lee, “Strengthening the Blockchain-Based Internet of Value with Trust,” 2018 IEEE International Conference on Communications (ICC), 2018, pp.1-7.

[3] F. Alam and A. Paul, “A computational model for trust and reputation relationship in social network,” 2016 International Conference on Recent Trends in Information Technology (ICRTIT), 2016, pp.1-6.

[4] M. Jäger, S. Nadschläger, and J. Küng, “Concepts for Trust Propagation in Knowledge Processing Systems - A Brief Introduction and Overview,” 2018 17th IEEE International Conference On Trust, Security And Privacy In Computing And Communications/ 12th IEEE International Conference On Big Data Science And Engineering (TrustCom/BigDataSE), 2018, pp.1502-1505.

Perceived Benevolence Trust, Perceived Competence Trust, and Onshore Information Sytems Development Project Success

The Mediating Effect of Knowledge Transfer

Solomon A. Nurye, Temtim A. Desta
Information Systems Track
Addis Ababa University
Addis Ababa, Ethiopia
e-mail: Selemonabe@yahoo.com
e-mail: abtemtim@gmail.com

Shegaw A. Mengiste
School of Business
University of South Eastern Norway
Borre, Norway
e-mail: sme@usn.no

Abstract— **Despite the increased organizational spending on information systems outsourcing, delivering business values from outsourcing initiatives is still a challenge for business managers in a developing economy. In recent studies, there has been much interest in addressing the challenge from a relational perspective. This study examines whether perceived benevolence trust and perceived competence trust affect knowledge transfer, which, in turn, impacts onshore information systems development outsourcing success within the context of Ethiopia. Drawing from the social exchange theory, knowledge transfer, and information systems literature, a conceptual model is developed and it reveals that knowledge transfer mediates the effects of perceived benevolence trust and perceived competence trust on onshore information systems development outsourcing success. The findings contribute to research and practice in information systems outsourcing relationships.**

Keywords-Perceived Benevolence Trust; Perceived Competence Trust; Outsourcing; Information Systems.

I. INTRODUCTION

Information Systems Development (ISD) has become an important organizational activity for strategic and operational purposes [1]. Due to the highly competitive and rapidly changing business environment, organizations have been under great pressure to seek out strategies for the successful development and delivery of Information Systems (IS) products and services [1]. One of the popular strategies devised by client organizations is outsourcing [2].

Information Systems Development Outsourcing (ISDO) refers to a contractual agreement between a client and a vendor organization for the provision of IS development and/or implementation services, whereby the client contracts all or part of its ISD activities to the vendor [3]-[5]. ISDO approaches and practices are becoming well established and accepted business practices for reducing operational costs while gaining business value [6]. In the year 2017, worldwide Information Technology Outsourcing (ITO) contracts that worth USD 137.2 billion were signed [7]. The growth rate of ITO is estimated to be 2.4% Compound Annual Growth Rate (CAGR) from 2017 to 2021 [8]. Besides, a market survey by Gartner shows that ITO has a 60% contribution in the worldwide IT services market and with its higher contribution the market is estimated to reach $1.1 trillion in 2021 [9]. A rising trend of ITO in some developing countries like India, China, Brazil, Russia, and Malaysia has also been observed in recent years. On the other hand, the revenues from the outsourcing sector in Africa reached nearly US$ 2 billion in 2014, projected to grow at 30–40% annually, but Ethiopia has yet to reap the benefits from the sector [10].

Although ISDO market in Ethiopia is immature, most software development projects are undertaken by means of onshore outsourcing [11]. For example, in the five-year strategic plan (2011-2015), the Government of Ethiopia had shown a commitment for the implementation of 219 e-government projects with an estimated budget of 201.5 Million US dollars [12] by inviting local vendors to some of these ISD projects. Nevertheless, Information Systems Outsourcing (ISO) failures are reported in developing countries [13] [14].

In spite of the high failure rate of ISDO projects, business managers have continued to increase their ISDO investments, as they perceive value in it [15]. However, exhibiting the values of outsourcing remains a challenge for both the service provider and the client organizations [16] [17]. For example, Nuwangi et al. [18] described ISDO as complex process mainly due to multiple, and often conflicting client requirements, incongruence in interpreting client requirements, changes and uncontrolled growth in a project's scope and the existence of many user groups. Primarily, ISD is a knowledge-intensive work [19] and the required knowledge is dispersed across domains of specialization (e.g., business and technical knowledge) [20] [21]. Clients have rich business domain knowledge, but shallow technical knowledge. On the other hand, technical knowledge is mainly owned by vendor organizations, but they typically lack business domain knowledge [22]. Due to these factors, providing the agreed deliverables on time and with the required quality has become extremely difficult for vendors [23]-[25].

Prior studies have given attention to exploring the values of ISDO from the relational perspective because building and sustaining a flexible relationship can help outsourcing partners to overcome outsourcing challenges [17][26]. To successfully build the system, therefore, outsourcing partners need to interact and cooperate with each other [21] [26]. Their interaction and cooperation are highly required for exchanging knowledge about business needs, preferences, approaches to problems, as well as use and technical possibilities of the new information system [26] [27].

Some knowledge transfer can take place between outsourcing partners due to contractual obligations [16]. However, it is harder to formalize and communicate tacit knowledge (e.g., business processes and technical know-how) [28]. This type of knowledge creates difficulties on actors to formalize as well as to communicate as it is deeply rooted in action, commitment and involvement in a specific context [16] [29]. Hence, contractual requirements are insufficient for effective knowledge transfer to occur between parties engaged in ISO deals [17]. Lee et al. [17] further argued that it is difficult to specify every rule and agreement in a contract due to the complexity of outsourcing contracts. As a result, outsourcing partners need to pay heed to unwritten contracts to supplement the more formal contracts to achieve a successful outsourcing relationship. According to [30], trust is one of the intangible factors that could not be easily captured in the formal contract.

Trust has been widely studied in the social exchange literature as one of the relational factors that lead to successful business relationships [17]. As clients and vendors rely on each other's knowledge, trusting each other enables partners to work together and to transfer the necessary knowledge during the outsourced information systems development projects. Ko [26] suggests that trusting relationships lead to greater knowledge exchange as it facilitates voluntary exchange, which promotes knowledge transfer activities.

Although several scholars demonstrated the importance of clients' trust in vendors for successful knowledge transfer (e.g., [17] [26]), the impact of the perceptions of the vendors being trusted by their clients on knowledge transfer to the clients is a potentially critical, but overlooked issue. According to Serva et al. [31, p. 627], "trust forms in the mind of the trustor", and therefore others cannot observe it. In the client-vendor relationship, the vendor is the main source of technical knowledge (e.g., technical know-how and ISD methodology) and the client is the recipient of the vendor's technical knowledge. In this study, the vendor is a knowledge source and the client is a knowledge recipient. During their relationships, the vendor may or may not feel trusted by the client although the client has trust in its vendor. This unidirectional conceptualization of trust (i.e., knowledge recipient's trust in a knowledge source) cannot provide a complete picture of the knowledge transfer behavior of actors engaged in a social exchange relationship. Knowledge recipients' trust in the knowledge sources needs to be expressed in actions so that knowledge sources can aware of recipients' trust in them and get actively involved in the knowledge transfer process. Thus, it is the observed trust-related actions of a partner that influence the level of trust formed in another partner [31].

Furthermore, literature so far has mainly focused on knowledge transfer in the offshore information systems development context of developed countries [2], where both the outsourcing markets and knowledge transfer experience are relatively matured when compared with that of developing economies. In addition, there appears to be a major shift toward domestic outsourcing [1]. Addressing this gap from the context of a developing economy is significant to create an understanding of outsourcing practitioners on how to facilitate knowledge transfer successfully across organizational boundaries and to drive greater business value from their ISO initiatives. Therefore, it is necessary to examine the kinds of social contexts in a developing economy in general, and Ethiopia, in particular, that can enhance knowledge sources' perception of being trusted by their recipients and how this felt trust is related to knowledge transfer and ISDO success. Therefore, this study seeks to address the following research question: To what extent does knowledge sources' perception of being trusted in their competence and benevolence by their recipients impact knowledge transfer, and, ultimately, onshore ISDO success?

In the following sections, a presentation of the conceptual underpinnings of the theoretical model that draws upon multiple areas of research, including information systems, trust, and social exchange theory is made. Then, the research model is developed and hypotheses are formulated. Thereafter, a plan for further study is briefly described. Finally, the paper concludes with a discussion of the implications of the study.

II. BACKGROUND LITERATURE

A. *Information Systems Outsourcing Success*

Defining information systems outsourcing success has been a challenge for the field of IS. Previous studies defined ISO success in different ways. For instance, outsourcing success is described as the attainment of strategic, technological and economic benefits through outsourcing activities [32]. By extending Grover et al.'s [32] model of outsourcing success, Lee and Kim [33] introduced business perspective and user perspective as dimensions of outsourcing success. Additionally, overall satisfaction is integrated into the ISO success definition [34]. In sum, different studies show that ISDO success is a multi-dimensional construct consisting of strategic, economic, technological, and relational benefits and overall satisfaction from the ISDO arrangements.

B. *Trust*

Due to the complex nature of trust, prior research has given diverse interpretations of trust. According to McAllister [35], there are two key dimensions of trust: (1) affect-based, or benevolence trust, and (2) cognitive-based, or competence trust. Affect-based is relationship-oriented [36] and it is largely based on ''emotional'' bonds between individuals [37]. This dimension of trust is the belief about reciprocated care and concern [35]. In contrast to affect-based, cognitive-based trust is the belief about exchanging partner's competency [35]. It is mainly task-oriented [36]. According to Chowdhury [37], a separate investigation of these two dimensions of trust is important as each has a distinct pattern of association with knowledge transfer. Besides the complexity of trust, the literature is ambiguous about the multilevel nature of trust [38]. Zaheer et al. [38] empirically find that the effects of trust in the inter-organizational context are distinct from the individual level of analysis. Thus, this study focuses on inter-organizational perspective of trust.

Earlier IS studies have examined trust as an antecedent of knowledge transfer [17] [26]. In order to ensure successful transfer of knowledge, the existence of trustful relationship between outsourcing partners is necessary [39]. Knowledge transfer as a mediator factor is introduced between trust and onshore ISDO success. This assumption is consistent with prior works (e.g., [17] [26]). Empirical evidences have also shown that both benevolence and competence trust have a positive influence on knowledge transfer at the dyadic, team, and individual levels [37] [40] [41]. Accordingly, this paper proposes a trust-based relationship model (see Figure 1) for onshore ISDO success.

III. SOCIAL EXCHANGE THEORY (SET)

There are a number of theories to be used by researchers to gain a comprehensive understanding of the relationships among trust, knowledge transfer, and ISDO success. Social exchange theory (SET) is one of the most prominent theories to understand the social behavior of humans in an economic context. According to SET, actors exchanging resources voluntarily via a social exchange relationship by expecting some future returns [42]. SET builds on essential social norms' constructs, for example, trust. Trust is one of the relational exchange variables that leads to a successful exchange relationship [43]. It assumes that both parties involved in the exchange relationship invest without any guarantee that such an investment will produce a future return so that the risk of this investment requires trust [44]. While the origin of SET is at the individual level, it has also been used to explain inter-organizational behavior during economic undertakings [42]. Creating inter-organizational relationships helps organizations cope with resource scarcity while achieving goals of reducing vulnerability and uncertainty [45].

Social exchange theory has served as an underlying theoretical model for examining outsourcing relationships and client-vendor exchanges [45]. In ISDO relationships, clients and vendors carry out different tasks for one another and exchange valuable resources [45]. Here, resources could consist a variety of things including knowledge, ISD methods and approaches, and software packages. In the context of this particular research, the resource exchanged between clients and vendors would be knowledge and the outsourced ISD project is viewed as an economic undertaking. It is often argued that clients bring in business knowledge and vendors bring in technical knowledge [30]. In addition to the social exchange of knowledge, clients and vendors need to act on each other's knowledge, combine it during the development of the outsourced project [46] or implementation of the system [26] [47].

In conclusion, this paper proposes a trust-based relationship model (see Figure 1) for onshore ISD outsourcing which includes (1) perceived benevolence trust, (2) perceived competence trust, (3) knowledge transfer as a mediator between perceived benevolence trust, perceived competence trust and onshore ISD outsourcing success, (4) onshore ISD outsourcing success as the dependent variable.

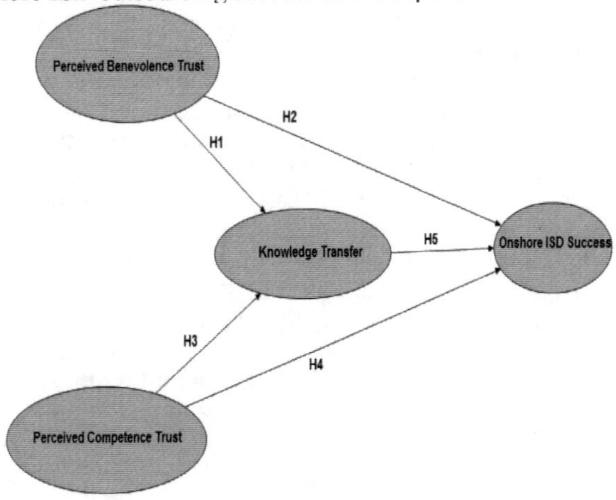

Figure 1. Conceptual Model

IV. RESEARCH MODEL AND HYPOTHESES

The research model as illustrated in Figure 1 proposes that knowledge transfer mediates the relationship between perceived benevolence and perceived competence trusts and onshore ISD success.

A. *Perceived Benevolence Trust*

In this paper, with respect to the knowledge source, perceived benevolence trust is defined as the perception of the knowledge source being trusted by the recipient to have goodwill or positive intentions toward it [31]. When a client is perceived to have benevolence (goodwill) to the vendor, the vendor will be more sensitive to its clients' needs and expectations and more willing to help the client [41]. For example, when clients engage in risk-taking behaviors such as reduced controlling and monitoring of vendors' system development activities, vendors can get signals about how much clients trust them, and this felt trust could have positive exchange outcomes [48]. Hence, such perception of trust will alleviate the problem of knowledge hoarding and motivate the vendor to engage in the knowledge transfer process [41].

Conversely, when vendors' felt not trustworthy about their benevolence, they tend to be less interested to know the knowledge requirements of a client firm, which, in turn, impacts the quality of knowledge to be transferred to the client. In this regard, Chini [49] argues that effective knowledge transfer necessitates proper identification of the knowledge requirements of a knowledge recipient by a knowledge source. By doing so, the knowledge source can provide "what is appropriate, in a form that is appropriate" [49, p. 65]. Thus, it can be argued that when vendors perceived that their clients see them as not having goodwill or positive intentions to them, the vendors will not be encouraged to take risks by performing actions that result in their being vulnerable to the clients. Taking the above into consideration, the following hypothesis is formulated:

H1: Knowledge source's perceived benevolence trust is positively associated with knowledge transfer.

Additionally, a direct effect of perceived benevolence trust on onshore ISD project success is proposed. Vendors' perceptions of being trusted by their clients can contribute to outsourcing success as it improves openness and working relationship, gives room for flexibility, and reduces the cost of coordinating activities [50]. On the other hand, when vendors' perceived benevolence trust is low, they become skeptical of the sustainability of their relationships with their clients. Thus, they might give less attention to the acquisition of knowledge about the long-term business strategies of their clients. According to Lacity and Willcocks [51], vendors' deliveries of the promised high-quality software product is hampered by the inadequacy of knowledge about the long-term business strategy of the clients. In general, a short-term oriented relationship of vendors will hamper the values to be derived from the ISO initiatives of the client firms. However, vendors seeking long-term relationships with their clients are committing resources to an ISD project and investing extra time and effort on it [52]. These vendors strive for improving customer value. They give priority to achieving client satisfaction by properly managing their customer value improvement process which is aimed at showing their competence and gain their market reputation [52]. This will generate value and enhance the outsourcing performance to clients.

Feeling of not trusted can also make vendors' development efforts limited to the officially agreed technical systems specifications. In other words, the vendor will be reserved to come up with innovative technical solutions to the client's business problem as the outsourcing service provider may feel that it will be harmed in this particular relationship. Sedera et al. [6] suggest that client satisfaction in outsourcing deals doesn't necessarily mean the delivery of the formal specifications, rather it entails delivering business value beyond that, for example, the introduction of new business processes and adding new software components. Therefore, only the clients' trust in the vendors is not leading to a successful transfer of knowledge to clients, which, in turn, affects ISO success. Rather, the trust-related behaviors exhibited by the recipient matters. Clients can be shared the value generated by vendors [53] when their trust in vendors is practically demonstrable, for example, alignment of risks and incentives associated with contracts. Thus, it is hypothesized that:

H2: Knowledge source's perceived benevolence trust is positively associated with onshore ISD success.

B. Perceived Competence Trust

Empirical studies in ISO settings show that knowledge recipient's perception of a knowledge source's expertise is positively associated with knowledge transfer (e.g., [26] [54]). However, it is unclear what will happen to knowledge transfer to the recipient when the knowledge source has the perception of not trusted by the recipient. Concerning the knowledge source, perceived competence trust is defined as the perception of the knowledge source being trusted by the client about its expertise to accomplish outsourcing tasks and reliability to carry out its promises [35] [55]. Vendors as knowledge sources are more likely to show positive knowledge transfer behavior when they felt trusted by their clients. For instance, if vendors' perception of being trusted by their clients about their competence is high, they tend to be motivated to work together and to put in extra effort for transferring the necessary knowledge to the client [17]. Moreover, vendors' willingness to assist clients to understand their technical knowledge during the IS development activities will be increased, thus knowledge transfer to clients will be facilitated [56]. Vendors' perception of being trusted in their competence will facilitate knowledge transfer to clients as it increases vendors' willingness to transfer knowledge and collaborate whenever necessary [57]. Positive perception of being trusted by clients will improve the client-vendor relationship. This trusting relationship will increase the vendor's engagement with the client's business problem and lead to a greater amount of knowledge transfer to the client [47].

Contrarily, when vendors felt that their clients are in lack of trust about their development capability, they will be less motivated to work collaboratively with the client. This lack of collaboration can create difficulties in outsourcing partners to properly identify and implement the most efficient and applicable technical solution for the problem at hand [6]. Based on the above arguments, the following hypothesis is proposed:

H3: Knowledge source's perceived competence trust is positively related to knowledge transfer.

In this paper, the direct effect of trust on ISO success is also proposed. Empirical studies show that a high level of competence trust in a social exchange relationship improves ISO performance (e.g., [26]). However, the effect of vendors' perceptions of being trusted by their clients about their competence on successfully accomplishing onshore ISD projects is not empirically investigated. A higher level of vendor's felt competence trust makes the vendor cooperative and willing to work closely with the client [50]. As a result, the vendor tends to provide immense support to its client. Besides, the vendor is more likely to work hard to meet its client expectations. These trust related actions of the vendor will motivate the client to engage in a more open and effective communication [50], which enables the vendor to obtain a better understanding of its client's expectations on its tasks and to achieve a higher task performance. Taking the above into consideration, it can be argued that when vendors felt trusted by their clients, they tend to act more responsibly to fulfill the expectations of their clients, thus it leads to higher ISO success. Hence, the following hypothesis is formulated:

H4: Knowledge source's perceived competence trust is positively associated with onshore ISD success.

C. *Knowledge Transfer and Onshore ISD Success*

Studies on information systems suggest that knowledge transfer is one of the key factors that impacts ISO success. In this study, onshore ISD success refers to the overall organizational benefits obtained from outsourcing by a client firm [58]. These include the client's satisfaction with the developed system, delivery of the project within the agreed time in the contract, derived values from the outsourcing relationship, relationship satisfaction, and overall satisfaction. On the other hand, knowledge transfer is defined as the flow of knowledge from a knowledge source so that it is applied by a recipient [47]. Table I summarizes the definitions of each construct of the research model.

TABLE I. CONCEPTUAL DEFINITION OF THE CONSTRUCTS

Construct	Definition	Reference
ISDO Success	The overall organizational benefits obtained from outsourcing by a client firm.	[58]
Knowledge Transfer	The flow of knowledge from a knowledge source so that it is applied by a recipient.	[47]
Perceived Benevolence Trust	The perception of the knowledge source being trusted by the recipient to have goodwill or positive intentions toward it.	[31]
Perceived Competence Trust	The perception of the knowledge source being trusted by the client about its expertise to accomplish outsourcing tasks and reliability to carry out its promises.	[35, 55]

Knowledge transfer in ISO relationships increases the level of shared knowledge [59], reduces development costs, and creates a strong relationship between partners [57]. When essential knowledge is transferred effectively between clients and vendors, they can better practice their outsourcing activities and develop a long term outsourcing relationship [17] [60]. Moreover, Teo and Bhattacherjee [16] argue that transferred knowledge will generate value for clients when it is effectively utilized. Similarly, Park and Lee [54] suggest that knowledge transfer can improve information systems development performance due to improved decision making and coordination. In sum, a successful transfer of knowledge will increase the chance of ISO success [61]. Taking the above into consideration, the following hypothesis is proposed:

H5: Knowledge transfer is positively related to onshore ISD success.

V. A PLAN FOR FUTURE WORK

The proposed research model will be tested empirically with data collected through a survey of client and vendor project managers in a matched-pair sample. A step-by-step procedure recommended by MacKenzie et al. [62] will be used to develop the survey instrument. Measures of ISO success will be adapted from Xu and Yao [63]. For the knowledge transfer, the instrument developed by Teo and Bhattacherjee [16] will be adapted. The measures of perceived benevolence trust and measure perceived competence trust will be adapted from Ko [26]. All constructs of this survey will be measured using multi-item scales with seven-point Likert rating scales.

The unit of analysis of this study is onshore information system development outsourcing projects in Ethiopia. Therefore, project-level data on each project will be collected from two members from the same project: a client project manager and a vendor project manager. The data will be analyzed by using Smart-PLS 3.0. Using the Smart-PLS software, data will be analyzed at two stages. In the first stage, the measurement model will be tested to ensure that the constructs had sufficient psychometric properties (i.e., reliability and validity of the measures). In the second stage, an assessment of the structural model will be done to test and provide statistics on the strength of the hypothesized relationships among the constructs.

VI. CONCLUSION

This study aims to examine the extent to which the effects of perceived benevolence trust and perceived competence trust on onshore ISD project success are mediated by knowledge transfer in a client-vendor dyad. The conceptual model is an attempt to provide an alternative lens for viewing trust in a client-vendor relationship. This study is expected to have implications for theory and practice. Theoretically, this paper extends prior trust research by introducing the concepts—perceived benevolence trust and perceived competence trust— as essential aspects of trust in a dyadic business relationship. Moreover, it shows that knowledge source's perceived benevolence and perceived competence trusts play important roles in influencing knowledge transfer to the recipient that in turn affects onshore ISD project success. Practically, the results of the study are expected to provide useful insights on how IS/IT managers of a developing economy can create trusting relationships with outsourcing partners for effective knowledge transfer to take place and to ensure onshore ISD project success. First, the study shows that an outsourced IS development project is knowledge-intensive work and its success depends on the successful transfer of the requisite knowledge. This can be achieved through a trusting relationship between outsourcing partners that encourages closer cooperation & open discussions and avoids opportunistic behavior. Second, this study shows the importance of paying due attention to tacit knowledge that is difficult to codify and articulate, but outsourcing practitioners can only transfer it successfully through their direct interactions.

REFERENCES

[1] L. Kappelman, E. McLean, V. Johnson, R. Torres, C. Maurer, and K. Kim, "The 2018 SIM IT Issues and Trends Study," MIS Quarterly Executive, vol.18, no.1, pp. 51-84, 2019.

[2] J-J Wang, N. Sasanipoor, and M-M Wang, "How PMBOK standard and partnership quality influence IT outsourcing success: An investigation of the mediated moderation effects," Journal of Global Information Technology Management, pp. 1-19, 2018.

[3] L. Bergkvist and O. Fredriksson, "Outsourcing terms: A literature review from an ISD perspective," ECIS 2008 Proceedings, Paper 129, 2008.

[4] S. M. Nuwangi and D. Sedera, “Lessons from a filed IS outsourcing project,” Twenty-Third Pacific Asia Conference on Information Systems, 2019.

[5] S. U. Khan, M. Niazi, and R. Ahmad, "Barriers in the Selection of Offshore Software Development Outsourcing Vendors: An Exploratory Study Using a Systematic Literature Review," Information and Software Technology, vol.53, pp. 693-706, 2011.

[6] D. Sedera, S. Lokuge, H. Krcmar, and S. C. Srivastava, The future of outsourcing in the Asia-Pacific Region: Implications for research and practice—panel report from PACIS 2014, 2014.

[7] KPMG, "Global IT-BPO Outsourcing Deals Analysis: annual analysis for 2017," https://assets.kpmg/content/dam/kpmg/in/pdf/2018/05/KPMG-Deal-Tracker-2017.pdf (accessed July 25th 2017).

[8] A. Yan, “Effective outsourcing governance: A configurational approach,” PACIS 2018 Proceeding, 147, 2018.

[9] I. Gartner, “ Forecast: IT Services, Worldwide, 2015-2021, 2017 Update. Gartner, Stamford, USA,” URL: htttps://wwwgartner.com (visited on 16/01/2019).

[10] M. Lixi, and M. Dahan, "ICT as an enabler of ICT as an enabler of transformation in Ethiopia,", 2014, Washington, DC: World Bank Group, http://documents.worldbank.org/curated/en/938461468256731409/ICT-as-an-enabler-of-Transformation-in-Ethiopia (visited on 25/04/2019).

[11] S. A. Nurye, A. Molla, and T. A. Desta, “Factors Influencing Knowledge Transfer in Onshore InformationSystems Outsourcing in Ethiopia,” African Journal of Information Systems, vol.11, issue 4, article 2, pp. 279-298, 2019.

[12] United Nations Conference on Trade and Development (UNCTAD), 2013, retrieved January 30, 2019 from http://unctad.org/meetings/en/Presentation/CSTD_2013_WSIS_Ethiopia_E-Gov_Strategy.pdf.

[13] K. Billy Mathias BM, O. Oludayo O, and K. Ray M, "Identifying Critical Success Factors: the case of ERP Systems in Higher Education," The African Journal of Information Systems, vol. 6, issue 3, Article 1, 2014.

[14] D. Beyene, S. Negash, T. Bandyopadhyay, "Information Technology outsourcing Risk Management Practices in Higher Educational Institutes in Ethiopia-a qualitative study," Twenty-first Americas Conference on Information Systems, Puerto Rico, pp. 1-12, 2015.

[15] C. Schwarz,“Toward an understanding of the nature and conceptualization of outsourcing success,” Information and Management, vol.51, pp.152–164, 2014.

[16] T. S. Teo and A. Bhattacherjee, “Knowledge transfer and utilization in IT outsourcing partnerships: A preliminary model of antecedents and outcomes,” Information and Management, vol. 51, pp.176-186, 2014.

[17] J-N Lee, M. Q. Huynh, and R. Hirschheim, “An integrative model of trust on IT outsourcing: Examining a bilateral perspective,” Information Systems Frontiers, vol. 10, pp.145-163, 2008.

[18] S. M. Nuwangi, D. Sedera, and S. C. Srivastava, "Multi-layered Control Mechanisms in Software Development Outsourcing,” PACIS 2018 Proceedings. 167, 2018.

[19] A. Tiwana and E.R. McLean, " Expertise Integration and Creativity in Information Systems Development," Journal of Management Information Systems ,vol., no. 22, pp. 13–43, 2005.

[20] Y. Li, Yang, B. Yang, Y. Feng, and G. Li, "Organizational Structure and Absorptive Capacity in Offshore Outsourcing," PACIS 2014 Proceedings, 307, doi: aisel.aisnet.org/pacis2014/307.

[21] L-G. Pee, A. Kankanhalli, and H-W. Kim, "Knowledge Sharing in Information Systems Development: A Social Interdependence Perspective," Journal of the Association for Information Systems ,vol. 11, Issue 10, pp. 550-575, 2010.

[22] L.P. Willcocks, J. Hindle, D. Feeny, and M. Lacity, "IT and Business Process Outsourcing: The Knowledge Potential," Information Systems Management, vol. 21, no. 3, pp.7-15, 2004.

[23] R. T. Nakatsu and C. L. Iacovou, "A Comparative Study of Important Risk Factors Involved in Offshore and Domestic Outsourcing of Software Development Projects: A Two-Panel Delphi Study," Information and Management, vol.46, pp. 57-68, 2009.

[24] P. Savolainen, J. J. Ahonen, and I. Richardson, "Software Development Project Success and Failure from the Supplier's Perspective: A Systematic Literature Review," International Journal of Project Management, vol. 30, pp. 458-469, 2012.

[25] S. C. Srivastava and T. S. H.Teo, "Contract Performance in Offshore Systems Development: Role of Control Mechanisms," Journal of Management Information Systems, vol. 29, pp. 115-158, 2012.

[26] D-G Ko, "The mediating role of knowledge transfer and the effects of client-consultant mutual trust on the performance of enterprise implementation projects, Information and Management, vol.51, pp.541–550, 2014.

[27] I. Rus, and M. Lindvall, "Knowledge Management in Software Engineering," IEEE Software, vol. 19, no.3, pp. 26-38, 2002.

[28] E. Duggan,"An investigation into the impediments to tacit knowledge transfer," Level 3, vol. 12, issue 2, Article 3, pp. 1-14, 2015, doi: arrow.dit.ie/level3/vol12/iss2/3.

[29] A-L. Chua and L.S. Pan, "Knowledge transfer and organizational learning in IS offshore sourcing," Omega, vol. 36, pp. 267 – 281, 2008.

[30] T. Goles, "The Impact of the Client/Vendor Relationship on Outsourcing Success," Unpublished PhD Dissertation, University of Houston, Texas, USA, 2001.

[31] M. A. Serva, M. A. Fuller, and R. C, Mayer, “The Reciprocal Nature of Trust: A Longitudinal Study of Interacting Teams,” Journal of Organizational Behavior, vol. 26, no.6, pp.625-648, 2005.

[32] V. Grover, M. J. Cheon, and J. T. Teng,“The effect of service quality and partnership on the outsourcing of information systems functions,” Journal of Management Information Systems, vol.12, pp. 89-116, 1996.

[33] J. N. Lee and Y. G. Kim,“Effect of partnership quality on IS outsourcing success: Conceptual framework and empirical validation,” Journal of Management Information Systems, vol.15, pp. 29-61, 1999.

[34] C. Qi, "Relationship and contract issues of IT outsourcing — An empirical study in China," July 29, 2012, AMCIS 2012 Proceedings, Paper 3.

[35] D. J. McAllister, “Affect- and cognition-based trust as foundations for interpersonal cooperation in organizations,” Academy of Management Journal, vol.38, no.1, pp.24-59, 1995.

[36] V. Ribière and F. Tuggle, “The Influence of Organizational Trust on the Use of KM Systems and on the Success of KM Initiatives,” In: Knowledge management in Modern Organizations. Hershey: Idea Group Publishing, pp.96-120, 2007.

[37] S. Chowdhury, “The Role of Affect-an d Cognition-based Trust in Complex Knowledge Sharing,” Journal of Managerial Issues, vol. 17, no.3, pp.310-326, 2005.

[38] A. Zaheer, B. McEvily, and V. Perrone, "Does Trust Matter? Exploring the Effects of Inter-organizational and

Interpersonal Trust on Performance, Organization Science, vol. 9, no. 2, pp.141-159, 1998.

[39] K. D. Joshi, S. Sarker, and S. Sarker, "Knowledge Transfer Within Information Systems Development Teams: Examining the Role of Knowledge Source Attributes," Decision Support Systems, vol. 43, no. 2, pp.322-335, 2007.

[40] T. Mooradian, B. Renzl, and K. Matzler, "Who Trusts? Personality, Trust and Knowledge Sharing," Management Learning, vol. 37, no. 4, pp.523–540, 2006.

[41] W.-L. Wu, B-F Hsu, and R-S Yeh, "Fostering the determinants of knowledge transfer: a team-level analysis," Journal of Information Science, vol. 33, no. 3, pp.326–339, 2007.

[42] C.-C. Liu, T-P Liang, B. Rajagopalan, V. Sambamurthy, and J. C.-H. Wu, "Knowledge Sharing as Social Exchange: Evidence from a Meta-Analysis," Pacific Asia Journal of the Association for Information Systems, vol. 3, issue 4, Article 3 pp. 21-47, 2011.

[43] C. J. Lambe, C. M. Wittmann, and R. E. Spekman, "Social Exchange Theory and Research on Business-to-Business Relational Exchange," Journal of Business-to-Business Marketing, vol. 8, no.3, pp.1–36, 2001.

[44] P. M. Blau, Exchange and Power in Social Life, New York: John Wiley and Sons Inc, 1964.

[45] J. Goo, R. Kishore, K. Nam, H. R. Rao, and Y. Song, "An investigation of factors that influence the duration of IT outsourcing relationships," Decision Support Systems, vol.42, pp.2107–2125, 2007.

[46] Faraj, S. and Sproull, L., "Coordinating expertise in software development teams", Management Science, vol. 46, no. 12, pp. 1554-68, 2000.

[47] D.-G. Ko, L. J. Kirsch, and W. R. King, "Antecedents of knowledge transfer from consultants to clients in enterprise system implementations," MIS Quarterly, vol. 29, no.1, pp. 59-85, 2005.

[48] T.-Y. Kim, J. Wang, and J. Chen, "Mutual Trust Between Leader and Subordinate and Employee Outcomes," Journal of Business Ethics, 2016, doi 10.1007/s10551-016-3093-y.

[49] T. C. Chini, "Effective Knowledge Transfer in Multinational Corporations," Palgrave Macmillan, 2004.

[50] H. M. Khamseh, and D. R. Jolly, "Knowledge transfer in alliances: determinant factors," Journal of Knowledge Management, vol. 12, no.1, pp. 37-50, 2008.

[51] M. C. Lacity and L. P. Willcocks, "Information Systems and Outsourcing: Studies in Theory and Practice," Basingstoke, Hampshire: Palgrave Macmillan, 2009.

[52] J.-N. Lee, "Exploring the Vendor's Process Model in Information Technology Outsourcing," Communications of the Association for Information Systems, vol.22, no. 31, 2008.

[53] N. Levina, and J. W. Ross, "From the Vendor's Perspective: Exploring the Value Proposition in IT Outsourcing," MIS Quarterly, vol. 27, no. 3, pp.331-364, 2003.

[54] J.-G. Park and J. Lee, "Knowledge sharing in information systems development projects: Explicating the role of dependence and trust," International Journal of Project Management, vol.32, pp.153–165, 2014.

[55] R. Krishnan, X. Martin, and N. Noorderhaven, "When does trust matter to alliance performance?" Academy of Management Journal, vol. 49, no. 5, pp.894–917, 2006.

[56] P. J. Lane, J. E. Salk, and M. A. Lyles, "Absorptive Capacity, Learning, and Performance in International Joint Ventures," Strategic Management Journal, vol.22, pp.1139-1161, 2001.

[57] J. W. Rottman, "Successful knowledge transfer within offshore supplier networks: A case study exploring social capital in strategic alliances," Journal of Information Technology, vol.23, pp.31-43, 2008.

[58] J.-N. Lee, "The impact of knowledge sharing, organizational capability and partnership quality on IS outsourcing success," Information and Management, vol. 38, pp.323-335, 2001.

[59] S. Blumenberg, H. T. Wagner, and D. Beimborn, "Knowledge transfer processes in IT outsourcing relationships and their impact on shared knowledge and outsourcing performance," International Journal of Information Management, vol. 29, no. 5, pp.342-352, 2009.

[60] M. S. Al-Azad and J. Ahn, "A research framework of vendor firms body of knowledge (BOK) and its impact on offshore IT outsourcing performance," PACIS 2014 Proceedings, Paper 308, 2014.

[61] W. Wang and C. Gan, "Study on knowledge transfer in knowledge process outsourcing (KPO)," PACIS Proceedings, Paper 188, 2010.

[62] S. B. MacKenzie, P. M. Podsakoff, and N. P. Podsakoff, "Construct Measurement and Validation Procedures in MIS and Behavioral Research: Integrating New and Existing Techniques," MIS Quarterly, vol. 35, no. 2, pp.293-334, 2011.

[63] P. Xu and Y. Yao, "Knowledge sharing in offshore software development: A vendor perspective," Journal of Global Information Technology Management, vol. 16, no. 1, pp. 58-84, 2013.

Mechanisms to Discover the Real News on the Internet

Yuta Nemoto
Graduate Department of Computer and Information Systems
University of Aizu
Aizu-Wakamatsu, Japan
e-mail: m5231153@u-aizu.ac.jp

Vitaly Klyuev
Software Engineering Lab
University of Aizu
Aizu-Wakamatsu, Japan
e-mail: vkluev@u-aizu.ac.jp

***Abstract*— Over the last decade, news media on the Internet have been developing at a high pace. The latest advances in information technology have helped to influence the growth of the number of people searching for information from their mobile devices. On the other hand, the risk of incorrect or false information spreading has also become higher. This problem is serious on social media and users need to distinguish between what is true and what is false. Meaningful tools to support them are strongly demanded in today's society. In this paper, we discuss the implementation of a tool that helps users find real news on the Internet. The key feature is to encourage users to look at the information from an objective perspective. To achieve this, an approach based on the idea of the "metasearch engine" can be applied. Although the popularity of this instrument has declined since the rise of Google, the mechanism itself is effective in preserving the neutrality of search results.**

Keywords - Internet; fake news; metasearch; Web; development.

I. INTRODUCTION

Nowadays, the impact of the information provided by online news media on users is growing with a rapid increase in the number of people owning a mobile device. The largest portion of this growth is in the younger generation (Generation Z) because they are growing up in a highly sophisticated technological environment and becoming familiar with computers, specifically smartphones [1]. Most tend to satisfy their information needs through Internet media on their smartphones. In other words, they are living in the environment where they can always access the latest information sources. On the other hand, the risk of false information spreading on the Internet is growing because of the specific characteristics of online media: uncertainty and lack of responsibility for information sources, and the high speed of information delivery to recipients.

This situation has attracted scientists' attention since the US election in 2016 [2]. According to [3], more than 27 percent of American people who have the right to vote visited at least one website with fake news during that election campaign. The report also mentioned that social media, especially Facebook, played an integral role in exposing people to fake news. This means the issue of fake news is now a serious social problem that affects both politics and economics on a large scale. Tools to help users recognize and reject false information are strongly demanded.

In a modern highly mobile society, people of any age tend to use a smartphone for lots of different actions, such as making phone calls, taking pictures, communicating with peers via messenger app, searching for information in a browser, purchasing goods online, and writing blogs. The main tendency in this communication is to use one application. For many users, Facebook or Google are used. These information instruments analyze a user's query and provide relevant ads. Utilizing the same approach, they may hide key documents that are important for the user. This altering of the results may influence the view of the users on news stories, politicians, etc. Search engines may influence users in the decision-making process during election campaigns. Traditional search engines are not independent judges of document quality and hearings in the US Congress in December 2018 [17] illustrate this conclusion.

Increasing plurality in the search results and reducing biased searches is the main goal in our development. To achieve this, the proposed tool works in the manner of the metasearch engine [4] to propagate the user query to several general search engines. The merging mechanism should place representatives retrieved by these search engines on the first output page within the search results.

We discuss a practical method to implement this. We expect this tool to be helpful for users who want to find real news related to their information needs. The real vision of events, facts, etc. can be created by the user from the different pieces of information like a mosaic. These pieces of information will be created by the proposed tool.

The remaining part of the paper is organized as follows. In Section II, we look over other publications in this area. In Section III, we discuss how to develop the tool using the mechanism of the metasearch engine. In Section IV, we specify the requirements for the development, and report the current progress in Section V. In Section VI, we illustrate the usage scenario that we expect by using an example. We explain the difficulties in the development in Section VII. The concluding remarks are in Section VIII.

II. RELATED WORK

To see the bigger picture of the mass media news area, Yap et al. [5] presents and roughly classify solutions for the problem of fake news into two categories: proactive and reactive variants. Their final goal is the same: to minimize the effect of fake news. According to the proactive solutions, the study above explains that Internet users should educate themselves about the existence of fake news, and it is effective if they validate news by finding at least two or more sources to check the credibility of the researched information.

Klyuev [6] proposes an approach using the mechanism of the metasearch engine to simply provide the needed information to users. It can be an efficient way to allow mobile device users, who are the main players in the searching process, to have the information on their mobile device.

For the reactive solutions, as a major approach to curbing the expansion of misinformation especially on social networks, the most needed task is to identify the articles that require fact checking. Tschiatschek et al. [7] illustrate the possible approaches of detection using crowd signals: users vote for the candidates of online articles needing to be checked. Kim et al. [8] discuss the crowd-powered solution and presents an algorithm to assist in the decision-making processes. Also, the study by Reis et al. [9] discusses the system that successfully predicts the articles to be validated at an acceptable accuracy by clarifying the features of detection. However, it also points out that the final judgment depends on an expert. If the article is about sensitive issues such as politics, the decision is an even tougher task. This means that automating the process will be difficult, and the efficiency as a solution is limited in practice.

In this work, we focus on the approach to give an unbiased perspective to the users and propose a concrete schema of the tool that implements the mechanism of the metasearch engine. Its main idea is presented in [6].

III. Approach Overview

To design the system, we extend the proposition presented in [6]. The approach presents the following filtering schema for the search results.

- Only textual data are used as result items;
- The result items are classified into encyclopedias, famous news agencies, online newspapers, portals, and blogs, by matching the URL to the prepared list of news agencies and newspapers or by analyzing the content of the documents;
- The maximum number of result documents has the following limitations: no more than 9; the result should include an encyclopedia and 2 items for each category mentioned above;
- The latest documents (in terms of time) should be selected if there is more than one document from the same source;
- Previous steps form the pool of documents. The final list for presenting is created by picking up one or two documents of each category from the pool;
- The ranks of documents given by the search engines should also be reflected in the presented search results. They should be ordered randomly when multiple documents have the same rank.

This work defines the filtering schema for mobile devices and computers with a powerful CPU, by considering the difference of computing speed and response time. If the device is the computer equipped with high computational ability, the following step is added to the schema.

- Selection of highest-ranked and lowest-ranked documents is carried out if two or more documents are from the same source or the same category.

All search result items are shown on the screen after this selection process. They are ordered according to the ranks assigned to each document.

A different application will be used for mobile devices and PCs, with high processing ability, and the application will work as a stand-alone system. In other words, the applications can work without any server running the service. The program on the devices sends the query, collects and then orders the search results on the device. This explains the necessity to use different schemas for mobile devices and PCs.

IV. Implementation

The data process in this application consists of three layers: metasearch, selection of the result items to be presented, and presentation of the chosen information.

A. Metasearch Layer

According to [10], the metasearch engine's systems can be classified as follows.

- Real: They are similar to traditional search engines and work on the server.
- Semi-pseudo: They propagate queries to multiple search engines and present the results grouped by engines in a scrollable easy to read list.
- Pseudo: They open multiple search engine pages simultaneously in multiple browser windows/ frames.
- Client-side: Their components reside on a user's machine.

Although it needs frequent updating and client software installation, here we adopt the client-side metasearch approach because it is assumed that the form of online native applications for mobile devices is required by users ([11] reports that mobile Internet has grown more than 500% in daily media consumption since 2011).

To implement this part, we utilize the method of scraping in programming. Beautifulsoup [12] is one useful library to realize the scraping from multiple search systems. The created program sends requests to the predefined search engines, which include Google, Yahoo! and Bing. To send the query to these search engines, we need to prepare the methods that correspond with each engine to retrieve the search result pages. For example, in the case of Yahoo!, the search result page can be obtained by requesting the URL, "https://search.yahoo.com/search?p=[keyword]". When users send multiple keywords, the program needs to combine the words with '+'. The following example illustrates this: "hongkong+protest". After receiving the search result page, the HTML parser retrieves the needed elements for each result item on the page, such as the document (Web page) title, URL, page description, and rank in the search result.

```
Classification:
    if domain of the document URL is one of encyclopedia:
        encyclopedia category append document
    else if domain of the document URL is in famous agencies domain list:
        famous news agencies documents category append document
    else if domain of the document URL is in online agencies domain list:
        online news agencies documents category append document
    else if document source is specified as portal:
        portal category append document
    else:
        blogs category append document
```

Figure 1. Pseudo-code for the classification

The program packs a set of this documented information as the result item object and goes to the analyzing step of the layer. In the analyzing step, it classifies each document into 5 categories (as mentioned in the previous section) and carries it to the next layer. The pseudo-code for this process is shown in Figure 1.

To specify whether the specific document is classified as "Portal" or "Blog", the program checks the content of the item. If the document is installed by the owner, it is classified as the item from a portal. In other cases, it is considered a blog item. The lists of famous news agencies, online newspaper agencies, and encyclopedia for source specifications are created in advance. They can be edited by the user. The domain part of the source URL and the page descriptions are the important factors in this classification.

B. *Selection of the Result Items to be Presented to the User*

This layer is the key part of the application. It works for choosing the information to be presented to the user. The following concrete method is necessary to get a maximum of 9 items: an encyclopedia page, 2 items from famous news agencies, 2 from online newspapers, 2 from portals, and 2 from blogs. Also, as mentioned in the previous section, the method chooses 2 items in the case of a PC if multiple documents are presented from the same source or belonging to the same category. Fixing the numbers mentioned above is carried out by analyzing ordinary users' behavior: most users look only at the first page. If they are not satisfied with the results of the search, they change the query. The number of documents presented to the user by general purpose search engines is in the range of 10 to 15. To increase the polarity of views on the topic of user interests, the method selects two documents from each category: they have the highest and lowest ranks in the retrieved set. This process is shown in Figure 2.

```
Selection:
  for all categories except encyclopedia:
      if the category has multiple items which have the same domain:
          for duplicated source of items:
              if program for Mobile Device:
                  latest ← pick the latest item
                  remove all others
                  put latest back to category
              else:
                  high ← pick the highest-ranked item
                  low ← pick the lowest-ranked item
                  remove all others
                  put high and low back to category

  result list append 1 item randomly picked from encyclopedia category

  for all categories except encyclopedia:
      if the number of items in the category is 1:
          result list append the item in the category
      else:
          if program for Mobile Device:
              result list append 2 items randomly
                                    picked from the category
          else:
              high ← pick the highest-ranked item in the category
              low ← pick the lowest-ranked item in the category
              result list append high and low
  return result list
```

Figure 2. Pseudo-code for the selection

In the case of mobile devices, selection from the same source is completed by choosing the latest document. Yet, in the case of a computer with high processing ability, the process is more complicated: it selects 2 items with the highest rank and the lowest rank. For example, in the case of 3 Web documents published by the BBC: news A with rank 1, news B with rank 1, and news C with rank 3 are classified in the "items from famous news agencies" category. It picks up A or B randomly and C is added as the second item from this class.

C. *Presentation of Chosen Information*

Finally, the aforementioned items are presented to the user on the screen. In particular, the interfaces are different on mobile devices to the display on a PC. It is more desirable to prepare optimal presentation format (character size, size of the description text, back/ forward functions, etc.) appropriate to the assumed display size. The responsive design technology should be applied for this purpose.

V. CURRENT PROGRESS

By the time of submission of this paper, we have realized the stage of obtaining the search results, classification and function to select the result items.

To retrieve the search results from several search engines, we use a Python library, Beautifulsoup [12], and APIs from third parties.

The classification of blogs and portals is specified by their URLs. For example, if the document is provided by predefined domains, such as "news.yahoo.com", the item is classified as a portal document. The function to check its content is under development because the formats of the documents on the search results depend on the publishers.

For the selection method, the app preserves the ranks in the search result given by each engine. It also checks the published date of the document. However, this part is not yet complete. We need to consider how to manage items without any date information. The presentation layer is planned to be ready after solving all of the aforementioned issues.

VI. RESULTS OF THE EXPERIMENTS

To demonstrate the implemented features, we illustrate the outcomes of the system using an example scenario:

```
Query: iran nuclear deal
<Result for Mobile Devices>
[Encyclopedia] Iran nuclear deal framework - Wikipedia
    - https://en.wikipedia.org/wiki/Iran_nuclear_deal_fr...
    - retrieved from Bing
[FamousNews] The Iran nuclear deal explained — RT World ...
    - https://www.rt.com/news/425589-iran-nuclear-deal-e...
    - retrieved from Yandex
[NewsPaper] Trump Abandons Iran Nuclear Deal He Long Sco...
    - https://www.nytimes.com/2018/05/08/world/middleeas...
    - retrieved from Yahoo
[Portal] Iran nuclear deal - Conservapedia
    - https://www.conservapedia.com/Iran_nuclear_deal
    - retrieved from Yandex
[Blog] The Historic Deal that Will Prevent Iran from Acq...
    - https://obamawhitehouse.archives.gov/issues/foreig...
    - retrieved from Yahoo
...
```

Figure 3. Example output for mobile devices with the query "Iran nuclear deal"

```
Query: iran nuclear deal
<Result for Powerful Computers>
[Encyclopedia] Iran nuclear deal framework - Wikipedia
    - https://en.wikipedia.org/wiki/Iran_nuclear_deal_fr...
    - retrieved from DuckDuckGo
[FamousNews] Iran nuclear deal: Key details - BBC News
    - https://www.bbc.com/news/world-middle-east-3352165...
    - retrieved from Bing
[NewsPaper] Iran nuclear deal | World | The Guardian
    - https://www.theguardian.com/world/iran-nuclear-dea...
    - retrieved from Yandex
[Portal] The Iran nuclear deal explained | UK News | Sky...
    - https://news.sky.com/story/what-is-the-iran-nuclea...
    - retrieved from Bing
[Blog] The Historic Deal that Will Prevent Iran from Acq...
    - https://obamawhitehouse.archives.gov/issues/foreig...
    - retrieved from Yahoo
...
```

Figure 4. Example output for powerful computers with the query "Iran nuclear deal"

results for the query "Iran nuclear deal". The output for the query on mobile devices and for powerful computers is shown in Figure 3 and Figure 4. There are 41 items collected including duplicate items: 6 from Bing, 15 from Yandex, 10 from Yahoo! and 10 from DuckDuckGo. Table I shows the classification of documents obtained (uncounted items are non-textual sources, such as YouTube links). The "Blogs" category is retrieved with the predefined set of URLs. Overall, the result pages look balanced compared to every source search system. The outcome may be even better if the sources of search include diverse types of engines.

TABLE I. RETRIEVED RESULTS FOR THE EXAMPLE QUERY

Docs class	*Encyclo -pedia*	*Famous News Agencies*	*Online News Papers*	*Portal Websites*	*Blogs*
No. of items	4	18	7	8	2

The implicit limitation is that this selection criteria does not always reflect the importance of documents presented by search engines, especially for results on mobile devices. There is a search result item entitled "Iran nuclear deal: Key details – BBC News". It is retrieved by all 4 systems and classified as the "Document from famous news media". However, the result for mobile devices does not include the item in this trial because the final selection of the items to be presented to the user is random after arranging the documents by publication date. The accuracy of the calculation level and the output level of the application for mobile devices should be adjusted after tests on real devices.

VII. DISCUSSION

Scraping is implemented for Yahoo!, Bing, Yandex and DuckDuckGo. We have difficulty with this phase for Google and Baidu: Google officially prohibits the computational scraping of search results. Although there are several APIs to scrape the search results from Google published on GitHub, most of them do not work correctly because Google also takes measures against scraping actions.

Baidu is another search engine of this kind. All of the links written on the results page are URLs to the Baidu server. All of the original URLs on the results page are stored in the Baidu database and users need to request the real ones by accessing the URL on the Baidu server. To incorporate Baidu in our metasearch subsystem safely, we need to find another way to retrieve these links.

Another problem is the weight of the search result items obtained from search engines. Right now, we consider the 6 main search engines: Google, Bing, Yahoo!, Baidu, Yandex, and DuckDuckGo. They have the most search engine market share in the world. However, not all of them provide the actual search engine system which crawls the Web. For example, Yahoo! uses Bing as the source to present its search results [13][14] and Yahoo! Japan switched its search technology to use Google [15]. If several search engines present the result items from the same source and our system evaluates them equally, the results from one engine may skew the search results. To develop the tool to work correctly, we need to remove these duplicated items from the search engine list or reduce the weighting for such items.

The way to evaluate the quality of the search outcomes is one of the foreseen difficulties. The metasearch system gives users less-biased search results. Hence, the advantage of this application for mobile and PC devices is in the relatively better neutrality of search results. Normally, the measure TREC-Style Average Precision (TSAP) [16] is used to evaluate the score by analyzing the relevance of the top N result items as a traditional way to assess the performance of the search engine. The points to quantify are not only the relevance of the search results to the intention of the given query, but also the fairness of the given results. In other words, we require a method that evaluates the bias affecting the search results or different ways to penetrate opinions in the result items. This is especially true when the searched issue is about politics: the presented results should include as many views as possible. The computational indicator should thus evaluate the obtained results objectively. Still, in many studies this process depends on experts' judgments in practice.

VIII. CONCLUSION

To develop a practical approach to discover real news on the Internet, the implementation of information retrieval from multiple search engines, classification, and the selection layer are reported as a work in progress. There are general and technical problems with compiling search results. Still, the discussion on how to deal with the search platforms having the same search system is also insufficient.

The next step in the development of the classification layer is to classify the items in the portals and blogs categories. We consider the general factors of the documents or domains, such as the amount of text, grammar, functional contents on the page, and so on.

Finally, the assessment method for the whole work including the evaluation of neutrality of the search result content is needed. We look forward to identifying a measure to determine the score of the approach comprehensively.

REFERENCES

[1] M. Dimock, *Defining generations: Where Millennials end and Generation Z begins*. [Online]. Available from: http://tony-silva.com/eslefl/miscstudent/downloadpagearticles/defgenerations-pew.pdf, [retrieved: 1, 2020].

[2] D. M. J. Lazer et al., "The science of fake news," *Science*, vol. 359, issue 6380, pp. 1094-1096, Mar. 2018, doi: 10.1126/science.aao2998

[3] A. Guess, B. Nyhan, and J. Reifler, *Selective Exposure to Misinformation: Evidence from the consumption of fake news during the2016 U.S. presidential campaign*. [Online]. Available from: http://www.ask-force.org/web/Fundamentalists/Guess-Selective-Exposure-to-Misinformation-Evidence-Presidential-Campaign-2018.pdf, [retrieved: 1, 2020].

[4] S. R. Lawrence and C. L. Giles, "Meta Search Engine" United States Patent 6,999,959 B1, Feb. 14, 2006

[5] A. Yap, L. G. Snyder, and S. Drye, "The Information War in the Digital Society: A Conceptual Framework for a Comprehensive Solution to Fake News," *Academy of Social Science Journal*, vol. 03, issue 07, pp. 1214-1221, Jul. 2018, Available from: http://www.innovativejournal.net/index.php/assj/article/view/2202, [retrieved: 1, 2020].

[6] V. Klyuev, "Finding the Real News in News Streams," 2019 Amity International Conference on Artificial Intelligence (AICAI), Dubai, United Arab Emirates, 2019, pp. 21-24. doi: 10.1109/AICAI.2019.8701334

[7] S. Tschiatschek, A. Singla, M. G. Rodriguez, A. Merchant, and A. Krause, "Fake News Detection in Social Networks via Crowd Signals," Companion Proceedings of The Web Conference 2018 (WWW '18). International World Wide Web Conferences Steering Committee, Republic and Canton of Geneva, Switzerland, pp. 517-524, March 2, 2018. doi: 10.1145/3184558.3188722

[8] J. Kim, B. Tabibian, A. Oh, B. Schölkopf, and M. Gomez-Rodriguez, "Leveraging the Crowd to Detect and Reduce the Spread of Fake News and Misinformation," Proceedings of the Eleventh ACM International Conference on Web Search and Data Mining (WSDM '18). ACM, New York, NY, USA, pp. 324-332, November 27, 2017. doi: 10.1145/3159652.3159734

[9] J. C. S. Reis, A. Correia, F. Murai, A. Veloso, and F. Benevenuto, "Supervised Learning for Fake News Detection," *IEEE Intelligent Systems*, vol. 34, no. 2, pp. 76-81, March-April 2019. doi: 10.1109/MIS.2019.2899143

[10] M. Manoj and E. Jacob, "Information retrieval on Internet using meta-search engines: A review," *Journal of Scientific & Industrial Research,* vol. 67, pp.739-746, October 2008, Available from: http://ir.niist.res.in:8080/jspui/handle/123456789/1953, [retrieved: 1, 2020].

[11] A. Rodriguez, *The internet is finally going to be bigger than TV worldwide*. [Online]. Available from: https://qz.com/1303375/internet-usage-will-finally-surpass-tv-in-2019-zenith-predicts/ 2018.06.13, [retrieved: 1, 2020].

[12] Crummy, *Beautiful Soup*. [Online]. Available from: https://www.crummy.com/software/BeautifulSoup/ 2019.11.09, [retrieved: 12, 2019].

[13] BBC News, *Microsoft and Yahoo seal web deal*, July 29, 2009. [Online]. Available: http://news.bbc.co.uk/2/hi/business/8174763.stm 2009.07.29, [retrieved: 1, 2020]

[14] L. Dirk, "Living in a world of biased search engines," *Online Information Review*, vol. 39, issue. 3, pp. 278-280, June 8, 2015. doi: 10.1108/OIR-03-2015-0089.

[15] H. Tabuchi, *Yahoo Japan Teams With Google on Search*. [Online]. Available from: https://www.nytimes.com/2010/07/28/technology/28yahoo.html 2010.07.27, [retrieved: 1, 2020].

[16] D. Hawking, N. Craswell, P. Bailey, and K. Griffiths, "Measuring Search Engine Quality," *Information Retrieval (2001)*, vol. 4, issue. 1, pp. 33-59, November 28, 2000. doi: 10.1023/A:1011468107287

[17] D. Wakabayashi and C. Kang, *Google's Pichai Faces Privacy and Bias Questions in Congress*. [Online]. Available from: https://www.nytimes.com/2018/12/11/technology/google-pichai-house-committee-hearing.html 2018.12.11, [retrieved: 1, 2020]

New Tourism System Across Industries in Nikko, Japan

Yuko Hiramatsu, Fumihiro Sato
Faculty of Economics
Chuo University
Hachioji, Tokyo, Japan
e-mail: {susana_y, fsato} @tamacc.chuo-u.ac.jp

Yoshikazu Nagao
Department of Agriculture
Utsunomiya University
Moka, Tochigi, Japan
e-mail: ynagao@cc.utsunomiya-u.ac.jp

Atsushi Ito
Department of Information Science
Utsunomiya University
Utsunomiya, Tochigi, Japan
e-mail: at.ito@is.utsunomiya-u.ac.jp

Takeo Watanabe
A cooperative of livestock farming
Utsunomiya, Japan
e-mail: t-watanabe@tochiraku.or.jp

***Abstract*—Tourist phobia has become a serious problem in Japan. Too many tourists visit Japan's world heritage sites. Meanwhile, the population is decreasing in rural areas where there are beautiful natural features, farms, and animals. In conjunction with rural residents, we have devised a new scheme for enticing tourists away from famous places to a cattle farm in the mountains of Nikko, Japan. We plan to collect data about cows at the farm using sensors and LoRa technology, which is a spread spectrum modulation technique. Through a production information cooperation policy, these data, which reflect food quality, will be shared with restaurants near the world heritage sites. This is a gateway to learning about the rural area. Our goals are to develop regionally branded products, cultivate markets for them, and inform tourists of their availability. Such cross-sectional collaboration will create a new agritourism system.**

Keywords- Society 5.0; agritourism; tourism phobia; LoRa.

I. INTRODUCTION

A lot of things are interconnected, resulting in a great amount of virtual data that is analysed using Artificial Intelligence (AI). This information exposes us to a new world. Primary, secondary, and tertiary industries are no longer separate; they connect and perform not only in the context of seamless service by Internet, but also with regard to new businesses connecting and analysing multiple scenes. For example, through AI analysis of big data consisting of diverse information, such as personal allergies, information on food products, food products stored in family refrigerators, retail store inventories, and market conditions. In Japan, this is called Society 5.0. It was proposed in the 5th Science and Technology Basic Plan as a future society to which Japan should aspire. It follows the hunting (Society 1.0), agricultural (Society 2.0), industrial (Society 3.0), and information societies (Society 4.0) [1].

The 2020 Olympics will be held in Tokyo. A lot of tourists will visit there. Meanwhile, the rural population is diminishing. We suggest a new system for attracting tourists to rural areas using the connection of Society 5.0.

The rest of the paper is structured as follows. In Section 2, we identify some tourism problems in Japan. In Section 3, we present our new agritourism and Society 5.0 system. We conclude in Section 4.

II. TOURISM PROBLEMS

International visitors to Japan have been steadily increasing in the last years. The number spiked to 18 million in 2016—a significant step towards the long-term target of 25 million by the start of 2020 (2010 performance: 8.61 million, 2011 estimate: 6.22 million [2]). However, this exponential increase has been accompanied by what seems like tourism phobia. Nowadays, tourism phobia is a significant worldwide problem. Concrete problems that are associated with the phenomenon are mainly traffic and the rising costs of room rent and restaurant dining.

In addition, people who live in tourist areas feel uncomfortable, as though they are not in their own town. This feeling is amplified by the use of smartphones. Specifically, since many travellers use smartphone devices on their trips, they do not ask residents for directions to their destinations; rather, they use smartphone applications and take photos. Research has been conducted in Nikko, which is one Japan's world heritage sites. We developed applications to solve such kind of communication gap involving the area's residents using a Bluetooth low energy beacon [3][4]. In this work, we present a new system that will not only serve the people who live in the central area of Nikko and the tourists who visit famous places near the local station, but also the people who live farther away in the rural area. We collaborated with the Oozasa cattle farm at Kirifurihkogen in Nikko. This large, beautiful farm is located in the mountains.

III. A NEW AGRITOURISM AND SOCIETY 5.0 SYSTEM

Based on Society 5.0, we intend to develop a new system that widely involves members of the Nikko area. It follows the hunting, agricultural, industrial, and information societies (Society 1.0 to 4.0). Using Internet access, these can all be connected. The plan is as described in the upcoming paragraphs.

A lot of tourists limit their visits to famous places at the world heritage sites. They have lunch or dinner or buy souvenirs nearby. However, such places can trigger tourist visits to other rural areas in Nikko where they can experience new agricultural dishes or goods at the restaurants or shops. Many original products are made at local farms, including cattle farms. We can provide information about those areas.

In addition, we can send effective, pertinent messages. As shown in Figure 1, farms (primary industry), factories (secondary industry), and restaurants/shops (tertiary industry) communicate using information tools. This is Society 5.0 in Japan (Figure 2). In order to offer visitors a marvellous experience, we aim to construct a food chain using the information flow from raw products (such as milk, meat, and vegetables), thus bringing new value to the food. We will then entice tourists away from the busy main streets in Nikko to the serenity of the natural farms and high plains.

Food is one of the most important tourist attractions. For example, Travel Trade News reported that among Thai people's motivations for visiting Japan, television programmes or movies that featured Japan were responsible for 65%, closely followed by Japanese food at 61% [5]. Chinese people use Social Network Service (SNS) and they try to take new, original photos. They will receive information using our application and have a chance to visit rural areas.

In the world of Society 5.0, the type of information mentioned above is gathered via a sensor network using a low-cost wide area network such as LoRa and analysed using AI. It is then transferred to consumers via the Internet of Things (IoT). For example, through cooperation with the cattle farm, we intend to work to verify the quality of milk that their grazing cows make. It is said that the quality of milk that is produced by grazing cows is superior to milk

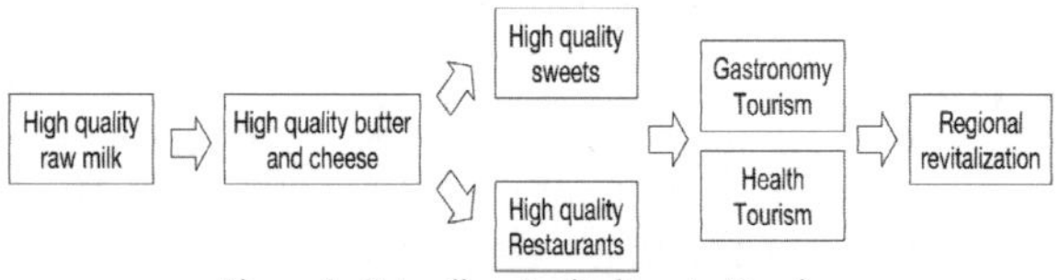

Figure 1. Extending Agriculture to Tourism.

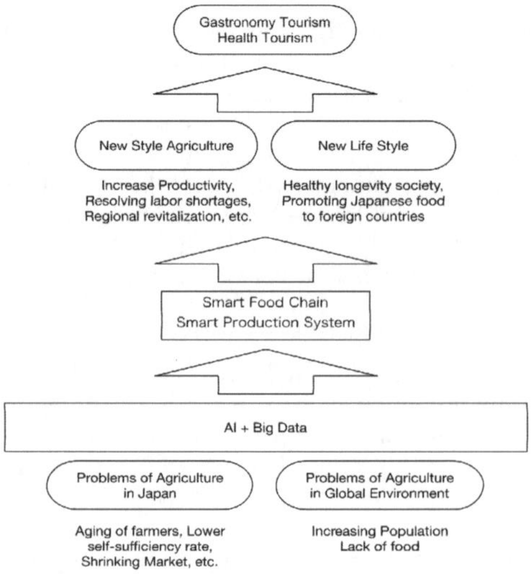

Figure 2. Society 5.0 in Nikko.

from cows that are housed in a barn; however, more information is needed to confirm this. To that end, using LoRa, which is suitable under the circumstances because it offers low-cost wide area communication features, we will collect data about each cow on the field at the cattle farm (200ha). The research has begun and 80% of the area can be covered now. We will place sensors on cows and prove the superiority of the farm's methods through data analysis. Quantification for the quality of milk can help the cattle farm and restaurants explain why their dishes are special, i.e., because the ingredients are sourced from a cattle farm in Nikko. Foreign tourists tend to choose authentic traditional Japanese food; however, milk is not a traditional Japanese food. For instance, foreign tourists like Japanese beef, which is known as Wagyu beef, despite the fact that beef, like milk, is not one of our traditional foods. In fact, Japanese beef is not much different from the American beef. Nevertheless, Wagyu has become a Japanese brand, and we intend to develop our project involving cows and milk in much the same direction. Furthermore, given that milk is a raw material for making cheese and butter, and milk is itself a basic food for making various dishes, the success of this project will benefit restaurants, cake shops, and supermarkets.

IV. CONCLUSION

Nowadays, many tourists are very interested in food quality. Rural areas are beautiful and often viewed as beneficial to visitors' health. However, instead of extending a direct invitation, we will attract tourists using clear data and information. Quantitative data is particularly persuasive. This project aims to connect natural, high-quality foods, mobility, and the cattle farm. By linking several industries using Information and Communication Technology (ICT), we will contribute to the whole area's activity level. This system will vitalise the local economy and support the modernisation of the countryside with an eye towards tourism.

ACKNOWLEDGMENT

A portion of the research results were obtained from commissioned research by the National Institute of Information and Communications Technology (NICT), JAPAN. This research is also supported by JSPS KAKENHI Grant Number JP17H02249 and JP18K11849.

REFERENCES

[1] Cabinet Office in Japan, *What is Society 5.0*, [Online]. Available from: https://www8.cao.go.jp/cstp/english/society5_0/index.html [Accessed February 2020]

[2] Japan Travel Agency, *The Tourism Nation Promotion Basic Plan*, [Online]. Available from: https://www.mlit.go.jp/kankocho/en/kankorikkoku/kihonkeikaku.html, 2017.2.16 [Accessed January 2020]

[3] Y. Hiramatsu et al., "A Service Model using Bluetooth Low Energy Beacons - To Provide Tourism Information of Traditional Cultural Sites", pp. 14-19, Service Computation 2016, March , Rome, Italy.

[4] Y. Hiramatsu et al.,"Outdoor Studying System Using Bluetooth Low Energy Beacon - To Feel Cultural Sites", HCII 2017, Part 1, pp. 340-352, July 2017, Vancouver, Canada.

[5] Japanese Travel Trade News, September 24, 2015 [Online]. Available from: https://www.travelvoice.jp/english/japan-tourism-marketing-survey-shows-the-ratio-of-thai-repeaters-to-japan-is-close-to-7, [Accessed December 2019]

A Web-Based Platform Prototype to Enhance e-Participation and e-Transparency in Local Government

Jose L. Cabrera-Guzman, Luis C. Villaverde-Hidalgo, Jorge R. Parra-Michel, Rafael Martínez-Peláez
Faculty of Information Technology
University of La Salle Bajio
León, México
e-mails: {jcg57968, lvh57920}@udelasalle.edu.mx, {jrparra, rmartinezp}@delasalle.edu.mx

Abstract— **In the last years, the number of Internet users in Mexico has increased, reducing the digital divide. As a consequence, the government has developed many Web-based applications and Web-based platforms to establish close communication with the citizens based on e-government policies. The e-government policies include the topics of participation and transparency. However, the real impact of e-government policies in society is low. For that reason, we developed a Web-based platform prototype to enhance the participation of citizens and promote the transparency of government.**

Keywords- e-participation; e-transparency; open government; society; Web-based application.

I. Introduction

The Internet has changed our world, providing the possibility to create new ways of communication and interaction with the environment. As a consequence, some group of visionaries have developed new technologies, called electronic services or e-services, to transform business, government, life, and the global economy.

The most popular e-services are e-commerce, e-banking, e-government, and e-learning due to the number of users or adopters, and their economic impact and social benefits [1]. The first reference related to the concept of e-government appeared in the seventies [2], where the government adopted information technology to perform office automation easier and faster. Twenty years later, e-government was defined by the Organisation for Economic Cooperation and Development (OECD) as "the use of information and communications technologies, and particularly the Internet, to achieve better government" [3].

According to Grönlund [4], the definition provided by the OECD makes sense from the society's perception in terms of usability and usefulness. For that reason, it is necessary the participation of different types of stakeholders (business, civil society, private sector, and universities) to achieve a better government. In this way, a better government based on Information and Communication Technologies (ICT) must offer citizen oriented applications [5], strategic management and more accessible services.

Nevertheless, the meaning of e-government does not incorporate public participation or citizen participation in the decision making process at any level of the government [6]. In this new perspective called e-participation [4], the concept of e-government should take into consideration an active citizenship [6] where citizens share their ideas, knowledge, and suggestions, using technology [6][7]. With citizen participation, the examination of problems should lead to policies based on real needs [8]. This means that government and citizenship need to work together for the benefit of the rest of society [6]-[8].

Although, e-participation reduces the bureaucracy and enhances communication among stakeholders, e-participation does not promote revealing data, information and processes from the government to citizens. The action where the government shares data, information, and processes to citizens is known as transparency [9]. According to Bertot et al. [10], transparency is essential to democratic participation because it offers trust in government and prevention of corruption, among other essential functions in society. In the context of e-government, transparency is called e-transparency [11]. The e-transparency contributes to the public administration reform, law enforcement and social change to reduce corruption [10].

The key contribution of this paper is the proposal of a new Web-based platform to improve e-participation and e-transparency to promote more collaboration among citizens. The structure of the paper is as follows. In Section II, we present the main concepts related to the contribution. In Section III, we describe the method used to develop our proposal. In Section IV, we describe the key components of our proposal. Finally, in Section V, we give our conclusions and future work.

II. Literature Review

In this section, we briefly explain the keynote concepts which are necessary to know the context of the proposal.

A. World Wide Web

One of the key components in the creation of e-services is the World Wide Web (WWW) created by Tim Burners-Lee in 1989 [12]. The first stage of the WWW is known as reading-only or Web 1.0, and it is based on global hypertext space, static HyperText Markup Language (HTML), client-server architecture, and Web forms. Web 2.0, defined by

Dale Dougherty, appeared in 2004 [12]. The second stage of the WWW is based on Extensible Markup Language (XML), Really Simple Syndication (RSS), peer-to-peer architecture, and Web applications, known as reading-writing or Web 2.0 [12].

The main differences between Web 1.0 and Web 2.0 are the flexibility of Web design, creative reuse, and collaborative content creation. In other words, Web 2.0 provides the possibility of an interactive collaboration among different people where they share experience, knowledge, and lessons learned [12]. The most relevant technologies created in this stage are blogs and social network sites by means of users working together to share data, resolving challenges and changing the world [13].

B. Web-based Platform

A Web-based application is a system with application components on the client-side which communicates with application components in a Web server for data processing based on the client-server architecture [14]. The data processing is carried out by the server because it has more resources than clients. Then, a Web-based platform is a Web-site, which provides two or more Web-based applications using different technologies [15]. In the context of e-government, a Web-based platform must fulfil the following requirements [15]:

- Interoperability – The Web-based platform must be accessible by any type of device using any type of communication based on international standards.
- Flexibility – The Web-based platform must be accessible by any citizen from anywhere and anytime.
- Inclusively – The Web-based platform must be accessible by any citizen with or without physical limitations.
- Scalability – The Web-based platform must have enough processing and storage capacity to process each request from citizens.
- Security – The Web-based platform must be based on security standards to provide authentication, confidentiality, integrity, and non-reputation in each transaction between the government and citizens.

C. Social Network Sites

A Social Network Site (SNS) is a Web-based service that allows individuals to construct a public or semi-public profile within a bounded system, articulate a list of other users with whom they share a connection, and view and traverse their list of connections and those made by others within the system [16]. For those reasons, SNS have been rapidly accepted by Internet users due to the possibility to keep in touch with family, friends and others [16]. In this scenario, Internet users have the option to share ideas, comments, and feelings with others, without barriers of time and space. Moreover, the messages published in SNS travel through the cyberspace faster than traditional media [17].

In the context of e-government, SNS allows different citizens to collaborate from any location via a virtual community to exchange information, knowledge, problems, and solutions without space and time limitations [13].

D. Corruption in Mexico

Transparency International publishes every year the corruption perceptions index. In the 2018 index, Mexico appears in the 138th position among 180 countries with 28 points out of 100 possible points [18]. In January 2019, Pring and Vrushi published the report "Tackling the crisis of democracy, promoting rule of law and fighting corruption" where they propose the following actions to reduce corruption and consolidate democracy: a) provide democratic checks and balances, b) bridge the gap between laws and their implementation, c) support public accountability, and d) press freedom [19].

More recently, Pring and Vrushi reported the citizens' perceptions about corruption in Latin America & the Caribbean, where they found that people think that corruption increased in the previous 12 months. In the particular case of Mexico, 45% of the people think that corruption has increased, and 90% of the people believe that corruption in government is a big problem [20].

E. Transparency

Transparency is not a new idea; it appeared around the 70s creating new laws and rules to share governmental information with citizens. As a consequence, citizens can get access to documents from government and non-governmental organizations [21]. Nowadays, the concept of transparency is linked to the concept of accountability to provide legitimate reasons for the way the public sector spends the budgets [22].

The information can be accessed in different ways, including a Web-based platform [9]. For that reason, local governments can take advantage of a Web-based platform to make available information and accountability without a specific request.

F. Participation in Public Administration

Participation in the context of public administration is known as collaborative governance, where citizens take part in the strategic decisions as well as promote accountability and responsiveness for the benefit of society. In this vision, citizens are partners of the government to enhance democracy and efficient governance [22].

Governments adopt new technologies to establish communication and interaction with citizens. The e-participation broadens the possibility for more citizens to be heard and to collaborate with the government [22].

G. Open Government

Open government is the consequence of transparency, accountability, and participation activities. In this new tendency, the public administration reveals documents using a public repository [23]. This action seems to be unidirectional; however, technology gives the possibility to create a bidirectional channel between government and citizens, creating a knowledge society.

The open government promotes the following activities related to democracy: monitor government, create policies and collaborate in developing new government services [24]. However, open government could be adopted by the following factors [25]: a) cause is the action to improve legitimacy and efficiency, b) constituents is the response to society caused by conflicting interests, c) content is the reaction to provide information as soon as possible, d) control is the conviction to share information, and e) context is related with the conditions of the environment.

III. Method

A. Problem Definition

According to the reports presented by Transparency International in 2018 and 2019 [18]-[20], Mexico has several problems of corruption which impacts all levels of society, from the top to the bottom, affecting the quality of life of more than one hundred millions Mexicans in terms of education, health, inequality, poverty, social welfare, civil and political rights.

Although the purposes of e-government, e-participation, e-democracy, e-transparency, and open government sound good, being useful in other countries, these do not work correctly in Mexico. Mexico has adopted, integrated, and transformed many processes and services to e-government [26][27], in the last nineteen years, as well as created and applied an open data policy since 2012, without reducing corruption. Moreover, many of the Web-based applications and Web-based platforms created by the Federal Government and Local Governments do not incorporate elements to establish real communication between authorities and people, leaving aside the participation of citizens.

B. Solution

In the State of Guanajuato, we can find some Web-based applications, Web-based platforms and Mobile-applications to connect citizens with the government; however, the previous solutions have the following limitations:

- Low incorporation of citizens in the definition of state strategic planning development, making it more inclusive.
- Low participation of citizens in strategic management to resolve problems.
- Poor or null notification of investment in public works and infrastructure as a policy to inform about the progress and total cost.

As a consequence, the government makes decisions based on a limited vision, and, sometimes, the government does not know the real necessities of citizens, carrying out an inefficiency distribution of resources and distrust in government.

For those reasons, we developed a Web-based platform where any citizen has the option to publish a complaint, idea, requirement, and solution related to the city of Leon Guanajuato, driving collaborative decision-making and promoting transparency.

C. Considerations

In recent years, information and communication technologies have changed the way people connect with people, companies interact with customers, and governments interact with citizens. Under these circumstances, it is common to request something, in both directions, to resolve a problem, to create a new service, to validate an idea, or to support an initiative that creates added value to society.

Our perception is based on the service delivery lifecycle [23][28]. In the first stage, the government consults citizens about public services and urban planning to define the state development plan. The purpose of this stage is to collect data from different points of view.

In the second stage, the government executes the activities providing services and resolving problems with the active participation of citizens. In this stage, public administration interacts with universities, non-governmental organizations, and the private sector to collect the knowledge from a different perspective, searching the best solution.

In the third stage, citizens can monitor the activities day-to-day, creating a culture of transparency and accountability in each action.

As a consequence, a technological solution needs to include each stage to bring added value for public services based on collaborative decisions and knowledge society.

IV. Prototype

In this section, we describe the main components and key functions of our proposal. The proposal is inspired by the first citizen-driven system for local public service called FixMyStreet.com [29].

We decided to develop a responsive Web-based platform because it is accessible by mobile devices and computers (or laptops) from anywhere and anytime. The prototype was developed using .NET and ASP.NET core frameworks, and MySQL as a DataBase Management System.

A. Entities

The Web-based platform has the following entities:

- Citizen – any person who lives in a city and has a proposal for the local government.
- Web-based platform – system managed for the government to enhance interaction with citizens for collecting relevant data.
- Responsible – is a member of the local government.
- System administrator – verifies the correct functionality of the Web-based platform, updates or deletes proposals, and performs the maintenance of the system.

B. Database

The database contains nine tables that start with tbl, as a rule (see Figure 1). The tblProblema table maintains the records related to the proposal, such as ID_Problem (PK), title, description, ID_status (FK), ID_Responsable (FK), and email. This table is the core of the proposal because it connects the other tables.

The table which contains the location of the problem is tblDireccion and it contains the following columns: ID_Problem (FK), street, number, district, and reference. This information is useful to identify the situation; however, it could be possible to identify it using a geolocation API. In the tblFoto table, the evidence of the problem is stored in image format. In this particular case, the evidence is used to provide a better explanation for any citizen and responsible.

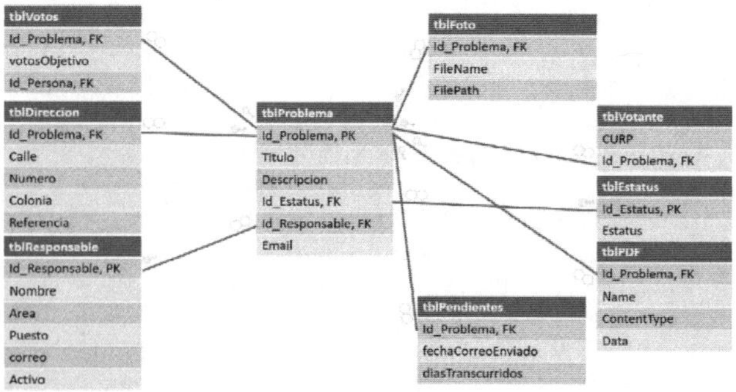

Figure 1. Design of the database.

The information related to each citizen is stored in tblVotante table. In this case, the citizen submits her/his Unique Population Registry Code or Personal ID code to the Web-based platform. When the Web-based platform receives the Personal ID code, it verifies its validity. This data is required every time the citizen wants to vote for any complaint, idea, requirement, and solution.

C. Generate a Proposal

The Front-end of the Web-based platform has a menu in the top right corner. The menu presents the option to create a report (see Figure 2).

Figure 2. Front-end of the Web-based platform.

After clicking the option to create a report, the Web form appears (see Figure 3). The citizen fills in the Web form with the following information: title, description, location, evidence, the area related to the report, and her/his email.

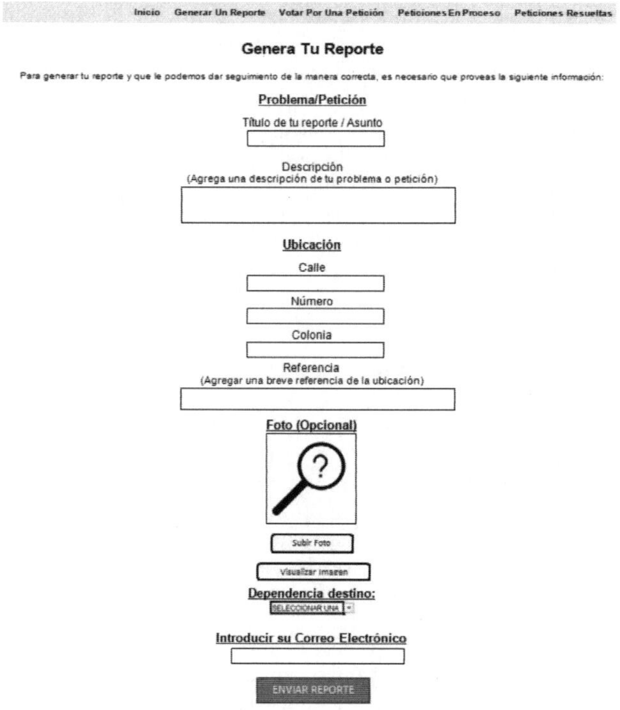

Figure 3. Web form to create a report.

Then, the system administrator verifies the information provided by the citizen. If the information is incorrect, the system administrator sends an email to the citizen explaining the mistake and giving him/her the possibility to update the information. If the information is correct, the system administrator accepts and publishes the report. As a particular case, if the system administrator identifies double reports, the duplicates are deleted.

D. Voting for a Request

When a citizen wants to see the list of reports, she/he needs to click on the options vote for a request located on the menu. As a response, the Web-based platform shows the entire request list, as shown in Figure 4.

Figure 4. Example of the list of citizen's request.

If a citizen wants to know more about a specific report, they need to click on the "see" button. The citizen can read the information without changing or modifying anything, keeping the integrity of the record. If the citizen wants to give his/her vote to this report, the Web-based platform requires the citizen's Unique Population Registry Code or Personal ID code. Finally, the citizen clicks the vote button to submit the vote to the Web-based platform. The Personal ID code is used to prevent double votes from a citizen, providing trust and legitimacy to citizens.

E. Request in Progress

Once the local government team receives a request from the Web-based platform, they need to resolve the problem as soon as possible because the Web-based platform counts the days that have passed since the report was created. As a result, citizens know the efficiency of local government action. Figure 5 shows the number of days, or the elapsed time, since the record was created.

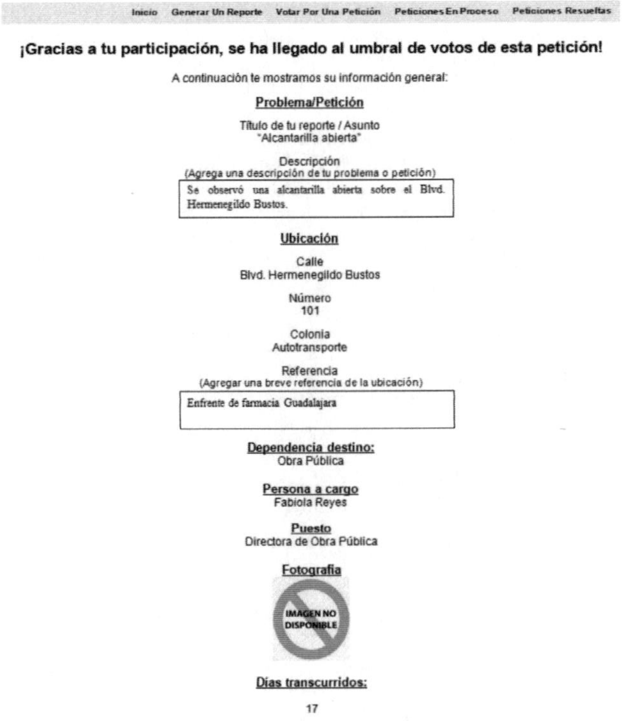

Figure 5. Example of the elapsed time in days.

In this way, the local government team can focus their effort on solving real problems that affect many citizens and avoiding the waste of time caused by the misassignments of tasks.

F. Request Made

After the local government team finalizes the request, they need to publish the final status and the following files: a) images related to the solution and b) PDF document with the financial information (see Figure 6). The evidence is public, promoting transparency and accountability as a social culture.

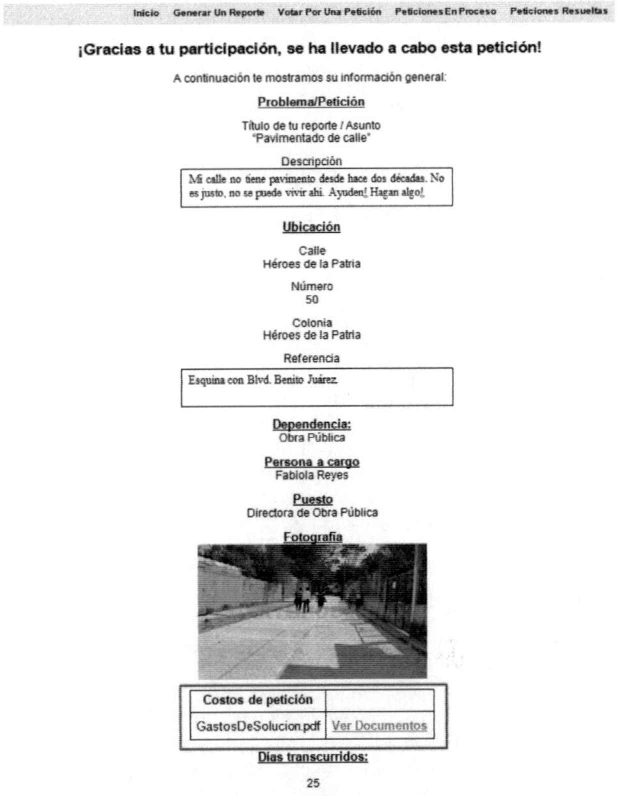

Figure 6. Example of transparency and accountability.

This process promotes the active participation of public administration in transparency and accountability, encouraging the transformation towards an open government. The information can be accessed and consulted by any citizen from anywhere, promoting constant monitoring in the government's work.

V. CONCLUSION

In a country where corruption is part of everyday life, it is clear that public administration requires increasing legitimization, efficiency, accountability, and transparency in collaboration with citizens to define an inclusive state development plan based on real requirements instead of unnecessary or excessive expenses when the budget is limited. One of the communication channels to collect data, interact with citizens, evaluate results, and receive feedback is a Web-based platform because it is a cheaper option than traditional options. Moreover, the Web system promotes bidirectional communication at any time. Also, the public administration can publish different types of files as evidence, giving more information to citizens. In this way, citizens have more elements to know how the public administration spends the budget and which are the entities receiving federal contracts.

We have presented the prototype of a Web-based platform whose purpose is promoting the collaboration between citizens and local government to resolve real problems for the benefit of society. The prototype requires active participation from citizens to define the priority to meet a request and to monitor the spending of time and budget. We are evaluating the prototype among citizens in the city of Leon Guanajuato, Mexico, in terms of usability and perception.

ACKNOWLEDGMENT

This work was partially supported by the University of La Salle Bajio in Leon, Mexico.

REFERENCES

[1] L. Révészová, J. Bucko, and P. Mihók, "Modelling of e-services," in Ambient Intelligence Perspective, vol. 1, IOS Press, pp. 203-2010, 2009.

[2] A. Grönlund and T. A. Horan, "Introducing e-gov: history, definitions, and issues,", Communications of the Association for Information Systems, vol. 15, pp. 713-729, 2004.

[3] OECD, "Implementing e-government in OECD countries: experiences and challenges, OECD, pp. 1-9, 2008.

[4] A. Grönlund, "Ten years of e-government: the 'end of history' and new beginning," Electronic government 2010. Lecture Notes in Computer, vol. 6228, Springer, Berlin, pp. 13-24, 2010.

[5] I. Ivan, B. Vintila, C. Ciurea, and M. Doinea, "The modern development cycle of citizen oriented applications", Studies in Informatics and Control, vol. 18, no. 3, pp. 263-270, 2009.

[6] M. Joao Simoe, "Sociological reflections on e-government," The Sixth International Conference on Digital Society, IARIA, pp. 29-34, 2012.

[7] S. Kim and J. Lee, "E-participation, transparency, and trust in local government," Public Administration Review, vol. 72, no. 6, pp. 819-828, 2012.

[8] R. A. Irvin and J. Stansbury, "Citizen participation in decision making: is it worth the effert?," Public Administration Review, vol. 64, no. 1, pp. 55-65, 2004.

[9] E. W. Welch and C. C. Hinnant, "Internet use, transparency, and interactivity effects on trust in government," 36th Annual Hawaii International Conference on System Sciences, pp. 1-7, 2003.

[10] J. C. Bertot, P. T. Jaeger, and J. M. Grimes, "Using ICTs to create a culture of transparency: e-government and social media as openness and anti-corruption tools for societies," Government Information Quarterly, vol. 27, no. 3, pp. 264-271, 2010.

[11] F. Bannister and R. Connolly, "The trouble with transparency: a critical review of openness in e-government," Policy & Internet, vol. 3, no. 1, pp. 1-30, 2011.

[12] S. Aghaei, M. Ali Nematbakhsh, and H. Khosravi Farsani, "Evolution of the world wide Web: from web 1.0 to web 4.0", International Journal of Web & Semantic Technology, vol. 3, no. 1, pp. 1-10, 2012.

[13] S. Ae Chun, S. Shulman, R. Sandoval, and E. Hovy, "Government 2.0: making connections between citizens, data and government", Information Polity, vol. 15, pp. 1-9, 2010.

[14] N.R. Dissanayake and G.K.A. Dias, "Web-based applications: extending the general perspective of the service of web," The 10th International Research Conference of KDU on Changing Dynamics in the Global Environment: challenges and opportunities, 2017.

[15] A. Kaliontzoglou, P. Sklavos, T. Karantjias, and D. Polemi, "A secure e-government platform achitecture for small to medium sized public organizations," Electronic Commerce Research and Applications, vol 4, no. 2, pp. 174-186, 2005.

[16] D. M. Boyd and N. B. Ellison, "Social network sites: definition, history, and scholarship," Journal of Computer-Mediated Communication, vol. 13, no. 1, pp. 210-230, 2007.

[17] P. Romero-Navarro, R. Martínez-Peláez, D. Toto-Jiménez, M. H. Juárez-Pérez, and C. A. Ochoa-Ortiz, "Knowing the tendency of an electoral candidate through facebook: a case study in municipal election in Miahuatlán de Porfirio Díaz, Oaxaca," Programación Matemática y Software, vol. 8, no. 2, pp. 8-16, 2016.

[18] Transparency International, "Corruption perceptions index 2018," Transparency International, pp. 1-26, 2018.

[19] C. Pring and J. Vrushi, "Tackling the crisis of democracy, promoting rule of law and fighting corruption," Transparency International, 2019.

[20] C. Pring and J. Vrushi, "Global corruption barometer: Latin America & The Caribbean 2019," Transparency International, ISBN: 978-3-96076-126-6, 2019.

[21] C. Ball, "What is Transparency?," Public Integrity, vol 11, no. 4, pp. 293-308, 2009.

[22] K. Soonhee and L. Jooho, "E-Participation, transparency, and trust in local government," Public Administration Review, vol. 72, no. 6, pp. 819-828, 2012.

[23] L. Schmidthuber, D. Hilgers, T. Gegenhuber, and S. Etzelstorfer, "The emergence of local open government: Determinants of citizen participation in online service reporting," Government Information Quarterly, vol. 34, no. 3, pp. 457-469, 2017.

[24] M. Gascó-Hernández, E. G. Martín, L Reggi, S. Pyo, and L F Luna-Reyes, "Promoting the use of open government data: Cases of training and engagement," Government Information Quarterly, vol 35, no. 2, pp. 233-242, 2018.

[25] E. Ruijer, F. Détienne, M. Baker, J. Groff, and A. J. Meijer, "The politics of open government data: understanding organizational responses to pressure for more transparency," American Review of Public Administration. [Online]. Available from: https://journals.sagepub.com/doi/full/10.1177/0275074019888065

[26] OECD, "Digital government in Mexico – The path towards a sustainable and inclusive digital transformation," OECD, pp. 1-5, 2018.

[27] UN, "E-government survey 2018 – Gearing e-government to support transformation towards sustainable and resilient societies," United Nations, pp. 1-300, 2018.

[28] D. Linders, "From e-government to we-government: defining a typology for citizen coproduction in the age of social media," Government Information Quarterly, vol. 29, no. 4, pp. 446-454, 2012.

S. F. King and P. Brown, "Fix my street or else: using the internet to voice local public service concerns," The First International Conference on Theory and Pracice of Electronic Governance (ICEGOV 2007), Dec 2007, pp. 72-80, ISBN: 978-1-59593-822-0.

Automatic Speech Intelligibility Assessment in Dysarthric Subjects

Ayush Tripathi, Swapnil Bhosale, Sunil Kumar Kopparapu
TCS Research and Innovation - Mumbai, India
Email: {t.ayush, bhosale.swapnil2, sunilkumar.kopparapu}@tcs.com

***Abstract*—Dysarthria refers to a group of neurogenic speech disorders characterized by abnormalities in the strength, speed, range, steadiness, tone, or accuracy of movements required for breathing, phonatory, resonatory, articulatory, or prosodic aspects of speech production. Proper evaluation of speech intelligibility is a key diagnostic step in identifying the effect of treatment on the patients. The proposed system has been developed so as to make this evaluation process simple for both the patient and the clinician. The system automatically estimates the intelligibility score on a scale of 0 to 100 along the lines of Assessment of Intelligibility of Dysarthric Speech (AIDS) score.**

Keywords–Dysarthria; Automatic Intelligibility Assessment; AIDS Score.

I. INTRODUCTION

Dysarthria is a motor speech disorder where permanent brain and/or nerve damage impacts speech-related muscles. These muscles either go limp and loose or become tight and rigid, thereby causing difficulty in speech production. Dysarthria is a common symptom in neurological disorders such as Parkinson's Disease (PD), Huntingtons Disease (HD), Amyotropic Lateral Scleoris (ALS), cerebral palsy or neurological trauma. Additionally, dysarthria may also arise after a traumatic head injury or a side effect of brain tumor. Reduction in intelligibility, audibility, naturalness, and efficiency of vocal communication are the major manifestations observed in dysarthric subjects which leads to slurred speech, hoarse and choppy sound, hypernasal voice and articulation errors [1] [2].

In order to analyze the patients progress and the effects of speech therapy and medication, accurate and consistent assessment of speech intelligibility at regular intervals is important. Traditionally, this assessment has been performed by a trained Speech Language Pathologists (SLP) who use different measures like Hoehn and Yahr scale, AIDS scale, etc. However, due to inter-listener differences, these methods are susceptible to errors and, therefore the development of a standardized method for intelligibility estimation is important [3].

In order to overcome these shortcomings in perceptual assessment, various automatic intelligibility assessment systems have been proposed in the past. In [4], the authors tackled the problem by using an i-vector based approach. A system based on audio descriptors was described in [5], where the features traditionally used to define timbre of musical instruments was modified to address the intelligibility assessment. More recently, spectral subspace analysis has been proven effective for such an assessment in [6]. An in-depth overview of objective assessment techniques for dysarthria intelligibility assessment has been addressed in [7]. It should also be noted that intelligibility assessment is a precursor to recognition of dysarthric speech [8].

A computer based system has the capability of being operated on recorded voice and does not require the patient to physically visit the clinician for intelligibility assessment. With the help of such a system, the patients progress can be electronically stored, analyzed remotely without the patient having to travel to the clinic. In this paper, we propose a novel system for automatically estimating the intelligibility scores from a few utterances of dysarthric speech on a scale of 0 to 100 along the lines of AIDS score. Our main aim is to develop a usable system, which requires minimum effort from the patient and the outcome of the system is easily interpretable by the clinician. This not only decreases the discomfort caused to the patient, but also reduces the errors caused by the previous listeners experience, which is the major drawback of perceptual evaluation.

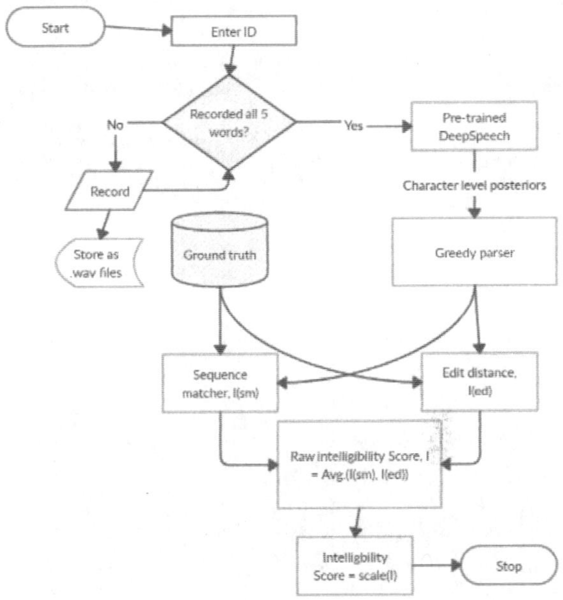

Figure 1. System flowchart.

The rest of the paper is organized as follows. In Section II, we describe the system in detail. In Section III, we present the implementation of the system and we conclude in Section IV.

II. SYSTEM OVERVIEW

The proposed system, in its final form, is very simple to use; we ask the patient to speak and record a set of *five words* which have been identified experimentally from a dataset of 455 words generally chosen for the task of intelligibility assessment [9]. Subsequently, the audio recording of the five words is analyzed to determine the intelligibility score of the patient. Figure 1 shows the complete functionality of the proposed system. From the usage perspective, the patient needs to enter a unique identity number assigned to them to start the assessment process. An audio recorder (sampling at 16 kHz) active for 3 seconds is enabled. This audio recording process is repeated for all the five words and processed by an end to end DeepSpeech (speech-to-character) engine resulting in a string of letters as output (say, o). This string of letters is then compared with the letters corresponding to the original word (say, r) using two different metrics, namely, Levenshtein distance ($l(ed)$) and Sequence Matcher ($l(sm)$) to obtain a raw intelligibility score. The raw score is

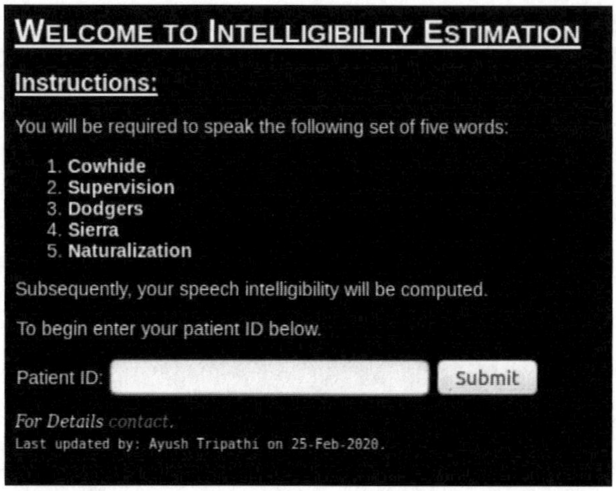

Figure 2. Assessment System Welcome Screen with instructions (Web based).

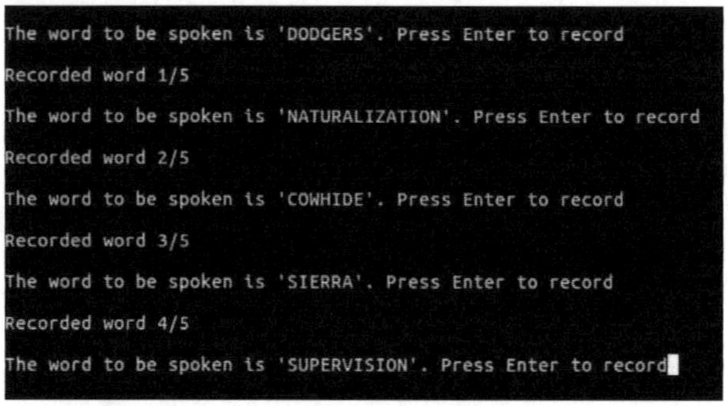

Figure 3. Audio Recording Process.

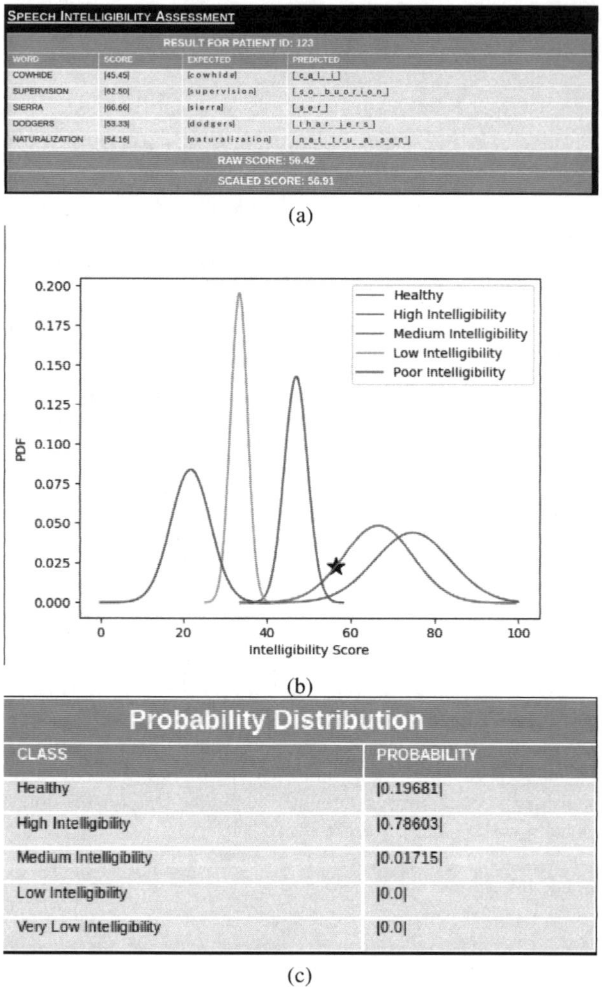

Figure 4. Web based Dysarthria Intelligibility Assessment System.

then normalized against a set of predefined baseline scores to obtain a scaled score. This scaled score is in the range 0 to 100 and is easily interpretable by the clinician who is familiar with the AIDS scale.

III. IMPLEMENTATION

The proposed system is implemented in Python, a general-purpose high level programming language. The system can be broadly divided into three major components, namely, (a) audio recorder, (b) speech-to-character engine and (c) intelligibility score estimator. Individual components are described in detail. The functional system welcome screen with instruction can be seen in Figure 2.

Audio Recorder: The main motivation of the proposed system is to estimate the speech intelligibility of a dysarthric patient by causing minimum discomfort, in terms of the number of words the patient needs to speak. For this purpose, we carefully choose a set of five words namely, DODGERS, NATURALIZATION, COWHIDE, SIERRA and SUPERVISION through extensive experimentation [9]. Notice that the articulation of these words involves a precise control of the *velum* and hence, patients with dysarthria have difficulty in producing these words. These words can be recorded by the patient by using a microphone attached to a desktop (a command line interface to record audio is shown in Figure 3) or can be recorded using any other audio recording utility and sent to the clinician.

Speech-to-character engine: The recorded audio samples are processed using DeepSpeech [10] [11], an open source speech-to-character engine to obtain a string of letters recognized by the Automatic Speech Recognition (ASR) process. Unlike in general purpose ASR, a language model is *not* used for decoding to retain the actual pronunciation of the patient. This pronunciation (or the lack of it) is crucial for identifying intelligibility errors.

Intelligibility Score Estimation: The obtained string of letters (o) is compared to the string of letters (r) corresponding to the original word by using two independent metrics. For example, r is `[c o w h i d e]` and o is `[c a l i]` as seen in Figure 4(a). The first metric is the *Levenshtein distance*, which computes the cost of converting a string o to the reference string r. The second metric is the *Sequence Matcher*, which gives a measure of the similarity between the two strings o and r. In order to find the longest continuous matching subsequence in o and r, sequence matcher is applied recursively to the sequences to the left and to the right of the matching subsequence. Similarity scores obtained from both the metrics are averaged to obtain a raw intelligibility score (see Figure 1) for the patient. Using the intelligibility scores marked by clinicians of 28 patients from UASpeech corpus [12], and the intelligibility raw scores determined by our system, we normalize the raw score to determine an intelligibility score between 0 and 100. Figure 4(a) shows both the raw and the scaled intelligibility scores. The 28 subjects are divided into 5 categories, namely, *Healthy*, *High Intelligibility*, *Medium Intelligibility*, *Low Intelligibility* and *Very Low* or *Poor Intelligibility*. We model each of these 5 classes with their mean and variance and can be represented as a Gaussian distribution, see Figure 4(b). The scaled intelligibility score is then used to assign a class among these five classes, with a confidence (or probability) of belonging to that class (see Figure 4(b)). So, for a given intelligibility score, we assign the probability of the patient belonging to each of the five classes. As can be seen in Figure 4(c), the patient belongs to the class *High Intelligibility* with probability or confidence 0.786, to the class *Healthy* with a probability of 0.197 and to class *Medium Intelligibility* with a probability of 0.017, thereby suggesting that the patient has a higher probability of belonging to the class *High Intelligibility*. The ability to graphically see the intelligibility score (Figure 4(b)) is advantageous and can be used by the clinician for getting a clear understanding of the patient's progress.

IV. Conclusion

Clinicians dealing with dysarthric patients are in need of an automatic intelligibility assessment system that is consistent, relate-able and usable. In this paper, we propose a working system that is easy to use by both the patient and the clinician. From the patient perspective, it is minimalistic in the sense that it requires the patient to speak only five words. From the clinician perspective, the intelligibility scores output by our system are very easy to interpret because they are relate-able by them to the well known and widely used AIDS score. The graphical representation of the intelligibility scores is an advantage too.

References

[1] P. C. Doyle et al., "Dysarthric speech: a comparison of computerized speech recognition and listener intelligibility." Journal of Rehabilitation Research & Development, vol. 34(3), July 1997, pp. 309–16.

[2] "Dysarthria," https://www.asha.org/public/speech/disorders/dysarthria/, accessed: 03-March-2020.

[3] R. Kent, "Some limits to the auditory-perceptual assessment of speech and voice disorders," American Journal of Speech Language Pathology, vol. 5, no. 3, 1996, pp. 7–23.

[4] D. Martinez, P. Green, and H. Christensen, "Dysarthria intelligibility assessment in a factor analysis total variability space," in ISCA Interspeech, 2013, pp. 2133–2137.

[5] C. Bhat, B. Vachhani, and S. K. Kopparapu, "Automatic assessment of dysarthria severity level using audio descriptors," in 2017 IEEE International Conference on Acoustics, Speech and Signal Processing, ICASSP 2017, New Orleans, LA, USA, March 5-9, 2017. IEEE, 2017, pp. 5070–5074. [Online]. Available: https://doi.org/10.1109/ICASSP.2017.7953122

[6] P. Janbakhshi, I. Kodrasi, and H. Bourlard, "Spectral subspace analysis for automatic assessment of pathological speech intelligibility," in ISCA Interspeech, 2019, pp. 3038–3042.

[7] R. Hummel, "Objective estimation of dysarthric speech intelligibility," Master's thesis, Queen's University, Kingston, Ontario, Canada, September 2011. [Online]. Available: https://qspace. library. queensu. ca/handle/1974/6779

[8] C. Bhat, B. Das, B. Vachhani, and S. K. Kopparapu, "Dysarthric speech recognition using time-delay neural network based denoising autoencoder," in Interspeech 2018, 19th Annual Conference of the International Speech Communication Association, Hyderabad, India, 2-6 September 2018, B. Yegnanarayana, Ed. ISCA, 2018, pp. 451–455. [Online]. Available: https://doi.org/10.21437/Interspeech.2018-1754

[9] A. Tripathi, S. Bhosale, and S. K. Kopparapu, "A novel approach for intelligibility assessment in dysarthric subjects," in International Conference on Acoustics, Speech and Signal Processing, 2020.

[10] A. Y. Hannun et al., "Deep speech: Scaling up end-to-end speech recognition," CoRR, vol. abs/1412. 5567, 2014.

[11] Mozilla, "Deep speech 0.4.0," https://github. com/mozilla/DeepSpeech/releases.

[12] H. Kim et al., "Dysarthric speech database for universal access research," in ISCA Interspeech, 2008, pp. 1741–1744.

Mobile Application Developed According to Accessibility Design Guidelines

Felipe Luna Tersi
Eldorado Research Institute
Campinas – São Paulo, Brazil
email: felipe.luna.tersi@gmail.com

Ilana de Almeida Souza Concilio
Eldorado Research Institute
Campinas – São Paulo, Brazil
email: ilana.concilio@eldorado.org.br

Abstract—**Despite the existing accessibility technologies, mobile applications are not being developed accordingly or are not even minimally using these resources. People with disabilities end up having difficulty or even are unable to use applications that in principle would serve as something to make everyone's life easier, becoming a serious problem that deserves attention. For this purpose, an iOS application was developed correctly addressing the implementation of tools for accessibility to all users. This paper shows the development process of an iOS application (Palpite Olímpico) following two accessibility guidelines with the aim of promoting inclusion of blind people and users with low vision and/or visual processing disorders.**

Keywords-mobile applications; iOS; accessibility; guidelines.

I. INTRODUCTION

Mobile devices have become part of people's daily lives and applications are being developed with the intention of promoting a better quality of life for their users. According to the Enders Analysis Institute [1], while the number of users grows exponentially, so does the number of people with difficulties who also use these technologies to access information and facilitate communication. However, the development of accessible applications does not keep pace with the improvement of devices' technology, becoming inaccessible to people with disabilities. Kane et al. [2] say that, despite the accessibility tools available in them, there is still a lack of adequacy of technologies focused on people with disabilities, making it difficult to use these devices and consequently their applications.

Hammel and Magasi [3] emphasize that the accessibility of mobile communication does not mean simply keeping users connected with other people; it also means offering them more security and autonomy, aiming to be socially independent and an integral part of society.

According to a report by the United Nations [4], it was registered that there are more than 1 billion people living with some type of disability in the world. The World Health Organization (WHO) [5] estimates that 39 million are affected by blindness and that 246 million suffer of moderate or severe loss of vision. Given this information, focusing on developing accessibility resources for these users becomes relevant, allowing them to use technology in their daily life.

With this motivation in mind, this paper shows the development of a mobile application for iOS according to accessibility design guidelines, aiming to meet the needs of these people who have visual disabilities. With more efficient interactions, it should bring them autonomy and make them independent on third parties for their use.

Palpite Olímpico is a mobile application developed for the 2020 Olympics, to allow to guess the matches of each game in the competition. This application presents a calendar containing all games matches, so the user would search for the match of his favorite sport and category and guess which country would win the selected match. According to the correct answers, the user would accumulate points and rise in the ranking among other users.

This paper outline is as follows. Section II describes the accessibility guidelines to help the development of accessible mobile applications. Section III shows the methodology used in the presented project and the results are described in Section IV. In Section V, we describe some preliminary user tests, followed by the conclusions in Section VI.

II. MOBILE ACCESSIBILITY AND DESIGN GUIDELINES

Accessibility of mobile devices refers to the ability to interact properly with the operating system of the devices (Android, iOS, Windows Phone, among others). To ensure that visually impaired people interact properly with mobile devices, there are a number of accessibility tools available in the operating systems of these devices, such as a screen reader, magnifier and contrast control [6].

There are some accessibility standards available in order to guide the development of applications accessible to users with special needs.

A. Web Content Accessibility Guidelines

The Web Content Accessibility Guidelines (WCAG) was developed by the W3C (World Wide Web Consortium - the main standardization organization on the World Wide Web) [7]. It aims to provide guidance to create accessible content in a standardized way for the web for people with special needs. It does not specifically address mobile applications, but the principles and success criteria outlined in WCAG is relevant to mobile apps [8].

WCAG consists of four principles [7]:

- Perceptible: Information and interface components must be presented to users so that they can perceive them. The idea is to provide text information for non-text content, such as images and buttons;
- Operable: Interface components and navigation should allow users to use them without difficulty. For example, providing keyboard access to all functionalities to include users that do not use mouse for interaction;
- Understandable: The information and the interface must be understood by all users. For example, all text should be readable and understandable and the interaction should be intuitive and predictable;

- Robust: Content needs to be robust enough to be concisely interpreted by a variety of user tools, including assistive technologies.

For each principle, there are a number of secondary recommendations that indicate how to address the primary ones. In total, 61 standards make up the normative part of the WCAG and three levels of compliance can be achieved if they are met [7]:

- Level A: It is the minimum level of criteria met in general accessibility barriers, but does not guarantee a highly accessible application;
- Level AA: Meeting the requirements at this level already guarantees a very accessible application for most users and use of most technologies;
- Level AAA: It is the most rigorous criterion to be reached, as it has already passed through level A and AA. At this moment, it is necessary to refine the technologies for very specific situations of accessibility, unique cases and unfortunately few applications apply criteria at level AAA.

B. Human Interface Guideline

Developed by Apple [9], the Human Interface Guideline (HIG) is a guideline that offers a series of recommendations, in order to improve the user experience through more intuitive, didactic and consistent interfaces. It was created to enrich the development of applications for all Apple mobile devices.

In the HIG, there is the Accessibility section, which addresses the four main categories of disabilities: visual impairment, hearing loss, physical and motor disabilities, literacy and learning disabilities [9].

The first categorized disability, visual impairment, comprises blindness, color-blindness, all forms of vision loss and situations that make viewing the screen uncomfortable or difficult to read. For these users, Apple offers VoiceOver, a tool that translates all information present in the interface in speech; color inversion to change how content is displayed; font size configuration that allows users to set the size of the text; screen zoom that enlarges the screen and a feature that uses the device's camera as a magnifying glass.

The second category of disability is hearing loss. In those cases, there are alternatives to aural interaction, such as closed captions, visual and haptic notifications and typing for Siri.

People with physical and motor disabilities fall into the third category, which impacts the ability to hold or manipulate devices. These people are provided with features, such as Switch Control integrating devices adaptable to the iPhone, iPad, Mac and Apple TV. Users may use Siri to control the devices and applications using their own voice and also Assistive Touch that facilitates the interaction through standard gestures.

The fourth category falls under the issue of literacy and learning disabilities, comprising difficulty in speaking and reading, managing complex things and staying focused. In order to reduce cognitive load and support these users, the operating systems provides features such as Speak Screen - the system reads a text for the user; Typing Feedback - while typing, user receives feedback as well as speak text corrections and word suggestions; and Safari Reader - isolating text without distractions, such as advertisements.

III. METHODOLOGY

For the development of this project, the Challenge Based Learning (CBL) methodology was used. This methodology helps finding solutions to real problems, in a fully collaborative way, regardless of the area and situation of the problem, it consists of three different interconnected phases and each one presents unique activities to raise questions and information that would gather essential data for the future solution of a problem [9]. All these phases are documented and reflected at each stage of the process (Figure 1): Engage, Investigate and Act. CBL is a circular process, that is, it does not have a middle and an end; all research can come and go during its phases [10].

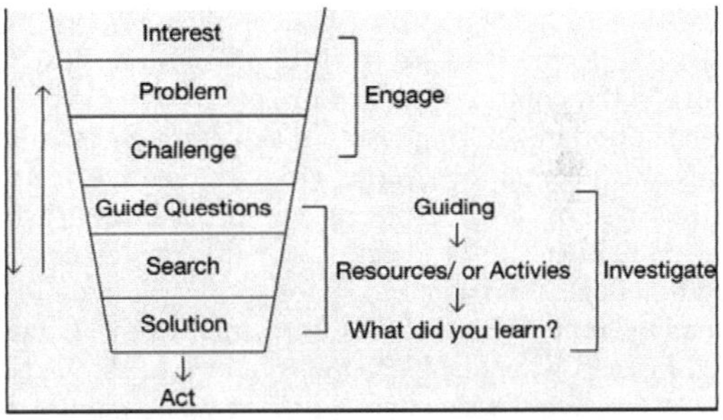

Figure 1. Challenge Based Learning Processes.

The first phase is Engage and, at this moment, it is necessary to choose a large area of activity known as Big Idea. In the project described in this paper, the area was "Accessibility". Next, a more specific problem is chosen - an essential question which would be the focus of research and from this problem, it should follow to a concrete challenge. As the objective of this work, the challenge was "To develop a mobile application that could meet most of the disabilities and needs of users with accessibility features".

In the second phase called Investigate, based on the challenge, a series of questions were raised that would help understanding the problem and would be fundamental to find an optimal solution to it. They are known as Guiding Questions and some of them were: "*What guidelines to study to use as a basis for the development of this application?*", "*What accessibility resources can we focus on in the study and development that will bring greater value to users?*", "*How to correctly apply these resources and technologies?*". After researching and answering all of the questions, it was possible to understand more about both guidelines of Human Interface Guideline and WCAG.

Finally, the Act phase is precisely the implementation of the solution defined as a result of the investigation phase. The solution consisted of the development of Palpite Olímpico, an iOS application for guessing the matches of each game in the Olympics. It is important to highlight that the focus of this challenge was not the development of the mobile app, but the creation of an accessible application. For this purpose, the proposed solution should support Voice Over, Dynamic Type and Color technologies Contrast Checker.

After developing the solution, some preliminary tests were carried out with two representatives of the target audience: one with Cataracts disease and another with color blindness.

IV. RESULTS

This paper presents the beta version of Palpite Olímpico, an accessible iOS application, developed in a period of just two weeks, following each phase of the CBL methodology. The proposal was to develop an accessible and inclusive application according to accessibility guidelines (WCAG and Apple's HIG).

For this purpose, it was decided to implement Voice Over to allow autonomous navigation by blind people; Dynamic Type for the ones with low vision to have better readability in all elements of the application; and Color Contrast for people who are color blind and have low vision to have a better contrast of the colors in the application.

It is important to emphasize that, although all of these features are offered by Apple's devices natively in their operating system, only few apps support them. For them to work correctly, it is necessary to implement them programmatically and adapt the applications accordingly.

The Dynamic Type tool was implemented throughout the application and when enabled, the font size of the text in the app must adapt to the size and weight specified in the device settings. As previously said, to work correctly in mobile applications, this feature must be manually implemented. With the necessary adaptations for the app, it should accommodate larger fonts dynamically, keeping the text legible and clear when enlarged and also making it bold.

Figure 2 (a) and (b) shows the support of Dynamic Type. In Figure 2(a), it is possible to see Palpite Olímpico's home screen without the feature enabled, with a calendar at the top showing five days a week and below a collection of sports with three sports per row. Figure 2(b) presents the home screen with the Dynamic Type enabled at its maximum size. It can be noted that the distribution of the elements change, the calendar now shows only three days, and the sports categories are arranged in only one column instead of three. It was all developed to provide better readability of the information on the screen by people with visual impairment or loss of vision.

Regarding the colors chosen for the app, contrasting colors were selected in relation to the background, to better identify the elements. It was also provided a feature for users with color blindness to choose the color palette to be applied according to their type of color blindness.

To confirm the effectiveness of the color contrast, WCAG's Color Contrast Checker tool was used to calculate the contrast ratio between foreground and background elements. It also evaluates the font color of a text or icon and the color of the background element and Palpite Olímpico obtained the AAA level classification. It reached the most rigorous criterion and with the most refinement possible, in all the colors of the system, guaranteeing an ideal accessibility, for color blind people and people with low vision.

(a) (b)

Figure 2. Palpite Olimpico screens: a) Home screen of the application without Dynamic Type; b) Home screen with Dynamic Type enabled.

The Voice Over feature was also implemented, helping blind users to navigate the entire application. It allows navigability through touch providing an audio description to guide the interaction. The user may swipe left or right to navigate and double-click to select items. Every time Voice Over is activated, a black rectangle appears around the element the user interacts with, that also may help users with low vision to navigate.

All audio narrated by Voice Over was edited by a Pronunciation Editor, allowing to create phonetics corresponding to the subject, providing tips on how to interact with the selected element, describing images, texts and button actions. It is important to create good labels and image descriptions in order to provide a better experience to blind users while navigating through a mobile application.

V. PRELIMINARY TESTS

To prove the efficiency of the accessibility tools developed in this project, two usability tests were carried out. The first test performed was with Bruno Nogueira, a 56 years old man with Cataract disease. Cataracts are eye lesions that make the lens opaque and leave the vision blurred, as if there was a mist before the eyes. It causes difficulties in activities such as reading, driving, sewing and even walking due to vision difficulty [11]. Bruno stated that he often stops using his cell phone because he can not see almost anything on the screen.

The test consisted of three steps. The first step was asking him to try to use the application Palpite Olímpico with the standard font size of the operating system. The user could not see anything, just a blurry screen and he was unable to distinguish what was really being shown. In the second step, the largest font size that comes standard in the system was activated. At this moment, the user started to distinguish some texts and icons, but he was not sure what was written or what the icons represented. In the third step, Dynamic Type was applied in its largest font size and the user stated that he could read everything and also distinguish the icons, as he was using glasses and a magnifying glass. For this user, the color tone was also beneficial because his disease also affected the brightness of the colors. Bruno also stated that "it would be incredible if every application could place fonts of this size, because I often need to use the cell phones, but there is no one near me to help and I end up being dependent on others".

The second usability test was carried out with Guilherme Caiola, a 24 years old young man with the condition of color blindness which is a vision disorder that interferes with color perception. This condition can be of three types and, in this case, he has deuteranopia, which is the absence or decrease in green cones sensitive to medium-length waves. So, instead of green colors, he sees shades of brown [12]. In this test, Guilherme should browse the application Palpite Olímpico with the standard colors and it was clear that it was possible for him to see and understand everything. Guilherme pointed out the contrast between the texts and the images, thus confirming that the use of color contrast at the AAA level actually worked. He stated that "it would be very interesting if all applications were designed with the contrast of colors, because it is impossible for me to read and understand the interface otherwise".

V. Conclusions

The design of applications with accessibility does not keep pace with technological innovations. It may cause people with disabilities to end up once again suffering from the lack of efficiency of the applications, which in principle should bring them autonomy.

This work presents the development process of an iOS mobile application (Palpite Olímpico) concerning some accessibility features such as: Voice Over for blind people to be able to browse autonomously; Dynamic Type for users with low vision making font size adapt to the size set in the device; and the Color Contrast Checker at AAA level, to provide better experience for color blind and low vision users, enabling the correct choice of colors.

While developing this app, it was noticed that it is a really difficult and thorough process so that all accessibility features and tools have an efficiency and safety during their use. It is often necessary to make adjustments to the layout and even the navigation flow.

One of the biggest lessons while working in this project was learned during the usability test. Before this stage, the thought was that people who needed accessibility resources were people who had already been born with some type of disease or were used to their conditions. In fact, accessibility must be a concern for everyone, because at any moment a disability or illness can arise, and these resources may be needed.

All mobile developers should be aware of the importance to focus on accessibility because it also includes those who do not have difficulties, but at one time or another they may need it. It is a totally social cause that deserves attention.

As next steps, it is expected to carry out tests with a larger sample of users, to effectively prove the relevance of using accessibility guidelines in the design of mobile applications. It is also necessary to test the efficiency of the Voice Over feature and prove that it allows navigation autonomously and without error for this type of user.

Acknowledgment

The authors of this paper would like to thank the Eldorado Research Institute and all the instructors and colleagues of Apple Developer Academy for the support of this work.

References

[1] Institute Enders Analysis, "The mobile explosion" [Online]. Available from: http://www.endersanalysis.com/. 2020.10.21.

[2] S. K. Kane, J. O. Wobbrock, and R. E. Ladner, "Usable Gestures for Blind People: Understanding Preference and Performance" Proceedings of the SIGCHI Conference on Human Factors in Computing Systems, New York, NY, USA, pp. 413–422, 2011.

[3] J. Hammel and S. Magasi, "What does participation means? An insider perspective from people with disabilities" Disabil. Rehabil. 30(19), pp. 1445–1460, 2008.

[4] ONU, "Realization of the Sustainable Development Goals by, for and with persons with disabilities" UN Flagship Report on Disability and Development, 2018. [Online]. Available from: https://www.un.org/development/desa/disabilities/wp-content/uploads/sites/15/2018/12/UN-Flagship-Report-Disability.pdf 2020.10.21.

[5] OMS, "WHO says there are 39 million blind people in the world", 2018. [Online]. Available from: https://nacoesunidas.org/oms-afirma-que-existem-39-milhoes-de-cegos-no-mundo/ 2020.10.21.

[6] B. Leporini, M. C. Buzzi, and M. Buzzi, "Interacting with Mobile Devices via VoiceOver: Usability and Accessibility Issues". In Proceedings of the 24th Australian Computer-Human Interaction Conference, New York, NY, USA, pp. 339–348, 2012.

[7] WCAG, "Web Content Accessibility Guidelines (WCAG) 2.0" https://www.w3.org/Translations/WCAG20-pt-br/ 2020.10.21.

[8] J. Avila, "What Accessibility Standards Apply to Mobile Applications? Level Access", 2013. [Online]. Available from: https://www.levelaccess.com/what-accessibility-standards-apply-to-mobile-phone-applications/ 2020.10.21.

[9] Human Interface Guideline, "Accessibility". [Online]. Available from: https://developer.apple.com/design/human-interface-guidelines/accessibility/overview/introduction/ 2020.10.21.

[10] M. Nichols, K. Cator, and M. Torres, "Challenge Based Learner User Guide". Redwood City, CA: Digital Promise, 2016.

[11] BRASCRS, "What is Cataract?", 2020. [Online]. Available from: https://brascrs.com.br/publico/o-que-e-catarata/ 2020.10.21.

[12] M. H. Varella, "Color Blindness", 2020 [Online]. Available from: https://drauziovarella.uol.com.br/doencas-e-sintomas/daltonismo/ 2020.10.21.

Smart Streets: Definition, Principles, and Infrastructural Elements

Theo Lynn
Irish Institute of Digital Business,
Dublin City University,
Dublin, Ireland.
Email: theo.lynn@dcu.ie

Pierangelo Rosati
Irish Institute of Digital Business,
Dublin City University,
Dublin, Ireland.
Email: pierangelo.rosati@dcu.ie

Grace Fox
Irish Institute of Digital Business,
Dublin City University,
Dublin, Ireland.
Email: grace.fox@dcu.ie

***Abstract*—Shopping streets are the lifeblood of rural towns performing a number of important economic, social, and environmental functions. Streets represent a public realm that is actively and passively consumed depending on how it is structured as a public space. These structures result from historic forces and planning processes that highly influence the norms for how such a space evolves, is moved through, and consumed by individuals or groups. In recent decades, stakeholders have sought to leverage technological advances to combine traditional elements of the public realm with cyber-physical systems to generate intelligence from data analysis in order to modify behaviour and optimise operations and services. While the overwhelming focus of existing research and policy focus is on "smart cities", there are significant potential benefits for rural communities. However, for many rural towns, the investment required for a "smart town" initiative is prohibitive. We posit that a smart street is more feasible and manageable for rural towns. This paper presents a working definition of a smart street, proposes a series of principles for smart street design, and identifies exemplar infrastructural elements to deliver widely accepted policies and behaviours.**

Keywords–Smart Cities; Smart Towns; Smart Street; Street.

I. INTRODUCTION

Over the next three decades, there is expected to be a decline in rural living as rural dwellers migrate to cities; the UN forecasts over 68% of the worldwide population will live in urban areas by 2050 [1]. The growth in urbanization is resulting in significant strain on housing, transportation, energy systems and other infrastructure [1]. Smart city initiatives that leverage advances in sensor, cloud computing, networking, and data science technologies are widely cited as a key solution to rapid, global urbanization [2][3]. Extant Smart City research projects focus on wide variety of domains including:

- Business – advertising, agriculture, entrepreneurship and innovation, enterprise management, logistics, and transactional commerce;
- Citizen - education, entertainment, health, public transport, traffic management, and tourism;
- Environment – building, housing, pollution control and waste management, public space, renewable energy and smart grids, and waste management;
- Government – city monitoring, e-government, emergency response, public safety, public service and transparency [4][5].

The quality of *smartness* is derived from the use of (i) near-real-time data obtained from physical and virtual sensors; (ii) the interconnection between different services and technologies within the urban area; (iii) the intelligence from the analysis of the data and the process of visualising it; and (iv) the optimisation of operations resulting from this analysis [6]. While the overwhelming focus of existing research and policy focuses on *smart cities*, such technology can benefit any urban area seeking to use data to optimise operations [6]. This includes rural towns and more granular spaces, including streets. Indeed, some researchers propose that smart streets are the building blocks of any smart city architecture [7].

Streets are not merely thoroughfares that connect one point with another. The public perform a wide range of activities in streets that can be categorised as mandatory (e.g., going to work or school), selective (shopping, wandering or sitting and watching street life), or social (having conversations) [8]. Human behaviour in streets can be classified as moving, visual perception, and resting behaviours, and can occur discretely, successively, and concurrently [8]. As such, it is a public realm that is actively and passively consumed depending on how it is structured as a public space. These structures highly influence the norms for how such a space is moved through and consumed by individuals or groups [9]. Streets comprise a number of tangible and intangible elements that need to be taken in to account (see Table I).

TABLE I. ELEMENTS OF THE STREET (ADAPTED AND EXTENDED FROM [10][11])

Tangible Elements	Primary	Vertical	Buildings, railway bridges, etc.	
		Horizontal	Floors	Roadbeds, footpaths, etc.
			Ceiling	Skyline, covering, etc.
			Underground	Utility channels, etc.
	Secondary	Street furniture	Benches, lamp posts, waste receptacles, storage units, utility cabinets, signage, etc.	
Intangible Elements	Natural	Short term	Light, seasons, organic growth, etc.	
		Long term	Precipitation, wind, etc.	
	Human	Administrative, economic, social, culture history, etc.		
	Behavioural	Humans, moving objects		

Shopping streets are the lifeblood of rural towns. In addition to connectivity, they perform a number of important economic, social, and environmental functions. They not only serve the functional and utilitarian needs of local residents but can attract tourists and day trip shoppers thus supporting a greater range of shops than the local population could support alone [12]. After decades, if not centuries, of resistance to the impact of global economic and societal change, the resilience of main streets of rural towns worldwide are being threatened by urbanization, online shopping, and now, COVID19. Cyber-physical infrastructure in the public realm can attract new users to a street, and decrease or increase (un)desired use and behaviour, depending on policy priorities. However, such infrastructure does not impact all activities and behaviour in the same way (see Table II).

TABLE II. HUMAN BEHAVIOUR IN THE STREET (ADAPTED FROM [8], [10])

		Moving	Behaviour Visual Perception	Resting	Impact of Public Realm
Activity	Mandatory (must be performed)	Going somewhere	Seeing out of necessity	Stopping or resting on the way to somewhere	Not significant
	Selective (undertak at will and as space allows)	Wandering for something	Seeing out of interest	Stopping or resting out of interest	Sensitive
	Social (undertake because they are in a public space)	Going to do something	Seeing to do something	Stopping or sitting to do something	More active in a conductive environment than a poor one

This paper has three objectives. Firstly, to address the gap in the literature on smart streets, we seek to define a smart street in Section II. Secondly, we present a series of design principles to guide the design of smart street initiatives in Section III. While we focus on rural shopping streets, these principles can be generalised for any street. Thirdly, to identify exemplar infrastructural elements for smart streets that support the proposed design principles, and deliver on widely accepted policies and behaviors (Section IV).

II. Towards a definition of a Smart Street

There have been numerous attempts to define a smart city (e.g., [13][14]). To arrive at a unified definition of a *smart city*, Ramaprasad et al. [14] suggest that such a definition comprises conceptualisations of *smartness* and *city* by stakeholders (e.g., Citizens, Professionals, Communities, Institutions, Businesses, and Governments) and their desired outcomes (e.g., Sustainability, Quality of Life, Equity, Livability, and Resilience). For Ramaprasad et al. [14], this quality of *smartness* comprises structures (architectures, infrastructure, systems, processes, etc.), functions (sensing, monitoring, communicating etc.), one or more foci (economic, social, infrastructural, etc.), and semiotics (data, information, and knowledge). They identify 22,500 components that can be instantiated in innumerable different ways to deliver a *smart city*. We posit that while academically sound, this approach is unwieldy and impractical on the ground. Similarly, while other papers define the quality of *smartness* in a broad way to include sustainability and inclusion, amongst other concepts [15], [16], these definitions typically focus on regional or urban development. We focus on streets because they are a defined and manageable unit with boundaries that all stakeholders can understand and work within. In the same vein, we focus on smartness as a quality derived from the use of (i) near-real-time data obtained from physical and virtual sensors; (ii) the interconnection between different services and technologies within a street; (iii) the intelligence from the analysis of the data, and the process of visualising it; and (iv) the optimisation of operations resulting from this analysis [6].

Smart streets seek to combine the traditional elements of the public realm with basic elements of cyber-physical systems. Extant research and definitions of smart streets focus on smart lighting systems as the basis for smart street projects (e.g., [7]). However, smart streets include a wide variety of potential infrastructural objects and services independent of lighting including space management, structural health, traffic management, environmental monitoring, and waste management, amongst others [17]. Similarly, *urban* is increasingly conflated with *city* whereas it is equally applicable as a characteristic of a town.

For the purpose of this paper, we define a smart street as a basic unit of urban space that leverages cyber-physical infrastructure to provide enhanced services to stakeholders, and through stakeholder use of the street, generates data to optimise its services, capabilities, and value to stakeholders. This definition aligns with existing definitions of smart cities, accommodates a wide range of potential activity, while at the same time recognising that street are a more atomised, and as a result more manageable, unit of development.

III. Principles for Smart Street Design

A. People First

The Design Manual for Urban Roads and Streets (DMURS) [18] emphasises the need for more walkable communities for sustainability, public health, and social equity. In line with DMURS and the Global Designing Cities Initiative (GDCI) Global Street Design Guide [19], the public should be at the heart of any smart street strategy. Both DMURS and GDCI propose a hierarchy of priorities as follows - pedestrians first, then cyclists, then public transport, then people doing business or carrying out public services on the street, and lastly, personal motorised vehicles [18][19]. Putting people first means designing streets and selecting cyber-physical investments that meet a wide range of objectives including public health and safety, quality of life, environmental and economic sustainability, and social equity.

B. Place Second

There has been a general shift in approaches from a primary focus on the movement of traffic, typically vehicular, to what DMURS refers to as multi-modal movement and streets as a "sense of place". GDCI [19] suggest that designing streets for place means considering the local culture and context. This includes the built and natural environment, the social and cultural context, and the economic environment. For DMURS [18], sense of place, while difficult to define has a number of attributes including:

- Connectivity - the creation of vibrant and active places requires pedestrian activity and consequently, should be walkable, connected and easily navigated.
- Enclosure - a sense of enclosure spatially defines streets and creates a more intimate and supervised environment.
- Active edge - an active frontage enlivens the edge of the street creating a more interesting and engaging environment.
- Pedestrian activity/facilities – an enclosed street with an active edge creates a sense of intimacy, interest

and overlooking and enhances a pedestrian's feeling of security and well-being.

When considering the digital analogue for this "sense of place", one must consider how digital technologies and cyber-physical infrastructure augment or reinforce these attributes, but equally what the digital analogue of connectivity, enclosure, an active edge, and pedestrian activity and facilities might be.

C. From Inputs to Impacts

Where limited resources are being invested, care needs to be taken to ensure inputs translate into impacts. Cyber-physical features and interventions must have associated measurement systems that provide more timely data from which decisions can be made and resources allocated to mitigate, remediate or optimise strategies to meet prioritised objectives. Digital technology allows stakeholders collect, process and analyse data in near-real time and, where appropriate, actuate decisions autonomically. Measuring and communicating impacts of interventions helps inform better decisions on resource allocation but also communicate progress to policymakers and the community, thereby building both political and community support for future funding and other projects. Baseline metrics must be collected before any intervention so that data collected post-implementation can be benchmarked against prior conditions. Furthermore, agreed success criteria must be determined in advance, and ideally, systems put in place to establish causal relationships between digital enhancements and changes in outcomes. In many smart street use cases, benchmarking may not be possible as historic data simply does not exist.

Based on GDCI [19] recommendations, smart street projects should focus on three categories of metrics:

1) *Cyber-physical and operational changes* – short-term quantitative results on progress towards meeting cyber-physical infrastructural targets e.g., new or improved facilities, technologies or infrastructure.
2) *Shifts in use and function* – medium-term quantitative and qualitative results on how a street is used differently as a result of the project e.g., changes in behaviour, new users of street or cyber-physical infrastructure, changes in transit flow and type, and improved functions.
3) *Resulting impacts* - long-term cyber-physical physical, operational, and functional changes that impact the overall performance of the street, and whether the investment and associated implementation is achieving the desired outcomes agreed with funding bodies.

D. Connectivity Counts

With sensors and machine learning, ubiquitous network connectivity is a foundational building block of digital transformation in the public realm. It is well established the broadband coverage, connectivity, quality, and adoption contribute to GDP and local economic growth [20][21], the location and development of clusters of knowledge-intensive firms [22], and rural employment [23], amongst others. In particular, research on free public Wi-Fi access suggests that it contributes to economic growth [24][25], promoting tourism [26][27], social inclusion [28], public safety [28][29], and improved public services [27][30]. The importance of digital connectivity for EU regional and social development is evident from the inclusion of access to digital communications in the European Pillar of Social Rights. However, rural broadband coverage continues to be lower than national coverage across EU Member States; just over 52.3% have access to high-speed next generation services [31].

E. Available and Accessible 24/7/365

Many rural areas experience weather conditions that may keep people indoors, lead them to choose to drive rather than walk or cycle, and otherwise adversely affect mobility and outdoor activities. Communities around the world have implemented weather mitigation strategies so that the public can spend more time outdoors in the public realm, generating social, economic and public health outcomes that may otherwise be lost due to climate. Similarly, in line with being "people first", improving accessibility and the quality of experience for those most vulnerable in society is key in a modern, inclusive society. This consideration is particularly pertinent against the backdrop of COVID19. While social distancing needs to be maintained, research suggests that COVID19 is less likely to be transmitted outdoors due to greater air ventilation [32]. Similarly, to counter the adverse impacts of public health interventions such as social distancing and social isolation, experts have called for further investment in public realm nature experiences that research suggests results in benefits to cognitive functioning, emotional well-being, and other dimensions of mental health [33][34].

F. A Flexible Programmable Public Realm

Thriving shopping streets are both social spaces and commercial spaces, with not only clusters of similar retail outlets but also featuring other diverse retail and social activities [12]. The physical and visual quality of the public realm including pedestrian friendliness, appropriate pavement widths, walkability and urban furniture, complemented by active shopfronts and communal facilities (bars, cafes, etc.) can transform shopping streets in to social spaces [35][36]. It is the combination of location centrality, retail mix use, and social vitality that attracts higher volumes of more diverse people to a street, resulting in sustainable long-term success. Against this backdrop, a key challenge in urban design is to make the public realm more flexible and dynamic, and encourage both traditional and new uses and behaviours of that space. Technology can be used to dynamically create time- and use-based flexible outdoor mixed-use spaces from wall to wall in the public realm. This can be used to attract more footfall, social, and ultimately commercial activity to the benefit of all stakeholders.

G. Open, Not Closed

Open government data is concerned with making public sector information freely available in open formats and ways that enable public access and facilitate exploitation [37]. The benefits of open data are summarised in Table III. It is important to note that open data, on its own, has little intrinsic value but value is created by its use [38].

The EU Public Sector Information (PSI) Directive (Directive 2003/98/EC) and subsequent revisions (Directive 2013/37/EU and Directive (EU) 2019/1024) were designed to encourage member states to provide access and encourage the reuse of PSI. Smart street projects provide stakeholders with

TABLE III. OVERVIEW OF BENEFITS OF OPEN DATA [38]

Category	Benefits
Political and Social	More transparency; Democratic accountability; More participation and self-empowerment of citizens (users); Creation of trust in government; Public engagement; Scrutinisation of data; Equal access to data; New government services for citizens; Improved citizen services; Improved citizen satisfaction; Improved policy-making processes; More visibility for the data provider; Stimulation of knowledge development; New public sector insights; New (innovative) social services.
Economic	Economic growth and stimulation of competitiveness; Stimulation of innovation; Contribution toward the improvement of processes, products, and/or services; Development of new products and services; Use of the wisdom of the crowds: tapping into the intelligence of the collective; Creation of a new sector adding value to the economy; Availability of information for investors and companies.
Operational and Technical	The ability to reuse data/not having to collect the same data again and counteracting unnecessary duplication and associated costs (also by other public institutions); Optimisation of administrative processes; Improvement of public policies;Access to external problem-solving capacity; Fair decision-making by enabling comparison; Easier access to data and discovery of data; Creation of new data based on combining data; External data quality checks (validation); Sustainability of data (no data loss); The ability to merge, integrate, and mesh public and private data.

the opportunity to accelerate their open data initiatives. With sufficient promotion, this can attract interest from industry and researchers with a view of leveraging the massive time series data that smart streets can generate to generate scholarly insight and socio-economic outcomes in towns and beyond. At the same time, smart street projects need to consider the significant ethical and legal implications of the substantial data being collected from such projects, particularly where such data is collected ambiently without explicit consent from the public [39].

H. Evolution, Not Revolution. Leading Edge, Not Bleeding Edge

While there is a temptation to be at the cutting edge of smart city technology, care needs to be taken so rural smart street projects are at the "leading edge" and not the "bleeding edge" of technology adoption. This is particularly the case where resources are limited. In every country, there are projects and schemes that need to be taken into account. Therefore, the adoption of potential technologies and proposals should acknowledge and build on best practice, existing systems and processes where possible, to minimise waste and maximise learning, within budget constraints.

I. Managing a Complex Stakeholder Environment

In order to meet the requirements of a diverse group of stakeholders, it is essential to fully understand the current barriers to change including apathy, fear, relevance, and inconvenience, and to design and select projects that seamlessly address these across a number of key themes, using a combination digital and urban design interventions. There is a rich tapestry of local, regional, national and International initiatives and programmes with recommendations and targets that can be used to inform decisions. Adopting this bottom-up approach rather than a top-down approach focused solely on the achievement of local targets should result in a programme that has greater awareness, relevance and longevity than those developed in isolation of citizen requirements.

IV. THE ELEMENTS OF A SMART STREET

A. Connectivity Corridor

A connectivity corridor is a substrate of network connectivity, power and associated hardware. As discussed, increased broadband speed and coverage is linked to a wide variety of direct and indirect socio-economic outcomes including reduced operational costs, increased GDP, increased jobs, retail and tourism visitor satisfaction, and social inclusion. Many rural towns and streets feature legacy utility wiring and street furniture that may adversely impact the visual identity of the street. By leveraging (i) existing wired infrastructure, (ii) upgrading access points to the state-of-the-art, and (iii) replacing legacy street furniture with multi-purpose units, much of the existing street overhead wiring can be eliminated or moved underground. Connectivity, both telecommunications and power, could be monitored for the street through one interface however this is unlikely. Consequently, smart streets require coordination and collaboration with existing infrastructure providers.

B. Smart Street Information Systems

There are a wide number of urban information systems that can inform a smart street project depending on the responsible agency and contractor at a national, regional, and local level. Table IV summarises some of the main urban information systems.

Given the idiosyncrasies of funding, utility management, and administrative responsibilities in rural towns, Urban Data Platforms (UDPs) are proposed as the priority for smart streets. By focussing on UDPs, the data generated can be used to stimulate future traffic control and demand management systems, mobile apps for citizens, and inform urban and strategic planning. Specifically, the data from a UDP can be used inform a more flexible and programmable public realm. Such a platform requires the ubiquitous connectivity assumed in Section IIID. Building in the needs of a UDP, including network, power, storage, sensor mounts, and APIs in to infrastructure will avoid expensive disruptive piecemeal retrofits in the future.

Sidewalk Labs, considered at the cutting edge of urban system thought leadership, view urban data platforms and associated tools for measuring, analysing, modelling and visualising this data as the first step in improving efficiency and the quality of life in urban environments [41]. The ability to collect data on fixed and moving things through sensors, video and beacon data will enable rapid low-cost analysis and testing interventions using scenario-based modelling thus avoiding the cost, inconvenience associated with live testing. Furthermore, it will allow the granular real-time evaluation of the impact of the redevelopment and enable optimisation or remediation, as necessary. Finally, the vast amount of data generated from one street can stimulate both scientific and economic activity in the street through entrepreneurial and research engagements with this open data.

C. Traffic and Transit Management

A significant part of the general public experience on a street takes place on the footpath. Footpaths are a conduit for pedestrian movement and access to properties located

TABLE IV. SUMMARY OF SMART CITY INFORMATION SYSTEMS (ADAPTED FROM [40])

System	Description
Urban data platform (UDP)	UDPs enable and stimulate a proper understanding of how infrastructure is used in different domains, the interdependencies between different elements of infrastructure and the effects of external drivers.
ICT as a planning support	Theze are quantitative tools and analytical methods in the form of step-by-step guidance that assess which issues and trade-offs that need to be addressed in decision-making as well as methodological processes for optimising opportunities and minimising risks. Decision support tools address all key actors, including consumers, producers and utilities and assess the benefits (or risks) for each actor under different scenarios.
Strategic urban planning (SUP)	SUP builds on understanding and developing all aspects of an urban area, integrating technical, environmental, political, social and economic interests. Its general objectives include clarifying which city model is desired and working towards that collective vision for the future by coordinating public and private efforts, involving citizens and stakeholders, channeling energy, adapting to new circumstances and improving the living conditions of the citizens affected. Furthermore, SUP provides a methodology which helps cities identify their strengths and weaknesses, while defining the main strategies for local development.
Traffic Control Systems (TCS)	TCS help to improve traffic flow and to regulate speed within a clean high-quality public transport corridor. A TCS includes real-time traffic data online, strategic traffic control and management, public transport acceleration measures, and information management.
Traffic demand management (TDM)	TDM describes the strategies and policies aiming to achieve more efficient use of transportation resources and to reduce travel demand by giving priority to public transit, car-sharing, car-pooling, etc. It puts focus on the movement of people and goods, rather than on motor vehicles. It includes trip scheduling, route, destination or mode reduction in the need for physical travel through more efficient land use or transportation substitutes.
Energy demand response	Energy demand response is the intentional modification of normal energy consumption patterns by end-use customers in response to incentives from grid operators, peaks of renewable energy generation or some compensation to reduce their power consumption at times of peak demand. The main objective of demand response is to maximise the integration of renewable energy systems while maintaining or improving today's levels of electricity supply reliability, energy security, economic growth and prosperity.
Mobile applications for Citizens	By using mobile applications, citizens can easily gain access to different services and open data. This offers new opportunities for the intelligent management of service demand and can enhance the quality of life in urban areas. Mobile applications help citizen to access information and make informed decisions in various domains.
Neighbourhood energy management systems (NEMS)	NEMS aim to integrate the different consumers and producers with the main electrical and heating grids at district level. These systems are essential to approach ultralow or net zero energy districts, controlling the energy consumption either by reducing it either shifting during the day to flat the demand shape. These systems, supplying predominantly residential buildings and districts, are able to de-couple fluctuations in the heat demand of buildings from the network conditions without perceptible changes in comfort. This allows the network's heat demand to be stabilised, energy efficiency to be improved, and heat (or cooling) loss in the supply network to be reduced.

on a street, they enhance connectivity and promote walking [19]. Footpaths have been shown to enhance general public health and maximise social capital. GDCI [19] suggests that footpaths should have four distinct zones. The frontage zone is the section of the footpath directly in front of a building. It comprises the façade and the space immediately adjacent to the building can be used as an extension of the building e.g., for sandwich boards or as additional seating. The clear path is the primary pathway running parallel to the street, typically 1.8-2.4 metres wide. The street furniture zone is situated between the kerb and the clear path; it is used for lighting, benches, kiosks, utility poles, greenery, cycle parking, etc. Finally, a footpath may have a buffer zone or enhancement for optional elements including parking, cycle racks, cycle-sharing stations, and kerbside cycle paths.

Rural towns can increase the multi-functional use of the public realm through a combination of designated areas, footpath widening, automated street bollards, sensors (including video cameras for Automated License Plate Recognition - ALPR), and embedded or overhead lighting in roads and footpaths. Together, these can be used to dynamically change the usage of a street at different times of the day, week and year giving priority to different street users depending on the time or weather conditions. For example, parts of or the whole street could be pedestrianised by raising automated retractable bollards at either end or the median of the street. Different uses (at different times in the day and week) can be signalled using data-driven programmable LED lights in pavement tiling. Technologies that combine advanced video camera technology and deep learning, for example ALPR, can be used to provide access and lower bollards, record infringements, identify stolen vehicles, and enforce regulations including fines and payment. In addition, adaptive smart traffic light systems can be implemented that identify and prioritise pedestrians and cyclists. These can be integrated with smart furniture and pedestrian crossings.

Sensors in parking spaces can direct people to available parking spaces, signal availability for specific purposes (e.g., Electric Vehicle - EV - parking and charging, accessibility or carsharing), record usage or signal pricing. Furthermore, parking spaces could be dynamically re-purposed and used for parklets, reservable, removable, transient pop-up retail or social spaces. Such systems could also support dynamic pricing and prioritised parking for retail customers, the most vulnerable, and EV owners (near charging points).

By being able to limit use of different sections of a street at different times in the day, it can be used as an innovative testbed for new forms of public transport and freight transit. For example, telepresence robot technology has developed and become more robust. These smartphone- or tablet-operated units allow people located remotely move, hear, see and speak via a tablet attached to a retractable unit with ruggedised wheels. They can be powered down and charged in relatively small docking stations. This can be used for tourists to visit remotely, potential customers to visit shops without being physically present, enable remote guides to interact with people, or for other teleworking scenarios. Similarly, zones can be reserved for transit by drone or autonomous vehicle (AV). For example, the Renault EZ series include AVs for freight, passenger transit and most recently, micro-mobility. These AVs are designed for low electric energy consumption and relatively small dimensions. The EZ-Pod is a small robo-vehicle (3 square metres – 32.3sq. ft.) with electric propulsion designed to transport people and goods over short distances and at very low speeds (sub-6kph). It could be used for transporting goods, the elderly or infirm and/or drone and robot delivery, and autonomous waste collection.

D. Accessibility, Security and Safety

Accessibility and safety issues can result from blocked, narrow or lack of footpaths, lack of accessible crossing, lack of protection when crossing streets particularly for those moving at slower paces, lack of cycle facilities, poor intersection designs, and other surface hazards [19]. Increasing accessibility has a number of outcomes including improving the quality of life of all citizens, regardless of age, size and ability, by providing a safe and inclusive environment. Furthermore, it increases mobility thereby contributing to public health outcomes.

In addition to eliminating permanent obstructions, supporting measures exist for integrating audio and signal cues along the street. These may be designed in street furniture or involve a system of Bluetooth beacons that provide audio or text messages to smart phones, or local visual signals to alert those in need. For example, Southern Cross Station in Melbourne, Australia uses Bluetooth and a free GPS smartphone app, BlindSquare, to create a beacon navigation system [42]. Users can receive audio cues via their smartphones, providing directions or real time information about issues such as escalator outages [42]. Additionally, object detection systems can be used to identify unpermitted obstructions, water pooling or other seasonal or anomalous issues without first notification from the public. It is worth noting that accessibility is not just about removing obstruction. Research suggests that benches to rest on and designing pavements and footpaths with clear separation of pedestrians and cyclists are high priority concerns for older citizens [43]. Furthermore, as mentioned previously, micro-mobile AVs can be used as taxibots to transport those who qualify short distances, and smart technologies can be used to prioritise parking for those accessibility issues.

Security cameras managed by local authorities can help monitor speeding vehicles, prevent crime, support access management, enable payment transactions (e.g., parking), and either deter or identify unwanted activities, with reduced labour costs and human error [19]. Notwithstanding this, there is a tension between personal privacy rights and the public interest. Any such implementation requires compliance with the General Data Protection Regulation (GDPR) and a persistent and consistent enforcement of clear data management policies. While recognising public concerns about mass surveillance, cameras and software can be configured for semi-anonymous analysis, i.e., an individual can be tracked but their individual personal information is never stored, or that only objects are tracked e.g., license plates.

E. Smart Street Furniture

Street furniture is designed primarily for passive consumption. It typically includes benches, transit stops and other shelters, waste receptacles, and public toilets. Smart street furniture re-imagines street furniture as not only a passive object but an active part of the street experience supporting different activities and behaviours to meet social, economic and public health outcomes. For example, in the current COVID-19 pandemic, it is worth noting the smart kiosks that have been implemented as part of variety of health initiatives to facilitate dialogue with health professionals and public health announcements. Street furniture can be categorised in a variety of ways including production method, function, target cohort, and public space typology.

1) Smart Lamp Posts

As per DMURS, good quality lighting promotes safer and secure environments by making it easier for all stakeholders to see each other and potential obstructions. Furthermore, it encourages greater mobility. State-of-the-art smart lamp posts operate a master and slave system and are designed for street illumination and telecommunications. As such, they include

TABLE V. CATEGORIES OF STREET FURNITURE (ADAPTED AND EXTENDED FROM [44])

Production method	Standardised	Designed for mass production but can be adapted for a specific place.
	Atypical	Designed for a specific place and often artistic in nature.
	Digital	Designed for connectivity.
	Sustainable	Designed for environmental sustainability.
Function	Service	Shelters, sunshades, waste receptacles, public transit stops, etc.
	Safety	Public lighting, protective railings, bollards, etc.
	Information	Signage, Information panels, etc.
	Relaxation	Benches, tables, cycle racks, drinking fountains, play areas, etc.
	Aesthetic	Artistic and architectural elements.
Target group	Younger	Street furniture should be sited and designed to take in to account the needs, limitations, safety and security of vulnerable populations.
	Older	
	Disabled	
Public space type	Urban	Street furniture is exposed to greater strain e.g., greater use and greater likelihood of dirt and destruction.
	Village	Less strained street furniture.

LED-smart lights and built-in GPS, Wi-Fi, telecommunications antennas and switchboards. Furthermore, many feature programmable NEMA controllers that can also be used for traffic signal and pedestrian crossing. Additional functionality includes CCTV, telemetry, and EV charging units. In addition to those mentioned, smart lamp posts are typically designed for extensibility thus ideal for supporting a wide range of other cyber-physical interventions including environmental sensing, security, ALPR use cases (e.g., speed, access, payment and demand management), vehicular, cyclist and pedestrian signals. It should be noted that existing legacy lampposts can be enhanced through a network of sensors, such as University of Chicago's Array of Things (AOT). AOT can be mounted to existing lampposts and other infrastructure to collect environmental data about temperature, humidity, light, air quality, wind, precipitation, noise levels, vibrations, proximity detection of Bluetooth- and Wi-Fi-enabled devices including measuring vehicular and pedestrian traffic [45].

2) Smart Kiosks

Modern smart kiosks are a form of multifunctional street furniture that features hardware and software components for sensing different environmental conditions, multi-modal interaction with users, and for capturing and transmitting data for analysis locally or in the cloud [46]. Media poles have similar functionality but with a conventional pole form which may restrict display and associated advertising. Smart kiosks often include much of the functionality of previous generations of related technology including digital signage, media poles and other wayfinding technologies.

Smart kiosks are increasingly adopted as part of smart city initiatives for a variety of use cases including as:

- Information points e.g., public services and related announcements, transit information, weather, route and wayfinding, town or city guide, and local events.
- Transaction points e.g., bicycle sharing, voter registration, seasonal transactions, parking, transit or other event tickets.
- Communication points e.g., emergency contact, public telephone access, and social interactions through

machine agents.

- Connectivity points e.g., relaying or providing access to Wi-Fi.
- Device charging points e.g., EV or USB charging
- Sensing points e.g., collecting passive environmental, traffic or security data through sensors and cameras.
- Research points e.g., collecting active survey data from citizens.
- Advertising points e.g., displaying advertising for sponsors, local retailers and events or other advertisers.

It is important to note that smart kiosks have the potential to be customisable, movable and more critically, a multi-modal experience in that they are interactive and can display visual information and broadcast sound, if required. They also typically include sensors to alert the authority to tampering. Security can be provided through secured WPA/WPA2 or an encrypted network thus requiring proprietary network keys. The CityBridge Link System has been rolled out in New York City and London, in conjunction with local authorities and utility providers providing free Wi-Fi access with speeds up to 1Gb per second, funded through advertising [47]. Each Link Kiosk provides coverage from 150-400ft. Some functionality was disabled due to misuses e.g., unlimited content browsing directly through the kiosk [48].

Smart kiosks can also become a destination in themselves thus attracting people to their location. Research suggests that smart kiosks incentivise local retail activity through proximity and assist people, especially visitors, to discover and navigate local businesses in different business categories [47]. Smart kiosks provide a vital bridge in crossing the digital divide by providing vulnerable communities with access to free Wi-Fi and public services and therefore support social inclusion [49].

3) Smart Benches

Modern smart street benches can include a wide range of functionality that encourage different street uses. For example, they can include additional functionality such as shelter, lighting, CCTV, USB and EV charging, bicycle parking and air pressure, as well as video displays that can be used for information, advertising, and entertainment e.g., games and other programming. Increasingly, smart benches can power themselves completely or partially using solar panels.

In addition to the functionality of the smart bench, three other factors warrant consideration by smart street designers. First, the location and orientation of smart benches can be a determining factor on successful outcomes, use and utility. In effect, local authorities make a decision about what a member of the public will look at and how close they will be to other elements of the street including retail outlets, waste receptacles, junctions, etc. For example, if a local authority wishes to use the smart benches for EV charging, then this determines location and proximity to car parking spaces and the associated impact that such activity has relative to the bench. Second, the design and placement of smart benches can include or exclude those with mobility limitations including participation by wheelchair users, or those with strollers, and accessibility on the footpath for other street users. Third, in addition to services for local stakeholders, smart street benches can provide additional functionality to support the connectivity corridor by housing multiple radio access units, backhaul equipment, power supplies and antennas [50]. Additionally, they can be located at convenient intervals between smart lampposts thereby boosting the coverage and strength of wireless signals.

4) Other Smart Furniture

Waste receptacles are a form of smart street furniture with a primary function. While necessary, they can adversely affect the visual identity of the street, and introduce accessibility issues. Smart waste solutions can be autonomous and robot-based or fixed. The former include making standardised waste containers (organised by organic, recyclable and landfill material) available and having robots that move these containers to centralised units for compaction and removal by type. The EU-funded projectm, FP6-Dustbot, and subsequent ROBOSWEEP projects, resulted in an autonomous street cleaning robot [51]. Similarly, the Lumebot is used to sweep and vacuum pavements, move snow, sweep and steam clean pavements, and dispense salt, sand and gravel [52]. Others have proposed more 'fun' designs. For example, Giant Food Stores has rolled out "Marty" to 172 stores, a robot that identifies spills and other dangerous obstructions [53].

There are a variety of fixed waste collection systems. Vacuum-based systems involve users throwing their waste bags into accessible waste inlets located indoors or outdoors and it is then stored in closed underground screw tanks which are linked together with docking points and a network of underground pipes. The docking points are positioned on the periphery so that the truck picking up the waste does not have to drive into gardens or narrow streets. More conventional smart bin designs are increasingly solar-powered waste receptacles with built-in compactors. Sensors signal the need for collection, as well as recording data on volume, fill rate and collection activity for analysis and chargeback.

Electronic storage units are another form of street furniture that can be used by public services, street vendors, and members of the public to store items. They can also be used by retailers and the public to deliver and collect goods and products out of hours. This may be particularly useful in the context of competing against online trading and limitations due to COVID19. Such units increasingly include advertising displays, reservation and payment, thereby facilitating income generation. Smart solutions also exist for (i) public toilets including access management, intelligent wash disinfection, and other related systems, and (ii) smart public drinking fountains that monitor usage, water quality and hygiene.

F. Climate Protection, Environmental Monitoring, and Weather Mitigation

As discussed, local climate conditions can discourage mobility and outdoor activities. Two achievable interventions include (i) weather monitoring and prediction capabilities, and (ii) support for a variety of weather mitigation strategies that can be triggered based on data, that (i) block wind, and (ii) provide shelter from precipitation, and (iii) shade from the sun. As previously mentioned, AOT is an experimental urban measurement system that provides programmable, modular "nodes" with sensors and computing capability for measuring climate, air quality, noise levels, flood and water levels, as well as counting the number of vehicles at an intersection (and then deleting the image data rather than sending it to a data center) [45]. Use cases today include consumer recommender systems for healthiest and unhealthiest walking times and routes, real-time detection of urban flooding, and micro-climate measurement and analysis [45].

In addition to monitoring the natural environment, sensor technology can be used to monitor the built environment including use and building decay. Smart street development provides the opportunity to embed sensors and other infrastructure systems for monitoring purposes. This includes footpaths, roadbeds, water pipes and electricity systems, providing operators with proactive and predictive maintenance and management systems to ensure usage and costs are within expected ranges, potential and actual anomalies, for example leaks, are detected and resolved, and that service levels are met through cleaning, repair, augmentation and other interventions.

Weather and traffic data can be used to actuate zonal public realm management including weather mitigation strategies. Such strategies may include fixed retractable umbrellas, retractable smart awnings or umbrellas managed and maintained by property owners (retailers), or even street use prioritisation during different weather conditions, in combination with increased tree canopy coverage. However, such technologies can represent a significant investment in themselves. The ultimate outcome of weather mitigation strategies will be to catalyse new uses for a street year-round including markets, events and other activities. As well as the socio-economic impact, it benefits public health by increasing mobility and street use by pedestrians and cyclists.

G. Environmental Sustainability

It is widely accepted that private motor vehicles are the most significant challenge to sustainable travel [54]. In rural communities, it may be infeasible to restrict conventional vehicles from shopping streets for parking or transit, particularly where local public transit alternatives are limited. As discussed, an alternative is to invest in the public realm digital fabric to enable a programmable flexible and adaptive system that prioritises roadbed use and parking space for pedestrians, cyclists, EVs, ride sharing and other sustainable practices. Similarly, reducing barriers to mobility including accessibility, security and safety measures will result in reduced carbon emissions. Implementation of a sensor network for collecting environmental data, for example via the AOT [45], will provide enhanced climate and environmental measurement capabilities and inform local decision making.

A number of the proposed interventions can make use of alternative energy sources e.g. solar power street furniture. To reinforce the sustainability of the street and proposed innovations, dedicated space on streets can be reserved for installing and demonstrating pavement interventions that encourage physical activity and convert alternative energy into off grid electrical energy to power lighting, kiosks, digital signage and other smart furniture. For example, even a relatively small strip of Pavegen tiles can generate 6 to 8 joules of off-grid electrical energy [55]. Bluetooth beacons in the system connect to smartphones, rewarding users for their steps and generating permission-based analytics. Furthermore, it can be integrated with other platforms using APIs. Technologies like Pavegen can be used in different scenarios including powering kiosks and lighting walls. A variety of alternative energy harvesting technologies can be used to store and power innovative street furniture and systems. These include specially- designed light-tiles at pedestrian crossings that only appear when pedestrians or cyclists approach and photovoltaic road cells that convert sunlight into energy. Dutch company, Energy Floors, has designed a number kinetic and solar-powered floors that serve dual purposes as both lighting and interactive street art, interactive games for kids, and dancing [56]. The Korea Advanced Institute of Science and Technology (KAIST) has run trials using induction coils embedded in roads to charge public transit vehicles [57]. Similarly, a UK project is developing smart roads that generate power using piezoelectricity and hydro-mechanical dynamics from passing cars, trucks and buses [58]. The electricity harvested is stored by roadside batteries to power street lamps, road signs, air pollution monitors, plus sensors that detect when potholes are forming, and generate data on vehicle speeds, the types of vehicle travelling along the roads, as well as other information on traffic flows [58]. Israeli company, Innowattech, has experimented with piezoelectric sensors to capture energy created by the weight, motion and vibration of passing trains [59]. While some of these technologies may not be feasible for long-term use, particularly on busy roads, dedicated plug and play areas can be made available to companies wishing to test their technologies in a live environment, and space for power storage supporting hardware as part of redevelopment plans.

H. Street Activity

Research suggests that while street-improvement projects can increase the level of pedestrian satisfaction, they may fail to increase pedestrian volume without specific interventions to invite greater street activity [60]. Inviting street activity is key to the sustainability of shopping streets. As discussed in Section I, thriving shopping streets are both social spaces and commercial spaces, with not only clusters of similar retail outlets but also other diverse retail and social activities [12]. The redevelopment of rural shopping streets should not only serve the needs of existing stakeholders but attract new businesses, customers, visitors and users. The public realm, and in this case one infused with cyber-physical infrastructure should be a destination in itself.

Local retail activity can generate greater economic activity through higher traffic (due to free Wi-Fi and other services) and proximity to smart street furniture (e.g., kiosks, benches and cycle parking and sharing). It can also assist people, especially visitors, to discover and navigate local businesses [47] and thus add value to existing businesses. The siting of such furniture should consider the types of audience a community wishes to attract, move through, and/or stay at different parts of the street, and where they wish to encourage more use at different hours of the day. Geo-fencing can be used in conjunction with smart street furniture to create a sense of digital enclosure and create dialogue with users of street, as well as promote social and commercial activities and retailers on the street. In addition, it can provide income generation through data trading and advertising.

In addition to inherent functionality, street furniture can be augmented with software-enabled solutions to make them interactive using machine learning, if connected, or QR and AR codes, when offline. Advances in intelligent chat technology and even simple conversational technologies can transform street furniture in to a social experience. For example, the Hello Lamp Post project demonstrated how the public could interact with everyday street objects through text messaging providing a fun and novel way for street interaction. More advanced conversational technologies may be used for stimulating interaction with at risk communities. Research also suggests that AI-based conversational technologies provides "valuable practice" and coaching to help older adults navigate challenging conversations and improve both their health and quality of life [61]. Such initiatives can be low cost and attract visitors for this interaction alone.

In conjunction with a more flexible programmable public realm, public projection and sound systems can transform the public space for outdoor events and extend after hours activity including in evenings. In addition to retractable awnings, this may represent another opportunity for the existing retail community on a street to contribute to a smart street through sharing off-peak use of their physical infrastructure. Retailers could be encouraged or incentivised to integrate smart glass and related initiatives. Smart glass takes many forms, often based on liquid crystal technology, to transform storefronts by allowing window glass for projection e.g. it can switch to opaque, transparent, for projecting media including advertising, or even using it as a mirror. Smart glass and motion sensor natural user interfaces can transform how the public engages with retail frontage, even out of hours. Such innovations provide 100% glass window utilisation out of hours including monetisation through advertising. When multiple units are linked together with a street sound system, they can be used for creating multimedia experiences and shows to attract visitors. In effect, they provide the opportunity to turn passive retail units in to information kiosks, entertainment systems, and digital out of home advertising.

Encouraging new uses, particularly transient uses, requires changes to the geometry of a street. Smart technologies can use digital technologies to experiment with using specific zones on the street as reservable outdoor spaces for short-term uses for regular or seasonal retail, performances, community and personal events (e.g., markets, school activities or hackathons), and food trucks. As well as systems to delineate these areas (e.g., automated retractable bollards and digital signage), utilities (power and water), and storage for pop-up stall units and street vendors and performers. New pop-up configuration and designs are emerging that can be used for multiple purposes such as street seating, movable and collapsible units. Similarly, historically unused or redundant space can be can be used for smart delivery and distribution centres (storage lockers) where citizens can have goods delivered or retail outlets can leave goods for customers to collect out of hours. Parklets, planters and dedicated units could also be used for Urban Farm projects with local schools.

V. Conclusion

Forecasts suggest that by 2050, over 68% of the world's population will live in cities [1]. Rural towns, communities, and their citizens are in danger of being left behind. The sustainable management of urban growth involves investments in smart city technologies and improving the lives of urban dwellers, however an alternative is improving the quality of life and attractiveness of rural living to reduce migration to urban centers, and ideally changing the flow. Digital technologies can play a significant role in sustaining and revitalising rural towns, and building economic and social linkages between urban and rural areas. We suggest the first step in the digital transformation of rural towns is sustaining rural shopping streets, often the economic core of rural communities. Smart streets are a manageable and feasible investment for rural towns that can sustain rural shopping streets while enhancing the lives of those who live in and around rural towns.

Acknowledgment

This work is partially funded by Wexford County Council and by the Irish Institute of Digital Business.

References

[1] United Nations Department of Economic and Social Affairs, "Revision of world urbanization prospects," 2018. [Online]. Available: https://bit.ly/2K8Sy6o

[2] D. Hoornweg and M. Freire, "Building sustainability in an urbanizing world: A partnership report," 2013. [Online]. Available: https://documents.worldbank.org/en/publication/documents-reports/documentdetail/622651468320375543/main-report

[3] Global Future Council on Cities and Urbanization, "Agile cities: Preparing for the fourth industrial revolution," 2018. [Online]. Available: http://www3.weforum.org/docs/WP_Global_Future_Council_Cities_Urbanization_report_2018.pdf

[4] Sánchez-Corcuera et al., "Smart cities survey: Technologies, application domains and challenges for the cities of the future," International Journal of Distributed Sensor Networks, vol. 15, no. 6, 2019, p. 1550147719853984.

[5] C. Yin et al., "A literature survey on smart cities," Science China Information Sciences, vol. 58, no. 10, 2015, pp. 1–18.

[6] C. Harrison et al., "Foundations for smarter cities," IBM Journal of research and development, vol. 54, no. 4, 2010, pp. 1–16.

[7] P. Přibyl and O. Přibyl, "Definition of a smart street as smart city's building element," in 2015 Smart Cities Symposium Prague. IEEE, 2015, pp. 1–6.

[8] S. Jung, J. K. J. Lee, and J. Ha, "A study on analysis of user behavior in urban central street: On the dongsung street in daegu," Journal of the Regional Association of the Architectural Institute of Korea, 2009, p. 300.

[9] M. Dellenbaugh, "Normative properties of street furniture," 2020. [Online]. Available: https://bit.ly/2P5SVOw

[10] J.-H. Lee and W.-J. Lee, "A study on the impact of ubiquitous street furniture on human behavior-based on media poles installed on seoul's gangnam boulevard," Journal of Asian Architecture and Building Engineering, vol. 12, no. 2, 2013, pp. 181–188.

[11] D. Song, "A study on the planning direction of street furniture in urban-street space–focused on the dae-chung road in busan city," Journal of the Regional Association of Architectural Institute of Korea, vol. 8, no. 3, 2006, p. 60.

[12] C. Jones, Q. Al-Shaheen, and N. Dunse, "Anatomy of a successful high street shopping centre," Journal of Urban Design, vol. 21, no. 4, 2016, pp. 495–511.

[13] G. Maccani, B. Donnellan, and M. Helfert, "A comprehensive framework for smart cities," in 2nd International Conference on Smart Grids and Green IT Systems. SciTePress, 2013.

[14] A. Ramaprasad, A. Sánchez-Ortiz, and T. Syn, "A unified definition of a smart city," in International Conference on Electronic Government. Springer, 2017, pp. 13–24.

[15] V. Yadav, "An overview of smart and sustainable regions' development," Sustainable Regional Development, 2020, p. 1.

[16] L. Naldi, P. Nilsson, H. Westlund, and S. Wixe, "What is smart rural development?" Journal of rural studies, vol. 40, 2015, pp. 90–101.

[17] S. H. Ahmed and S. Rani, "A hybrid approach, smart street use case and future aspects for internet of things in smart cities," Future Generation Computer Systems, vol. 79, 2018, pp. 941–951.

[18] J. Lahart, P. Kelly, A. Kiernan, S. McGrath, D. Taylor, and J. Taylor, "Design manual for urban roads and streets," Irish Department of Transport, Tourism and Sport and Irish Department of Housing, Planning and Local Government, 2019.

[19] Global Designing Cities Initiative, "Global street design guide," 2016. [Online]. Available: https://globaldesigningcities.org/publication/global-street-design-guide/

[20] R. Katz and F. Callorda, "The economic contribution of broadband, digitization and ict regulation," ITU, 2018.

[21] M. Minges, "Exploring the relationship between broadband and economic growth." World Bank, 2015.

[22] E. A. Mack, "Broadband and knowledge intensive firm clusters: Essential link or auxiliary connection?" Papers in Regional Science, vol. 93, no. 1, 2014, pp. 3–29.

[23] J. Kolko, "Broadband and local growth," Journal of Urban Economics, vol. 71, no. 1, 2012, pp. 100–113.

[24] G. S. Yovanof and G. N. Hazapis, "An architectural framework and enabling wireless technologies for digital cities & intelligent urban environments," Wireless personal communications, vol. 49, no. 3, 2009, pp. 445–463.

[25] F. Bar and H. Galperin, "Geeks, bureaucrats and cowboys: Deploying internet infrastructure, the wireless way," The Network Society From Knowledge to Policy, 2005, p. 269.

[26] A. Picco-Schwendener, "Social dimensions of public large-scale wi-fi networks," Ph.D. dissertation, Università della Svizzera italiana, 2018.

[27] P. Ballon, L. Van Audenhove, M. Poel, and T. Staelens, "Business models for wireless city networks in the eu and the us: Public inputs and public leverage," in Telecommunication markets. Springer, 2009, pp. 325–340.

[28] K. A. Chesley, "The future of municipal wireless in the united states and europe," Available at SSRN 1408808, 2009.

[29] A. H. Tapia, L. Kvasny, and J. A. Ortiz, "A critical discourse analysis of three us municipal wireless network initiatives for enhancing social inclusion," Telematics and Informatics, vol. 28, no. 3, 2011, p. 215.

[30] T. Heer et al., "Collaborative municipal wi-fi networks-challenges and opportunities," in 2010 8th IEEE International Conference on Pervasive Computing and Communications Workshops. IEEE, 2010, pp. 588–593.

[31] IHS Markit and Point Topic, "Study on broadband coverage in europe 2018," 2019. [Online]. Available: https://ec.europa.eu/digital-single-market/en/news/study-broadband-coverage-europe-2018#:~:text=The%20results%20of%20the%20study,the%20EU%20reached%2096.7%25%20households&text=87.4%25%20of%20rural%20EU%20homes,high%2Dspeed%20next%20generation%20services.

[32] H. Qian et al., "Indoor transmission of sars-cov-2," medRxiv, 2020.

[33] J. Wang, "Why time outdoors is crucial to your health, even during the coronavirus pandemic," 2020.

[34] G. N. Bratman et al., "Nature and mental health: An ecosystem service perspective," Science advances, vol. 5, no. 7, 2019, p. eaax0903.

[35] J. Gehl et al., "World class streets: Remaking new york city's public realm," 2008.

[36] V. Mehta, The street: a quintessential social public space. Routledge, 2013.

[37] E. Kalampokis, E. Tambouris, and K. Tarabanis, "A classification scheme for open government data: towards linking decentralised data," International Journal of Web Engineering and Technology, vol. 6, no. 3, 2011, pp. 266–285.

[38] M. Janssen, Y. Charalabidis, and A. Zuiderwijk, "Benefits, adoption barriers and myths of open data and open government," Information systems management, vol. 29, no. 4, 2012, pp. 258–268.

[39] L. Edwards, "Privacy, security and data protection in smart cities: A critical eu law perspective," Eur. Data Prot. L. Rev., vol. 2, 2016, p. 28.

[40] European Commission, "Smart cities," 2020. [Online]. Available: https://bit.ly/3hL24rS

[41] Sidewalk Labs, "Sidewalk toronto: Vision sections of rfp submission," 2017. [Online]. Available: https://www.sidewalktoronto.ca/documents/

[42] M. Dunn, "Melbourne introduce pilot trial for technology allowing blind people to navigate public spaces," 2017. [Online]. Available: https://bit.ly/307Ptt1

[43] H. Wennberg, A. Ståhl, and C. Hydén, "Older pedestrians' perceptions of the outdoor environment in a year-round perspective," European Journal of Ageing, vol. 6, no. 4, 2009, p. 277.

[44] M. Mrázek et al., "Street furniture for seniors," Acta Universitatis Agriculturae et Silviculturae Mendelianae Brunensis, vol. 68, no. 1, 2020, pp. 81–94.

[45] University of Chicago, "Array of things," 2020. [Online]. Available: https://arrayofthings.github.io/

[46] O. Gómez-Carmona, D. Casado-Mansilla, and D. López-de Ipiña, "Multifunctional interactive furniture for smart cities," in Multidisciplinary Digital Publishing Institute Proceedings, vol. 2, no. 19, 2018, p. 1212.

[47] S. Sobolevsky et al., "Impact of urban technology deployments on local commercial activity," arXiv preprint arXiv:1712.00659, 2017.

[48] J. Brodkin, "After "lewd acts," nyc's free internet kiosks disable web browsing," 2016. [Online]. Available: https://bit.ly/3jQt9Mn

[49] C. L. de Camargo Penteado, P. R. E. de Souza, I. Fortunato, and S. A. da Silveira, "Connectivity public policy in the network society: The case of "wifi livre sp"," 2016.

[50] L. Manholm, J. Fridén, and B.-E. Olsson, "Deployment considerations for 60 ghz backhaul using smart street furniture," in 2015 9th European Conference on Antennas and Propagation. IEEE, 2015, pp. 1–3.

[51] Robotech srl, "Dustclean," 2020. [Online]. Available: https://www.robotechsrl.com/dustclean-en-robot-sweeper/

[52] Lumebot, "Autonomous street clearning robots," 2020. [Online]. Available: https://lumebot.com/

[53] P. Holley, "Giant food stores will place robotic assistants at 172 locations, company says," 2019. [Online]. Available: https://wapo.st/305fby9

[54] European Union Directorate-General for the Environment, Reclaiming city streets for people: chaos or quality of life? Office for Official Publications of the European Communities, 2004.

[55] E. M. Nia, N. A. W. A. Zawawi, and B. S. M. Singh, "A review of walking energy harvesting using piezoelectric materials," in IOP Conference Series: Materials Science and Engineering, vol. 291, no. 1. IOP Publishing, 2017, p. 012026.

[56] R. Saifan, L. A. Ali, A. A. Shreikh, and S. H. Alnabelsi, "Smart walk: Case studies on hybrid power generation system of piezoelectricity and solar power," in 2019 International Conference on Electrical and Computing Technologies and Applications. IEEE, 2019, pp. 1–6.

[57] J. Huh and C.-T. Rim, "Kaist wireless electric vehicles-olev," SAE Technical Paper, Tech. Rep., 2011.

[58] A. Frost, "Smart city project aiming to harvest energy from passing traffic," 2019. [Online]. Available: https://bit.ly/3f5Rgmn

[59] A. Qabur and K. Alshammari, "A systematic review of energy harvesting from roadways by using piezoelectric materials technology," Innov Energy Res, vol. 7, no. 01, 2018, pp. 1–6.

[60] H. Jung, S.-y. Lee, H. S. Kim, and J. S. Lee, "Does improving the physical street environment create satisfactory and active streets? evidence from seoul's design street project," Transportation research part D: transport and environment, vol. 50, 2017, pp. 269–279.

[61] S. Z. Razavi, L. K. Schubert, K. A. Van Orden, and M. R. Ali, "Discourse behavior of older adults interacting with a dialogue agent competent in multiple topics," arXiv preprint arXiv:1907.06279, 2019.

Addressing the Urban-Town-Rural Divide: The Digital Town Readiness Assessment Framework

Theo Lynn
Irish Institute of Digital Business,
Dublin City University,
Dublin, Ireland.
Email: theo.lynn@dcu.ie

Pierangelo Rosati
Irish Institute of Digital Business,
Dublin City University,
Dublin, Ireland.
Email: pierangelo.rosati@dcu.ie

Grace Fox
Irish Institute of Digital Business,
Dublin City University,
Dublin, Ireland.
Email: grace.fox@dcu.ie

Declan Curran
DCU Business School,
Dublin City University,
Dublin, Ireland.
Email: declan.curran@dcu.ie

Colm O'Gorman
DCU Business School,
Dublin City University,
Dublin, Ireland.
Email: colm.ogorman@dcu.ie

Edel Conway
Irish Institute of Digital Business,
Dublin City University,
Dublin, Ireland.
Email: edel.conway@dcu.ie

***Abstract*—Economic growth, job creation, better public services, and improved quality of life are just some of the benefits from the digital transformation of society. Policymakers worldwide are not only investing in the infrastructure to deliver this digital future but measurement and benchmarking to assess digital progress. These benchmarks are, for the most part, national benchmarks heavily influenced by broadband connectivity and an increasing focus on cities and metropolises. Against the backdrop of global urbanisation, towns outside the functional urban area of cities are in danger of both being depopulated and disconnected. This paper proposes a definition for a digital town and outlines eight rationales for digital towns. Based on these rationales and a review of existing benchmarking frameworks for digitisation, we present a framework for measuring digital readiness at a town level. The framework can be used by local stakeholders and regional and national policymakers to understand digital town readiness and digital competitiveness; compare a town against selected national and international benchmarks; and stimulate stakeholder engagement on digital strategies for town development.**

Keywords–Rural Development; Digital Town; Smart Cities; Smart Towns; Government Policy; Framework.

I. Introduction

"The Digital Society" is the latest sobriquet in a long list for a society whose social structures and activities, to a greater or lesser extent, are organised around digital information networks that connect people, processes, things, data and networks [1]. There is near-universal agreement that, at a national level, progress towards such digitisation and the societal and economic consequences are beneficial. As such, policymakers have invested heavily in Information and Communication Technologies (ICTs) to support digital agendas. To assess and benchmark performance and progress, a wide range of country-level and city-level indices have been developed and introduced by international organisations, industry bodies, firms, and academics.

Concurrent with the introduction and evolution of the digital society, there has been a significant rise in the proportion of the population that live in cities, from 37% in 1975 to 48% today [2]. This urbanisation has been driven by city expansion, city densification, and rural migration driven by economic opportunities and higher quality of life [2][3]. While the larger population results in an agglomeration of resources that attract economic activity, government investment, and opportunities for socio-cultural and political participation, greater population density has an adverse impact on sustainable development [2]. In an effort to reduce pollution and crime, limit exposure to natural hazards, transition to a low-carbon economy, and more recently curb the spread of infectious diseases such as COVID19, there has been an increased focus on the use of ICTs at a city level, so-called "smart city" technologies. Given the level of investment in smart cities, it is unsurprising that smart city indices have emerged including the Horizon 2020-funded CITYkeys indicators for smart city projects and smart cities, and the more recent IMD Smart City Index.

The term "digital divide", in reality, refers to two inter-related digital divides - (i) divides resulting from inequalities in the technological infrastructure required to support digital connectivity, and (ii) socio-economic digital divides [4]. These aspects have been explored in the urban-rural context for over two decades [4]–[6]. A substantial number of studies from around the world suggest this divide exists due to inadequate infrastructure [4][7][8], however more recent studies in highly digitised countries such as South Korea and Australia suggest that the digital divide extends to a difference in use by and perceived benefits for rural users [9][10]. In addition to broadband availability and geographic remoteness, suitability and social exclusion are also factors that have been cited as barriers to digital adoption and use in rural areas [8]–[10]. These inter-related factors may not be capable of being addressed by the market or government intervention alone, particularly where geographic conditions make broadband deployment commercially infeasible or unattractive. Community-led multi-stakeholder initiatives have been suggested as a solution to the urban-rural digital divide, however such initiatives need to overcome access to technical expertise, volunteerism, and funding arrangements, as well as geographical conditions, to ensure success [7].

While national and global definitions tend to agree on what cities are, national definitions tend to disagree on the classification of towns, semi-dense areas and rural areas [2]. This definitional ambiguity reduces comparability at all levels - international, national, regional, city, town, and other levels - and does not recognise fundamental differences in governance. While countries and cities have both policy making and investment capabilities, towns and rural areas may not, or if they do so, such capabilities are limited. This has been recently addressed by the European Union, the Food and Agriculture Organization of the United Nations (FAO), the International Labour Office (ILO), the OECD, UN-Habitat and the World Bank by the introduction of two new definitions, the degree of urbanisation and the Functional Urban Area (FUA) which proposes three classes instead of the traditional two - (i) cities; (ii) Towns and Semi-dense Areas (TSA); and iii) rural areas [2]. With the adoption of these definitions, new research is required to explore whether these categorisations provide new insights and identify a need for renovation of existing theories, measurement frameworks, and interventions that delineate between cities, towns and semi-dense areas, and rural areas so that the efficacy of digital policy and investment can be assessed and compared for these important and discrete parts of society. This paper presents preliminary work on a digital readiness framework to support towns (outside FUAs) and semi-dense areas in the assessment of digital readiness, benchmarking against national and international indicators, and the development of multi-stakeholder digitisation strategies.

The remainder of this paper is structured as follows. Next, we discuss the rationales for digital towns and propose a definition of a digital town based on extant literature. In Section 3, we review existing national and smart city frameworks for assessing digital performance and progress. We then briefly present the Digital Town Readiness Assessment Framework in Section 4. The paper concludes with a discussion of the current status of the project.

II. Defining and Rationalising Digital Towns

While there is extensive literature on smart cities, there is a paucity of research on the digital transformation of towns [11]. This can be partly explained by the attractiveness of cities to researchers and policymakers as a focal topic due to their size, impact and profile. This is not the only reason. A number of researchers and projects have focussed on *smart towns* [11]. While the term *smart city* focuses attention on cities, it does not necessarily preclude other urban areas, including towns, that use smart city technology and data to optimise the operation and services in that area [12]. Notwithstanding this, while towns face similar issues to cities albeit at a smaller scale, they have a number of local contextual challenges including availability of infrastructure services, geographic remoteness, smaller population sizes, amongst others [13][14]. In this paper, we do not focus on the quality of *smartness* as this derives from the use of (i) near-real-time data obtained from physical and virtual sensors; (ii) the interconnection between different services and technologies within the urban area; (iii) the intelligence from the analysis of the data, and the process of visualising it; and (iv) the optimisation of operations resulting from this analysis [12]. Instead, we focus on *digital* as a quality as we are interested in the transformations triggered by widespread adoption of digital technologies that generate, process, share and transfer information, in all aspects of life.

In addition, and as previously discussed, towns, until recently, were inconsistently classified as urban or rural thus preventing international comparisons. These factors are evident even in the limited literature on digital towns. For example, Aveiro in Portugal pioneered a "digital town programme" in the late nineties [15]. At the time, it had a population of over 75,000 people and today is an urban agglomeration with a population of over 120,000. Similarly, Fujisawa, a prominent Japanese *smart town* project is an urban area with a population of over 420,000 people [16]. At the other end of the scale, researchers and projects have focussed on smart and digital villages [17]–[19]. Again, definitional consistencies abound. The Digitale Doerfer project in Germany includes Billerbeck with a population of 450 people and Bodenheim with a population of over 20,000 [20]. In arriving at a usable definition of a Digital Town, we must recognise and account for the increasing expansion of cities and accommodate the new higher resolution OECD definitions, while also recognising existing perspectives on digital towns, and both general and local contextual rationales for digital adoption and use at a town level. As mentioned earlier, the OECD has adopted two definitions - the degree of urbanisation and the FUA. The degree of urbanisation reflects an urban-rural continuum and proposes three classes (i) cities; (ii) TSAs; and iii) rural areas [2]. The FUA recognises that cities are metropolitan areas comprising the city itself and surrounding areas that are connected to the city in terms of labour market interactions (commuting zones) [21]. These definitions provide new insights in to population change. As discussed, population share in cities has increased to 48% with a corresponding drop in towns and semi-dense areas, and rural areas. However, overall population growth has meant that the population has increased in all area classifications. More importantly, research by the OECD on 111 countries suggest that social and economic opportunities follow an urban gradient including life satisfaction, income premia, employment opportunities, economic mobility, educational attainment, internet and mobile access and use, and the provision of public services [2]. Consequently, we focus on towns and semi-dense areas outside of the FUA of cities, and exclude low density rural areas. As such and to enable future comparability, we adopt the definition of town as per the revised OECD [2] definition:

1) Cities consist of contiguous grid cells that have a density of at least 1,500 inhabitants per km^2 and are at least 50% built up with a a population of at least 50,000.
2) Towns and semi-dense areas consist of contiguous grid cells with a density of at least 300 inhabitants per km^2, are at least 3% built up, and have a total population of at least 5,000.
3) Rural areas are cells that do not belong to a city or a town and semi-dense area, and for the most part have

a density below 300 inhabitants per km^2.

Based on analysis of existing community network and digital town projects, we identify at least eight rationales for digital towns that can be organised along a socio-economic spectrum - Social, Accessibility, Vocational, Sustainability, Quality of Service, Catalytic, Economic - and an over-riding Opportunistic rationale. The Social Rationale recognises that towns are part of a wider Digital Society and digital technologies help towns and their residents participate and function more fully in such a Digital Society [15][22][23]. In many instances, this revolves around the provision of online platforms where stakeholders can share and consume information, services, and transact through marketplaces [20][24]. The Accessibility and Vocational Rationales also relate to participation in society. The former posits that the adoption and use of digital technologies can increase accessibility to services and opportunities to those who may be disadvantaged or vulnerable in society [15], while the latter assumes that digital technologies help town residents prepare to work in a Digital Society [19][22]. This includes embedding digital technologies in educational institutions, the provision of education and training on digital technologies and related topics, and the overall digital competencies for the entire community [22][23]. For example, Aveiro had a specific focus on training and providing employment opportunities for citizens with special needs in their digital town programme [15]. Unsurprisingly, environmental sustainability is a common rationale for digital town projects. Here, the adoption and use of digital technologies is seen as a means for towns to reduce adverse environmental impacts and build a resilient habitat for existing and future residents [16][19][25][26].

A number of digital town objectives can be categorised under a Quality of Service Rationale. This rationale assumes that digital technologies may increase the range, quality and efficiency of service delivery whether public services including health services, commercial services, or community services [15][23][27]. A common theme in digital town projects is that role of digital technologies as a catalyst of other innovations from all parts of the community [11][15][23] (Catalytic Rationale). Indeed, in the case of Parthenay, a specific objective of the digital town programme was to explore whether citizens were capable of co-inventing services with the public and commercial sponsors [23]. Many digital agenda and digital town initiatives are driven, at some level, by an Economic Rationale. This rationale posits that the availability, quality (including broadband speed), adoption and use of digital technologies may attract greater economic growth and employment to a town [23]. This includes increased tourism and retail activity in addition to potentially attracting digital industry investment and teleworkers [27]. For example, in the German Digital Doerfer project, the platform includes a service for ordering and delivering local products and services [20]. Finally, although somewhat implicitly, digital towns appear to be motivated by an Opportunistic Rationale in that the adoption and use of digital technologies can differentiate a town from other towns and may make it a more attractive place to live, work or visit, or competitive from an economic and investment perspective, when compared to other towns. This rationale has a dual purpose in that towns not only seek to attract new residents, workers and visitors to the town but retain existing residents and mitigate the risk of depopulation [24].

These rationales are reflected in three prevailing perspectives found in the literature which we label as infrastructure-centric, service-centric, and community-centric. The Infrastructure perspective of a digital town emphasises the local availability and appropriation of ICT infrastructure as a prerequisite for the connection of a town as a node in a national/global network. The Service perspective emphasises the provision of local information services for citizen's everyday lives and visitors. Finally, the community perspective emphasises platforms for communities of interest to support work in a geographical and information space where users can interact, sharing knowledge, experience and mutual interests [23]. In reality, a digital town is all of these things. Consequently, we define a digital town as a geographic and information space that adopts and integrates information and communication technologies in all aspects of town life.

III. Measuring Digital Readiness

The emergence of frameworks for assessing digital adoption and use emerged in the mid-nineties with the emergence of the World Wide Web and wider use of the Internet by the general public [28]. Unsurprisingly, given that telecommunications connectivity is a key enabling technology in the digital value chain, research and measurement frameworks initially emphasised the availability, quality, adoption and use of broadband as a key digital indicator [28]. For example, the International Telecommunications Union (ITU) ICT Development Index (IDI) seeks to assess country-level progress towards becoming an information society by measuring the level, evolution, and differences over time of ICT developments in countries and the experience of those countries relative to other countries [29]. First developed in 2008 and revised in 2018, IDI comprises three sub-indices - ICT Access (infrastructure availability and access), ICT Use (level of ICT usage and intensity), and ICT Skills (capabilities of the citizens) comprising 14 indicators in total [29]. ICT Access and ICT Use each have a weighting of 40%, the ICT skills sub-index has a weighting of 20%; discrete indicators within each sub-indices have equal weightings [29]. While commonly referenced, this index places a significant emphasis on Internet, and specific broadband and mobile connectivity, and is relatively simplistic. For example, ICT skills indicators primarily relate to enrollment in schools with only one indicator on specific ICT skills. Other than education, it does not delineate between different actors in a given country.

In the last decade, frameworks have expanded to reflect the wider transformative impact of digital technologies on society at different levels - country, city, and to a lesser extent towns and other rural areas. These include the European Union (EU) Digital Economy and Society (DESI) Index, the Digital Capital Index, the Digital Evolution Index, and the Digital Ecosystem Development Index, to name but a few. DESI [30] is a composite index designed for monitoring and benchmarking the digital competitiveness of EU Member States in digital competitiveness. DESI [31][32] measures performance across five dimensions:

1) Connectivity: the deployment of broadband infrastructure and its quality i.e., broadband take-up, fixed broadband coverage, mobile broadband and broadband prices;
2) Human Capital: the Internet user and advanced skills needed to take advantage of the possibilities offered by a digital society;

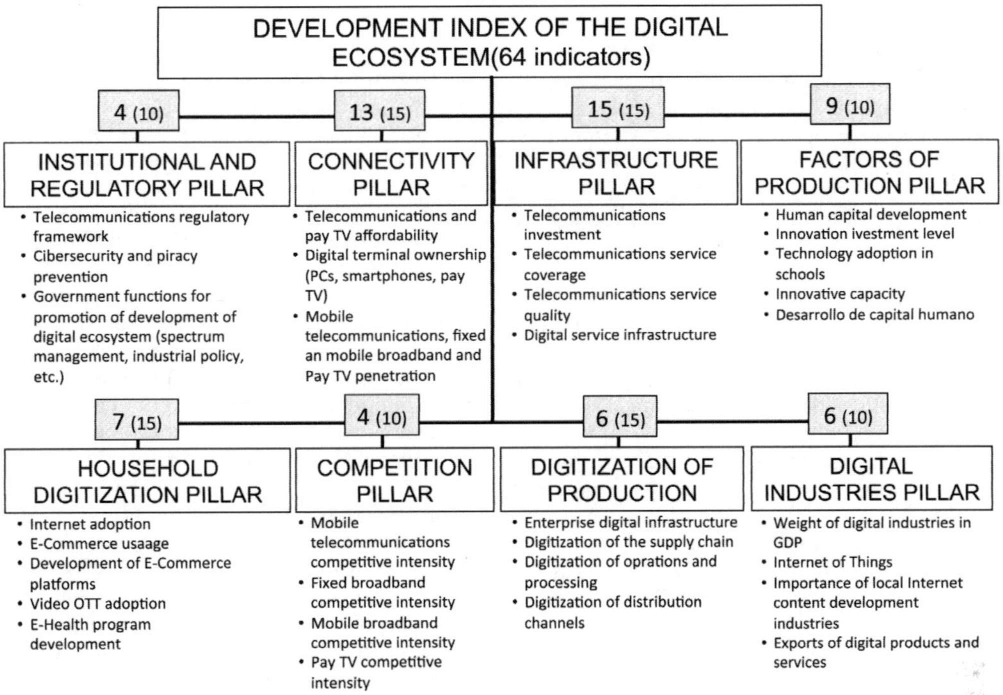

Figure 1. Structure of the Digital Ecosystem Index [28]

3) Citizen use of Internet and online transactions: the variety of activities performed by citizens already online;
4) Business digitisation and e-commerce: the digitisation of businesses and development of the online sales channel;
5) Digital public services: the digitisation of public services. It should be noted that DESI 2020 does not include ehealth as part of the Digital Public Services report as no new data was reported in [33]. It is unclear whether this is a consequence of the COVID19 pandemic or not.

Since 2018, an international version of DESI (I-DESI) was produced comparing the 28 countries in the EU with 17 non-EU countries [32]. DESI is based on data regularly collected by EU member states however in some cases, for example rural data, this may be based on aggregating a number of towns, semi-dense and sparsely populated rural areas based on the Nomenclature of Territorial Units for Statistics (NUTS). NUTS is a geocode standard for referencing the subdivisions of a country for statistical purposes. It aggregates towns and regions at a resolution level that may not be useful for town-level strategic planning.

Similar to DESI, the Digital Capital Index (DCI) focuses specifically on the digital evolution of a population. In the context of the DCI, digital capital is defined as an accumulation of both digital competencies and digital technologies (or digital access). The former seeks to measure the individual abilities of citizens based on the European Digital Competence Framework for Citizens i.e., information and data literacy, communication and collaboration, digital content creation, safety, and problem solving. The latter, digital access, includes indicators on the access to digital equipment, connectivity (quality and place), historical time spent online, and support and training. While not specifically focusing on towns or rural areas, Ragnedda, Ruiu and Addeo [34] find that urban users are more likely to have higher digital capital than rural users.

The Digital Evolution Index (DEvI), introduced in 2015, is an attempt to assess the progress and benchmark country-level progress towards a digital economy [35]. In the DEvI, the competitiveness of a country's digital economy is a function of two factors - (i) its current state of digitisation based on four drivers (supply conditions, demand conditions, institutional environment, and innovation and change) comprising between 99 and 170 indicators, and (ii) its pace of digitisation (momentum) over time measured by the growth rate of a country's digitisation score over a ten-year period (2008—2017) [36]. Based on these two factors, digital progress can be categorised as (a) rapidly advancing, (b) steadily advancing, (c) slow moving, and (d) declining [36]. Similar to the DEvI, Katz and Callorda developed the Digital Ecosystem Index (DEcI) [28] to address limitations in country-level frameworks that overly focussed on telecommunications infrastructure or a subset of an economy. The DEcI comprises 64 indicators organised in to eight pillars as per Figure 1.

More recently, there has been an effort to assess the state and evolution of digital progress at a city level. These efforts are largely in the *smart city* domain and as such often conflate both digital and environmental sustainability themes. The Smart City Index (SCI) assesses the adoption of smart technologies in a given city. SCI comprises two pillars, Structures and Technology, and each pillar is evaluated from five perspectives - health and safety, mobility, activities, opportunities, and governance. For comparison purposes, cities are also categorised against four groups based on the UN Human Development Index (HDI) score of the economy they are part of, and are ultimately given a rating for each pillar and overall, an overall ranking. Similarly, the EU-funded CITYkeys project propose a benchmarking framework, indicators, and associated data collection procedures for monitoring and benchmarking smart city solutions across European cities [37]. The CITYkeys smart city indicator framework is organised around five themes:

1) People - health, safety, access to services, education, diversity and social cohesion, quality of housing and the built environment;
2) Planet - energy and mitigation, materials, water and land, climate resilience, pollution and waste, ecosystem;
3) Prosperity - employment, equity, green economy, economic performance, innovation, attractiveness and competitiveness;
4) Governance - organisation, community involvement, multi-level governance; and
5) Propagation - scalability and replicability [37].

CITYkeys is the basis for the ETSI technical specification for standardised key performance indicators for sustainable digital multiservice cities [38].

As can be seen from the aforementioned indicators, many of the indicators are not within the control of local communities or municipal authorities at a town-level. Furthermore, the discussion of smart cities and related technologies is often conflated or combined with environmental sustainability and associated outcomes. Additionally, where indicators might be relevant, data may not easily be available or required at regional or national levels and therefore are not collected or easily accessible for town stakeholders. While we could not find robust town-level indicators for digital readiness, those we identified, for example Kalinka et al. [39], are designed for sustainable local area planning rather than digitisation purposes.

IV. The Digital Town Readiness Framework

The Digital Town Readiness Assessment framework was developed by the Irish Institute of Digital Business and the IE Domain Registry, the Irish national registry for ".ie" domains, to support stakeholders in towns outside FUAs to rapidly and cost-effectively:

- Understand current digital town readiness and digital competitiveness;
- Compare a town against national and international benchmarks; and,
- Stimulate stakeholder engagement on digitisation.

Based on desk research of existing frameworks for measuring digital adoption and use and consultation with stakeholders in target areas, an initial framework was developed. The framework comprises eight dimensions as per Figure 2, namely Connectivity, Digital Citizen, Digital Education, Digital Civil Society, Digital Business, Digital Public Services, Digital Tourism, and Horizontal Integration.

A. Connectivity

Based on extant indices and literature, we include a connectivity dimension with nine sub-dimensions relating to the deployment, quality, adoption and use of broadband. Firstly, we include two sub-dimensions relating to the availability of documented plans for both fixed and mobile broadband connectivity for the town. Secondly, in line with DESI [30], we include five sub-dimensions relating to equal access to fixed, mobile, wireless, and next generation access technologies in the town. As per [28], we assume greater competition between broadband and mobile phone services will result in lower prices to access these services as well as higher quality of service. Consequently, we include local competition levels between telecommunications service providers as a factor. Literature suggests that municipal and free public Wi-Fi access contribute to economic growth [40][41], promoting tourism [42][43], social inclusion [44][45], public safety [45]–[47], and improved public services [43][48]. Similarly, a number of commentators have emphasised the need for local economic policy to focus on encouraging teleworking in rural areas [49]–[51]. As such, we include two sub-dimensions relating to the availability of free public Wi-Fi and public Internet access in public and co-working spaces in the town.

B. Digital Citizen

The Digital Citizen dimension focuses on the competence and usage of digital technologies by citizens in a town. Again, we include two sub-dimensions relating to the availability of documented town-level plans for increasing digital competencies and usage by citizens in the town. To allow country-level and international comparability, we adopt and expand the sub-dimensions and indicators used in DESI and the European Commission Digital Skills Indicators. This includes the number and complexity of activities involving digital technologies including the Internet, as well as the availability of more advanced skills and development, and use of internet services, e-commerce, digital public services, and health and care services. Again, reflecting recent emphasis in scholarly literature and policy, we include a sub-dimension for teleworking, freelancing and other sharing economy work.

C. Digital Education

It is increasingly accepted that digital technologies and related affordances can directly change the nature of teaching and learning; this is particularly poignant against the backdrop of the COVID19 pandemic. The Digital Education dimensions relates to the support for use and sophistication of digital technology in education and the provision of training and education in digital technologies for all levels. Extant general digitisation measurement frameworks either focus nearly exclusively on Internet access and computer availability in schools as in DEcI [28] or, as per DESI [30], do not include digital adoption and usage in education at all. There are numerous benchmarking studies on ICT adoption by education which primarily focus on schools and higher education. These include reports and studies by the UNESCO Institute for Statistics [52], European Schoolnet [53], and more recently the European Commission's DG CONNECT [54]. As digital adoption and use are heavily influenced by the experience and skills of the user population, and older citizens may not have had the same opportunity to

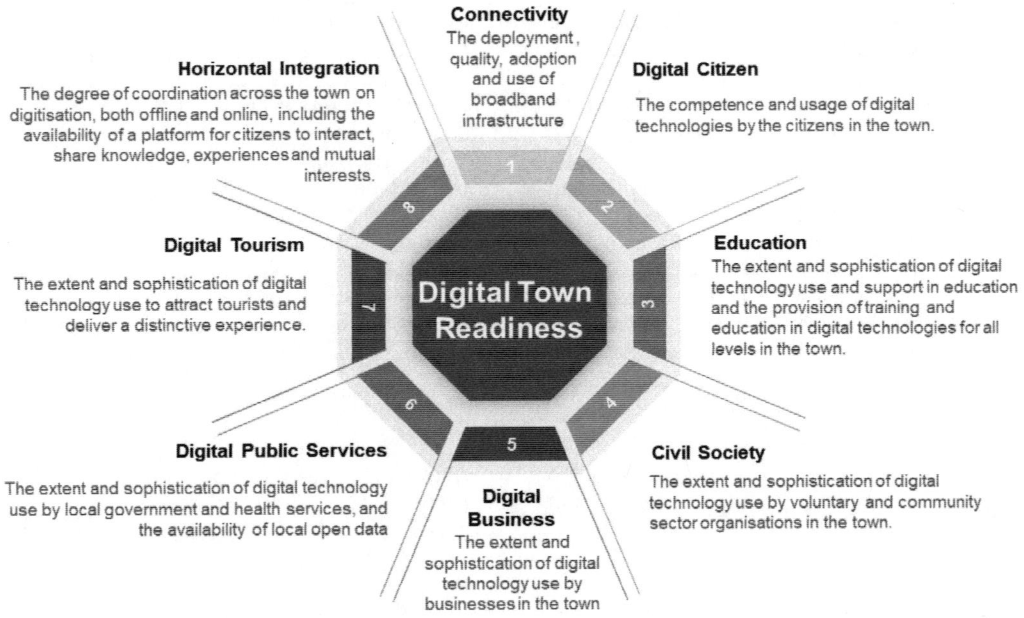

Figure 2. The eight dimensions of the Digital Town Readiness Framework

acquire these skills, we include the availability of documented plans at both a town-level and institution-level for digital skills provision and integration for all levels of education and age levels. As such we include all education providers including pre-school, primary, post-primary, and other digital skills education providers including training provided by community organisations, local, regional and national agencies, and commercial organisations. To aid comparability, we adopt and extend sub-dimensions from extant benchmarks for ICT in Education including access to and use of digital technologies, digital activities and digital confidence of educators and students, ICT-related professional development for educators, and the availability of digital policies, strategies, and plans at town and institutional levels.

D. Digital Civil Society

Digital Civil Society refers to the use and sophistication of digital technologies by Voluntary and Community Sector Organisations (VSCOs) in a town. These include charities, sports and social clubs, political parties etc. While there are indices to measure digital social innovation, for example the DSI Index [55], these indices typically focus specifically on innovation or social entrepreneurship ecosystems rather than the use of digital technology more generally by civil society, and specifically VSCOs, in their day to day activities. Again, such indices are often at a country- or city-level. VSCOs are rarely included in the mainstream digital indices. Similar to the literature in the commercial domain, extant literature suggests that digital technologies can transform VSCOs' organisational capacity and stakeholder engagement [56][57]. Like commercial organisations, VSCOs can generate value and exploit the same opportunities digital technologies present including cost savings, process efficiencies, new revenue generation, and improved quality of service [56]–[58]. Notwithstanding this, extant literature suggests that digital adoption by VSCOs is limited [59], with a substantial focus on the use of digital technologies for communication [57][59]–[61]. We include similar sub-dimensions as those for businesses adapted for the VSCO context in our framework e.g., the range of digital technologies used by VSCOs and their use of e-commerce. In 2019, more than half of charities (52%) surveyed in the UK didn't have a digital strategy. As such, we include a sub-dimension on the availability of a documented plan for towns and individual VSCOs on the use of digital technologies. Research has suggested digital adoption by VSCOs has been hindered by digital experience and skills [56][57][60][61] and that this has been especially damaging during the COVID19 pandemic [61]. Consequently, we include sub-dimensions on the confidence of VSCO officers and their completion of digital skills training in the previous two years.

E. Digital Business

It is widely accepted that the adoption and use of digital technologies by business can generate business value and improve competitiveness. So-called third platform technologies - cloud computing, Big Data analytics, social media and mobile technologies - can create new revenue generation opportunities through e-commerce, introduce new business models and faster time to market, reduce costs, generate and provide faster time to insight, and enable intelligent infrastructure [62]. This can often be accomplished with lower upfront investment, reduced risk, and improved organisational agility and efficiency [63]–[66]. The positive impact of broadband and ICT infrastructure, websites, e-commerce, social media, CRM, and other digital business technologies on small-to-medium sized businesses is well established [67]. However, a digital divide between urban and rural SMEs is also noted in the literature [67]. In line with DESI [30], the Digital Business dimension relates to the use and sophistication of digital technology use by local businesses. We include two sub-dimensions related to the availability of a documented plan to increase use of digital technologies by businesses in the town and the prevalence of firm-level plans for digital business. As per DESI [30], we include sub-dimensions on business digitisation and e-commerce but also the availability of digital equipment and next generation technologies e.g. blockchain, the Internet of Things, 3D Printing etc. We expand the indicators on business digitation to include indicators for data protection, website security, and international business readiness. To capture the human capital dimension, we include sub-dimensions on employee confidence in their digital competences, and the recency of digital skills training.

F. Digital Public Services

Similar to DESI [30], we define digital public services as the use and sophistication of digital technology by local government and health services, and the availability of local open data.

1) E-government

E-government is commonly defined as *"the use of IT to enable and improve the efficiency with which government services are provided to citizens, employees, businesses and agencies"* [68]. There is an extensive literature both on the measurement of the maturity of e-government [69] and relatedly the performance assessment of e-government projects [70]. Most e-government maturity models do not focus on local government and town-level e-government which often includes inherited national and regional e-government systems, as well as local initiatives. In their review of performance assessment frameworks for e-government projects, Singh et al. [70] note the importance of placing the citizen at the centre of e-government performance assessment. In particular, the note the prevalence of user satisfaction, and specifically ease of use and usefulness in e-government performance assessment. In our assessment of e-government readiness, we take citizen-centric approach largely following Belanger and Hiller's five-level maturity framework i.e., (i) information, (ii) two-way communication, (iii) transaction, (iv) integration, and (v) participation [71]. In addition, we include both mobile and desktop usability as an indicator of readiness. For comparability, we use similar indicators to DESI [30].

2) eHealth

eHealth can be defined as *"the use of Information and Communication Technologies (ICT) across the whole range of healthcare functions"* [72]. eHealth comprises a wide range of applications that can benefit citizens, healthcare professionals and organisations, and public authorities by improving medical practices, simplifying the prescription of diagnostic procedures, producing alerts and reminders, and reducing errors [73]–[76]. At a macro level, studies suggest that eHealth can result in significant cost savings and improved service quality [77]. In rural communities, local doctors play a central role in facilitating access to, and delivery of, care [78][79] as they represent the main point of contact between the healthcare system and citizens. As such, they are in the position to gather important information which would constitute the basis of an IT-enabled integrated healthcare system [80]. For this reason, the EU, prior to 2020, mostly focused on the adoption of eHealth services such as e-Prescribing and data exchange by GPs when it comes to measuring the digitisation of healthcare across different countries [81]. However, other actors like pharmacies and specialised doctors (e.g., physiotherapists, orthodontists, etc.) may also play a critical role in fostering the adoption of eHealth services within communities [82]–[84]. As DESI, at least up to 2019, only recorded the eHealth adoption rate by GPs, this may lead to a partial picture of the current status of eHealth. To address this we expand eHealth indicators to include all medical practitioners and related actors.

3) Open Data

Open data is commonly defined as "data that can be freely used, shared and built-on by anyone, anywhere, for any purpose" [85]. Open Government Data (OGD) is specifically concerned with making public sector information freely available in open formats and ways that enable public access and facilitate exploitation [86]. Open data is heralded as means of delivering a wide range of political and social, economic, and operational and technical benefits [87]. Claims about OGD are equally effusive. For example, the EU impact assessment on the reuse of Public Sector Information (PSI) suggests PSI has the potential to achieve 1.7 billion in cost savings through better policy making, generate up to 52 billion in economic value, as well as bridging the gap between government and citizens in terms of information, and, in general, leading to increased social inclusion and empowerment, civic participation, and improved personal decision-making capabilities [88]. Due to the nascency of the OGD movement, there is limited evidence to support these claims however OGD remains an indicator in country-level digital indices including DESI [30]. With this in mind, we include an open data component that seeks to uncover evidence of local government availability of an open data plan, a systematic approach to collecting and publishing town level open data on local and/or national open data portals.

G. Digital Tourism

The travel and tourism industry has been at the front line of both digital disruption and transformation [89]. Tourism is a major contributor to rural economies and has long been seen as a counter-measure to the decline of traditional agrarian industries [90]. Digital Tourism is the use and sophistication of digital technology to attract tourists and deliver a distinctive experience. Typically, tourism is not addressed discretely from other industry sectors. However, given the idiosyncrasies of digital disruption to travel and tourism, its emphasis in rural economic development literature and policies, and the opportunities for digitisation both of tourism businesses and destinations, we include digital tourism as a discrete dimension. In line with other dimensions, we include the availability of a tourism plan for the town with specific digital aspects. For comparability, we adapt the sub-dimensions used for digital businesses above for the tourism sector including indicators relating to tourism-specific technologies including booking engines and reviews. We include a dimension relating to the availability of information online relating to local events and popular tourism destination sites, and a separate dimension relating to the availability of a dedicated website for the town and the quality of the information, features and functionality of that site. Smart tourism involves the use of digital technologies to create more intelligent, meaningful and sustainable connections between tourists and the destinations [91]. It includes digital signage and wayfinders, augmented and virtual reality integration, digital kiosks, amongst other technologies that are embedded and accessible in the public realm of a town. Consequently, we include smart tourism as a sub-dimension in the framework. Research has suggested that availability of free public Wi-Fi contributes to tourism promotion, [42][43] we include this as an additional sub-dimension at the destination site level.

H. Horizontal Integration

Reflecting the experience of existing digital town initiatives [7], we take the position that digital towns require a broad concept of community governance that, as per Leach and Percy-Smith [92], involves multi-agency working and self-organising networks that cut across organisational and stakeholder boundaries. In the Digital Town Readiness Framework, horizontal integration relates to the degree of coordination across the town on digitisation, both offline and online, including the availability of a platform for citizens to interact, share knowledge, experiences and mutual interests. In this way the sub-dimensions reflect the the UK Department of the Environment, Transport and the Regions definition of community strategy [93] in that we seek to identify and assess the existence of a governance mechanism, e.g., a Digital Town Working Group, a shared digital vision and documented strategy for the town and its inclusion in municipal and regional plans, and arrangements for monitoring progress of the plan against targets. Furthermore, recognising the role online town-based portals and platforms play in digital town initiatives [15][23], we assess the availability and quality of an online platform for stakeholders to interact, share knowledge and mutual interests.

V. Conclusion

This paper recognises the need to differentiate between digital policy interventions and planning for cities, towns outside of the functional urban area of cities, and rural areas. We propose a definition of a digital town and outline eight rationales for digital towns. Based on a review of extant literature, and digital benchmarking frameworks and indices, we present an initial framework for assessing the digital readiness of towns based eight dimensions. The framework was designed to address the need for community-based planning and to provide a tool for understanding the status of digital readiness in a town, comparing towns against domestic and international benchmarks, and stimulating multi-stakeholder engagement on digitisation. At the time of writing, an easy-to-use checklist for self-assessment has been developed for use by towns, and a process and enabling workflow has been developed for a more comprehensive assessment. The latter includes two versions, a rapid and full assessment. The rapid assessment has been piloted in five towns in Ireland reflecting different regional contexts and population trends. Furthermore, data was collected both pre- and post-COVID19 to enable an assessment of the short-term impact of the COVID19 pandemic on digital adoption and use in those towns. Further work is required on the weighting of dimensions, sub-dimensions and indicators before wider rollout.

Acknowledgment

This work is partially funded by IE Domain Registry (IEDR) and by the Irish Institute of Digital Business.

References

[1] T. Lynn, P. Rosati, and P. T. Endo, “Toward the intelligent internet of everything: Observations on multidisciplinary challenges in intelligent systems research,” in Coloquio Doctorados: Tecnología, Ciencia y Cultura: una visión global, 2018.

[2] OECD and European Union, “A new perspective on urbanisation,” 2020.

[3] M. Lerch et al., “Urban and rural fertility transitions in the developing world: a cohort perspective,” Max Planck Institute for Demographic Research, Rostock, Germany, Tech. Rep., 2017.

[4] L. Philip, C. Cottrill, J. Farrington, F. Williams, and F. Ashmore, “The digital divide: Patterns, policy and scenarios for connecting the ‘final few’in rural communities across great britain,” Journal of Rural Studies, vol. 54, 2017, pp. 386–398.

[5] D. B. Hindman, “The rural-urban digital divide,” Journalism & Mass Communication Quarterly, vol. 77, no. 3, 2000, pp. 549–560.

[6] L. Townsend, A. Sathiaseelan, G. Fairhurst, and C. Wallace, “Enhanced broadband access as a solution to the social and economic problems of the rural digital divide,” Local Economy, vol. 28, no. 6, 2013, pp. 580–595.

[7] F. H. Ashmore, J. H. Farrington, and S. Skerratt, “Superfast broadband and rural community resilience: Examining the rural need for speed,” Scottish Geographical Journal, vol. 131, no. 3-4, 2015, pp. 265–278.

[8] M. Afshar Ali, K. Alam, and B. Taylor, “Do social exclusion and remoteness explain the digital divide in australia? evidence from a panel data estimation approach,” Economics of Innovation and New Technology, 2019, pp. 1–17.

[9] S. Park and G. Kim, “Same access, different uses, and the persistent digital divide between urban and rural internet users.” TPRC, 2015.

[10] S. Park, “Digital inequalities in rural australia: A double jeopardy of remoteness and social exclusion,” Journal of Rural Studies, vol. 54, 2017, pp. 399–407.

[11] S. Hosseini, L. Frank, G. Fridgen, and S. Heger, “Do not forget about smart towns,” Business & Information Systems Engineering, vol. 60, no. 3, 2018, pp. 243–257.

[12] C. Harrison et al., “Foundations for smarter cities,” IBM Journal of research and development, vol. 54, no. 4, 2010, pp. 1–16.

[13] S. Hess, M. Naab, M. Trapp, D. Magin, and S. Braun, “The importance of mobile software ecosystems in smart rural areas,” in 2015 2nd ACM International Conference on Mobile Software Engineering and Systems. IEEE, 2015, pp. 164–165.

[14] P. Neirotti, A. De Marco, A. C. Cagliano, G. Mangano, and F. Scorrano, “Current trends in smart city initiatives: Some stylised facts,” Cities, vol. 38, 2014, pp. 25–36.

[15] N. P. da Rocha, “Aveiro—digital town,” in Advances in Digital Government. Springer, 2002, pp. 305–314.

[16] M. Sakurai and J. Kokuryo, “Fujisawa sustainable smart town: Panasonic’s challenge in building a sustainable society,” Communications of the Association for Information Systems, vol. 42, no. 1, 2018, p. 19.

[17] M. Trapp and S. Hess, “Digitale dörfer,” in Biologische Transformation. Springer, 2019, pp. 371–387.

[18] A. Visvizi and M. D. Lytras, “It’s not a fad: Smart cities and smart villages research in european and global contexts,” 2018.

[19] European Network for Rural Devlopment, “Smart villages - revitalising rural services,” 2018. [Online]. Available: https://enrd.ec.europa.eu/sites/enrd/files/enrd_publications/publi-enrd-rr-26-2018-en.pdf

[20] Digitale Doerfer. Die digitalen doerfer. [Online]. Available: https://www.digitale-doerfer.de/die-digitalen-doerfer/ (2020)

[21] L. Dijkstra, H. Poelman, and P. Veneri, “The eu-oecd definition of a functional urban area,” 2019.

[22] H. McQuillan, "Ennis information age town: Virtuality rooted in reality," in Kyoto Workshop on Digital Cities. Springer, 2001, pp. 139–151.

[23] K. Hervé-Van Driessche, "Parthenay, the digital town: myth or reality?" Telematics and Informatics, vol. 18, no. 1, 2001, pp. 5–15.

[24] V. Zavratnik, A. Kos, and E. Stojmenova Duh, "Smart villages: Comprehensive review of initiatives and practices," Sustainability, vol. 10, no. 7, 2018, p. 2559.

[25] M. Ghosal, A. Bobade, and P. Verma, "A quadcopter based environment health monitoring system for smart cities," in 2018 2nd International Conference on Trends in Electronics and Informatics (ICOEI). IEEE, 2018, pp. 1423–1426.

[26] H. N. Hsieh, C. Y. Hou, and P. C. Chia, "A study of smart town development strategies," in 2011 International Conference on Multimedia Technology. IEEE, 2011, pp. 6684–6689.

[27] J. Wichmann, M. Wißotzki, and K. Sandkuhl, "Toward a smart town: Digital innovation and transformation process in a public sector environment," in Human Centred Intelligent Systems. Springer, pp. 89–99.

[28] R. Katz and F. Callorda, "The economic contribution of broadband, digitization and ict regulation," International Telecommunication Union, published in Switzerland, Geneva, 2018.

[29] International Telecommunications Union, "The ICT Development Index (IDI) methodology, indicators and definitions (as of February 2019)," 2019. [Online]. Available: https://www.itu.int/en/ITU-D/Statistics/Documents/statistics/ITU_ICT\%20Development\%20Index.pdf

[30] Digital Economy and Skills Unit, "The digital economy and society index (desi)," 2020. [Online]. Available: https://ec.europa.eu/digital-single-market/en/desi

[31] ——, "The digital economy and society index 2020 - thematic chapters," 2020.

[32] P. Foley, D. Sutton, I. Wiseman, L. Green, and J. Moore, "International digital economy and society index 2018," Publications Office of the European Union: Brussels, Belgium, 2018.

[33] Digital Economy and Skills Unit, "Desi 2020 - digital economy and society index (desi) 2020 questions and answers," 2020. [Online]. Available: https://ec.europa.eu/commission/presscorner/detail/en/qanda_20_1022

[34] M. Ragnedda, M. L. Ruiu, and F. Addeo, "Measuring digital capital: An empirical investigation," new media & society, vol. 22, no. 5, 2020, pp. 793–816.

[35] B. Chakravorti, C. Tunnard, and R. S. Chaturvedi, "Where the digital economy is moving the fastest," Harvard Business Review, vol. 19, 2015, pp. 102–101.

[36] B. Chakravorti and R. S. Chaturvedi, "Digital planet 2017: How competitiveness and trust in digital economies vary across the world," The Fletcher School, Tufts University, vol. 70, 2017, p. 70.

[37] P. Bosch, S. Jongeneel, V. Rovers, H.-M. Neumann, M. Airaksinen, and A. Huovila, "Citykeys indicators for smart city projects and smart cities," CITYkeys report, 2017.

[38] ETSI, "Access, terminals, transmission and multiplexing (ATTM)," 2020. [Online]. Available: https://www.etsi.org/deliver/etsi_ts/103400_103499/10346301/01.02.01_60/ts_10346301v010201p.pdf

[39] M. Kalinka, S. Geipele, E. Pudzis, A. Lazdins, U. Krutova, and J. Holms, "Indicators for the smart development of villages and neighbourhoods in baltic sea coastal areas," Sustainability, vol. 12, no. 13, 2020, p. 5293.

[40] G. S. Yovanof and G. N. Hazapis, "An architectural framework and enabling wireless technologies for digital cities & intelligent urban environments," Wireless personal communications, vol. 49, no. 3, 2009, pp. 445–463.

[41] F. Bar and H. Galperin, "Geeks, bureaucrats and cowboys: Deploying internet infrastructure, the wireless way," The Network Society From Knowledge to Policy, 2005, p. 269.

[42] A. Picco-Schwendener, "Social dimensions of public large-scale wi-fi networks," Ph.D. dissertation, Università della Svizzera italiana, 2018.

[43] P. Ballon, L. Van Audenhove, M. Poel, and T. Staelens, "Business models for wireless city networks in the eu and the us: Public inputs and public leverage," in Telecommunication markets. Springer, 2009, pp. 325–340.

[44] C. A. Middleton, "A framework for investigating the value of public wireless networks." TPRC, 2007.

[45] K. A. Chesley, "The future of municipal wireless in the united states and europe," Available at SSRN 1408808, 2009.

[46] A. H. Tapia and J. A. Ortiz, "Keeping promises: Municipal communities struggle to fulfill promises to narrow the digital divide with municipal community wireless networks," The Journal of Community Informatics, vol. 4, no. 1, 2008.

[47] A. H. Tapia, L. Kvasny, and J. A. Ortiz, "A critical discourse analysis of three us municipal wireless network initiatives for enhancing social inclusion," Telematics and Informatics, vol. 28, no. 3, 2011, pp. 215–226.

[48] T. Heer, R. Hummen, N. Viol, H. Wirtz, S. Götz, and K. Wehrle, "Collaborative municipal wi-fi networks-challenges and opportunities," in 2010 8th IEEE International Conference on Pervasive Computing and Communications Workshops (PERCOM Workshops). IEEE, 2010, pp. 588–593.

[49] B. Moriset, "Developing the digital economy in france's rural regions: A new era for telecenters?" in Association of American Geographers Annual Meeting, 2010.

[50] M. Meyn, "Digitalization and its impact on life in rural areas: Exploring the two sides of the atlantic: Usa and germany," in Smart Village Technology. Springer, 2020, pp. 99–116.

[51] R. Gallardo, Responsive countryside: The digital age and rural communities. Mississippi State University Extension, 2016.

[52] UNESCO Institute for Statistics, "Guide to measuring information and communication technologies (ICT) in education," 2008.

[53] P. Wastiau, R. Blamire, C. Kearney, V. Quittre, E. Van de Gaer, and C. Monseur, "The use of ict in education: a survey of schools in e urope," European Journal of Education, vol. 48, no. 1, 2013, pp. 11–27.

[54] Deloitte and IPSOS MORI, "2nd survey of schools: ICT in education," 2019. [Online]. Available: https://ec.europa.eu/digital-single-market/en/news/2nd-survey-schools-ict-education#:~:text=or%20analytical%20thinking.-,The%20results%20of%20the%202nd%20Survey%20of%20Schools%3A%20ICT,coding%20or%20programming%20at%20school.

[55] J. Bone, C. Cretu, and M. Stokes, "A theoretical framework for the dsi index," Brussels, Belgium: European Commission, 2018.

[56] J. O'Grady and P. Roberts, "The digital transformation of irish non-profit organisations." in AICS, 2019, pp. 388–399.

[57] P. Ehnold, E. Faß, D. Steinbach, and T. Schlesinger, "Digitalization in organized sport–usage of digital instruments in voluntary sports clubs depending on club's goals and organizational capacity," Sport, Business and Management: An International Journal, 2020.

[58] T. Walker, S. Esmene, L. Colebrooke, C. Leyshon, and M. Leyshon, "Digital possibilities and social mission in the voluntary sector: the case of a community transport organisation in the uk," Voluntary Sector Review, vol. 11, no. 1, 2020, pp. 59–77.

[59] N. Dufft and P. Kreutter, "Digitization in non-profit organizations: strategy, culture and competencies in digital change," in future-oriented foundation management. springer, 2018, pp. 105–115.

[60] Z. Amar and L. Clough, "Charity skills report 2019," 2019.

[61] ——, "Charity skills report 2020," 2020.

[62] F. Gens, "The 3rd platform: Enabling digital transformation. usa: Idc," 2013.

[63] M. Armbrust et al., "A view of cloud computing," Communications of the ACM, vol. 53, no. 4, 2010, pp. 50–58.

[64] S. Marston, Z. Li, S. Bandyopadhyay, J. Zhang, and A. Ghalsasi, "Cloud computing—the business perspective," Decision support systems, vol. 51, no. 1, 2011, pp. 176–189.

[65] T. Leimbach et al., "Potential and impacts of cloud computing services and social network websites," Publication of Science and Technology Options Assessment, 2014.

[66] T. Lynn, J. G. Mooney, P. Rosati, and G. Fox, "Measuring the business value of cloud computing," 2020.

[67] W. Richmond, S. Rader, and C. Lanier, "The "digital divide" for rural small businesses," Journal of Research in Marketing and Entrepreneurship, 2017.

[68] F. Bélanger and L. Carter, "Digitizing government interactions with constituents: an historical review of e-government research in information systems," Journal of the Association for information Systems, vol. 13, no. 5, 2012, p. 1.

[69] F. Iannacci, A. P. Seepma, C. De Blok, and A. Resca, "Reappraising maturity models in e-government research: The trajectory-turning point theory," The Journal of Strategic Information Systems, vol. 28, no. 3, 2019, pp. 310–329.

[70] H. Singh, P. Grover, A. K. Kar, and P. V. Ilavarasan, "Review of performance assessment frameworks of e-government projects," Transforming Government: People, Process and Policy, 2020.

[71] F. Belanger and J. S. Hiller, "A framework for e-government: privacy implications," Business Process Management Journal, vol. 12, no. 1, 2006, p. 48.

[72] European Union Directorate-General for the Environment, Reclaiming city streets for people: chaos or quality of life? Office for Official Publications of the European Communities, 2004.

[73] R. Bodell, H. D. Covvey, and C. Fader, "Achieving a" therapeutic dose" of it." in Medinfo, 2004, pp. 1348–1351.

[74] C. Delpierre, L. Cuzin, J. Fillaux, M. Alvarez, P. Massip, and T. Lang, "A systematic review of computer-based patient record systems and quality of care: more randomized clinical trials or a broader approach?" International Journal for Quality in Health Care, vol. 16, no. 5, 2004, pp. 407–416.

[75] R. Kaushal et al., "Return on investment for a computerized physician order entry system," Journal of the American Medical Informatics Association, vol. 13, no. 3, 2006, pp. 261–266.

[76] J. Øvretveit, T. Scott, T. G. Rundall, S. M. Shortell, and M. Brommels, "Implementation of electronic medical records in hospitals: two case studies," Health Policy, vol. 84, no. 2-3, 2007, pp. 181–190.

[77] C. Hackett, K. Brennan, H. S. Fowler, and C. Leaver, "Valuing citizen access to digital health services: applied value-based outcomes in the canadian context and tools for modernizing health systems," Journal of medical Internet research, vol. 21, no. 6, 2019, p. e12277.

[78] R. Atun, "What are the advantages and the disadvantages of restructuring a health system to be more focused on primary care services," WHO, 2004.

[79] J. Macinko, B. Starfield, and L. Shi, "The contribution of primary care systems to health outcomes within organization for economic cooperation and development (oecd) countries, 1970–1998," Health services research, vol. 38, no. 3, 2003, pp. 831–865.

[80] C. Codagnone and F. Lupiañez-Villanueva, "Benchmarking deployment of ehealth among general practitioners-final report," European Union. Luxembourg. Publications Office of the European Union: European Commission. Directorate-General of Communications Networks. Content & Technology, vol. 114, 2013.

[81] Digital Economy and Skills Unit, "Desi 2019 - digital public services," 2019. [Online]. Available: https://ec.europa.eu/newsroom/dae/document.cfm?doc_id=59975

[82] J. Gregorio, T. L. Ferreira, A. Cavaco, M. M. da Silva, C. Lovis, and L. V. Lapão, "Community pharmacies and ehealth services: barriers and opportunities for real primary healthcare integration," in Proceedings of the 26th IEEE International Symposium on Computer-Based Medical Systems. IEEE, 2013, pp. 393–396.

[83] S. Vorrink, C. Huisman, H. Kort, T. Troosters, and J.-W. Lammers, "Perceptions of patients with chronic obstructive pulmonary disease and their physiotherapists regarding the use of an ehealth intervention," JMIR human factors, vol. 4, no. 3, 2017, p. e20.

[84] D. Baines et al., "A scoping review of the quality and the design of evaluations of mobile health, telehealth, smart pump and monitoring technologies performed in a pharmacy-related setting," Frontiers in Pharmacology, vol. 9, 2018, p. 678.

[85] L. James, "Defining open data: Open knowledge foundation blog," 2013.

[86] E. Kalampokis, E. Tambouris, and K. Tarabanis, "A classification scheme for open government data: towards linking decentralised data," International Journal of Web Engineering and Technology, vol. 6, no. 3, 2011, pp. 266–285.

[87] M. Janssen, Y. Charalabidis, and A. Zuiderwijk, "Benefits, adoption barriers and myths of open data and open government," Information systems management, vol. 29, no. 4, 2012, pp. 258–268.

[88] European Commission, "Impact assessment accompanying the document - proposal for a directive of the european parliament and of the council on the re-use of public sector information," 2018. [Online]. Available: https://ec.europa.eu/newsroom/dae/document.cfm?doc_id=51644

[89] B. Weinelt and J. Moavenzadeh, "Digital transformation initiative: Aviation, travel and tourism industry," in Geneva, Switzerland: World Economic Forum, 2017.

[90] R. Sharpley and A. Vass, "Tourism, farming and diversification: An attitudinal study," Tourism management, vol. 27, no. 5, 2006, pp. 1040–1052.

[91] J. G. Molz, Travel connections: Tourism, technology, and togetherness in a mobile world. Routledge, 2012.

[92] R. Leach and J. Percy-Smith, Local governance in Britain. Palgrave, 2001.

[93] Department of the Environment, Transport and the Regions, "Preparing community strategies: Government guidance to local authorities," 2000.

The Multi Crane Scheduling Problem: A Comparison Between Genetic Algorithm and Neural Network Approaches based on Simulation Modeling

Naomie Bartoli, Roberto Revetria, Emanuele Morra
Department of Mechanical Engineering (D.I.M.E.)
University of Genoa, UNIGE
Genoa, Italy
e-mail: nani.bartoli@live.it, roberto.revetria@unige.it, emanuele.morra@edu.unige.it

Gabriele Galli, Edward Williams
Department of Industrial and Manufacturing System Engineering (I.M.S.E.)
University of Michigan - Dearborn
Dearborn, USA
e-mail: {ggalli, williame}@umich.edu

Maurizio Schenone
Department of Management and Production Engineering (D.I.G.E.P.)
Polytechnic of Turin, PoliTO
Turin, Italy
e-mail: maurizio.schenone@polito.it

Abstract— **The internal logistics for warehouses of many industrial applications, based on the movement of heavy goods, is commonly solved by the installment of a multi-crane system. The job scheduling of a multi-crane system is an interesting problem of optimization, solved in many ways in the past. This paper describes a comparison between the optimization by the use of Genetic Algorithms (GA) and introduce a framework for the solution of the problem using machine learning driven by Neural Networks (NN). Even though this last approach is not implemented in this paper, performances very close to GA ones are expected with NN. A case-study for steel coil production is proposed as a test frame for two different simulation software tools, one based on a heuristic solution and one on machine learning; performances and data achieved from reviews and simulations are compared.**

Keywords - Crane; Genetic Algorithm; Neural Network; Simulation.

I. INTRODUCTION

To move materials, particularly heavy or bulky ones, in warehouses, bridge cranes are often used. These bridge cranes frequently share runway girders. The presence of more than one overhead bridge crane sharing the same runway girders, virtually over the same served area, represents an enormous advantage in terms of efficiency for the operations, but also markedly increases the complexity of job scheduling, with relevant consequences for plant and workers' safety. The digitalization of production processes opens numerous research themes with the ultimate aim of reaching a higher level of repeatability and efficiency of the plant. In the context of the whole manufacturing factor, the bridge crane is a fundamental component of every plant, as it must guarantee the movement of the processed objects or its components from one workstation to another, minimizing delays and other inefficiencies. To date, the management of overhead traveling cranes is still done manually for many reasons, mainly related to the safety and extreme conditions of these systems such as temperature, dust, and the handling of generally heavy or unwieldy objects. Nonetheless, the latest developments in the field of sensors and the implementation of interventions today invite exploration of completely automatic management of the movement of the bridge cranes, in particular applied in the park area. This area is organized in large stacks containing different types of scrap and is dominated by a bay on which at least two bridge cranes move; their exact number depends on the size and complexity of the system. Their hooks (mechanical or magnetic) enable picking up and depositing the material.

In general, the scheduling of overhead crane movements is an optimization problem, given the data of a list of jobs (withdrawal-deposit); the goal is to find the best sequence with the assignment of single jobs to complete all the jobs in the shortest possible time. This theme is particularly interesting in the scrap stock area for coil steel production plant, where, unlike the melt shop, at a given time it is typical to have very long job lists to get a basket, so dozens of missions are needed for one goal.

Crane transport is the most important logistical transport method in the production of steel; the cranes must catch, hoist, and deliver scrap loads. The planning of the bridge crane has become the key to any production procedure and represents a decisive factor to ensure the production process operates with stability, reliability, and high efficiency in the workshop.

The programming problems of metallurgical cranes are mainly focused on how to solve the spatial conflict between cranes. Research methods based on mathematical programming methods, heuristic methods, simulation methods and intelligent hybrid programming algorithms have been used. It is, therefore, necessary to study a method that could simultaneously and effectively eliminate the spatial and temporal conflict between cranes [1]. Finding optimal solutions to planning problems is generally a difficult proposition, entailing combinatorial optimization and often being strongly nondeterministic polynomial (NP). The problem of programming cranes is no exception to this: it is an NP-hard problem. Therefore, simulation is a suitable tool for studying complex materials management systems.

In this paper, a comparison between two different approaches is proposed to be analyzed in parallel on a test frame offered by a simulation model: the first is given by the application of a wizard for optimization based on Genetic Algorithms and the second is the application of machine learning for piloting the multi crane by a Neural Network. The comparison is currently still on a qualitative level and this paper proposes a test frame for further performance comparisons. Quantitative results from the Genetic Algorithm solution are shown, while hypotheses on the Neural Network approach results are described, taken from general evaluation and results by commercial solutions. The next development of this paper will be focused on the set up of a model based on the same test frame, but in which multiple cranes are moved by an artificial intelligence (AI) application. Hence a quantitative comparison between both will be available in future work.

The paper is organized as follows. First, a literature review about the cranes problem is presented, followed by a description of the problem (both a general description and the scheduling problem). Second, the methodology used (i.e. simulation, GA solution, and NN solution – the last one to be implemented later in a future follow-up paper) is explained. Third, an evaluation analysis of the paper is introduced. Lastly, a conclusion is provided.

II. STATE OF THE ART

Due to the growing need to accelerate warehouse handling operations, many recent studies have focused on programming multiple cranes operating simultaneously within the same area (typically understood to mean "bay;" i.e., the cranes share rails). A literature review was carried out according to the following stages:

1. identification of keywords and their combinations;
2. selection of a source database;
3. analysis of the results.

Regarding phase one, the following words were chosen: simulation, optimization problem, objective function minimization, bridge crane scheduling, genetic algorithms. The research was applied to the article title, abstract and keywords. In research phase two, Scopus and Google Scholar have been selected as source databases. At the end of this phase, about twenty articles were collected. During phase three, a new systematic analysis of the basic specifications was undertaken and specific papers in the references have been selected based on their content and availability.

The topic was already covered in the early 2000*s*, during which proposals arose to study the programming of cranes in a port environment with spatial constraints with the goal of finding the crane-job combination that maximizes productivity. Zäpfel et al. [2] presented new ideas with the aim of increasing the efficiency of the steel supply chain, by improving warehouse management, concerning the handling of different types of steel coils with the help of overhead cranes subject to time constraints. This study aimed to minimize processing time, the last order completion time during the planning period and labor costs. To do this, due to the complexity of the study, a mixed-integer mathematical-nonlinear optimization model was created. Furthermore, the problem was formulated in terms of job shops to represent all the dynamic situations of the warehouse processes (logistics center). Graunke et al. [3] studied the sequencing problem that was based on a multi-crane programming problem in a coils warehouse. Indeed, for problems on a larger scale, the heuristic algorithm generates quick, robust and acceptable solutions. The genetic algorithms were also used for the optimization of the integrated programming of overhead cranes and storage platforms at the automated container terminals. This article introduced a genetic algorithm capable of performing integrated programming of quay cranes, automated guided vehicles and handling platforms; in particular, this work is oriented towards container terminal applications. In fact, this study aimed to optimize the container stacking process, which is the motivation to save space. The results obtained with the genetic algorithm method have shown higher performance when the programming horizon increases. The programming of the movements of the bridge cranes over time has therefore been studied with different methods and approaches; only some of the methods used in different work environments will be reported below.

The use of machine learning and AI in multi-crane driving is as yet a task unconsolidated in the literature, although early studies and commercial solutions based on model simulation are appearing on the market. On the contrary, job scheduling problems in manufacturing have been studied via machine learning for many years. The works by Jain et al. [4] and by Weckman et al. [5] are expressions of this and specific system architectures in this direction have been evaluated. Results emphasize that the solution through a Neural Network scheduler provides performances very close to a Genetic Algorithm scheduler, with the well-known capabilities of AI to learn and adapt to variations in initial conditions.

Xie et al. [6] considers a multi-crane programming problem commonly encountered in real warehouse operations in steel companies' warehouses of steel coils. A certain set of coils must be recovered from the designated places: if a requested coil is in the upper or lower level without being blocked, it can be taken directly to its designated place; otherwise, the blocking coils must first be moved to another position. The study is to consider at the same time the problem of mixing and the problem of programming the overhead crane since the simultaneous approach could accurately take into account the routing and the time of movement of the crane; therefore an improvement in the utilization of the crane could also improve the completion time of the operations. To clearly describe the problem studied, it was first formulated as a mixed Model of Integer Linear Programming (MILP); after which some feasible and optimal properties were identified for the assignment of the bridge cranes to avoid collisions. Since a particular case of the problem has proved to be strongly NP-hard, a heuristic algorithm has also been proposed to solve the aforementioned problem efficiently. In the heuristic algorithm program, for each crane, a detailed sequence specifies the order of all the necessary coils and the position of each block coil to be repositioned. To evaluate the performance of the heuristic, three lower limits are obtained according to the different cases. Furthermore, the strategy of the composite constraint of the lower limits has been adopted to converge toward an optimal value as they are mutually complementary and no one lower limit can dominate the others. Based on the tighter lower limit, the worst performance limit of the proposed heuristic algorithm is analyzed. The results showed that for small-scale problems, MILP can achieve slightly better high-quality solutions than heuristic solutions. For problems on a larger scale, the proposed heuristic algorithm can quickly generate robust and acceptable solutions.

In order to solve the NP-hard problem of overhead crane programming, the work by Ma et al. [1] presents a method of simulating crane programming in the steelworks workshop based on the Multi-Agent System (MAS). The scheduling system mainly includes groups of agents for overhead cranes, groups of agents for workstations and agents for managing coordination. MAS can decompose a complex and large system into many simple agents that have a simple structure, can interact with each other and can be easily managed. MAS introduces the global objective to match the programming strategies and operating results of the overhead crane with the global objective and the production practice in the workshop. Based on the analysis of the production process, on the methods of organizing production and on the characteristics of the current programming of the cranes in the steelworks workshop, the MAS applied in the operation of the steel bridge cranes is feasible because:

1. The MAS uses the "bottom-up" design method, which agrees with the rule of formation of the overhead crane programming system;
2. The MAS corresponding to the structural characteristics of the different levels is in accordance with the distributed structure of the bridge crane programming.
3. The autonomy and adaptability of MAS agree with the intelligence of each unit in the overhead crane programming system;
4. MAS can combine with various types of advanced information technology, artificial intelligence technology and so on, which then complement each other.

Each agent has its corresponding rules. The research shows that the simulation method based on the MAS is feasible and can meet the demand of the bridge crane in a timely and effective way. Furthermore, it can reduce the average transit time of materials and also describe the characteristics of the overhead cranes in the steel mill efficiently [1].

The document by Lim at al. [7] examines the programming of overhead cranes for ports through the Tabu Search (TS) method, a search procedure that proceeds iteratively from one solution to another by moving to a "neighborhood space" with the help of adaptive memory. Probabilistic Search for Tabu (PTS) is a variant of the basic TS, which places more emphasis on randomization than the basic TS. TS operates through neighborhood shifts, which proceed from one solution to another at each iteration. In the basic TS method, some shifts are taboo-marked and prohibited, unless they lead to highly desirable results. Rather than using deterministic strategies, PTS can be used to select movements based on the status and ratings assigned to them by the basic TS principles. The basic approach is to create move assessments that include references to the taboo status and other relevant prejudices of TS strategies using penalties, modifying the decision criterion and selecting the next move among the neighborhood moves that are based on values of different evaluation. From the experiments, the comparison and the above analysis, it is, therefore, believed that the Tabu Probabilistic Research is a good heuristic method to find good solutions to the programming problem of the bridge cranes.

The paper by Yuan et al. [8] proposes an efficient network flow model based on events and time spaces with lateral constraints for the problem of programming the overhead crane in a coil warehouse when the overhead crane must undertake a series of requests for storage, recovery and mixing of the reels, and determine the sequence of management of these requests as well as the positions to which the reels are moved. The goal is to minimize the makespan (the time needed to execute *all* the requests); in fact, the problem of programming the overhead crane is optimized by minimizing the actual working time to avoid unnecessary movements. Not only optimization for the handling time of each request, but also for the space in which for storing the reels is required; so, a new space-time network flow model is required, that uses the strategy of continuous time modelling in a space-time network, which can be optimally solved by a conventional Mixed Integer Program (MIP) solver for small cases and medium size in one minute. Due to the NP-hard characteristic of the problem, a dynamic programming approach has been designed exploiting the structure of the problem, on the basis of which an Approximate Dynamic Programming algorithm (ADP) is developed to obtain almost optimal solutions. The results, through computational experiments, showed that the proposed model for space-time network flow can be solved much faster than the traditional planning model and the standard model for space-time network flow.

Xie et al. [9] solve the programming problem of a bridge crane as presented in the warehouse of cold rolling material in a steel company. The goal, as before, is to minimize the makespan. Since the problem is NP-hard, a genetic algorithm has been presented to offer a reasonable quality of the solution. The exploration process is performed by two genetic operators: the crossover and the mutation. GA starts with a population of individuals and each solution is called a chromosome, which is made up of genes that represent decision variables. The chromosome representation used in this work shows that each coil in the program is a chromosome gene. Ten instances have been resolved to test the performance of the proposed GA. For most smaller cases, GA can achieve an optimal solution. As the problem size or space usage increases, the GA solution time is longer. The performance of this algorithm has been demonstrated efficiently and effectively. It provides a solution to improve the efficiency of the bridge cranes and the productivity of the steel company in the warehouse. In the work proposed, simulation has been used together with GA in order to explore a sub-system of solution and to reduce the computational time accordingly. This is a crucial point since three cranes are assumed; hence, the computational complexity is markedly higher than that of reference.

III. MATERIALS AND METHODS

A. *General Description*

The steel plant is divided into several bays and, in this elaboration, we have focused on the analysis of the scrap park which represents the area where the material is stored awaiting loading into the kilns. The shed analyzed is characterized by several stalls (sheet pantograph, turning, pre-reduced, naval, etc.) and each of these represents a possible starting point for the scrap. In addition, there are three preparation points where the scrap baskets are then prepared.

To move, after loading the scrap in the various stalls, and unloading it subsequently in the baskets, there are three overhead traveling cranes that travel on a single track. The real dimensions for the shed are the length of runway (213m) and the respective width of runway (63m).

B. *Scheduling Problem*

In the scrap park, overhead cranes must manage mainly:

- The supply of scrap, moving it from trucks/flights to stacks in dedicated bays,
- Loading the scrap, moving it from the stacks to the baskets (or conveyor belts) which then deliver the scrap to the melting furnace, following a suitable and predetermined succession by type.

Three overhead cranes share the same runways and are engaged by the simulation scheduling system. The task of the system is to provide scrap materials to specific baskets, starting from different sources according to a specific recipe, needed for the final product (steel type) to be produced. The overall process flowchart is shown in Figure 1.

C. *Simulation Model*

As previously described, the plant studied is a scrap park and is characterized by several areas that represent the possible starting points for the scrap handling. The transport of the scrap from the different areas to the baskets takes place by means of three overhead cranes that move on one set of rails. A standard object from a common simulation software library is used. In particular, the software used is Tecnomatix Plant Simulation [10]. The real features of the shed have been attributed to the model frame, so the geometric scale is one-to-one relative versus the model. An initialization function called at the beginning of the simulation loads into a column of a data table all the portal cranes desired and creates their frame logic and 3D counterparts. The portals need other functions to take the mobile unit (hoist load), then the object, and take it from the originating station to the arrival station. In the specific case, it allows removing the scrap from the various stalls and taking it to the scrap baskets. The scrap park is made up of several stations, so there are more starting points where the scrap is available. These areas are modelled as buffers with an infinite capacity assigned. A structure is therefore built in and the starting points are arranged in matrix format. The same procedure is used to represent the scrap baskets which, unlike the scrap pick-up points, are connected to a drain block and then are to be deleted. The base is to create recipes and a function that reads recipes data from a table is provided. This table refers to one of the preparation points; therefore, in this specific case to the three scrap preparation points which are the baskets. This table consists of two columns: a first column where each row represents a location, i.e. a scrap pick-up point (i.e. the buffers), and a second column that contains a number, which indicates the number of catches that must be done in that location.

A queue is created for each portal crane with the following features:

- A function to take the first object of the queue, which is then removed;
- A function which allows the analyst to add an object;
- A function to take the first object at the top without removing it; therefore, the analyst can examine it as often as necessary.

The recipes are provided for more than one basket depending on the type of steel to be made. The scrap pick-up location and the number of pick-up tasks for each location will be provided for each recipe. The traveling salesman problem can be compared to the scheduling problem for the loading of scrap baskets. In the traveling salesman problem, the aim is to find an optimal sequence of points to visit such that the sum of the distances to go from one point to another is minimal. The problem relating to the loading of the scrap baskets is similar, in the sense that there is a sequence of operations to be carried out, specifically the movements with the bridge crane, with the difference that the sum of the times necessary to load the baskets must be minimized, in contrast to minimizing the sum of the distances to be covered. To do this, genetic algorithms will be used for their properties in this first customization of the test frame for the comparison with the Neural Network approach. A table that indicates the sequence of tasks and a function that indicates the goodness of our solution are created. In the case studied, the function will be the completion time of the baskets which, to minimize it, must optimize the problem and then sequence the baskets. For the fitness function, a method will be created to communicate with the GA optimization tool from the software library described in the next paragraphs. The table, which will be used to configure the model to read the sequences, will define the sequence in which we will prepare the baskets. The assignment of the basket target is needed, since in the system studied there are three places to prepare them.

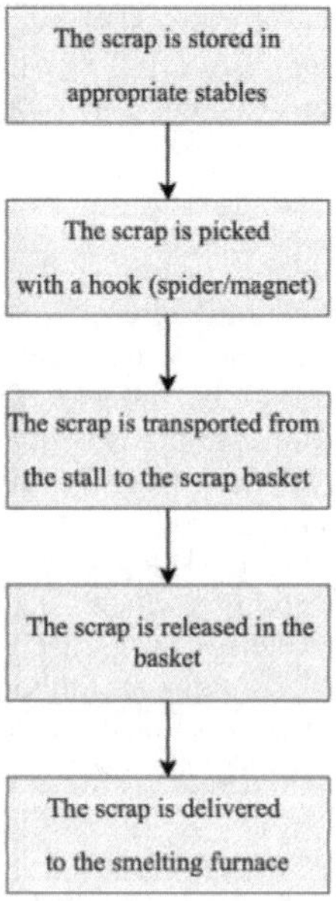

Figure 1. Process flowchart

D. *Genetic Algorithm Solution*

The use of Genetic Algorithm is an efficient solution because the optimization task at hand has a large number of variants of different solutions. In the specific case, a GA wizard is instantiated to integrate genetic algorithms into the test frame of the simulation model. Table I summarizes the inputs to and the outputs of the optimizer. In terms of inputs, we assume N missions (*OrderID* column) are carried out in a time span. A recipe (*RecipeID* column) and a to-fill-basket (*Basket* column) are assigned to each mission. This recipe tells how many times the scrap must be taken from a stall point; hence, the mission will end only when all the scrap planned in the recipe is taken. After assigning a recipe to each mission, a deadline (*DueDate* column) is provided. This is the time the mission must be completed. The solutions generated by the Genetic Algorithms wizard object are passed to the simulation model, which in turn will be configured accordingly. Standard libraries from the simulation software are used. At the end of the simulation run, the test frame model transfers the resulting fitness value to the GA wizard object. When the Genetic Algorithms creates individuals, who define the same parameterization, the GA wizard recognizes it and uses the fitness values of the individuals already evaluated. Performing optimization therefore does not waste additional time for multiple assessments of an individual. A first important advantage compared to classical methods is the immunity of genetic algorithms to the number of variables, whereas classical numerical methods are often imprecise due to rounding errors which increase rapidly as the number of variables increases. GA are often used in problems where the objective function depends on a large number of variables, typically five or more. A second, but no less important, property of these algorithms is that the method of finding the solution does not presuppose any type of linearity of the problem, so it is also possible to face problems in which one or more non-linearities exist, possibly also in the form of constraints. Practically, the GA wizard object will do the sequencing, as well as the optimization, starting from the initial orders list; this sequencing represents the initialization of the simulation.

E. *Neural Network Solution*

The Neural Network approach under study requires specific work, intended as an extension of the present paper. The scheduler will be created using the system architecture in Figure 2.

The Neural Network suitable for this aim is the Multi-Layer Perceptron (MLP) with one hidden layer and trained using a back-propagation algorithm. Regarding the simulation model, the test frame will be implemented with the following scheme:

- Creation of a connection between the model and the external neural network, to be developed on a software-specific platform (data must be collected continuously in the simulations before specified actions);
- Use of the model test frame to test the NN training algorithm;
- Testing the NN driving system for cranes on the same data set used for the GA solutions.

IV. Results and Discussion

A. *Genetic Algorithm Performance Evaluation*

The results from the model simulation for the case study are shown in Table I. The solution represents the best sequence of operations that minimize the fitness function which is intended as the sum of process and delay times contained in the column *Delay*. Intuitively, the shorter the delays, the better the configuration obtained. The objective function, also called the fitness function, is the sum of the *Delays* and the minimum is obtained for Generation Four which reaches a value of roughly 28.55, as shown by the red curve in Figure 3. More quantitative details of the optimization output are included in Table II.

To reach the optimal value, 15 generations with 20 individuals per population and five generations per individual have been chosen empirically. Multiple solutions for each generation are shown in Figures 4 through 8.

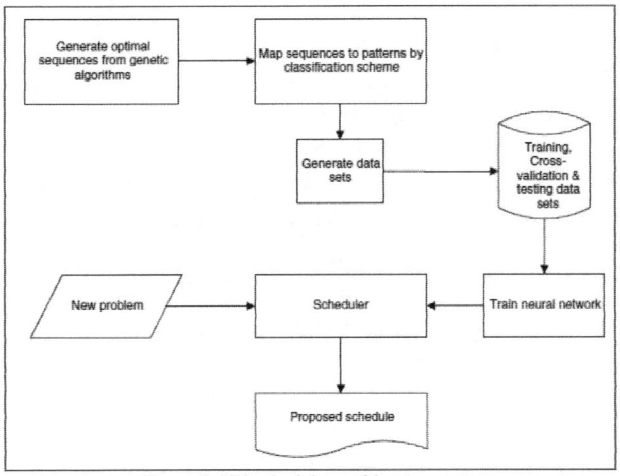

Figure 2. NN scheduler architecture system

TABLE I. Optimization Scheduling

OrderID	*RecipeID*	*Basket_Seq*	*StartTime*	*EndTime*	*DueDate*	*Delay*	*Elapsed*
9	Recipe4	Basket1	2018/01/01 00:02:38	2018/01/01 00:28:41	2018/01/01 01:00:00	0.00	26.04
8	Recipe1	Basket3	2018/01/01 00:00:56	2018/01/01 01:27:15	2018/01/01 01:10:00	17.25	86.31
4	Recipe3	Basket1	2018/01/01 00:33:21	2018/01/01 02:06:48	2018/01/01 02:30:00	0.00	93.45
6	Recipe1	Basket1	2018/01/01 02:10:31	2018/01/01 03:38:04	2018/01/01 03:40:00	0.00	87.56
3	Recipe2	Basket3	2018/01/01 01:31:43	2018/01/01 03:12:17	2018/01/01 04:55:00	0.00	100.56
5	Recipe2	Basket1	2018/01/01 03:39:45	2018/01/01 05:51:18	2018/01/01 05:40:00	11.30	131.55
1	Recipe4	Basket3	2018/01/01 03:16:55	2018/01/01 04:46:51	2018/01/01 04:50:00	0.00	89.93
10	Recipe4	Basket2	2018/01/01 00:01:25	2018/01/01 00:19:17	2018/01/01 00:40:00	0.00	17.87
2	Recipe2	Basket2	2018/01/01 01:25:52	2018/01/01 01:31:11	2018/01/01 01:35:00	0.00	65.32
7	Recipe1	Basket2	2018/01/01 01:35:28	2018/01/01 02:43:12	2018/01/01 02:45:00	0.00	67.72

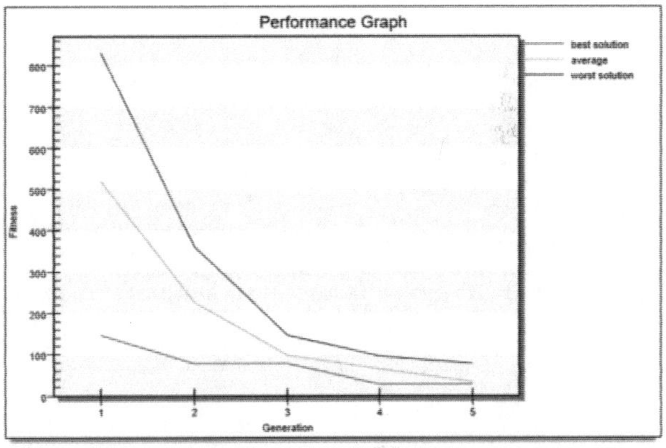

Figure 3. Fitness function trend for different solutions

B. *Experimental NN performances evaluation*

In the hypothesis of this paper, performances very close to GA ones are expected with the neural network approach. A peculiar expected result, to be quantitatively inspected, is the capability of the NN scheduler to quickly react to scenarios never seen before. From commercial feedback collected so far, a performance gain of 50% to 70% is expected, compared to other optimization methods.

V. Conclusions

The use of Genetic Algorithms has proven to be a good method for solving NP-hard problems, hence also the problem related to the scheduling of the movements of the overhead cranes for loading scrap baskets in the steel industry. Certainly, of fundamental importance is the creation of the model because in order to avoid errors or to avoid obtaining results that differ too much from reality, it is necessary to make the virtual model as equivalent as possible to the real one, creating a Digital Twin. This overhead crane scheduling problem has received attention in the literature and different methods have been used (network flow model, Tabu research, MAS based), but the performance of the Genetic Algorithms is considered the best. Even in the case of multiple gantries, the method based on Genetic Algorithms provides a solution to improve their efficiency and the introduction of the GA Wizard object improves the preparation times of the scrap baskets for melting furnaces; consequently, also an improvement of the overall performance of the steel company is achieved.

The most important achievement of the paper is the development of a challenging test frame to compare GA results with the ones expected by the use of a neural network technique. Further studies will complete the comparison proposed.

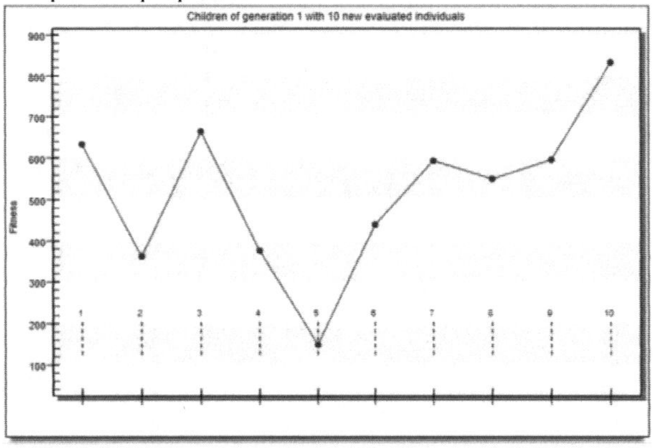

Figure 4. Children of generation 1 with 10 new evaluated individuals

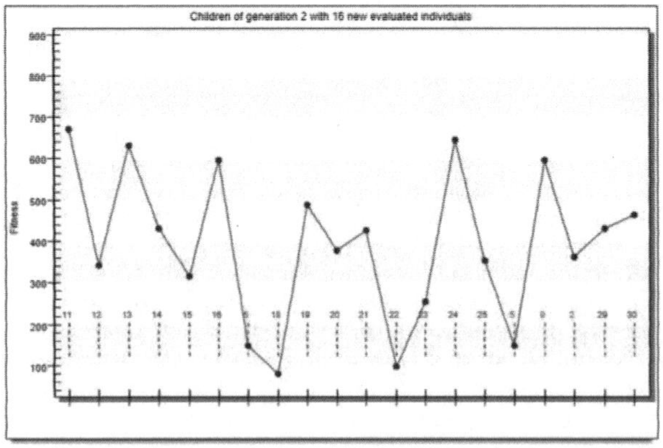

Figure 5. Children of generation 2 with 16 new evaluated individuals

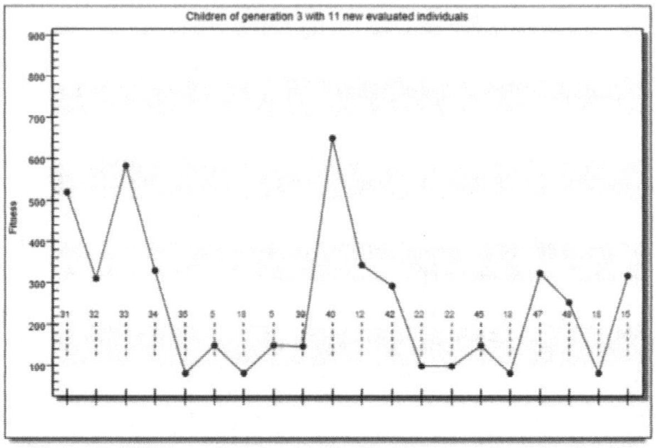

Figure 6. Children of generation 3 with 11 new evaluated individuals

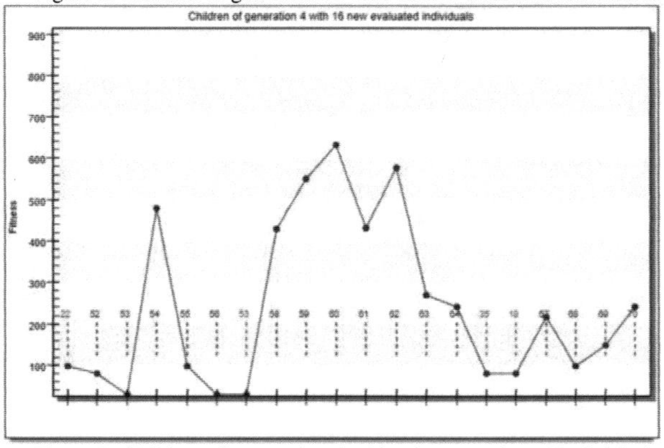

Figure 7. Children of generation 4 with 16 new evaluated individuals

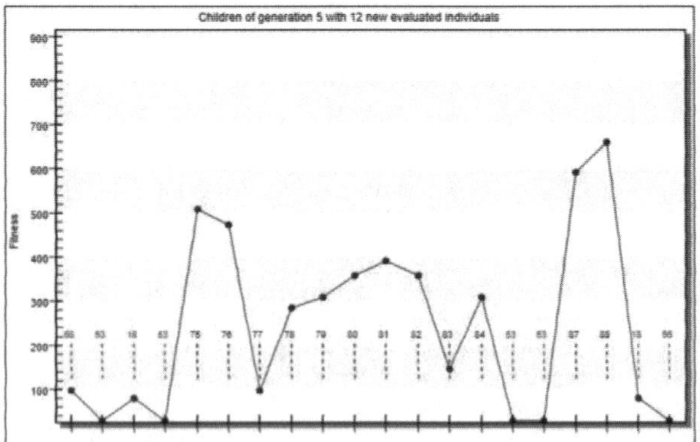

Figure 8. Children of generation 5 with 12 new evaluated individuals

TABLE II. BEST INDIVIDUAL FOR GENERATION FOUR

Individual	Fitness	Chromosomes	Observations
Gen 4 Ind 3	28.55409	Chrom 1	Fitness 53
Gen 4 Ind 6	28.55409	Chrom 1	Fitness 56
Gen 2 Ind 8	78.70279	Chrom 1	Fitness 18
Gen 3 Ind 5	78.70279	Chrom 1	Fitness 35
Gen 4 Ind 2	78.70279	Chrom 1	Fitness 52

ACKNOWLEDGMENT

The authors would like to acknowledge Genoa University for the support.

REFERENCES

[1] C.B. Ma, D.F. Zhu, H. Wang, Y.Q. Zhao, and J.X. Xu, "Simulation model for crane scheduling in workshop of steel-making plant based on MAS," *2010 International Conference on Computer Application and System Modelling* (ICCASM 2010), vol. 5, pp. V5-404, 2010.

[2] G. Zäpfel and M. Wasner, "Warehouse sequencing in the steel supply chain as a generalized job shop model," *International Journal of Production Economics*, vol. 104(2), pp. 482-501, 2006.

[3] A. Graunke, G. Burnett, C. Hu, and G. Wirth, "Decision support model to evaluate complex overhead crane schedules," *Proceedings of the Winter Simulation Conference* 2014, pp. 1608-1619, 2014.

[4] A.S. Jain and S. Meeran, "Job-shop scheduling using neural networks," *International Journal of Production Research*, vol. 36(5), pp.1249-1272, 1998.

[5] G.R. Weckman, C.V. Ganduri, and D.A. Koonce, "A neural network job-shop scheduler," *Journal of Intelligent Manufacturing*, vol. 19(2), pp.191-201, 2008.

[6] X. Xie, Y. Zheng, and Y. Li, "Multi-crane scheduling in steel coil warehouse," *Expert Systems with Applications*, vol. 41(6), pp. 2874-2885, 2014.

[7] A. Lim, B. Rodrigues, F. Xiao, and Y. Zhu, "Crane scheduling using tabu search," *14th IEEE International Conference on Tools with Artificial Intelligence*, pp. 146-153, 2002.

[8] Y. Yuan and L. Tang, "Novel time-space network flow formulation and approximate dynamic programming approach for the crane scheduling in a coil warehouse," *European Journal of Operational Research*, vol. 262(2), pp. 424-437, 2017.

[9] X. Xie, Y. Zheng, and Y. Li, "Genetic algorithm and its performance analysis for scheduling a single crane," *Discrete Dynamics in Nature and Society*, 2015.

[10] M.R.K. Mes, "Simulation Modeling using Practical Examples: A Plant Simulation Tutorial," University of Twente, 2017 https://www.utwente.nl/en/bms/iebis/staff/mes/plantsimulation/tutorialplantsimulation13v20170726.pdf .

Data Privacy for AI Fraud Detection Models

A framework for GDPR compliant AI

Kadir Ider
Delivery Hero SE
Berlin, Germany
email: kadir.ider@deliveryhero.com

Andreas Schmietendorf
Berlin School of Economics and Law
Berlin, Germany
email: andreas.schmietendorf@hwr-berlin.de

Abstract—**Although the European General Data Protection Regulation (GDPR) is technology neutral, it indirectly imposes strict processing rules for personal information in Artificial Intelligence systems. As fraud detection becomes more sophisticated and complex, the challenge to manage the trade-off between privacy and accuracy of such systems arises concurrently. This paper identifies and presents key components for a GDPR compliant design and development of Machine Learning supported fraud detection solutions.**

Keywords - Fraud detection; GDPR; transparency; automated decision making; AI.

I. INTRODUCTION

According to a global economic crime and fraud survey in 2020, the financial damage in the US is estimated to amount to USD 42 billion, with a large fraction contributed by cybercrime [13]. Nearly half of businesses have been affected by fraud attacks within a 24 months period. At the same time false credit card declines amount to almost USD 120 billion that is three times higher than the detection of actual fraud cases [9].

Thus, there is a great interest in increasing the accurate detection of true positive and decreasing false positive fraud cases to achieve both, minimize monetary losses, but also accelerate business. Roughly 50% of affected corporations employ Artificial Intelligence (AI) fraud detection systems, but struggle to harness the benefits of such tools. In order to fight fraud effectively, algorithms must be provided with adequate input data that include personal identifiers to some extent.

The European Data Protection authorities are aware of this trend and increasingly publish guidelines on the lawful usage of personal Identifiable Information (PII) as well as to prevent the "black box problem" [12]. The phenomenon of black box algorithms is due to increasing sophistication and complexity of Machine Learning (ML) solutions making it difficult to transparently process PII and ensure accountability [15].

Particularly when sensitive PII pursuant to Art. 9 GDPR [16] is processed, the data processing may not be valid if the legal basis is not given and if it is not consistent with the initial purpose of the data collection. Compliant fraud detection systems can therefore act as an instrument to meet accountability requirements by identifying unlawful and non-compliant usage of PII.

The body of the paper is divided into six sections. In Sections 2 and 3, a segmentation of fraud activities and models generate structural insights and define the research scope. Section 4 evaluates relevant papers and identifies the research need for the framework development. Section 5 formulates the framework components, based on the underlying requirements. In Section 6, further specification is provided on the framework applicability. The final section highlights and discusses the trade-off of privacy requirements and usage of AI and ultimately closes with the conclusion.

II. FRAUD ACTIVITIES AND METHODS CLASSIFICATION

Frequent online fraud activities include identity theft, account takeovers, abuse of promotions, fake reviews or listings [2]. All have monetary consequences in common, i.e., financial losses due to fraud and potential fines imposed to the data controlling entity as a consequence of the data theft. Fraud detection methods include

1) blacklists,

2) rule engines and

3) AI solutions.

Blacklists could contain user data, such as name, email, IP address and device data that are associated with fraudulent activities and therefore will be blocked from using online services. In the scope of promotion code abuse, such lists may be effective if users have already created an account and where one or more variables are matching the blacklist. Due to its static characteristic, the list may only be effective after a fraud attempt has been made, thus may have already caused damage at the stage of detection. Such a reactive approach is therefore not sufficient as a standalone solution. Blacklists may be considered as the most simple rule engine.

More complex, but also manually written rule engines employ several rules, check multiple conditions and incorporate weight scorings. Such rules are frequently employed in the detection of fraudulent activities in the scope of money transactions. For example, multiple small instead of large transactions conducted by different people from an unusual location or having the same beneficiary would be probably rejected as the transaction would violate one or many rules [11]. The downside is that the larger the number of rules, the greater the maintenance. Moreover, rules may cancel each other out. Both options are suitable for identifying obvious fraud cases, are computationally cheaper, but require more manual work to maintain their effectiveness. On the upper end of proactive fraud detection approaches are Supervised Machine Learning algorithms (SML), such as Decision Trees, Support Vector Machine (SVM) or Artificial Neural Networks (ANN) [11]. To overcome the burden of maintaining rule engines, SML models learn from existing patterns and identify fraud in unstructured data, learn and predict fraud activities, despite a multitude of input features [1].

III. Scope and Definitions

In order to limit the research scope and ensure thorough analysis, the assessment will focus on the development of an AI compliance framework, but will not further elaborate the design of a comprehensive Data Protection Management System (DPMS). Subsequently, according to Figure 1, the third-party management will not be assessed further as it belongs to the DPMS framework.

No matter which fraud detection algorithm is used, all are gaining popularity due to their ability to exploit large amounts of personal data, conduct automated decision making and create profiles. Such activities provide competitive advantage and leverage business activities. However, these kinds of processing activities require additional security measures to protect PII, pursuant to Art. 22 and 35 GDPR [16]. As not only data of identified, but also identifiable persons are affected, the GDPR sets strict requirements on such activities. For example, in the design and development process of fraud detection technology, data protection by design and by default, in accordance with Art. 25 GDPR [16], requires enterprises to design the solution in such a way that the flow of personal data is protected by Technical and Organizational Measures (TOMs) at any point in time during the processing, as stated in Table 1. The integration of cloud solutions - whether internally or externally developed and/or hosted - must additionally protect data in rest and transition.

In order to consistently demonstrate compliance and accountability in the entire data lifecycle, monitoring and incident response management plans for the detection of fraudulent activities must be documented, even after implementation of technologies. Non-compliance may result in data breaches that could compromise the identity of data subjects and lead to increased risks to the rights and freedoms of individuals, pursuant to Recital 75 GDPR. Monetary penalties could arise for the data controlling and processing enterprise and amount to €20 million or 4% of the total worldwide annual turnover of the preceding financial year, whichever is higher, according to Art. 83 (5) GDPR [16].

The British Information Commissioner's Office (ICO) has published guidelines and frameworks for AI audits which will be used to a large extent for the development of a comprehensive framework, including specifications for the proposed control areas.

IV. Literature Review

In related publications, either the development, assessment of features, comparison of fraud detection algorithms performance or the issue of an increased digital footprint and its data protection implications are elaborated. A comparison of privacy preserving fraud detection methods [1] provides an understanding on the performance of algorithms by measuring their efficiency. GDPR or data protection aspects are marginalized. Other publications assess elements of trustworthiness in the usage of AI or look into specific AI models including respective classification techniques, such as for ANN, aiming to improve their prediction accuracy [7][10]. The mentioned articles do not highlight the importance of transparency and accountability for PII adherent to the GDPR. Thus, the fraud detection algorithms proposed in the articles disregard the fact that the usage of such technology introduces new risks to data, but more importantly to individuals, which leads to the development of a framework to close the present shortcomings. The development shall further improve the accountability requirements pursuant to Art. 5 (2) GDPR [16].

V. Assessment Method

In the following assessment process, a GDPR compliant AI audit framework will be presented. Subsequently, a common data lifecycle process is analyzed independent of a particular fraud detection model as the framework is equally applicable. The ICO's proposal for a compliant AI framework includes an assessment of the general governance and accountability aspects and AI specific control areas [14]. The model's drawback is the lack of an ethical control area, which will be compensated by incorporating key requirements into the framework based on the Hambach Declaration on Artificial Intelligence [5].

The proposed AI Privacy Design Framework enhances an already existing DPMS [17]. The AI component is split into nine elements and looks as depicted in Figure 1.

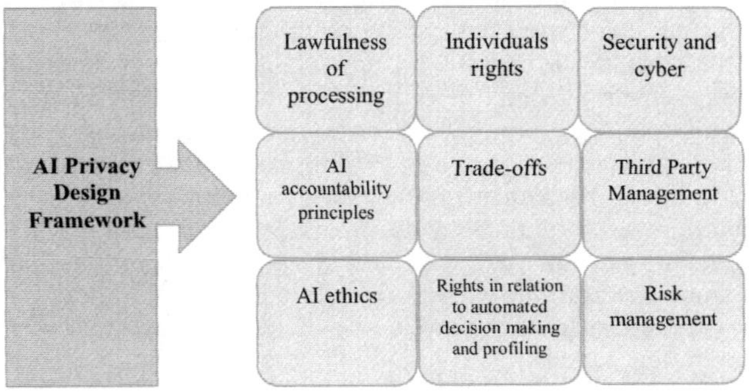

Figure 1. AI Privacy Design Elements. Source: own elaboration.

Each element is a standalone feature, which increases the compliance with GDPR, when considered in the framework. However, removing an element immediately reduces the quality of the framework's proficiency, overall. The composed elements and corresponding specifications are non-exhaustive and should be adjusted according to the business needs. The elements displayed in Figure 1 are further specified in Table 1 (see Appendix 1). The framework can be effectively used for the definition of guidelines or development of maturity assessment models.

VI. Privacy Preserving Design Aspects

The three parties that play an essential role in the process are data subjects, data controller and data processor. The data controller pursuant to Art. 4 (7) GDPR [16] is the entity that defines the purpose and means of processing and is liable for any data incident, while the processor is another party that processes the data upon instructions of the controller. Typically, the processor is an entity that either hosts the data in large data centers (on behalf of the controller) or provides cloud services, such as - pretrained - fraud detection models.

That concludes that the controller is in the obligation to design and ensure a privacy preserving procedure throughout the PII usage lifecycle. In accordance with the framework presented in Table 1, the lifecycle begins with the determination and definition of the lawful basis associated with the data subject rights on the subsequent data processing. Most relevant lawful basis in the scope of fraud detection are legitimate interest and data subjects consent. Processing PII for training and testing based on legitimate interest provides the controller the broadest legitimate ground. It allows the utilization of PII to its full extent for testing various fraud detection purposes, their prediction accuracy as well as use the data for a wider range of AI-based models. Yet, because of its flexibility, it may not be the most accurate ground for processing.

A three-stage-test should be performed to test the fitness of this legitimate basis and involves [8]:

1) identify a legitimate interest (the 'purpose test');

2) show that the processing is necessary to achieve it (the 'necessity test'); and

3) balance it against the individuals interests, rights and freedoms (the 'balancing test').

If the conclusion favours the interests of the controller, the legitimate interest may be appropriate.

Reliance on consent is appropriate in cases where the deployment of fraud detection is in the immediate context with the data subject, e.g., the prevention of customer account or credit card misuse. Processing PII requires the collection of separate consent as each activity has a different purpose and might require the processing of different PII.

Pursuant to Art. 7 GDPR [16], the conditions for obtaining valid consent are:

1) freely given,

2) specific,

3) informed and unambiguous,

4) clear affirmative act of the individual (e.g., clicking "I consent").

The downside is that the number of different purposes increases the difficulty to ensure the conditions of Art. 7 GDPR [16] are effectively met. The data subject has the right to restrict the processing or withdraw the consent completely at any time. Consequently, the immediate discontinuation of the data processing for the fraud detection purpose must be ensured (see Table 1 "Individuals rights").

Besides determining the lawful basis, the controller must challenge whether or not the intended data is needed for the development and deployment of the fraud detection model in accordance with the minimization principle presented in the section "AI accountability principles" in Table 1. Common data categories selected in the feature engineering process include identity, orders, payment method, location, network data and [2]. These parameters are all considered as PII, as all data are in association with an individual.

Acquiring fraud detection services from external suppliers does not release the controller from the duty to adhere to GDPR compliance. The obligation involves defining and communicating the requirements down to the processor.

In order to strengthen the protection of PII, it is suggested to implement additional security mechanisms, such as homomorphic encryption [6]. The original dataset will be encrypted, but still provides the ability (for the algorithm) to perform computations on the encrypted data. However, depending on the homomorphic encryption method, i.e., full, somewhat or partial, the computational overhead may slow down the entire fraud detection process [3]. The optimal trade-off between model complexity and PII security must therefore be balanced out. Nevertheless, encryption is considered as a pseudonymization of PII, as a re-identification is possible with the corresponding decryption key, at any time.

VII. Advantages and Limits of AI Set by Privacy Regulations

Compliance with GDPR is at the ultimate forefront of advantages. The chapters highlight that, by adhering to the data protection law, AI deploying enterprises demonstrate thorough understanding of their models. A transparent documentation of fraud detection models will not reveal secrets about the underlying algorithm and thus, will not jeopardize businesses intellectual property, but rather enable affected users to understand the processing of personal information. From a business continuity point of view, a compliance and thus transparent documentation increases the maintainability of fraud detection models, particularly in areas with higher employee turnover rates.

A clear limitation of AI models is set by the consistent challenge to measure the trade-offs between the level of privacy and model accuracy. Implementing security layers, such as homomorphic encryption elevate the data security, but come at the expense of speed and required computation resources. These factors may decrease the appeal for smaller and medium enterprises with fewer tech- and privacy experts as well as financial resources. Companies that deploy application programming interface (API) based fraud detection models must additionally monitor user queries, implement rate-limiting and other security layers [8]. Moreover, deploying externally developed models bindes to their bias and therefore might not effectively detect the fraud as the degree of influence in the development is limited and set by the provider.

VIII. Conclusion

The foregoing analysis presented a framework for a GDPR compliant development of fraud detection models. Incorporating privacy and ethics into technology goes beyond the mere understanding of the 99 GDPR articles. The challenge is - irrespective of the underlying Machine Learning model - to translate the regulation requirements into operable measures. Due to the GDPR's technology neutrality, enterprises face the great challenge to identify and integrate appropriate technology in order to comply. The proposed framework must therefore not be seen as a standalone solution. The eight control areas defined are rather modules to be incorporated in the scope of AI development and where PII is involved. In subsequent studies, the implementation and assessment of this framework on various fraud detections, but also other AI supported models in different industries will eventually reveal its long-term effectiveness. In this context, an empirical validation of the proposed framework elements will be further conducted.

References

[1] M. P. Bach, N. Vlahović, and J. Pivar, "Fraud Prevention in the Leasing Industry Using the Kohonen Self-Organising Maps." *Organizacija* 53, no. 2, May 2020, pp. 128–45. https://doi.org/10.2478/orga-2020-0009.

[2] M. Beals, M. DeLiema, and M. Deevy, "Full-Taxonomy-Report" [retrieved: 10, 2020]. http://162.144.124.243/~longevl0/wp-content/uploads/2016/03/Full-Taxonomy-report.pdf.

[3] R. Canillas et al., "Exploratory Study of Privacy Preserving Fraud Detection." In *Proceedings of the 19th International Middleware Conference Industry on - Middleware '18*, pp. 25–31. Rennes, France: ACM Press, 2018. https://doi.org/10.1145/3284028.3284032.

[4] Data2.eu, "What Technical and Organisational Measures Do We Need to Take? - GDPR Processing Index." [retrieved: 10, 2020]. https://data2.eu/en/gdpr/what-technical-and-organisational-measures-do-we-need-to-take.

[5] Datenschutzkonferenz (DSK), "Report on Experience Gained in the Implementation of the GDPR." [retrieved: 10, 2020]. https://www.datenschutzkonferenz-online.de/media/dskb/20191213_evaluation_report_german_dpa_s_clean.pdf.

[6] T. Graepel, K. Lauter, and M. Naehrig, "ML Confidential: Machine Learning on Encrypted Data", In *Information Security and Cryptology – ICISC 2012*, edited by T. Kwon, M.-K. Lee, and D. Kwon, 1–21. Berlin, Heidelberg: Springer Berlin Heidelberg, 2013.

[7] C. W. L. Ho, J. Ali, and K. Caals, "Ensuring Trustworthy Use of Artificial Intelligence and Big Data Analytics in Health Insurance." *Bulletin of the World Health Organization* 98, no. 4, Apr. 2020, pp. 263–69. https://doi.org/10.2471/BLT.19.234732.

[8] Information Commissioner's Office, "Guidance on the AI auditing framework." [retrieved: 10, 2020]. https://ico.org.uk/media/about-the-ico/consultations/2617219/guidance-on-the-ai-auditing-framework-draft-for-consultation.pdf.

[9] J. Khodos, "Mastercard Rolls Out Artificial Intelligence Across Its Network." [retrieved: 10, 2020]. https://newsroom.mastercard.com/press-releases/mastercard-rolls-out-artificial-intelligence-across-its-global-network/.

[10] A. K. Patience and J. V. N Lakshmi. "A Study on Credit Card Fraud Detection Using Machine Learning." *International Journal of Trend in Scientific Research and Development (Ijtsrd)* 4, no. 3, Apr. 2020, pp. 801–804.

[11] M. M. Rahman and A. R. Saha, "A Comparative Study and Performance Analysis of ATM Card Fraud Detection Techniques." *Journal of Information Security* 10, no. 03, Jul. 2019, pp. 188–97. https://doi.org/10.4236/jis.2019.103011.

[12] A. Rai, "Explainable AI: From Black Box to Glass Box." *Journal of the Academy of Marketing Science* 48, no. 1, Jan. 2020, pp. 137–41. https://doi.org/10.1007/s11747-019-00710-5.

[13] K. Rivera, C. Rohn, J. Donker, and C. Butter, "PwC's Global Economic Crime and Fraud Survey 2020," 2020. [retrieved: 10, 2020]. https://www.pwc.com/gx/en/forensics/gecs-2020/pdf/global-economic-crime-and-fraud-survey-2020.pdf

[14] B. Reuben and V. Gallo, "An Overview of the Auditing Framework for Artificial Intelligence and Its Core Components." [retrieved: 10, 2020]. https://ico.org.uk/about-the-ico/news-and-events/ai-blog-an-overview-of-the-auditing-framework-for-artificial-intelligence-and-its-core-components/.

[15] M. Veale, R. Binns, and L. Edwards, "Governing Artificial Intelligence: Ethical, Legal and Technical Opportunities and Challenges." *Philosophical Transactions of the Royal Society A: Mathematical, Physical and Engineering Sciences* 376, no. 2133, Nov. 2018, 20180080. https://doi.org/10.1098/rsta.2018.0080.

[16] EU General Data Protection Regulation (GDPR): Regulation (EU) 2016/679 of the European Parliament and of the Council of 27 April 2016 on the protection of natu-ral persons with regard to the processing of personal data and on the free movement of such data, and repealing Directive 95/46/EC (General Data Protection Regula-tion), OJ 2016 L 119/1.

[17] A. Rai, "Explainable AI: From Black Box to Glass Box." *Journal of the Academy of Marketing Science* 48, no. 1, Jan. 2020, pp. 137–41. https://doi.org/10.1007/s11747-019-00710-5.

APPENDIX 1

TABLE I. AI PRIVACY DESIGN FRAMEWORK

Areas and controls		*Specification*
Lawfulness of processing		Pursuant to Art. 6 GDPR [16]
	Assessment of lawful basis	• Determine lawful basis depending on the fraud systems purpose: ○ Determination before processing starts ○ Document the decision process ○ Lawful basis must not be changed after processing starts ○ Communicate lawful basis with affected individuals (e.g., via privacy policy)
AI accountability principles		Pursuant to Art. 5, 13, 14 and Recital 60 GDPR [16]
	Fairness and transparency in profiling	• Specification of person/team in charge of AI system (responsibility and accountability) • Explanation of models unbiased decision making ability • Address (e.g., in privacy policy) the associated risks of using AI ○ Providing a summary of a data protection impact assessment (DPIA)
	Accuracy (of used data)	• Specification of data used in AI system (classification in categories and detailed listing of dates, e.g., Identification Data: name, surname; Technical Data: IP address, device ID) • "Binning" (e.g., continuous) variables into discrete ranges in the pre-processing phase may alter the accuracy of data (pursuant to Art. 5 (1) lit. d GDPR [16] and subsequently the accuracy of the prediction (e.g., instead of processing individuals age "54", he/she will be "binned' into the age group "50-60")
	Data minimization and purpose limitation	• Ability to explain why AI is required for the specific purpose (e.g., "detect the abuse of promo codes", instead of just stating "fraud detection") • Aiming for usage of minimum amount or anonymous data, if sufficient enough for achieving a specific legitimate purpose
AI ethics [5]		Pursuant to Art. 5, 12, 22, 24, 25, 32, 35 and Recital 71 GDPR [16]
	AI must not turn human beings into objects	• Automated decision-making with legal consequences for individuals must be used in a limited scope with appropriate safeguarding measures in place (see TOMs) • Intervention into the automated decision-making process: individuals have the right to request a human intervention (see Individuals rights) • Ability to provide explanation of solely automated decision after it is been made
	AI may only be used for legitimate purposes and may not abrogate the requirement of purpose limitation (see purpose limitation)	• PII may only be used for the purpose communicated to and limited to the data acquired from the individuals • Extended purposes must be closely associated with the original purpose • Specifications must include information on the usage of individuals PII for train and/or test data ○ Specify which data of the individual will be used for train/test purposes ○ Specify bias mitigation measures incorporated in the model ▪ State the means by which you ensure that the data is representational
	AI must be transparent, comprehensible and explainable	• Transparency of processing is associated with the ease of understanding of the processing activity. It is not enough to explain the result, but rather the end-to-end processes and the decisions made that lead to the result.
	AI must avoid discrimination	• Data input sources and data quality must be consistently evaluated to ensure that the principle of fairness, the processing according to the legitimate purpose and the adequacy of the processing is in pace • DPIA results should be evaluated prior to data processing • If data on individuals consist of outlier and model has not been trained such data, incorrect predictions might take place
	The principle of data minimisation applies to AI	• Demonstration that the PII is necessary for AI (train/test) purposes and proving the effects to privacy and accuracy if data is not used (e.g., there is no need to collect health information, if the purpose of the fraud detection model is the identification of money laundering transactions)
	AI needs responsibility	• Obligation of the controller to demonstrate accountability end-to-end • Ensuring data subject rights • Security and controllability of processing • Conduct DPIA
	AI requires technical and organizational measures (TOMs)	• TOMs must be defined for the end-to-end protection of individuals, as the processing of large amounts of data does not dilute the identity of individuals (see Technical and Organizational Measures for further details)
Individuals rights		Pursuant to Art. 12 - 23 GDPR [16]
	to be informed	• Informing individuals about the usage of their data for fraud detection purposes supported by AI models before data processing begins • If data is not obtained directly from individuals, they must be notified within one month at latest accordance with Art. 14 GDPR
	of access	• Providing individuals access to their data in accordance with Art. 15 GDPR [16]
	to rectification	• Wrong data on individuals must be rectified, this is applicable to data stored in the database/raw data and for the pre-processed training data • Attention: a wrong date (e.g., age 32 instead of 23) is not likely to affect the model performance. Nonetheless, the right of an individual must not be disregarded
	to erasure	• Erasure of PII in any data processing system, including training datasets Remember: Erasure of one or few individual's

Areas and controls		*Specification*
		data is unlikely to affect the models performance
	to restrict processing	• Individuals have the right to restrict processing of their PII • If automated decision making is involved, be able to provide information on how human intervention can replace fully automated decision making procedures
	to data portability	• Individuals have the right to request their original data in a machine-readable form • Data that has been modified in the pre-processing phase may count as PII, but is not affected by the portability request
	to object	• Individuals can object the usage of their data for AI purposes • This may impact their rights to use engage with data processing entities (see Assessment of lawful basis)
Trade-offs		
	Data privacy compliance vs. model accuracy	• identify and assess any existing or potential trade-offs, when designing or procuring an AI system, and assess the impact it may have on individuals • consider available technical approaches to minimize the need for any trade-offs • consider any techniques which you can implement with a reasonable level of investment and effort • have clear criteria and lines of accountability about the final trade-off decisions. This should include a robust, risk-based and independent approval process • Accuracy with respect to privacy: demonstrating the correctness and consistency of personal data • Accuracy with respect to statistics: predicting the correct answer; high statistical accuracy (high probability) of predicting the correct answer • AI system demonstrate compliance with the fairness principle: higher prediction accuracy means data is PII the o GDPR requires maintenance of correct data (see right to rectification) [8] • Be aware of discrimination: o If model discriminates minorities, due to lack of data about a subject group (e.g., less data on fraud cases associated with woman from particular countries are in dataset; model may lead to wrong prediction) o Statistical accuracy (prediction quality) may be increased by feeding more data on minority cases, but may impose higher risks to their privacy, due to additional data o A clear process of weighting the interests of privacy rights and statistical accuracy must be defined to mitigate risks
Rights in relation to automated decision making and profiling		Pursuant to Art. 22 GDPR [16]
	Automated decision making models	• Explanation, if model will entirely make a decision in the respective fraud detection process • Demonstrating the ability to provide human intervention on case-by-case basis • Demonstrating transparency on the underlying data (see Data minimization and purpose limitation)
Security and cyber		Pursuant to Art. 32 GDPR [16]
	Technical and organizational measures (TOMs) [4]	• Access control: e.g., Access to server rooms only with key or chip card, office rooms secured with alarm • Integrity: e.g., user authorizations are restricted to tasks (marketing department only newsletter, accounting also HR data) • Pseudonymization: e.g., Replacement of user-related data by random codes • Encryption: e.g., Hard disk encryption or cloud solution with encryption • Transmission control: e.g., SSL certificate for websites (https: //) to transfer data within forms • Confidentiality: e.g., password policies • Recoverability: e.g., backups that are regularly checked for successful recovery • Evaluation: e.g., annual review of technical and organisational measures on effectiveness and plausibility
	Cross-border data transfer security	• Appropriate safeguards for data stored outside the EU or in transmission from/to EU must ensure that data is pseudonymized, through o encryption when stored o encryption in transmission (e.g., transfer takes place via API) o TOMs implemented on both ends, i.e., data storage and consumption location o Identity and access management guidelines
Risk management		
	Risk appetite	• Understanding, evaluating and documenting o risks arising from usage of AI models for the respective processing activity (e.g., risks of ANN for evaluation of new account sign-ups and promo code abuse) o risks for the rights and freedom of individual (likelihood and severity) • Mitigation of above mentioned risks
	Special data categories	• State in a transparent manner how the usage of following data in an AI system will not discriminate individuals o Age o Disability o Gender reassignment o Marriage and civil partnership o Pregnancy and maternity o Race o Religion and belief o Sex o Sexual orientation

SEAL Project: User-Centric Application of Linked Digital Identity for Students and Citizens

Francisco José Aragó-Monzonís
Universitat Jaume I
Castellón, Spain
e-mail: farago@uji.es

Laura Domínguez-García
Universidad de Málaga
Málaga, Spain
e-mail: lauradomg@uma.es

Victoriano Giralt
Universidad de Málaga
Málaga, Spain
e-mail: victoriano@uma.es

Basurte-Durán, Alberto
Universidad de Málaga
Málaga, Spain
e-mail: abasurte@uma.es

Raúl Ocaña
Universidad de Málaga
Málaga, Spain
e-mail: raulocana14@uma.es

***Abstract*— The SEAL (Student and Citizen Identity Linked) project targets two important aspects of identity management: give the users control over their own data, and facilitate the reconciliation of the multiple electronic identities citizens have across public and private institutions. Through a modular, extensible, and scalable design, the SEAL service empowers the citizen to build his own persistent and unique identity, while still having control over the anonymity and traceability. This citizen empowerment is due to the exploration of the Self-Sovereign Identity concept, which reduces data exposition and critical dependencies, building a bridge between the federated data world and the Self-Sovereign Identity new horizons. In this paper we describe the paradigm that SEAL proposes for dealing with identity reconciliation issues and its contribution to secure digital identities, and how users can control all of this through the SEAL service dashboard.**

Keywords-identity reconciliation; self-sovereign identity; identity federation; know your customer; eIDAS.

I. INTRODUCTION

SEAL has been born amidst a complex situation. The rapid growth in online service usage and needs in the last decades greatly exceeded the organisational capacity of the regulatory bodies, producing an environment where users own personal data in a myriad of different and non-interoperable sources. This situation has been tackled partially through different aspects, like for example the authentication. In the academia sector, the eduGAIN (Education Global Authentication Infrastructure) network [1] facilitated an effective sharing of online services and resources among higher education and research institutions using SAML2 (Security Assertion Markup Language v2) standard [2], and later, the European Commission has taken a similar approach to produce a framework for cross-border acceptance of state-issued electronic identities [3]. However, this tendency is not limited to authentication: EMREX project [4] created a framework for the trusted exchange of academic records, to support students moving abroad in getting credit recognition. The main common factor behind these initiatives is a user-centric approach, in accordance with the evolution of the data protection legislation that aims at giving the users full sovereignty over the personal data.

The increasing demand for integrated online user services requires trusted, effective data interoperability. At the centre of this lies a key but usually ignored issue: how to determine if two sets of data identified by non-matching identifiers belong to the same individual. The usual solution to this lies in trusting the users' statement of ownership. However, on many high-profile use cases (especially on official administrative procedures), this is not an option, as the users can benefit from counterfeiting data. This would not be an option in the context of trusted infrastructures, but the blind spot of non-matching identifiers in data sources can open the door to borrowing data from another citizen. Ensuring the ontological relationship between two sets of data and an individual requires a process of comparing contextual data of the subject of both sets (i.e., comparing name, surname, date of birth, etc.). This process is costly and probabilistic, requiring human interaction in many edge-cases, especially if the trust standards are high. This is the reason for the growth of specialised Know-Your-Customer (KYC) companies that provide this identity reconciliation service. However, this is still a chaotic and non-standard field.

SEAL tries to build a key element to formalise the management of data and their relationships, by coordinating the different involved actors to let the users be in the centre of it, bringing the data under a virtually unified and persistent identity, while still guaranteeing all his rights and giving full control over the traceability and anonymity. The SEAL service develops a modular and extensible framework that allows plugging in to sources of identity and data, KYC providers and data consumers, to let the users collect her data sets, establish trusted links among them, and deliver them to the consuming parties, namely university user services.

This work is organised in two main sections: SEAL innovation as digital identity, which shows SEAL architecture, and user-centric management for students, where the user-centric approach of the SEAL project is detailed and the users' experience interaction -web and mobile- is described.

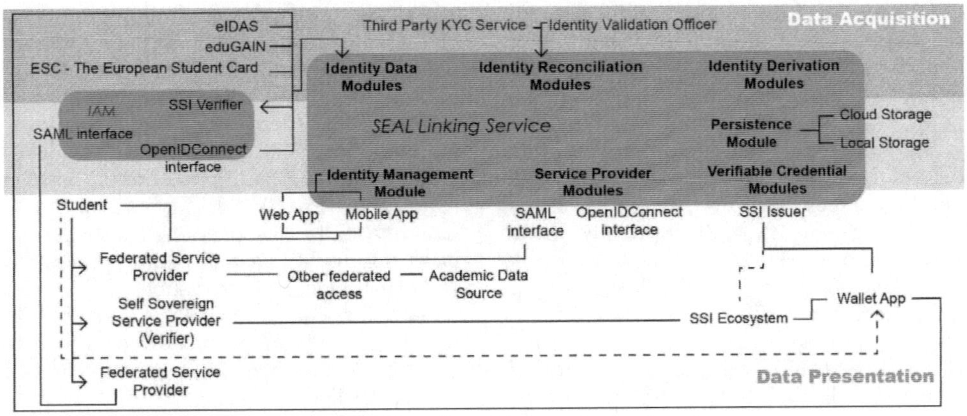

Figure 1. SEAL service architecture structure layout.

II. SEAL INNOVATION AS DIGITAL IDENTITY

SEAL proposes an innovative framework aimed at creating a standardized and holistic way of dealing with an often disregarded issue: identity reconciliation. Only in the latest years, the growth in the demand for online services, has brought into light this missing piece, that hinders the establishment of online services and procedures(especially in the public sector and in banking) that show a big potential demand but also need to establish with a high level of trust that two identities refer to the same individual citizen, without having to trust the citizen for that. This has brought to the appearance of KYC companies that develop complex assurance procedures to establish this fact, and sell their services to interested companies, and also the approval of specific regulations, like eIDAS (Electronic Identification Authentication and trust Services) [5] regulation, that settle the legal grounds for the public acceptance of said methods.

The state of the art, shows independent KYC providers dealing with independent consumer entities, doing specific and no-portable integrations. The SEAL project has recognised this gap and proposes a structured, common and standardised approach to create a common ground that brings together all the actors in this scenario: KYC providers, data providers, data consumers, and builds it around the user, to ensure the protection of the users' rights regarding data management. And it tries to do so in a manner to open the way for standardization of procedures, and minimisation of efforts for the implied stakeholders, coordinating the actions of all of them in the most efficient way.

A. Architecture

SEAL is not a new data transport infrastructure, but a support framework. It minimises the reconciliation effort for data consumers by centralising this management on the SEAL service and allowing the reuse of this effort by storing the trusted links on secure storage areas. SEAL is divided in three layers, with information flowing from top to down, as shown in Figure 1. First, we find a data acquisition layer, where we find three specific interfaces that allow data into SEAL: identity data access, identity reconciliation and identity derivation. Of these interfaces, multiple pluggable implementations can be provided to support almost any source of data or KYC provider. Out of the box, SEAL provides integration with eduGAIN and with eIDAS, and internal automated and manual KYC support procedures.

On the middle layer, we find the management and storage interfaces. SEAL allows any API (Application Programming Interface) compliant client to allow users to connect and interact, to retrieve data and establish links. Two clients are provided: a mobile and a browser-based client. The storage can be performed on a series of locations under the control of the users: mobile storage, local storage on the computer or, cloud storage services. Stored data is encrypted, so only the users can decrypt it and decide when it is decrypted and fed into SEAL, but also the data is signed to ensure the users do not tamper with it, breaking the chain of trust: the user owns the data, however, SEAL does not trust the users.

The lower layer is the data presentation layer. There, any data consumer can access the data users want to deliver through multiple ways, divided into two main blocks: federated access and self-sovereign access. On the federated access, the relaying party sends a request to SEAL using a standard delegation protocol: SAML2 and OIDC (Open ID Connect) [6], having this last one more fitted with the concept of user-centric federated identity management [7]. Then, the users are requested to access their storage to retrieve the required data and send it back to the relaying party. On the self-sovereign access, SEAL acts as an issuer of verifiable claims. These claims are stored on a user wallet (similar to the SEAL storage, but designed as an independent agent) that the users can carry around and deliver to data consumers, that will verify the integrity and trust on those claims through validation data published on a distributed ledger. This access model skips the SEAL service once the data has been issued, removing critical central points in the processing, which is the base of the self-sovereign concept.

III. USER-CENTRIC APPLICATION MANAGEMENT FOR STUDENTS

A user-centric approach allows for general-purpose infrastructures supporting a wide array of use cases, because the users interact with the components. They can be properly informed and can request their consent over any operation that needs to be performed on their data, asked to discover the sources, and is able to follow and cut the process at any point.

This concept has evolved into the self-sovereignty of the data, which advocates for the users to be the keeper and have an effective control over their data, not just a formal one. The concept has been gaining strength, especially in the context of the increasing risks and costs for private companies to secure the sensitive user data being kept in their systems: if the users keep their own data and offer it to be processed only when needed, the window of risk is greatly reduced, and companies become less appealing targets. SEAL linked identity offers key advantages regarding privacy and security of High Education Institutions (HEI) students in their operations and interactions as users of educational, institutional and private services. In this regard, there are some potential features to be addressed not only from the student perspective, but also from the whole academic community. The SEAL project is an example of how compatible data of interest can be linked as other projects previously did, like Europeana [8] focuses on electronic resources data aggregation, to fulfil citizens needs providing a secure user-controlled digital identity framework.

The European Blockchain Services Infrastructure (EBSI) specifies four use cases for 2019: Notarisation, Diplomas, European Self-Sovereign Identity and Trusted Data Sharing [9]. The SEAL service covers all these cases and can contribute to secure the process, resulting in a reduction of the verification costs and an improvement of the authenticity trust between organizations [10]. The potential of the SEAL service lies in its power to create and utilise the user-centric service features of digital identity to improve the user experience of accessing restricted personal digital areas among institutions or e-Government authorities. Facilitating the authentication process improves the user experience by avoiding nowadays long administrative processes. This has been addressed by A. Crespo et al. [11] as the offering of cross-border services allows access to new services with credentials that the citizen already possesses and without the need for issuing local ones.

A. Dashboard application and user interaction

As described by X. Liu et al. [12] the Web has undergone toward a highly user-centric environment where millions of users can participate and collaborate for their own interests and benefits. Thus, the SEAL dashboard allows users to lead their actions. The SEAL service can be used from different devices and two service applications have been designed: a web dashboard and a native mobile application compatible with Android and iOS (iPhone Operating System) systems.

1) Access methods and data storing: Two access options are offered: centralised and decentralised. Both of them fulfil the security requirements established for the SEAL service and the same privileges are granted. The centralised Personal Data Store (PDS) access requires the user's password. Nevertheless, as personal data is a complex issue, not all the attributes are available to users as linked ones [13]. This access method offers two options for storing the data file: local and cloud, both of them require the user's password, and when locally stored, the file is saved in the user device's system.

The decentralised Self-Sovereing Identitty (SSI) access method uses a Distributed Ledger Technology (DLT) to assure and verify the identity of a person, together with the integrity of the personal data. As suggested by A. Benzekri et al, this could avoid uploading official documents during the registration process, which is tedious and degrades the users' experience, especially with mobile [14]. This access method requires an external mechanism to connect, read and generate data over the DLT infrastructure, and it behaves as an intermediary between the SEAL service and the ledger: the uPort [15] API. Since this API needs a local wallet [16] to fulfil the users' credentials, which in turn authorise the operations over the DLT, the SSI access method can be seen as a conjunction of the dashboard, the uPort API and the DLT infrastructure.

2) SEAL Dashboard functionalities: Linked digital identities can be defined as linked data capable of storing data and allowing a service to tie linked resources into a worldwide network [17]. The SEAL service uses this new technology to retrieve different identities, link them and expand users' feature options while strengthening the authentication process; as this is the major advantage of Linked Data technology [18].

The soul of the service in terms of identity collection is the Identity Reconciliation functionality, which allows the users to link two identities (manually or automatically) and create a new one. In order to assure the users' privacy, the identity reconciliation only takes place when the users select a suitable pair of identities and start the process. The users can check its progress thanks to the Reconciliation Status function. Besides, the SEAL service offers the possibility of loading a new identity and including it among those from the Identity Reconciliation functionality. The Retrieve Identity Data function performs the data collection and its storage in the session. Thus, the users can display the loaded identities data and store the current session. About the storage, the Configuration Data Store functionality presents the two options: local and cloud; the selected one will remain for future access.

Concerning the DLT operations, the Manage Verifiable Claims functionality allows the users to create, retrieve and store a Verifiable Credential (VC), which is a set of tamper-resistant claims made by an issuer (the SEAL service in this case) where each claim asserts a set of properties about a subject [19]. The last feature of the Identity Manager interface is the Derive Identifier functionality. It can generate a new identifier from a current stored identity.

B. Mobile – Desktop interoperability

In today's world, smartphones have become a central technology. For this reason, the SEAL service is designed to be accessible from a mobile perspective. The SEAL App provides all the web service functions to cover the users' needs when using their digital identity. This is possible as the digital identity is linked to the web app via the SEAL servers. Besides, the SEAL App can be combined with a personal wallet for decentralised authorisation and identification process. Thus, the verification and certification of personal data can be done on demand basis.

IV. CONCLUSIONS

The SEAL project addresses security and assurance, the two critical issues of cloud computing in public sectors as described by D. Shin [20]. SEAL-linked digital identity can be used as a multiple identity detector becoming a keystone in the EU ecosystem. Its platform allows both authorities and users to obtain limitless digital resources from authentication and identification mechanisms. Furthermore, features and functionalities of the SEAL service are designed from a user-centric approach, focusing on the final user' benefits and the compliance of the service interoperability with the EU information systems.

The SEAL service offers an easy-to-use user experience, ending up in a better users' interaction of their digital linked identities, giving the users the full control of their single lifetime identity and data across borders - in a trusted and secured manner. SEAL, more than competing with existing infrastructures, tries to fill a gap in the management of identities: the reconciliation of identities. Moreover, it tries to do so in a manner to open the way for standardization of procedures and minimisation of efforts for the implied stakeholders, coordinating the actions of all of them in the most efficient way.

REFERENCES

[1] J. Howlett, V. Nordh, and W. Singer, "Deliverable DS3. 3.1: eduGAIN service definition and policy Initial Draft," GÉANT. Deliverable DS3.3.1, May 2010, URL: https://geant3.archive.geant.org/Media_Centre/Media_Library/Media%20Library/GN3-10-081-DS3_3_1_eduGAIN_service_definition_and_policy.pdf accesed: 2020-11-05.

[2] S. Cantor et al., "Assertions and Protocols for the OASIS Security Assertion Markup Language (SAML) V2.0," Oasis Standard, March 2005, URL: https://docs.oasis-open.org/security/saml/v2.0/saml-core-2.0-os.pdf accessed: 2020-11-05.

[3] European Commission, "eID Documentation," URL: https://ec.europa.eu/cefdigital/wiki/display/CEFDIGITAL/What+is+eID accessed: 2020-11-05.

[4] T. Fridell, "EMREX The User-centered Solution for Electronic Transfer of Student Data," URL: https://emrex.eu/wp-content/uploads/2020/09/Emrex-EUNIS2019-16-9.pdf accessed: 2020-11-05.

[5] European Commision, "Trust Services and Electronic identification (eID)," URL: https://ec.europa.eu/digital-single-market/en/trust-services-and-eid accessed: 2020-11-05.

[6] R. Sakimura, N. Bradley, J. Jones, M. De Medeiros, and C. Mortimore, "Openid connect core 1.0.," The OpenID Foundation S3, February 2014, URL: https://openid.net/specs/openid-connect-core-1_0-final.html accessed: 2020-11-05.

[7] R. Laborde et al., "A User-Centric Identity Management Framework based on the W3C Verifiable Credentials and the FIDO Universal Authentication Framework," IEEE 17th Annual Consumer Communications & Networking Conference (CCNC), January 2020, doi: 10.1109/CCNC46108.2020.9045440. URL: https://ieeexplore.ieee.org/abstract/document/9045440 accessed: 2020-11-04.

[8] A. Isaac, R. Clayphan, and B.Haslhofer, "Europeana: Moving to Linked Open Data," Information Standards Quarterly, vol. 24, Jun. 2012, pp. 34–40, doi: 10.3789/isqv24n2-3.2012.06 URL: https://www.niso.org/niso-io/2012/06/europeana accessed: 2020-11-04.

[9] European Commission, "European countries join Blockchain Partnership," April 2018, URL: https://ec.europa.eu/digital-single-market/en/news/european-countries-join-blockchain-partnership accessed: 2020-11-04.

[10] European Commission, "Introducing the European Blockchain Services Infrastructure (EBSI)," URL: https://ec.europa.eu/cefdigital/wiki/display/CEFDIGITAL/EBSI accessed: 2020-11-05.

[11] A. Crespo, N. Rodríguez, F.J. Aragó, and V. Andreu, "Feasibility Study on Cross-border Use of eID and Authentication Services (eIDAS compliant) to support Student Mobility and Access to Student Services in Europe," doi: 10.2759/735197. URL: https://op.europa.eu/en/publication-detail/-/publication/c0bc89a9-437b-11e8-a9f4-01aa75ed71a1/language-en/format-PDF/source-69424735 accessed: 2020-11-05.

[12] X. Liu, G. Huang, and H. Mei, "Discovering Homogeneous Web Service Community in the User-Centric Web Environment," IEEE Transactions on Services Computing, vol. 2, nº. 2, 2009, pp. 167–181, doi:10.1109/TSC.2009.11. URL: https://ieeexplore.ieee.org/abstract/document/4912192 accessed: 2020-11-05.

[13] H. L. Moulaison and A. J. Million, "The disruptive qualities of linked data in the library environment: Analysis and recommendations," Cataloging & Classification Quarterly, vol. 52, nº. 4, 2014, pp. 367–387, doi: 10.1080/01639374.2014.880981 URL: https://www.tandfonline.com/doi/abs/10.1080/01639374.2014.880981 accessed: 2020-11-05.

[14] A. Benzekri et al., "Know Your Customer: Opening a new bank account online using UAAF," IEEE 17th Annual Consumer Communications & Networking Conference (CCNC), January 2020, doi:10.1109/CCNC46108.2020.9045148 URL: https://ieeexplore.ieee.org/document/9045148 accessed: 2020-11-05.

[15] uPort Mobile, "uPort Project," Github page. URL: https://github.com/uport-project/uport-mobile accesed: 2020-11-05.

[16] O. Johnston-Watt, "DLT is your passport to work," URL: https://medium.com/blockchaintp/dlt-is-your-passport-to-work-e0183457b54b accessed: 2020-11-04.

[17] E. Miller, U. Ogbuji, V. Mueller, and K. MacDougall, "Bibliographic Framework as a Web of Data: Linked Data Model and Supporting Services," Washington DC: Library of Congress, 2012 URL: https://www.loc.gov/bibframe/pdf/marcld-report-11-21-2012.pdf accessed: 2020-11-04.

[18] T. Baker et al., "Library linked data incubator group final report," W3C Incubator Group Report, vol. 25, 2011 URL: https://www.w3.org/2005/Incubator/lld/XGR-lld-20111025/ accessed: 2020-11-05.

[19] D.W. Chadwick et al., "Improved Identity Management with Verifiable Credentials and FIDO," IEEE Communications Standards Magazine, December 2019, doi:10.1109/MCOMSTD.001.1900020 URL: https://ieeexplore.ieee.org/document/9031543 accessed: 2020-11-04.

[20] D. Shin, "User centric cloud service model in public sectors: Policy implications of cloud services," doi: 10.1016/j.giq.2012.06.012, URL: https://www.sciencedirect.com/science/article/pii/S0740624X13000099 accessed: 2020-11-05.

Towards an Empirical Analysis of Trustworthiness Attributes in the Context of Digitalization

Sandro Hartenstein
Berlin School Of Economics And Law
Berlin, Germany
email: sandro.hartenstein@hwr-berlin.de

Steven Schmidt
DB Station&Service AG / Berlin School Of Economics And Law
Berlin, Germany
email: s_schmidts19@stud.hwr-berlin.de

Andreas Schmietendorf
Berlin School Of Economics And Law
Berlin, Germany
email: andreas.schmietendorf@hwr-berlin.de

***Abstract*— This idea paper describes the current perception of the terms trust and trustworthiness in technical and sociological systems. Related works are examined and put into relevant context for the proposed research. The main goal is to show the missing link between those two extrema. Thus, proposed future works aim to further identify systems aspects connecting sociological and technical trustworthiness. The focus lies on socio-technical systems. Therefore, the proposed empirical research concentrates along this spectrum. The thorough examinations in the proposed study fields benefit a holistic model of trustworthiness attributes for digital systems through enrichment of empirically evaluated and compared trustworthiness attributes.**

Keywords-Trustworthiness; Digitalization; Information Systems; Society.

I. INTRODUCTION

The richness of provided services in the digital world is ever evolving and rapidly growing through the establishment of digitalized aspects in everyday life, private or professional. The consumption of digital services relays on trustworthiness in a significant way [1]-[3]. Yet, the terms trust and trustworthiness are perceived differently across multiple academic and industrial disciplines, as well as the related attributes.

This idea paper aims to present a possible approach on analyzing significant factors of trustworthiness through different empirical examinations of different fields. Those *trustworthiness attributes* may vary heavily from field to field, but the general assumption is that those attributes mainly only differ in weight, relative to the observed field they are significant to.

In Section 2, different terms and viewpoints on the topic of trust and trustworthiness are described to explain the motivation for this approach. In Section 3, past and current related work is then examined, to demonstrate the variations of the current understanding and related contexts that have been evaluated. Section 4 describes what could be done to achieve a generic and general model of trustworthiness attributes and associated weights according to the area under study. The conceptional procedure to accomplish this idea is described in detail, as well as what fields are going to be involved as part of the planned project to enable this work. The fields and their individual empirical approach, thus, are presented briefly to demonstrate the general idea of the approach.

II. TERMS AND VIEWPOINTS

A definition of trust is:

"Trust by definition entails a willingness by the [trustor] to make herself vulnerable to the possibility that another will act to her detriment" [4, p. 28]

A definition of trustworthiness for software is:

"Software trustworthiness is a key enabler of IoT trustworthiness, which is the degree of confidence that a system will perform as expected. Trustworthiness is based on five characteristics—safety, security, privacy, reliability and resilience, which directly and in combination provide protection against hazards and threats related to environmental disturbances, human errors, system faults and attacks." [5, p. 6]

The digitization is depending on the well-being of the users. Entrusting data and work steps to computer systems is viewed critically by the user. Besides the advantages, there are also disadvantages. Trust is a key to the acceptance of digitised services and thus also to the increase in productivity through digitisation. This idea paper shows the dimensions of trust. These need to be addressed by the provider. There are several participants with different interests and understandings of trust and trustworthiness. The needs of the stakeholders in the context of trustworthiness of digital services are consumer, provider and third-party trustee. The consumer is striving to use a service that is as trustworthy as possible, as the effects of data misuse are becoming increasingly apparent. Digital service providers need consumer confidence in their products. They also need trustworthy supply services. The third independent authority can confirm the trustworthiness of digital services to the user, as long as it has the confidence of the users and can verify the services.

From the point of view of the service, two main elements are decisive for its reputation with consumers. User trust and the trustworthiness of the service are these two factors. In the research project that is named OPerational Trustworthiness Enabling Technologies, in short

OPTET, the prerequisite for trust in the context of web-based services was determined. The result is that trust can be personal, transferred and based on core trust, for example in institutions. The trustworthiness of the service is based on its attributes and on those confirmed by third parties. These correlations and their influences were summarized in Figure 1 [6]-[8].

The structure of the known Social-, Technological-, Economic-, Environmental-, Political-, Legal- and Ethical-environment analyses, in short STEEPLE, was used to classify the trust building measures as a view from outside [9, pp. 80-84]. From the authors' point of view, the environment analysis for a digital service is essential for its trustworthiness and the trust of its consumers. For this reason, the influencing factors can be classified with STEEPLE.

This idea paper focuses on the social, economic and technical factors that influence trust in digital services. Based on the analysis of trust and trustworthiness, the following influencing factors can be assigned. The social factors are distinguishable by personal, referral and derived trust. Personal trust is characterised by emotions, e.g., browser certifications status colour (red – danger, green – ok) or knowledge, e.g., knowledge about the two-factor authentication procedure. Referral trust is based on a third party who is trusted. Derived trust is often shaped by experience with institutions and their status. The technological factors are the trustworthiness attributes of the services. These should be measured objectively during development and operation or confirmed by third parties. The economic factors are characterised by the expectation of profit. The provider aims to offer trusted digital services. He can achieve this by optimising all factors, but there must be a minimum level of each factor. For example, a service may be technically perfect, i.e., fully trusted, but the provider has a bad reputation, so the derived trust is low and the service is not fully trusted. One factor influencing the consumer is the absence of risk or low risk. If the stakes are low, the service will be trusted more because the potential loss is manageable. However, many users are not aware of the value of the user data. A risk assessment is therefore useful for all stakeholders.

III. Related Work

The research on trust goes back a long way; basics were already interesting in the 50s. More recent research has commercial reasons [10]. For trust in software and its use, this section introduces the most important concepts briefly.

The social drivers for trust are honesty, integrity and reliability of the interaction partners. It is the nature of trust to address these interpersonal relationships. That's also the basis for stability in social institutions and markets. It is undisputed that trust is the fundament of the interactions of the daily life.

Simmel sees the generation of trust on the expected result [11]. If it is good, trust is created. If it is bad, trust is destroyed. Trček highlights the emotional aspects and the behaviour of the participants as important influencing factors [12]. The change in perceived competence appeared to occur largely for citizens with high trust and little knowledge and a shift in perceived benevolence could mainly be noted among citizens with low knowledge and low trust. [13]

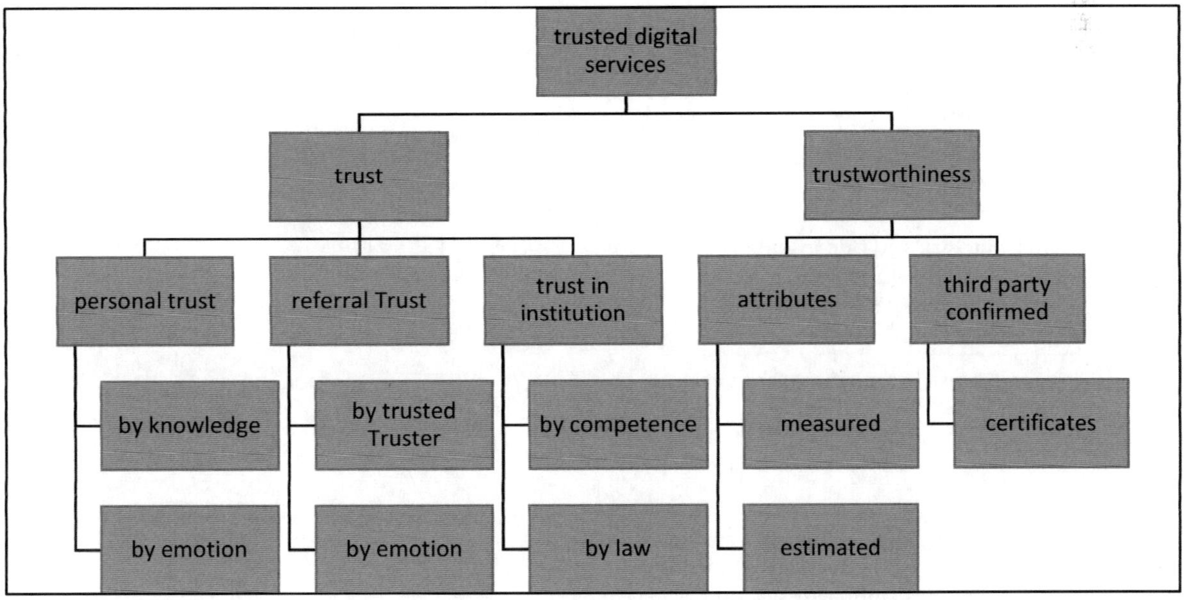

Figure 1. Trust and trustworthiness for digital services [own representation based on [6]-[8][14]]

In the commercial context, Patrick and his team have determined that cognitive and emotional dimensions of trust are strong, independent and interconnected in building trusting relationships with firms [10]. Grimmelikhuijsen and Meijer examined the relations with public institutions and found that they are considered more trustworthy than private companies [15]. In 2001, McKnight brought together the various aspects and their dependencies on trust in one design. This is illustrated in Figure 2. Basically, he distinguishes in trust in the institution through psychology and sociology, which influences the personal trust.

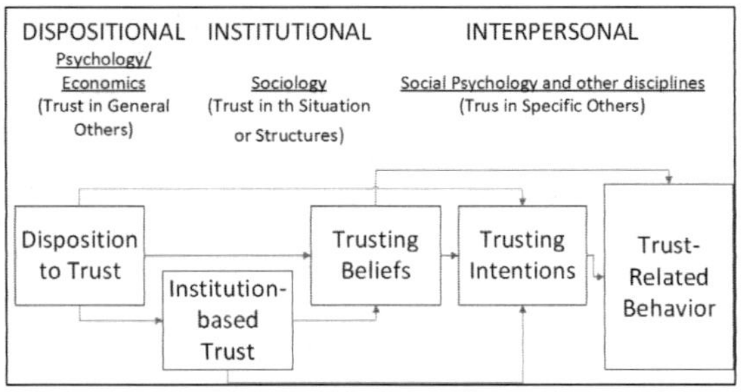

Figure 2. Interdisciplinary model of trust constructs [recreated from 16, p. 33].

Robbins shows a modern trust-risk-act-model, called relational trust in the year 2016 [17, p. 985]. It is illustrated in Figure 3 and visualizes the connections between trust, risk assessment and the relation to activities. The factors influencing trust are the characteristics of the actors and the relationships between the actors and external parties.

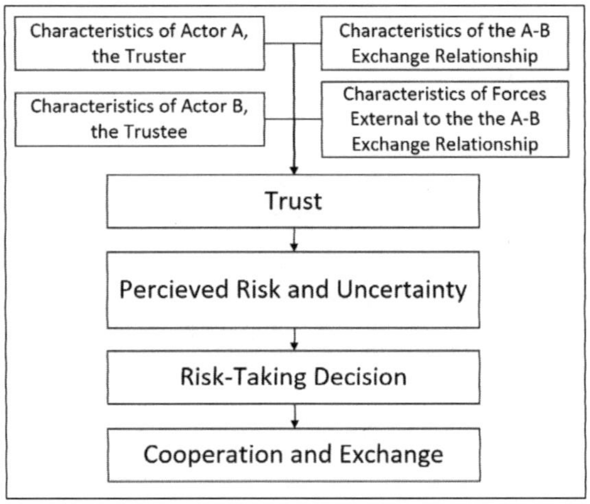

Figure 3. Structural-cognitive model of trust [recreated from 17, p. 982].

The technical drivers for trust are characterized by the trustworthy properties of the service. By evaluating 72 scientific articles on trustworthiness and corresponding quality categories, the attributes were determined within the OPTET project (EU FP7-project from 2012 till 2015). These are shown in Figure 4. [18, p. 24][19, p. 236]

Figure 4. Trustworthiness attributes [19, p. 236].

The attributes have context-specific influence on the trustworthiness. The domain and the type of the Social-Technical- System, in short STS, are relevant. The attributes are measurable and can map the influence with a weighting. The top three attributes of the study of 72 relevant papers by Mohammadi et. al are Security, Dependability and Usability. In almost 2/3 of the literature, security is mentioned as the most important attribute. Reliability is mentioned in almost half of them. 1/4 of the papers mention usability as an important attribute for trustworthiness. All attributes and their relevance are shown in Figure 5. [18, p. 25]

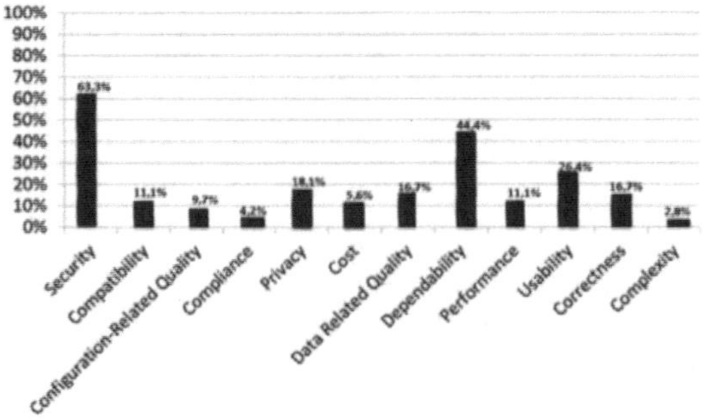

Figure 5. Classified trustworthiness attributes [18, p. 24].

IV. Conclusion and Future Work

The description of related works shows that the focused dimensions range from very technological to very sociological but fail to respect both extremes equally. Trust is related to many more fields than solely sociology or technology. Different legal or political institutions might perceive trustworthiness different than individuals and therefore evaluate the same systems attributes dissimilar with varying implications on the systems evaluation and consumption of its services.

Considering classical environmental approaches such as the STEEPLE analysis would enable a system that models trustworthiness and related attributes to take different aspects of the systems whole environment into account. The systems attributes in relation to different environments is important especially for the socio technical view, as the connection of these two fields is the main motivation for the intended research project in the context of digitalization and its impacts. The width of all fields enables a greater richness for the model itself in terms of representativeness and – if examined – empirical argumentation.

This thought leads to the proposed idea regarding the planned feature works related to trustworthiness and trustworthiness enabling attributes to achieve a generalized set of empirical evaluated and weighed attributes examined in different fields of the project to model trustworthiness. The architecture shall be designed to be extended through further research in different fields across the socio technical spectrum through the views of the STEEPLE dimensions. The first fields and respective systems which will be observed, are as follows:

S1 - Simulation of a trustworthy scrum process

The observation concentrates on the impacts of different trustworthiness enabling attributes along a simulated software engineering process. The aim is to examine weights of different attributes to achieve a high trustworthiness score.

S2 – Trustworthy public WiFi

The empirical assessment in this field emphases trustworthiness attributes in public WiFis through questionnaires and compared interviews between user groups of different services with different suspected trustworthiness levels.

S3 – Trustworthy AI-Webservices

This research area is concerned with determining and evaluating the trustworthiness of web services that use artificial intelligence.

S4 – Trustworthy web presence of mediators

Similar to the previous field, a variety of web presences of self-established mediators is examined to gain a collection of empirical validated trustworthiness attributes in this field, to enrich the overall proposed model with weights unique to this field.

Figure 6 shows the planned research goal in a schematic diagram. Each empirically determined trustworthiness attribute (Ai) per examined system (Sj) should be weighted. In addition, these attributes are categorized according to the STEEPLE dimensions and thus enable the formation of clusters. This is helpful to create the general model. Each further investigation of similar or different systems will contribute to the overall set, but also add information on different weights, unique per examined field.

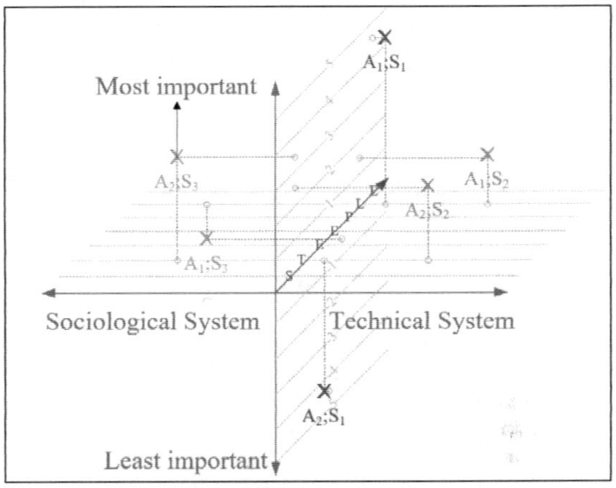

Figure 6. Visualization of the proposed approach

The empirical research and contribution of insights to the proposed system shall be established at the Berlin School of Economics and Law as a research project abbreviated as EUMoVe – Empirische Untersuchung der Modelierung von Vertrauenswürdigkeit (Empirical Examination Of Modeling Trustworthiness). The main objective of the planned research project is to achieve the said model, enriched with a static set of attributes empirically weighted per domain and thus applicable to most of the socio-technical spectrum of systems.

Without sufficient confidence in appropriate solutions, problems of acceptance or even difficult to resolve conflicts arise. Accordingly, the question arises as to what a systemic approach to improving customer-related trust in the discourse of digital solutions can look like.

We see here a combination of organizational, sociological and technological approaches to solving problems, whereby potential conflicts of involved parties are monitored immanently (if necessary, also algorithmically) by a mediatory approach and solved if necessary. The aim is to establish intelligent conflict resolution strategies as an integral part of digital products and services. On this basis, customer-centered trust can be ensured through transparency, control options, conflict resolution strategies and considered liability issues.

References

[1] S. Utz, P. Kerkhof, and J. van den Bos, "Consumers rule: How consumer reviews influence perceived trustworthiness of online stores," *Electronic Commerce*

Research and Applications, vol. 11, no. 1, pp. 49–58, 2012, doi: 10.1016/j.elerap.2011.07.010.

[2] European Commission, *Trustworthy AI.* [Online]. Available: https://ec.europa.eu/digital-single-market/en/news/trustworthy-ai-brochure [retrieved: 10, 2020].

[3] World Economic Forum, *Our Shared Digital Future Building an Inclusive, Trustworthy and Sustainable Digital Society: Insight Report.* [Online]. Available: http://www3.weforum.org/docs/WEF_Our_Shared_Digital_Future_Report_2018.pdf [retrieved: 10, 2020].

[4] C. A. Hill and E. A. O'Hara O'Connor, "A Cognitive Theory of Trust," *SSRN Journal*, 2005, doi: 10.2139/ssrn.869423.

[5] M. Buchheit, F. Hirsch, S. Rix, M. Hermeling, and B. Martin, *Software Trustworthiness Best Practices.* [Online]. Available: https://www.iiconsortium.org/pdf/Software_Trustworthiness_Best_Practices_Whitepaper_2020_03_23.pdf [retrieved: 10, 2020].

[6] S. van der Graaf, W. Vanobberghen, M. Kanakakis, and C. Kalogiros, "Usable Trust: Grasping Trust Dynamics for Online Security as a Service," vol. 9190, pp. 271–283, 2015, doi: 10.1007/978-3-319-20376-8_25.

[7] A. Chakravarthy *et al.*, "OPTET D2.4 Socio-economic evaluation of trust and trustworthiness," OPTET. Accessed: Oct. 16 2020. [Online]. Available: https://www.researchgate.net/publication/317488309_OPTET_D24_Socio-economic_evaluation_of_trust_and_trustworthiness.

[8] S. Wiegand *et al.*, "D2.5 – Consolidated report on the socio-economic basis for trust and trustworthiness," OPTET, 2015. Accessed: Oct. 16 2020. [Online]. Available: https://www.researchgate.net/publication/317488377_OPTET_D25_-_Consolidated_report_on_the_socio-economic_basis_for_trust_and_trustworthiness.

[9] G. Johnson, K. Scholes, and R. Whittington, *Strategic Management [orig.: Strategisches Management]: An Introduction; Analysis, Decision and Implementation [orig.: Eine Einführung; Analyse, Entscheidung und Umsetzung]*, 9th ed. München: Pearson Studium, 2011, ISBN: 9783868940565.

[10] A. Patrick, S. Marsh, and P. Briggs, "Designing Systems That People Will Trust," *Security and Usability*, NRC 47438, pp. 75–99, 2005. [Online]. Available: https://www.researchgate.net/profile/Pamela_Briggs/publication/44081283_Designing_Systems_That_People_Will_Trust/links/00b7d5344d8b27f675000000.pdf.

[11] G. Simmel, *The sociology of Georg Simmel: Selected writings*. New York: Free Pr, 1964, ISBN: 9780029289204.

[12] D. Trček, "A Brief Overview of Trust and Reputation over Various Domains," in *SpringerBriefs in Information Systems, Trust and Reputation Management Systems: An e-Business Perspective*, D. Trček, Ed., Cham: Springer International Publishing, 2018, pp. 5–19.

[13] T. Nguyen, "Trust and Sincerity in Art," *Ergo*, 2020. [Online]. Available: https://www.researchgate.net/publication/343239976_Trust_and_Sincerity_in_Art.

[14] N. Gol Mohammadi *et al.*, "An Analysis of Software Quality Attributes and Their Contribution to Trustworthiness," *Proceedings of the 3rd International Conference on Cloud Computing and Services, Science*, pp. 542–552, 2013.

[15] S. G. Grimmelikhuijsen and A. J. Meijer, "Effects of Transparency on the Perceived Trustworthiness of a Government Organization: Evidence from an Online Experiment," *JOPART*, vol. 24, no. 1, pp. 137–157, 2014, doi: 10.1093/jopart/mus048.

[16] D. H. McKnight and N. L. Chervany, "Trust and Distrust Definitions: One Bite at a Time," in *Lecture Notes in Computer Science*, vol. 2246, *Trust in Cyber-societies: Integrating the Human and Artificial Perspectives*, R. Falcone, M. Singh, and Y.-H. Tan, Eds., Berlin, Heidelberg: Springer, 2001, pp. 27–54.

[17] B. G. Robbins, "What is Trust? A Multidisciplinary Review, Critique, and Synthesis," *Sociology Compass*, vol. 10, no. 10, pp. 972–986, 2016, doi: 10.1111/soc4.12391.

[18] N. G. Mohammadi *et al.*, "Trustworthiness Attributes and Metrics for Engineering Trusted Internet-Based Software Systems," in *Communications in Computer and Information Science, Cloud Computing and Services Science*, M. Helfert, F. Desprez, D. Ferguson, and F. Leymann, Eds., Cham: Springer International Publishing, 2014, pp. 19–35.

[19] S. Paulus, N. G. Mohammadi, and T. Weyer, "Trustworthy Software Development," in *Lecture Notes in Computer Science, Communications and Multimedia Security*, D. Hutchison et al., Eds., Berlin, Heidelberg: Springer Berlin Heidelberg, 2013, pp. 233–247.

eParticipation for Lurkers and Stand-by Citizens?

Evaluating a Norwegian Rapid Feedback eParticipation Solution

Marius Rohde Johannessen
School of Business
University of South-Eastern Norway
Horten, Norway
email: marius.johannessen@usn.no

Lasse Berntzen
School of Business
University of South-Eastern Norway
Horten, Norway
email: lasse.berntzen@usn.no

Abstract— **This paper presents an evaluation of an eParticipation solution for rapid feedback and dialogue between citizens and politicians. The solution consists of a mobile application with survey-like functionality and a methodology for politicians' use of the app. We report the findings from our evaluation of a pilot study involving five Norwegian municipalities. Our findings clearly show that this type of solution has the potential to engage so-called lurkers and standby citizens to provide feedback on politicians' concrete issues. Further, the solution's complexity level places it between existing solutions for open/unstructured debate and more complex solutions. Both politicians and participating citizens report that they were happy with the pilot results and would like to continue using the solution. A test of an extended version of the solution is planned in 2021.**

Keywords - eParticipation; implementation; survey; pilot study; implicit participation; evaluation.

I. Introduction

Many technological systems have been, and are being, developed to further democracy. In the 1990s, open discussion forums were popular, but had limited success [1]. In later years, we have seen several complex and advanced systems designed top-down for decision-makers to receive input on concrete issues. The Seventh Framework Program (FP7) of the European Union had calls for the development of participation systems, and in the early to mid-2010s, many different tools were presented in academic journals and conferences (See, i.e., [2][3]), along with evaluations of pilot projects [4]. The evaluations seem to conclude that such systems provide excellent feedback but are also complex and time-consuming and struggle to attract enough participants. In social media, participation threshold is lower and more people discuss politics [5][6]. Still, the quality of communication is lacking, and it is difficult to extract meaningful information and handle the conversation [7][8].

Arguably, there is a need for a middle ground between complex tailored systems and social media's anarchy. Hibbing and Theiss-Morse argue for what they call "stealth democracy" [9], claiming that most people want to be heard but are not interested in taking the time to read up on and understand complex issues. Instead, they argue that a good approach to participation is to ask simple questions about issues where citizens can form an opinion without reading hundreds of pages of documentation. While stealth democracy is an idea situated in a different context from the European and Norwegian democratic tradition, it nonetheless provides a starting point for discussing the merits of lightweight systems as a bridge between traditional deliberation and involvement and the sarcastic comments found in social media and news – a middle ground in terms of complexity and democratic outcome.

Amnå and Ekman [10] call for research on how we can involve citizens with low motivation for time-consuming activities. In this paper, we respond to this call by presenting findings from an evaluation of a Norwegian eParticipation system based on lightweight or stealth democracy ideas. The question is if this is a good and effective form of eParticipation, engaging otherwise passive citizens.

This paper's remainder is structured as follows: Section II presents related research on democracy models and implicit participation. Section III presents our research collection and analysis approach, while Section IV summarizes our evaluation findings. In Section V, we present the next steps of the project and outline some future research avenues.

II. Related Research

Signs are indicating that liberal democracy is struggling. Since 2015, Europe has experienced a major refugee crisis. Populists have been elected for president or prime minister positions, the yellow vests movement emerged in France, and Eastern Europe has seen an increase of "illiberal democracy." The Norwegian paper *Morgenbladet* created a map of authoritarian changes in the legal systems of European nations, which shows that several countries, including Western European ones, are moving away from liberal ideals [11]. This trend is aided by social media polarization, fake news, bots spreading propaganda, and an increasing number of activist websites positioning themselves as alternatives to mainstream media [12][13]. The so-called alt-right (alternative right) find each other in online fora, such as *4chan.org*, *tumblr.com*, and *8kun.top* to coordinate campaigns against political opponents. Disinformation is an issue high on the European Union agenda [14]. Hence, finding ways of engaging citizens is perhaps more important than ever.

In Norway, most of us still report high trust levels in the political system and institutions, but a significant minority is less trusting and chooses not to vote in elections [15]. Voter turnout is lower among the young, and few are actively trying to influence policy. Those who do tend to be in the high income/higher education demographic, which typically would be labeled as elites [16]. Earlier research shows several reasons for non-participation. eParticipation systems need a clear purpose and form [17], the concretization of the outcomes of participation [18], and feedback mechanisms allowing citizens to see the impact of participation [19], and failing in these has proven to alienate citizens from using the system.

A. Models of participation and democracy

eParticipation is defined as a range of actors conducting different activities with varying outcomes and effects, targeting different democratic ideal-types [20]. Fig. 1 shows the relationship between the actors, activities, and outcomes. This means that researchers should be clear about the type of democracy the system supports when discussing specific systems and applications.

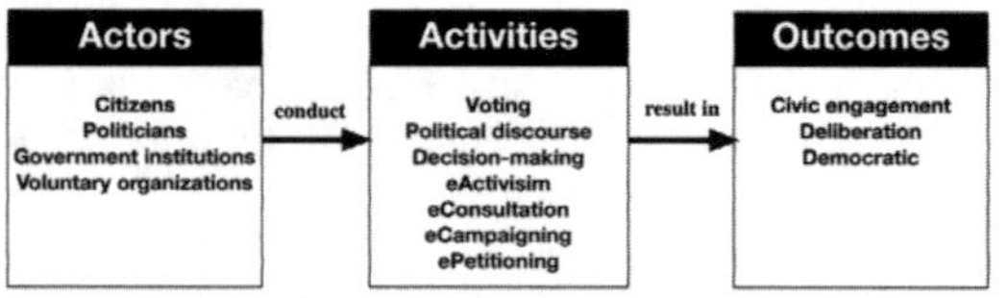

Figure 1. eParticipation actors, activities, and outcomes. Based on [20].

The activities and outcomes of participation can also be seen as a stage model. Arnstein [21] has shown how we can rate participation from low (voting, information) to high (direct democracy). The purpose of participation, according to Arnstein, is to reach as high as possible on what she calls the "ladder of participation" to empower citizens as much as possible.

Democracies should involve citizens through elections, political parties [22][23], and citizen/politician dialogue in various channels and media within the frames of representative democracy [24]. There are several models of democracy, with different normative criteria for participation. One example, proposed by Ferree and colleagues [25], describes four different models of democracy; *representative liberal*, *participatory liberal*, *discursive*, and *constructionist*. The models outline the amount of citizen participation, based on "who should speak, the content of the process (what), style of speech preferred (how), and the relationship between discourse and decision-making (outcomes) that is sought (or feared)." While some countries focus only on voting, others, such as Norway, see it as a democratic value that citizens engage in dialogue and are involved in decision-making between elections (participatory liberal model). Participation in the public debate is seen as a value in and of itself (Habermasian discursive model). The Norwegian constitution (§100, part 6) states that "government is required to facilitate open and rational public discourse." Even so, membership in political parties is in decline, with only 7 percent of the adult population being members of a political party [26]. Thus, there is a need to find new ways of communicating between politicians and citizens. We believe the system presented in this paper can support the participatory liberal model of democracy if politicians wish to do so.

B. Stealth democracy, lurking or standby citizens

In their book *Stealth Democracy,* Hibbing and Theiss-Morse [9] found that many American citizens were tired of politics and political debates as they play out in the media. Citizens report being tired of conflict, constant debates, and difficult-to-understand political compromise. They have little interest in how democracy works in practice and do not wish to become too involved. At the same time, citizens want to express their opinion and be heard, but without having to spend time reading long policy documents or become too involved. They are happy to participate in surveys or contribute in other ways, such as through FixMyStreet-type services related to their areas of interest [27].

Other researchers also look into the phenomenon of passive or observing citizens from a European perspective. Edelmann applies the concept of "lurking" – being a passive observer, or someone who only participates occasionally but is still interested enough to follow the conversation [28]. Amnå and Ekman [10] similarly define what they call "standby citizens": citizens with high political efficacy and interest, but rarely choose to participate actively in political discourse. This group chooses not to participate but can become active if the situation calls for it. In the Nordic countries, youth have both knowledge and skills. Still, they report a weaker sense of "participatory attitudes," in other words, typical standby or lurking behavior. In less stable and wealthy democracies, people report a higher level of motivation for engagement [29], perhaps because they see participation as a way of improving their living conditions.

Amnå and Ekman call for research on encouraging the standby citizen to become a more active participant [10]. Based on the survey of PostLocal, and previous research by Cruikshank, Smith, and Edelmann on how other low-complexity systems can transition citizens from standby to active [30], we believe the system presented in this paper can contribute to activating standby/lurking/stealthy citizens. It is designed as a low complexity/low time demand tool for consultation, where politicians ask questions, and the citizens answer them. The outcome is increased civic engagement and general democratic effects, depending on how the politicians decide to use the system. The findings we present below indicate that it could be seen as part of a participatory liberal model, as citizens are asked their opinion on matters being addressed by city councils.

III. RESEARCH APPROACH

This paper aims to present the initial findings from our evaluation of a system for lightweight participation. In addressing this, we applied a case study mixed-methods approach grounded in interpretivism. Our theoretical lens is that of stealth democracy and democracy models, and the case is the start-up PostLocal and their system for lightweight participation.

Data collection: The data collection period lasted approximately twelve months in 2018-19, covering development, implementation, and pilot testing. For the development and implementation phases, data is mainly qualitative in the form of participant observation [31] in project meetings and workshops with municipal, volunteer- and private sector stakeholders. Twelve mayors and fifty politicians were present in these workshops. We also conducted email interviews with politicians in the pilot municipalities and informal talks with colleagues researching media, democracy, and digitalization. In this process, we had an active role in the shaping of the system. For the pilot study, we distributed a survey to the pilot participants (N=389), receiving 189 answers. We had colleagues in the department verify the survey and tested it on five random users before distribution.

Data analysis: The analysis was based on stealth democracy and the system creators' idea of reaching those who do not normally participate in political processes. Field notes and interview questions were structured and coded accordingly. For the survey, we relied on literature discussing acceptance of technology. We was inspired by the constructs in the Unified Theory of Acceptance and Use of Technology (UTAUT) [32], adding trust and demographic variables as these have shown to be relevant for technology acceptance [33]. Finally, we were curious if gamification, found to be an effective incentive in similar applications [34], was important.

IV. FINDINGS

A. *Presentation of case and system*

In January 2018, we were approached by a small start-up who wanted to discuss the possibilities of a system for lightweight democracy. As their ideas corresponded well with our previous research, we agreed to provide input based on prior research and evaluate the pilot project. PostLocal consists of people with a broad background in business, the voluntary sector (youth sports), and the media industry. They used a local UX (User eXperience)/web company to build the app and ecosystem. They focused their efforts on their wide network of possible partners. They were extremely active in building a network of business-, government-, NGOs (Non-Governmental Organizations), and political partners, who stated their support for the system. This has likely been an important factor in the process, from idea to realization.

PostLocal's objectives for the system were as follows:

- Create a system that would ensure the "silent majority" could easily participate in political processes. The silent majority was defined as those not represented via organizations and rarely raised their hand in public meetings. Young citizens were targeted as being especially important.
- Develop an app where the mayor can consult with citizens on current issues (*In practice, it is not the mayor that decides on questions, it is more the executive council, but citizens relate to the mayor*).
- Citizens should spend no more than two-three minutes on each round of questions.
- So quick and easy to use that it can be done in the checkout queue at the supermarket.

Fig. 2 shows the system architecture, consisting of a common database, a back-end system for generating questions and analyzing responses, and a mobile app dialogue tool. Privacy is built-in, and external consultants have verified the GDPR (General Data Protection Regulation) compliance of the system.

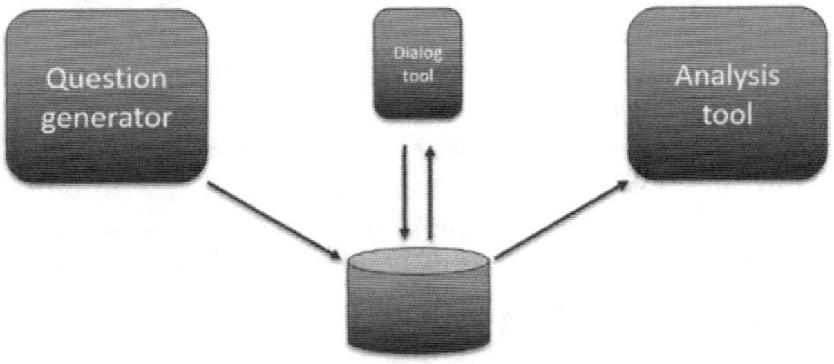

Figure 2. System architecture.

When logging in to the app, users choose their municipality and are greeted by a short video from the mayor, informing about the app's intentions and how to use it. Users can register to participate in all surveys or surveys on areas of interest. Participation is in the form of a simple survey with a few questions and the opportunity to reply more in-depth at the end. When the survey is completed, users get a "thank you" note and an option to contact the mayor with their concerns through the app. PostLocal is currently developing this part of the system (messages from citizens to politicians), but at the time of testing it was just implemented as a simple form.

Finally, users can see the responses of others. This was an important part of the app, as seeing others' opinions can aid mutual understanding [35]. After completing a set of questions, users get feedback from the mayor on how the results are being used (an option in the system, not mandatory but highly recommended). The methodology under development includes 1) ideas on how the municipality can apply this input, and 2) guidelines and functionality for using the system in physical public meetings. This was not ready for the pilot but is part of the ongoing work with creating a methodology and ecosystem for municipal participation, which is the project's ultimate goal. Fig. 3 presents screenshots from the app.

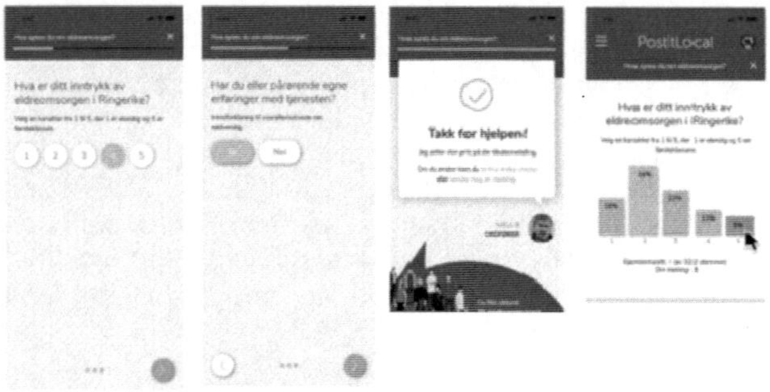

Figure 3. Screenshot from the survey.

B. Qualitative data from workshops

The workshops we observed revealed that the general issue of participation and democracy needs to be discussed more often. Several politicians stated that the workshop's most interesting part was that it gave them a space to discuss normative and fundamental democratic issues. These are often left out of hectic day-to-day politics. Besides, participants raised the following issues:

The need for improved communication: Almost all of the participants agreed that there is a need to reach out to a broader range of citizens, especially the young citizens and those who are not members of the organizations typically invited to hand in formal statements to policy processes. A small group of often older citizens tends to contact their local politicians, raise their hands in public meetings, etc. Several politicians say they have tried social media, but the tone and style of communication are not fostering a civil and rational debate. There was a general agreement that more needs to be done to reach the young and the silent, and politicians welcomed initiatives, such as PostLocal.

Ownership and organization: A lot of the discussion was related to practical issues, such as ownership, financing, and organization. Specifically, participants raised the following issues: *Who should be invited to participate?* Should there be a representative panel, or should everyone be invited to answer every survey? Ensuring representative and valid answers was also an issue. *Who should be in control of the system and act as the figurehead?* This raised heavy debate on the pros and cons of having the mayor act as front and controlling the questions being asked. This was discussed over several workshops, and the consensus seemed to be that mayors should front the app, as a human face tends to work better than a municipal logo. The internal organization should be up to a committee of politicians from the parties represented in the municipal government to avoid party politics coloring the questions and topics being addressed via the app.

Formulation of questions: Anyone who has attempted to create a survey from scratch knows how difficult it is to get the questions right. This was also a major area of concern among the workshop participants. The consensus was that simple questions about what [do you think about…] and how [should we handle…] acting as a temperature gauge on issues being discussed in the municipal government was the correct approach. Several politicians added they wanted to prioritize issues high on the agenda in local news and local social media groups. Issues of a more ideological nature should be avoided, as simple survey questions are less suited to address this type of debate.

Criticism: While most workshop participants were positive, some NGOs raised concerns about the democratic outcomes of PostLocal's system. They asked what kind of democracy this would facilitate. They discussed being heard vs. affecting policy outcomes, if the app was any different from a regular survey, and if this type of system manages to involve those who are not participating and the young.

As for the type of democracy, the workshops and previous research would put this in the "consultation" category. PostLocal is not designed to be a deliberative system for the reasons mentioned in the theory section. The difference between an app and using a polling agency is mostly related to costs and time. The system allows for a quick and easy round of temperature gauging related to current issues while using a polling agency would be more costly and more time-consuming. The expected outcome of participation and public interest is discussed further in the next section.

C. Survey – feedback from citizen test users

Background and demographic variables: Gender distribution is equal, with 47% female, 53% male respondents. When it comes to age distribution, there is a decent spread: 35 respondents are between 15-24 years old. 56 between 25 and 39, 56 between 40 and 54, and 36 are 55 years or older. Crosstab-analysis of age shows that age has little impact on the recorded responses. Young citizens are somewhat more active social media users and more positive towards gamification, while the older groups are more likely to sign a petition. Young adults (25-39) are the least politically active. When implementing the pilot, we found that youth in high school were the ones most positive towards the app, as they started out with little interest in both the app and politics, but in the end, was the group who was most positive – contacting the mayor and PostLocal to have more questions pushed out more frequently.

Our sample has a somewhat higher education level compared to the total Norwegian population [38], especially for the master's level (sample: 29%, population in 2019: 10.3%).

The respondents are also somewhat more politically active than the general population. 5% of the general population have written a political letter to the newspaper, vs. 13% of the respondents. 6% have attended a demonstration, vs. 8% of the respondents. 12% of the general population and 25% of our respondents say they have directly contacted a politician. Our questions differ from those of Statistics Norway, as we wanted a more detailed overview of political activity. However, the comparison still indicates that our respondents are somewhat more educated and politically active compared to the Norwegian population. Even so, most of our respondents are in the silent majority category, as they claim not to be politically active.

Gamification as a motivational factor: Gamification was discussed in both workshops and project meetings.

Existing studies of gamification show varying results but lean towards a positive direction (see, e.g., [34][36]). Our data do not provide a definite answer, as 34% are positive towards gamification, 37% are neutral, and 30% claim they do not see gamification as a motivational factor. However, age plays a role here, with 58% of the youngest respondents agreeing (somewhat or fully) that gamification is a motivational factor. At the same time, the 40+ group is neutral to negative and 55+ leaning even more towards negative. Fig. 4 shows the distribution of answers for the different age groups.

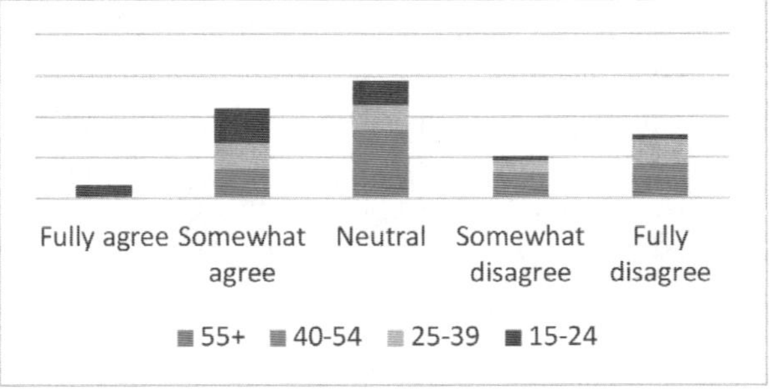

Figure 4. Age and gamification as a motivational factor.

Attitudes to personalization: Another important element that emerged from the workshop discussions was using the mayor as the front of the app vs. using the municipality logo. This was heavily debated, with politicians having strong opinions for and against. We chose to have the mayor present the app for the pilot, as there is a general trend towards politics becoming more person-oriented [37]. 70% of the respondents saw it as positive that the mayor's face was the first thing to greet them in the app. 65% also respond positively to the statement: "the mayor is a unifying force in my municipality." In Norway, mayors are expected to be mayor first and party member second; this seems to be the case in the five pilot municipalities.

Expectations towards outcome: As previous research has shown [18], being clear about the outcome of participation is important. As this was a pilot test, we were more concerned about mapping citizens' expectations in later full-scale use. 65% of the respondents reported that they expect the app outcome as "being heard and taken into account as part of the formal hearing process in policymaking," with only 6% expecting their input to have a direct consequence. 29% had no expectations whatsoever or were unsure what to expect.

Trust and intention to use: Trust, or a lack of trust, is one possible explanation for the current wave of populism and anti-elitist sentiment [15]. Our respondents are in line with the general population and show high levels of trust in local politicians and information from local government. Trust is positively correlated with respondents' intention to continue using the system. When asked if they intend to continue using the app if it becomes available after the pilot, 70% somewhat or fully agree that they would like this, while 25% are neutral/unsure. While there is some uncertainty about how this translates to the general population, this is still a good number, which shows a need and a market for this type of system.

V. CONCLUSION AND FUTURE WORK

In this paper, we have presented a selection of the findings from evaluating a system for lightweight participation. Our findings indicate that the test users were mostly happy with the system and have moderate expectations about how their input should be used (in line with representative democratic ideals). A majority are clear that they would like to use the system if it becomes available. Section IV B illustrates the complexity of eParticipation, even for a lightweight tool, such as this. Expectations, outcome, organization, and use are important factors that each municipality needs to define.

The literature review indicates that there is a link between system complexity and outcome. Systems with high complexity and time demands from the user have potentially valuable outcomes but few users. Systems that are easy to use have more users. Still, the democratic outcome is "lower" on a scale ranging from voting (requires little of the user) to deliberation and active participation (requires much of the user). Table 1, using Arnstein's "ladder of participation" [21] as a measure, illustrates this relationship.

TABLE I. PARTICIPATION LEVEL IN RELATION TO SYSTEM COMPLEXITY

	Participation level	
	Low: Voting	High: Deliberation
System complexity	Low complexity/time	High complexity/time

We argue that the system presented here has the potential to be a missing link between the open and unstructured debate found in social media and the more tailored and complex systems for participation. This acts as a middle-ground on the participation level/system complexity scale presented above. This supports a participatory liberal model where citizens are involved between elections [25].

Lightweight, "stealth" participation in the form of surveys, data analysis through sensors or apps, such as FixMyStreet, allow citizens to participate in a way that gives valuable insights to decision-makers without having to spend too much time and effort. Over the past few years, we have participated in several studies examining how lightweight participation can contribute to democracy. While this does not contribute directly to a discursive type of democracy [25], we still argue that this form of participation has a place in democratic practice. The workshops we attended indicate that we should rather see this as one important part of a broader set of tools for local democracy and perhaps as a way of activating the standby/lurking citizen.

The project will continue in its second phase, starting fall 2020. In future work, we will have to work harder to reach a sample in line with the general population to ensure validity and verify the pilot's results. Further, we intend to dig deeper into personalization and gamification as motivational factors through workshops and possibly track use in gamified vs. non-gamified situations. The extent to which the system manages to activate standby citizens and act as a bridge towards more discourse-based participation given the right methodology, is a further avenue for future research. We expect to build on the experiences from the pilot to create a methodology and framework for use by municipalities and to examine the extent to which this type of tool has an impact on local policymaking.

ACKNOWLEDGMENTS

This research was partially funded by a grant from the Oslofjord Regional Research Fund for the pilot project "Tools for dialog and methodology for citizen participation in local democracy," project number 289252.

REFERENCES

[1] Ø. Sæbø, J. Rose, and J. Molka-Danielsen, "eParticipation: Designing and Managing Political Discussion Forums," Social Science Computer Review, vol. 28(4), pp. 403-426, 2010.

[2] A. De Liddo and S. B. Shum, "New ways of deliberating online: An empirical comparison of network and threaded interfaces for online discussion," E. Tambouris, A. Macintosh, and F. Bannister (eds.) Electronic Participation. ePart 2014. Lecture Notes in Computer Science, vol. 8654, Springer, Berlin, Heidelberg, pp. 90-101, 2014.

[3] L. Porwol, A. Ojo, and J. Breslin, "A semantic deliberation model for e-Participation," Proc. 15th Annual International Conference on Digital Government Research (dg. o' 14), pp. 263-272, 2014.

[4] A. Taudes and H. Leo, "Determinants of the Willingness to Contribute to an eConsultation," Joint Proceedings of Ongoing Research, Posters, Workshop and Projects of IFIP EGOV 2014 and ePart 2014, IOS Press, pp. 13-19, 2014.

[5] G. S. Enli and E. Skogerbø, "Personalized campaigns in party-centred politics: Twitter and Facebook as arenas for political communication," Information, Communication & Society, vol. 16(5), pp. 757-774, 2013.

[6] E. Elvestad and M. R. Johannessen, "Facebook and local newspapers' effect on local politicians' popularity," Northern Lights Film and Media Studies Yearbook, vol. 15, Intellect, pp. 33-50, 2017.

[7] M. R. Johannessen, "Genres of Participation in Social Networking Systems: A Study of the 2017 Norwegian Parliamentary Election," N. Edelmann, P. Parycek, G. Misuraca, P. Panagiotopoulos, Y. Charalabidis, and S. Virkar (eds.) Electronic Participation. ePart 2018. Lecture Notes in Computer Science, vol. 11021, Springer, Berlin, Heidelberg, pp. 64-75, 2018.

[8] S. R. Majumdar, "The case of public involvement in transportation planning using social media," Case Studies on Transport Policy., vol. 5(1), pp. 121-133, 2017.

[9] J. R. Hibbing and E. Theiss-Morse, "Stealth Democracy: Americans' Beliefs About How Government Should Work," Cambridge University Press, Cambridge, 2002.

[10] E. Amnå and J. Ekman, "Standby citizens: diverse faces of political passivity," European Political Science Review, vol. 6(2), pp. 261-281, 2014.

[11] H. Ø. Jakobsen, M. B. Reinertsen, C. Belgaux, and S. Indregard. "Lovendringer i Europa som svekker demokratiet, (Legislative changes in Europe weakens democracy)," Morgenbladet 2019.03.22, 2019.

[12] C. R. Sunstein, "Republic divided: Divided democracy in the age of social media," Princeton University Press, Princeton, 2018.

[13] H. Allcott and M. Gentzkow, "Social media and fake news in the 2016 election," Journal of Economic Perspectives, vol. 31(2), pp. 211-236, 2017.

[14] European Commission High Representative of the Union for Foreign Affairs and Security Policy, "Joint Communication to the European Parliament, the European Council, the Council, the European Economic and Social Committee and the Committee of the Regions. Report on the implementation of the Action Plan Against Disinformation," JOIN(2019) 12 final, 2019.

[15] Ø. Kleven, "Nordmenn på tillitstoppen i Europa, (Norwegians are most trusting in Europe," Samfunnsspeilet, 2/2016, Statistics Norway, 2016.

[16] M. L. With, "Politiske ressurser og deltakelse," Slik har vi det - livskvalitet og levekår, 2017 edition, Statistics Norway, 2017.

[17] R. Hurwitz, "Who needs politics? Who needs people? The ironies of democracy in cyberspace," H. Jenkins, and D. Thorburn (eds.) Democracy and new media, MIT Press, Cambridge, Massachusetts, pp. 101-112, 2003.

[18] A. Kolsaker and L. L. Kelly, "Citizens' attitudes towards e-government and e-governance: a UK study," International Journal on Public Sector Management , vol. 21(3), pp. 723-738, 2008.

[19] A. Kolsaker, "Third Way e-Government: The Case for Local Devolution," M. Böhlen, J. Gamper, W. Polasek, and M. Wimmer (eds.), Proc. E-Government: Towards Electronic Democracy (TCGOV 2005), Lecture Notes in Computer Science, vol. 3416, Springer, Berlin, Heidelberg, pp. 70-80, 2005.

[20] Ø. Sæbø, J. Rose, and L. Skiftenes Flak, "The shape of eparticipation: Characterizing an emerging research area," Government Information Quarterly, vol. 25(3), pp. 400-428, 2008.

[21] S. R. Arnstein, "A Ladder Of Citizen Participation," Journal of the American Institute of Planners, vol. 35(4), pp. 216-224, 1969.

[22] J. Dewey, "The Public and its Problem," Swallow Press/Ohio University Press, Athens, 1927.

[23] F. E. Oppenheim, "democracy — characteristics included and excluded," The Monist, vol. 55(1), pp. 29-50 , 1971.

[24] C. Brooks and J. Manza, "Why welfare states persist: The importance of public opinion in democracies," University of Chicago Press, Chicago, 2007.

[25] M. M. Ferree, W. A. Gamson, J. Gerhards, and D. Rucht, "Four models of the public sphere in modern democracies," Theory and Society 31(3), pp. 289-324, 2002.

[26] Statistics Norway, "Få aktive medlemmer i politiske partier, (Few active members of political parties)," [Online]. Available from:https://www.ssb.no/kultur-og-fritid/artikler-og-publikasjoner/fa-aktive-medlemmer-i-politiske-partier 2020.11.01

[27] L. Berntzen, M. R. Johannessen, S. Böhm, C. Weber, and R. Morales, "Citizens as sensors: Human sensors as a smart city data source," Proc. Seventh International Conference on Smart Cities, Systems, Devices and Technologies (SMART 2018), pp. 11-18, 2018.

[28] N. Edelmann, "Reviewing the definitions of "lurkers" and some implications for online research," Cyberpsychology, Behavior and Social Networking, vol. 16(9), pp. 645-649, 2013.

[29] B. Hoskins, C. Villalba, and M. Saisana, "The 2011 civic competence composite indicator (CCCI-2): measuring young people's civic competence across Europe based on the IEA international citizenship and civic education study," European Commission Joint Research Centre, Institute for the Protection and Security of the Citizen, 2012.

[30] P. Cruickshank, N. Edelmann, and C. F. Smith, "Signing an e-petition as a transition from lurking to participation," J. Chappellet, O. Glassey, M. Janssen, A. Macintosh, J. Scholl, E. Tambouris, and M. Wimmer (eds.), Electronic Government and Electronic Participation, Trauner, pp. 275-282, 2010.

[31] H. S. Becker and B. Geer, "Participant observation and Interviewing: A Comparison," Human Organization, vol. 16(3), pp. 28-32, 1957.

[32] V. Venkatesh, M. G. Morris, G. B. Davis, and F.D. Davis, "User acceptance of information technology: Toward a unified view," MIS Quarterly, vol. 27(3), pp. 425-478, 2003.

[33] M. Naranjo Zolotov, T. Oliveira, and S. Casteleyn, "E-participation adoption models research in the last 17 years: A weight and meta-analytical review," Computers in Human Behavior, vol. 81, pp. 350-365, 2018.

[34] J. E. Coronado Escobar, A. R. Vasquez Urriago, "Gamification: an effective mechanism to promote civic engagement and generate trust?" Proc. 8th International Conference on Theory and Practice of Electronic Governance, ACM, pp. 514-515, 2014.

[35] S. Indregard, "Det som skiller oss (og ikke), (What divides us (and not))," Morgenbladet 2019.05.31, 2019.

[36] H. Nothhaft and J. Seiffert, "The Gamification of Democracy," W. T. Coombs, J. Falkheimer, M. Heide, and P. Young (eds.) Strategic Communication, Social Media and Democracy. Taylor & Francis Group, pp. 130-142, 2015.

[37] I. McAllister, "The personalization of politics," The Oxford handbook of political behavior. Oxford University Press, 2007.

[38] Statistics Norway, "Befolkningens Utdanningsnivå, (The Education Level of the Population)," [Online]. Available from: https://www.ssb.no/utniv/ 2020.11.01

Creating Innovative Structures in Workplace and Vocational Digital Learning to Ensure Social Distancing

Ileana Hamburg
IAT, Westfälische Hochschule, GE Gelsenkirchen, Germany
E-Mail: hamburg@iat.eu

Abstract—**The COVID-19 pandemic has influenced learning, including Vocational Education and Training (VET) and workplace learning in companies. Many people with special needs (social or disabilities) have not benefited from the e-learning systems used in this period, and emphasized the fact that digital innovations are necessary in all types of education. This paper highlights the importance of disruptive digital innovations in education, such as personalized e-learning and e-mentors, and presents examples of structures and social measures, which can be developed around improving learning during the COVID-19 crisis to ensure social distancing.**

Keywords-COVID-19; workplace learning; vocational education and training; disruptive innovation.

I. INTRODUCTION

The COVID-19 pandemic has influenced all types and levels of learning including Vocational Education and Training (VET) and workplace learning in companies: a generation of learners have seen their usual education and training processes disrupted [5][7].

E-learning systems and other digital tools change the way people approach learning and training and could offer access to learning content to everyone. They support learners to be more active and motivated, allowing them to choose how, when and where they learn. Learners can progress at their own pace and review what they have not understood. Such systems support life-long learning, allowing people to gain new skills and knowledge in order to adapt to a changing job market. During a pandemic, these digital systems may create new opportunities for stronger international collaboration. Adaptability will be crucial for the next generations to navigate through the present—and any future—pandemics.

Many people with special needs (social or disabilities) that limit learning activities should also be beneficiaries of e-learning systems because such systems offer the flexibility to adapt training programs to meet their specific needs. However, this has not happened. Special measures and disruptive innovations are necessary so that students and companies' employees do not suffer when continuity is not being ensured through distance learning.

In the first section of this paper, the necessity and importance of disruptive digital innovation in education is discussed and some examples are given. The next section includes structures and social measures, which can be developed around improving learning in the COVID-19 crisis to ensure social distancing, particularly in Germany. Such measures have been taken within a workplace-oriented learning program for companies developed and tested during the COVID-19 pandemic within a European project and adapted for VET. In addition, other measures taken in Germany to help teachers and trainers to move into their virtual classrooms and workplaces are also presented. Some conclusions for educational institutions, companies and governments to improve education in the existing pandemic crisis are given in the last section of the paper, with particular reference being made to e-learning.

II. DISRUPTIVE INNOVATION IN EDUCATION

Disruptive innovations in education are intended to break with an established model and to introduce an improved one. Ken Robinson underlines in [12] that, while economic, cultural and personal spheres have undergone enormous transformation over the last 50 years, education systems have not modified their syllabuses or their objectives. Curtis Johnson, co-author of the bestseller Disrupting Class: How Disruptive Innovation Will Change the Way the World Learns [4], explains that the current form of teaching "is unable to provide today's pupils with the skills they need to master in order to interact with and within the digital society" and so disruptive education is necessary that approaches learning in another way. However, innovators in the education segment have not disrupted the status quo significantly so far. In 2008's Disrupting Class, Christensen predicted great disruptions in the segment from online learning. However, while there has been much adoption of digital learning, this has not proved very disruptive; online education continues to reflect traditional models rather than a disruption.

Disruptive innovation has the capacity to improve education and outcomes. One condition is that educators embrace a free-market mindset [6]. Cooperation and new ways of thinking can also help to replace an obsolete schooling model of education [1]:

A. Disruptive innovation supports equitable access to mentors.

Mentoring is an old approach used within education, but it has not been equitably distributed [11]. Disruptive technological innovations enable the use of e-mentors who are accessible to the masses independent of location. This includes all students with social problems or disabilities, not just a few.

B. Disruptive innovation supports the creation of a personalized education system.

New digital technologies, also disruptive ones, support personalized e-learning through flexible online curricula, new staffing structures and personalized support, which is particularly important for people with special needs [16]. Some examples include [4]:

- Power MyLearning, which actively involves teachers in wraparound services and family engagement so that teachers' academic decisions can be sensitive to the non-academic factors present in students' lives.
- City Connects, which integrates a range of targeted poverty relief and afterschool services into schools.

These are an important reminder that, just as personalized instructional models focus on using instructional data to target learning, personalized support models also hinge on high quality, longitudinal non-academic data. Luckily, tools are starting to emerge to make these data-driven practices more feasible.

Education is a complex services business in which quality is difficult to define, particularly in times of Covid-19. However, innovative approaches, innovative methods and innovative formats are necessary. Universities and other training institutions have a big role in disruptive innovations in education – also in workplace ones – and they have to adapt to changes. Some milestones include [2][10]:

- Practice over theory: universities should concentrate their efforts on the acquisition of skills and abilities adapted to the new reality rather than to concepts.
- Multidisciplinary learning: the frontiers between disciplines no longer exist and training must be adapted and content-rich to create far-reaching professionals. Methods like Problem-Based Learning (PBL) should be used.
- Digital innovation: many universities now have their own virtual areas for training, partnerships and shared knowledge purposes.
- Closer links with the job market: universities should become platforms for connecting companies and students and promoting the entrepreneurial spirit.
- Making competitiveness a priority: universities must be ever more competitive in order to transform themselves into research leaders and new knowledge areas.

Turning to VET and workplace learning, VET teachers and trainers have an important role in companies, but they face difficulties in their efforts to respond to the current crisis [3]. COVID-19 consequences are seen at all levels of education, but seem more severe for the workplace learning and VET sector. The work-based component has been interrupted in companies offering apprenticeships due to closures in many European countries.

Teachers and trainers have to meet the new demands imposed on them during the crisis and to overcome the new challenges that they must now face, and they need more support and greater investment in their area. Only 60% of teachers received professional development in Information and Communication Technology (ICT) in the year preceding the Organization for Economic Co-operation and Development (OECD) survey [13] while 18% reported a great need for development in this area. These figures highlight that teachers need to renew their skills regularly in order to be able to innovate their practices and adapt to the rapid transformations inherent in the 21st century. This is even more important in the current context, where the COVID-19 health crisis has pushed teachers to adapt very quickly, especially in countries where they do not necessarily have the pedagogical and technical skills to integrate digital tools into learning.

Workplace learning in companies is emerging as one of the earliest and hardest-hit business activities [8]. Efforts are made to reskill employees, but companies cannot simply take a pause of critical workplace learning, even as they try to focus on employee safety first.

In connection with COVID-19, disruptive innovation in education should be combined with better socially oriented service models that are built around an improved educational program quality for all.

III. The Socio-Economic Impact of COVID-19 on the Most Vulnerable Learners and Contribution of E-Learning

Social distancing measures have a big impact on a large section of the population who do not have the means to protect themselves against the virus, which requires means and resources that a large section of the population lacks. Many people do not have access to suitable learning facilities or the required skills to use digital technologies and a large number of learners from disadvantaged backgrounds or with disabilities are missing education because they do not have access to the Internet or the digital skills to take part in online classes. As an example, in Gelsenkirchen, Germany, the unemployment rate is about 40% and there are many refugees and European migrants with big families and very limited digital skills [9]. This gap is seen across countries and between income brackets within countries. 95% of students in Switzerland, Norway and Austria have a computer to use for schoolwork, but only 34% in Indonesia (OECD Data). Therefore, the pandemic will widen the digital divide [14][15].

In Germany, the education ministers decided to provide financial support so that each teacher has a laptop (Notebook) and each student an Internet connection.

To continue to enable and deliver value-creating efforts, learning leaders have to consider taking a number of tactical steps to protect learners with social problems and/or disabilities, adapt programs and delivery, and establish and expand virtual live learning. E-learning programs were already on the rise before COVID-19 and there is a marked increase in such learning programs. Many younger employees embrace such approaches, but they should be available for all.

In the following, we describe some tactical steps and strategic measures, such as exploring alternative digital learning strategies, which managers can develop during this time of social distancing and thus avoid disrupting workplace learning.

Within the European Erasmus+ project [7], involving a consortium with higher education institutions and research organizations, chambers of commerce and Small and Medium Size Enterprise (SME) representative bodies from Germany, Ireland, Spain, Lithuania and Romania, a hybrid-training program for workplace-oriented learning has been developed, supported by a digital platform. Discussions have been held in Germany on how to adapt it for a special course within VET. A short time after starting the program, some companies and VET institutions closed due to the COVID-19 pandemic and later the program had to be continued exclusively digitally. Initially, 178 employees from all five-project partner countries registered for the learning program. In each country, 20 learners or more planned to take part. After their companies were closed (March 2020), only 30 learners wanted to continue.

To create a comprehensive picture of how to adapt the training to this new environment, a cross-functional response team composed of members of the German partner responsible for the project, managers of some interested companies and VET has been formed. Because some people with cognitive disabilities and migrants wanted to undertake the training, we invited two persons with knowledge in this context. Therefore, the COVID-19-response effort was coordinated within the project. Two e-mentors and one tutor supported the training program. The tutor particularly supported the learners with special needs, i.e. with registration, simplification of some activities and exercises, and e-mails to communicate more often with these learners. At the end of the project, (August 2020) 20 learners from Germany finished the course. It is planned that an adapted form of the e-learning program will be started at the company Flüchtlingshilfe Solingen that is embarking on a new project.

Turning to VET, in order to provide individual learning support for learners at risk during the pandemic in Germany, so-called "transition coaching" supports students at school to acquire general secondary education or to complete (assisted) VET or another form of upper-secondary education. In cooperation with the individual student, the coach prepares a transition plan. To ensure continuity of tailored support during this crisis, the transition coaches have adjusted their services, steering young people as much as possible towards individual guidance services by phone.

To support apprentices at risk in Germany, a programmer managed by PES Germany and co-funded by the European Social Fund offers a special form of support for disadvantaged young people to reduce early school leaving from VET, given this disruption to the apprenticeships of VET learners [3].

Germany celebrated Digital Day 2020 with many high-profile guests, such as government officials and business leaders, on 18 June 2020. The Digital Day is connected to 1,435 campaigns related to digitalization across Germany. The theme of the event was "Digital for all" with a focus on digital participation.

On September 22, 2020, the Federal Foreign Office, the Federal Ministry of Education and Research, the Federal Ministry for Economic Cooperation and Development and the German Commission for UNESCO held a digital event to present the 2020 UNESCO Global Education Monitoring Report: Inclusion and Education. It was highlighted that poverty is the main obstacle to success in education, that global partnerships for education have to be strengthened, and that inclusion needs well-trained teaching and training staff because they have a crucial role to play when it comes to ensuring participation in the education sector.

"Inclusion 4.0 Ruhr - Digital Support Systems for Employees with Cognitive Disabilities" is a network funded by the Federal Ministry of Education and Research to teach employees with intellectual disabilities to secure and expand their jobs in workshops and companies by using innovative digital assistance systems [9].

IV. CONCLUSIONS

The COVID-19 pandemic has created the largest disruption of education systems in history, affecting nearly 1.6 billion learners in more than 190 countries and on all continents [15].

During the COVID-19 pandemic, companies, VET institutions and other educational establishments have needed to address new issues. Massive efforts have been made in a short time to respond to the shocks to education systems and have showed that change is possible. However, the solutions were not always fit for purpose because the necessary – and not always available – equipment had to be found, including new online tools and resources. Many teachers and trainers have to be reskilled. Marginalized and vulnerable learners have to be involved in e-learning procedures. Educational institutions have to think carefully about their choices regarding e-learning, particularly personalized forms, e-mentors and inclusive education technologies. Disruptive innovations are necessary because the crisis has shown that no digital inclusion without measures to minimize social distancing exists [9]. Governments should consider focusing on equity and inclusion, reinforcing capacities for risk management at all levels of the system, enhancing consultation and communication mechanisms, addressing learning losses and preventing dropouts, offering skills for employability programs, supporting the teaching profession and teachers' readiness, and supporting flexibility across levels and types of education and training.

REFERENCES

[1] T. Arnett, "How disruptive education addresses 3 of education most critical issues", https://www.christenseninstitute.org/blog/how-disruptive-innovation-addresses-3-of-educations-most-critical-issues-today/ [retrieved: 10, 2020], 2020.

[2] E. Blass, A. Jasman, and S. Shelley, "Postgraduate research students: You are the future of the Academy." Futures 44:166, 2012.

[3] Cedefop, "Digital gap during COVID-19 for VET learners at risk in Europe. Synthesis report on seven countries based on preliminary information provided by Cedefop's Network of Ambassadors tackling early leaving from VET", 2020.

[4] C. Christensen, C. Johnson, and B. Horn, "Disrupting class: How disruptive innovation will change the way the world learns", McGraw-Hill, New York, 2008

[5] H. D'Orville, "COVID-19 causes unprecedented educational disruption: Is there a road towards a new normal? "Prospects. 2020. https://doi.org/10.1007/s11125-020-09475-0, 2020.

[6] FEE, "Education Entrepreneurs Are the Only Ones Who Can Disrupt the Status Quo", https://fee.org/articles/education-entrepre-neurs-are-the-only-ones-who-can-disrupt-the-status-quo/, [retrieved: 10, 2020], 2019.

[7] I. Hamburg, "Facilitating lifelong learning in SMEs towards SDG4.", in Advances in social sciences research journal 7, no. 9, p. 262-272, 2020a.

[8] I. Hamburg, "Supporting digital innovations by interdisciplinary entrepreneurial learning", in Advances in social sciences research journal 7, no. 4, p. 8-17. 2020b.

[9] I. Hamburg, "Digital Inclusion should be at the heart of response to COVID-19, Exploring the Meaning and Experience of Digital Inclusion Limerick Lifelong Learning Festival", 2020c.

[10] E. O'Brien, J. McCarthy, I. Hamburg and Y. Delaney, "Problem-based learning in the Irish SME workplace", in Journal of workplace learning 31, no. 6, pp. 391-407, 2019.

[11] B. Ragins and K. Kram, "The Handbook of Mentoring at Work." Thousand Oaks, CA: Sage, 2007.

[12] K. Robinson, "Creative schools: the grassroots revolution that's transforming education." New York: Viking, 2015.

[13] OECD survey, https://www.oecd.org/education/the-impact-of-covid-19-on-education-insights-education-at-a-glance-2020.pdf, [retrieved: 10, 2020], 2020.

[14] UNESCO, COVID-19 educational disruption and response. Paris: UNESCO. https://en.unesco.org/covid19/educationresponse, (2020a), [retrieved: 10, 2020], 2020.

[15] UNESCO, "Global education coalition." Paris: UNESCO. https://enunesco.org/covid19/educationresponse/globalcoalition, (2020b), [retrieved: 10, 2020], 2020.

[16] World Economic Forum, 4 ways "COVID-19 could change how we educate future generations." https://www.weforum/agenda/2020/03/4-ways-covid-19-education-future-generations, [retrieved: 10, 2020], 2020.